Lived Wisdom in Jewish Antiquity

Education, Literary Culture, and Religious Practice in the Ancient World

Series Editors
Sean A. Adams (University of Glasgow, UK) and
Catherine Hezser (SOAS, University of London, UK)

Editorial Board
Jim Aitken (University of Cambridge, UK), Jeanne-Nicole Saint-Laurent (Marquette University, USA), David Carr (Union Theological Seminary, New York, USA), Raffaella Cribiore (NYU, USA), Matthew Goff (Florida State University, USA), Marc Hirshman (Hebrew University of Jerusalem, Israel), Sylvie Honigman (Tel Aviv University, Israel), Jan Stenger (Julius Maximilian University of Würzburg, Germany)

This interdisciplinary series provides a space for the exploration and advancement of the study of education and literary culture in antiquity and its intersection(s) with religious practice. Specifically, it covers the geography of the Mediterranean basin from the beginning of literary culture until late antiquity. Books in the series are at the cutting edge of research, challenging traditional scholarly boundaries by engaging with the lived elements of literary culture, religion, and education.

By advancing theoretical and methodological approaches from inter/transdisciplinary perspectives, books in this series make important contributions to discussions of textuality, history, material culture, and cultural studies. Interactions with material and literary culture are core elements to this series and scholars will wrestle with how practices change over time and locality. Attention to interreligious and intercultural interaction will deepen our understanding of religious experiences, communities, institutions, and individuals in antiquity.

Lived Wisdom in Jewish Antiquity

Studies in Exercise and Exemplarity

Elisa Uusimäki

BLOOMSBURY ACADEMIC
LONDON • NEW YORK • OXFORD • NEW DELHI • SYDNEY

BLOOMSBURY ACADEMIC
Bloomsbury Publishing Plc
50 Bedford Square, London, WC1B 3DP, UK
1385 Broadway, New York, NY 10018, USA
29 Earlsfort Terrace, Dublin 2, Ireland

BLOOMSBURY, BLOOMSBURY ACADEMIC and the Diana logo are trademarks
of Bloomsbury Publishing Plc

First published in Great Britain 2021
This paperback edition published 2023

Copyright © Elisa Uusimäki, 2021

Elisa Uusimäki has asserted her right under the Copyright, Designs
and Patents Act, 1988, to be identified as Author of this work.

For legal purposes the Acknowledgements on pp.vi–vii constitute
an extension of this copyright page.

Cover design: Charlotte James
Cover image © Rawpixel/iStock

All rights reserved. No part of this publication may be reproduced or
transmitted in any form or by any means, electronic or mechanical, including
photocopying, recording, or any information storage or retrieval system,
without prior permission in writing from the publishers.

Bloomsbury Publishing Plc does not have any control over, or responsibility for,
any third-party websites referred to or in this book. All internet addresses given
in this book were correct at the time of going to press. The author and publisher
regret any inconvenience caused if addresses have changed or sites have
ceased to exist, but can accept no responsibility for any such changes.

A catalogue record for this book is available from the British Library.

Library of Congress Cataloging-in-Publication Data
Names: Uusimäki, Elisa, author.
Title: Lived wisdom in Jewish antiquity : studies in
exercise and exemplarity / Elisa Uusimäki.
Description: 1. | New York : Bloomsbury Academic, 2021. |
Includes bibliographical references and index. |
Summary: "Moving away from focusing on wisdom as a literary genre, the book
delves into the lived, embodied, and formative dimensions of wisdom as they are delineated in
Jewish sources from the Persian, Hellenistic, and early Roman eras. Considering a diverse body of
texts beyond later canonical boundaries, the book demonstrates that wisdom features not as an
abstract quality, but as something to be performed and exercised in the level of both an individual
and a community. The analysis specifically concentrates on notions of a "wise" person, including
the rise of the sage as an exemplary figure. It also looks at how ancestral figures and contemporary
teachers are imagined to manifest and practise wisdom, and considers communal portraits of a
wise and virtuous life. In so doing, the author demonstrates that the previous focus on wisdom
as a category of literature has overshadowed significant questions related to wisdom, behaviour,
and social life. Jewish wisdom is also contextualized in relation to its wider ancient
Mediterranean milieu, making the book valuable for biblical scholars, classicists, scholars of
religion and the ancient Near East, and theologians"– Provided by publisher.
Identifiers: LCCN 2021006814 (print) | LCCN 2021006815 (ebook) |
ISBN 9780567697950 (hardback) | ISBN 9780567697967 (pdf) | ISBN 9780567697981 (epub)
Subjects: LCSH: Judaism–History–Post-exilic period, 586 B.C.-210 A.D. |
Wisdom–Religious aspects–Judaism. | Wisdom literature–Criticism, interpretation, etc.
Classification: LCC BM176 .U97 2021 (print) |
LCC BM176 (ebook) | DDC 296.1/206–dc23
LC record available at https://lccn.loc.gov/2021006814
LC ebook record available at https://lccn.loc.gov/2021006815

ISBN:	HB:	978-0-5676-9795-0
	PB:	978-0-5676-9799-8
	ePDF:	978-0-5676-9796-7
	eBook:	978-0-5676-9798-1

Series: Education, Literary Culture, and Religious Practice in the Ancient World

Typeset by Integra Software Services Pvt. Ltd.

To find out more about our authors and books visit www.bloomsbury.com
and sign up for our newsletters

Contents

Acknowledgements	vi
Permissions	viii
1 Introduction	1
2 Living embodiments of wisdom: The sage as an exemplar	19
3 Learning and lifestyle: The everyday performance of wisdom teachers	49
4 Shared wisdom: Ideal ways of living in Jewish communities	83
5 Conclusions	117
Notes	126
Bibliography	177
Index of Ancient Sources	202
Index of Modern Authors	221

Acknowledgements

This book draws on the work, which I gradually began as a postdoc at the Hebrew University of Jerusalem (2014–15) and thereafter continued at the University of Helsinki, first as an Academy of Finland fellow (2015–18) and then as a researcher at the Helsinki Collegium of Advanced Studies (2018–19). In 2016–17, I also conducted research in Groningen and at Yale. I wish to thank John Collins, Mladen Popoviç, and Michael Segal for hosting my visits, which prompted much learning and provided me with new perspectives on work and life. I also thank Alex Jassen for helping me access some materials in New York.

In 2018–20, I have served as the PI of the research project "Early Jewish Conceptions of Virtue" at the University of Helsinki. I am grateful for the opportunity to have worked with two brilliant minds in the context of this project, and I thank Anna-Liisa Rafael and Sami Yli-Karjanmaa for thinking and writing with me both before and during this project. I also thank our research assistant, Riina Haapakorpi, for her work on the bibliography and indices.

This book was completed at Aarhus University, where I arrived in January 2020. My colleagues Miriam DeCock and Valeria Dessy were of immeasurable value in the final writing phase of the book; thank you for all the feedback that you delivered to me in our writing group, which was a true delight at the time of corona. I also thank my other colleagues in the School of Culture and Society for a warm welcome and for sharing an inspiring working environment.

Several colleagues have contributed to the research presented in this book over the years. I am particularly grateful to George Brooke, Bärry Hartog, and Hanna Tervanotko, who have read and commented on my texts on many occasions. Furthermore, I thank Martti Nissinen for all the opportunities offered to me and many others in the context of the Academy of Finland Centre of Excellence in "Changes in Sacred Texts and Traditions" (2014–20). In Helsinki, I also received astute feedback from Katri Antin, Rick Bonnie, Raimo Hakola, Jutta Jokiranta, Jessi Orpana, Mika Pajunen, and Hanna Vanonen. Finally, I extend my thanks to all of those who have commented on my presentations in seminars and conferences, as well as to the anonymous peer-reviewers whose sharp observations helped me finalize the book project.

It has been a pleasure to work with Bloomsbury. I thank Lucy Carroll for commissioning this book. I also thank her, Lily McMahon, and Karthiga Sithanandam for all their help during the publication process.

I am indebted to the PostDoc Pole, Academy of Finland, Helsinki Collegium for Advanced Studies, and the University of Helsinki Research Funds. Thank you for the financial aid that enabled the research that eventually also resulted in the publication of this book.

I thank my family in Finland for moral support and for making life so rich in nuance. I dedicate this book to Stephen, my home sage and my everything, who is always full of upekkha and insight. Thank you for travelling with me and for making me happy.

In Aarhus, Denmark, 12 November 2020

Elisa Uusimäki

Permissions

Parts of this book draw on the following articles, but the materials included in them have been reworked and reframed in order to make a case for approaching the phenomenon of wisdom in Jewish antiquity from the viewpoint of lived and embodied practices:

"Maskil among the Hellenistic Jewish Sages." *Journal of Ancient Judaism* 8/1 (2017): 42–68.

"The Formation of a Sage according to Ben Sira." *Second Temple Jewish "Paideia" in Context*. Edited by Jason M. Zurawski and Gabriele Boccaccini, 59–69. Beihefte zur Zeitschrift für die neutestamentliche Wissenschaft 228. Berlin: Walter de Gruyter, 2017.

"The Rise of the Sage in Greek and Jewish Antiquity." *Journal for the Study of Judaism in the Persian, Hellenistic and Roman Period* 49/1 (2018): 1–29.

"Local and Global: Philo of Alexandria on the Philosophical Life of the Therapeutae." *Henoch: Historical and Textual Studies in the Ancient and Medieval Judaism and Christianity* 40/2 (2018): 298–317.

1

Introduction

Numerous texts from the ancient world argue for an intimate link between wisdom or philosophy and the everyday life. Yet, how does one perform wisdom, or what does it mean to live wisely? In this book, I will delve into such questions of applied and lived wisdom in the context of Jewish antiquity, focusing on the Persian, Hellenistic, and early Roman eras. I will investigate how Jewish authors drew on and transformed the earlier Hebrew tradition for the sake of thinking about wisdom, and living wisdom out, in new contexts. While scholars continue to debate the category of "wisdom literature" and its defining criteria, I will approach wisdom in ancient Israel and early Judaism from another angle, that of "lived wisdom." Leaving aside the question of wisdom as a literary genre, and addressing wisdom's multiple loci in the Jewish tradition, I seek to explore embodied, formative, and performative dimensions of wisdom as they are delineated in the extant sources. In so doing, I hope to demonstrate that wisdom is far from an abstract quality; it appears as something to be exercised and executed at the level of both an individual and a community.

My aim in this book is to show that the previous focus on wisdom as a body of texts has overshadowed significant questions related to lived practices, behaviour, and social life. I wish to challenge the assumption that "wisdom" only or primarily stands for a literary genre in Jewish antiquity. Although scholars admit the great variety of wisdom-related texts, it is still common to think of wisdom as a type of literature. This obsession has prevented scholars from asking significant questions related to wisdom and the everyday life in antiquity. In this book, therefore, I will take another approach by setting out to explore Jewish wisdom from the viewpoint of lived ancient religion, i.e., as a phenomenon covering a myriad of daily practices.[1] I will argue that wisdom is an embodied phenomenon since the formation and lifestyle of a wisdom lover, as those are imagined in the extant literary sources, involve various bodily exercises such as study, contemplation, and prayer.[2] I will also argue that it is pertinent to characterize wisdom as performative because it has the effect of executing external actions. These actions range from ones undertaken within a specific communal setting (e.g., liturgical performance) to others affecting the society in general (e.g., prosocial deeds).[3]

My argument is indebted to several developments in recent research. In particular, scholars in biblical and cognate studies have acknowledged that wisdom does not represent a coherent category of literature, and they have begun to cultivate an interest in the formative functions played by the so-called wisdom texts. Scholars of Jewish antiquity have greatly advanced our understanding of the place of early Judaism in the ancient Mediterranean world, specifically prompting one to reject the artificial distinction between Judaism and Hellenism as binary categories. Scholars of religion, for their part, have turned to religion as lived in recent decades, whereas philosophers now conceive of ancient philosophy as a phenomenon involving a whole way of life. In the following sub-sections, I will discuss all these issues and their implications for the present study on lived wisdom in the ancient Jewish tradition.

Wisdom as a complex category

The concept of "wisdom" is multifaceted in ancient Israelite texts and thus difficult to pinpoint. The Hebrew term חכמה denotes several types of expertise, ranging from a mental capacity to particular skills; it may connote both abstract and mundane matters. In all cases, the question is about a faculty that enables appropriate action, allowing "one to assess a situation and choose effective means to carry out one's intentions," whether the question is about craftsmanship, erudition, or skills needed for success in social life.[4] The meanings of חכמה even fluctuate within the so-called wisdom books of the Hebrew Bible – i.e., the books of Job, Proverbs, and Qoheleth – although the term often stands for an ethical quality and virtue in them.[5] The considerable variety of meanings warns against narrow definitions of wisdom, and I will return to the term's multiple meanings in Chapter 2 on the figure of the wise person in the ancient world. In that context, I will demonstrate that the connotations of the Greek term σοφία ("wisdom") and its derivatives likewise vary. At this point, however, it suffices to observe that wisdom has several imports, and the purpose of the present book is to explore how those meanings intersect with the conception of wisdom as a lifestyle.

The idea of wisdom as a body of texts is equally ambiguous. The incoherence of the category is already visible in texts that were later included in the Hebrew

Bible or the Greek Septuagint. In addition to the three "wisdom books" of the Hebrew canon, the standard Jewish wisdom corpus is considered to include the book of Ben Sira, Wisdom of Solomon, and the hymn in the book of Baruch (3:9–4:4). The latter three, which belong to the Septuagint, differ from the materials of the Hebrew canon because of their distinct emphases. The books indicate that the idea of divine revelation and the historical experience of Israel became integral components of wisdom discourse over the course of time. This feature among others indicates that the ancient sources on wisdom do not represent a unified tradition.[6] They also do not constitute a single literary genre, but a "macro-genre" at the most, for they cover several sub-genres such as instructions, admonitions, speeches, dialogues, or poems.[7]

The discovery of the Dead Sea Scrolls has further highlighted the impossibility of conceiving of wisdom as a homogeneous class of literature that could be neatly separated from other types of writings.[8] The scrolls from Qumran and Masada, in particular, show that the idiom and figurative speech of earlier Hebrew wisdom texts lived on in the imagination of Jewish authors who wrote in the late second temple period, i.e., roughly between the second century BCE and the first century CE. These writers, however, were not driven by antiquarian aims, but they constantly reflected on and communicated contemporary meanings of wisdom. In so doing, they also drew inspiration and content from outside the earlier "wisdom books," as is shown by the frequent apocalyptic, prophetic, torah-devoted, philosophical, liturgical, and apotropaic colours and concerns of their texts.[9]

Wisdom, therefore, found its way to multiple literary contexts in antiquity. Considering the sprawling nature of the extant textual evidence, it is natural that the boundaries and defining criteria of Jewish wisdom literature are fuzzy and thus continue to be debated.

As a starting point, one must be aware that Jewish authors produced no native theory of literary genres or textual classification. In other words, wisdom literature is an etic category introduced by modern scholars, beginning in the middle of the nineteenth century.[10] The idea of wisdom literature may help one discern a constellation of ancient writings with points of contact, but it was neither explicated nor promoted by the ancient authors themselves. Wisdom literature is, as Matthew Goff explains, "an inductive category based on our reading of ancient literature, rather than a precise class of texts that was rigidly defined by their authors."[11] It is hardly surprising, therefore, that the process of identifying wisdom texts has typically been rather impressionistic, often based on the frequent occurrence of the term "wisdom" in them.[12] Yet, even this feature is not watertight as some texts from Qumran, like the book of Mysteries, avoid the Hebrew term חכמה and prefer related terms such as "understanding" (בינה), "insight" (שכל), or "knowledge" (דעת). This clearly adds an element of intuition to the task of textual categorization.¹³

The multiplicity of wisdom literature has prompted critical discussion on the helpfulness of the very category.¹⁴ While the idea remains somewhat problematic, most scholars recognize its value as long as the categorization does not distort or downplay the dynamic nature of the evidence. The imposition of a modern category or taxonomy is not necessarily a problem, but it can be seen as an intellectual act that can be done in meaningful ways. In recent years, the need to rethink the existence and defining criteria of wisdom literature has sparked various promising responses. Some scholars have sought to detect parallels between wisdom texts without imposing definite lists of genre criteria.¹⁵ Others have emphasized that the designation "wisdom text" does not need to be an exclusive one.¹⁶ Crucially, the intended genre of a text may be obscure, as is the case of many Qumran scrolls, which warns against forcing a given text into any predetermined class. Instead, one should acknowledge the manifestation of different literary features in a text and then consider their implications for textual classification, including the definition of a text's literary genre(s).

While the discussion on the essence and criteria of wisdom literature continues, the question is obviously about a vital collection of texts that resists strict generic classification. Furthermore, the wisdom corpus is heterogeneous regarding provenance, as the writings are rooted in a myriad of temporal, geographical, and intellectual settings. Recent studies have advanced our notion of wisdom texts in these respects, but they have nevertheless concentrated on wisdom as a type of literature. Choosing another path, I argue in this book that wisdom is more than a mode of literature and that the conception of wisdom as a genre is not the only type of taxonomy with an etic dimension that one can create based on the ancient textual evidence on wisdom. As I hope to demonstrate, new facets emerge when wisdom's lived, embodied, and performed aspects are placed at the centre of analysis.

To clarify, the selected focus on the phenomenon of lived wisdom does not mean that I would wish to end the discussion on wisdom as a category of literature. On the contrary, one may well continue to reflect on the conditions under which it makes sense to conceive of wisdom as a body of writings. Yet, I aim at showing that genre is not the only – or necessarily the most fascinating or productive – question that one may raise regarding wisdom in Jewish antiquity. As I hope to demonstrate, there are alternative pathways that help one uncover neglected aspects of wisdom and ensure that scholars are not stuck with perennial, and at times slightly tedious, debates. Ideally, the proposed way of reading wisdom would also serve to deconstruct disciplinary boundaries and communicate the relevance of Jewish wisdom to other scholars of the ancient world and beyond.[17]

In summary, the aim of this book is not to create an "either–or" setup, i.e., to argue that the time to approach wisdom as a body of literature would be over. It simply intends to introduce a complementary way of reading ancient Jewish texts on wisdom. One can also, but not exclusively, think of and conceptualize wisdom in terms of lived practices and lifestyle.

On the loci of lived wisdom

Where can (lived) wisdom be found? In order to reach the sources that bear relevance to the topic of this book, I need to deconstruct several boundaries between standard areas of research. First, I propose that it is necessary to rethink the loci of wisdom, as relevant materials appear outside the standard "wisdom corpus." Second, it would be intellectually dishonest to concentrate only on those texts that later came to be included in Jewish and Christian canons, which did not exist in the second temple era (*c.* 515 BCE–70 CE). Third, I wish to acknowledge that ideas of lived wisdom appear in both Semitic and Greek Jewish writings, which calls for analysing multiple cultural registers and for dismantling the outdated "Judaism vs. Hellenism" distinction.

Beginning with the loci of wisdom, the group of Jewish wisdom compositions remains difficult to specify. As discussed above, the texts on wisdom are not homogeneous regarding style, content, or provenance, which ought to deter one from focusing on a narrow body of sources such as the "wisdom books" of the Hebrew Bible or "instructional texts." Surely, many of the texts to be analysed in this book count as instructions, which is a typical understanding of wisdom literature,[18] but the selected sources are not limited to them. Rather, I will address and explore a range of writings that indicate an interest in wisdom and related concepts such as knowledge or virtue. In so doing, I wish to stress that wisdom figures in many types of texts, extending from autobiography to instruction, encomium, liturgical poetry, rule literature, and philosophical treatise.[19]

In other words, I actively promote an inclusive understanding of wisdom, which helps me leave aside the question of wisdom as a corpus of texts and proceed to ask alternative questions concerned with wisdom. This is not a book about wisdom literature, but about notions of lived wisdom, which means that any source with reflection on and engagement with wisdom and related ideas is potentially relevant. The rule texts from Qumran and Philo of Alexandria's writings, for example, are extremely relevant regarding wisdom, although they are not typically included in the standard corpus of Jewish wisdom literature.

While I will integrate various texts into the enquiry, one study obviously cannot cover everything pertaining to lived wisdom in Jewish antiquity. My purpose, therefore, is not to present an exhaustive treatment of the topic, but to address a set of questions in the light of selected sources. This does not mean that there would not be other sources or themes to make the argument. Rather, I have used my curatorial freedom to communicate essential aspects of lived wisdom by means of texts and topics that I consider to illustrate the issue under scrutiny. At the same time, even if my treatment of lived wisdom is not exhaustive, the corpus to be studied in this book is relatively vast, which creates the risk of superficiality. I will not be able to discuss all the materials in great depth, but my aim at this point is to introduce a new perspective and approach that is not limited by genre categories.

Second, in addition to promoting an inclusive notion of wisdom, it is necessary to deconstruct later canonical boundaries and to analyse the variety of Jewish wisdom regardless of them. Canonical divisions are not warranted, although they continue to have an undesirable effect on scholarship, creating a situation that Robert Kraft has characterized as the "tyranny of canonical assumptions."[20] In recent years, however, it has become increasingly clear that one needs to reject canonical presuppositions in order to grasp the vitality of texts in Jewish antiquity.[21] Authors in the late second temple era did not operate with a notion of a fixed and closed canon.[22] Hence, it is not intellectually sustainable for modern scholars to maintain later canonical boundaries as they think of the relevance and value of various texts for ancient Jewish communities. On the contrary, scholars are prompted to deconstruct the very idea of "the Bible" in the context of second temple Judaism.[23]

In this book, therefore, I will not prioritize canonical books over those that did not end up in Jewish and Christian collections of scripture in late antiquity. I am committed to examining individual texts, irrespective of their origin and author, in their wider intellectual contexts, and I seek to bring them into a dialogue with each other. This is crucial since the Hebrew Bible and the Septuagint offer but some evidence for the phenomenon of lived wisdom, which also presents itself in the Qumran scrolls and Greek Jewish materials. While this point may seem obvious to some scholars, I cannot take it for granted, as many scholars in the field of biblical studies continue to work on wisdom based on a very narrow set of sources known from the Hebrew and Greek canons, or from the former alone.

Third, I must address the question of Judaism and Hellenism at the outset. In this book, I do not seek to deconstruct only boundaries between "biblical" and "extra-biblical" sources, but also those between Jewish texts written in Semitic languages and those written in Greek. I am committed to bringing these sets of compositions into a dialogue with each other, in order to perceive (dis)continuities within ancient Jewish intellectual culture, which was vibrant both in Judea and the diaspora. As I hope to show, the sum of Semitic and Greek writings illustrates the multiple cultural registers in which ancient Israelite and early Jewish authors discussed wisdom and the good life.

By analysing both Semitic and Greek texts I join the overwhelming majority of scholars who wish to move beyond the binary distinction between Judaism and Hellenism, questioning the idea of "two essentially monadic cultures that were destined to collide like billiard balls."[24] In recent decades, scholars have come to characterize Hellenism as a process of cultural collaboration.[25] Lee Levine, for example, stresses that Jews had ongoing contact with "the outside world." They both cultivated their own tradition and incorporated new elements into it.[26] Similarly, Erich Gruen argues that Jews in the diaspora naturally came into close contact with Greek culture, but it also flourished in areas within the reach of those who lived in Judea, and ancient Jews did not have to choose between two options, i.e., either "succumbing" or "resisting."[27]

The widespread exposure to Greek culture does not mean that all of early Judaism was the same. On the contrary, there is much variety, which is to be anticipated, considering that Hellenism always implies a fusion or *mélange* of Greek and local cultures.[28] As set out by Levine, "the Hellenistic world was the scene of a veritable potpourri of cultural forces." Thus, Hellenization was not about assimilation and influence, but about "the interplay of a wide range of cultural forces on an *oikumene* (the civilized world as then known) defined in large part – but not exclusively – by the Greek conquests." Such an interplay resulted in the selective adoption of new ideas, mores, or institutions. Since all Jewish groups were affected by the process to some extent, one should avoid making simple yes/no or either/or claims and, instead, "formulate more subtle distinctions, determining how much, in which areas, and at what pace these changes took place."[29]

Even if scholars now recognize the mixture of diverse cultural elements in early Judaism, one still comes across the binary phrase "Judaism and Hellenism," as well as the related assumption that Hellenistic Jewish texts mean Jewish texts written in Greek. Furthermore, the nuanced discussion on Hellenism has not adequately shaped the analysis of Jewish wisdom in its wider cultural context. In this book, I will examine all late second temple sources as culturally Hellenistic, rejecting the idea that only some Jewish authors or groups would represent Hellenistic Judaism and others not. While Jewish wisdom drew on the ancient Near East, it lived on and flourished in new contexts, where Jews responded to and were moulded by Hellenism in fundamentally different ways.[30]

Beyond wisdom literature: A turn to lived wisdom

This book investigates "functional wisdom" in Jewish antiquity insofar as I am concerned with practices and activities mentioned in wisdom-related texts, thus seeking to understand what a person or a life characterized as wise looked like according to the ancient authors. By unearthing such embodied aspects of wisdom, I wish to introduce and promote a conception of lived wisdom. In what follows, I will briefly review the turn to "lived religion" in the field of religious studies and then explain how my present enterprise pertains to, or deviates from, this trajectory in current research.

In the past couple of decades, scholars of religion and anthropology, especially those working in North America, have carried on a vibrant discussion on the phenomenon of lived religion.[31] The term "lived religion," as it has been used in these circles, is not narrowly defined, but it enables a plethora of approaches. Robert Orsi, one of the pioneers of the approach, uses the term as referring to "religious practice and imagination in ongoing, dynamic relation with the realities and structures of everyday life in particular times and places."[32] He explains that the study of lived religion, which aims at rethinking "religion as a form of cultural work," takes into consideration a range of issues, including "institutions *and* persons, texts *and* rituals, practice *and* theology, things *and* ideas—all as media of making and unmaking worlds." As such, the approach aims at a holistic understanding of religion, specifically underlining its cultural and lived dimensions. The approach situates, as Orsi argues, "all religious creativity within culture and approaches all religion as lived experience."[33]

As these quotes from Orsi's work indicate, the turn to lived religion accentuates the value of everyday practices and signals a reconsideration of where religion happens and who its agents are. For the most part, studies on lived religion have highlighted daily forms of religious life and given voice to ordinary people, including women, instead of the official spokespersons or representatives of a religious tradition, who are often men. Accordingly, scholars of lived religion have aimed at analysing the practice, experience, and expression of religion and spirituality in everyday life.[34] On balance, embodied practices have been crucial in this enterprise since "religion-as-lived" is primarily based on them. It has been emphasized that lived religion requires "practical coherence," and Meredith McGuire explains the concept as follows: "It [religion] needs to make sense in one's everyday life, and it needs to be effective, to 'work,' in the sense of accomplishing some desired end."[35]

Scholars of contemporary religion first began the study of lived religion, but the approach is now gaining prominence in the study of the human past. Scholars of ancient religion, particularly those working on the Mediterranean region at the time of the Roman Empire, have applied the concept of "lived religion" to various sources, both texts and material culture, thus launching the oxymoronic concept of "lived ancient religion."[36] The model shifts attention away from practices undertaken in public or civic institutions, which have played a prominent role in the history of religion, and it has brought new issues to the focus of research, including interaction of individuals with religious specialists and traditions, forms of religious experience, and the question of embodiment. The area of research is only emerging, but its pioneers have already provided other scholars with tools and inspiration by arguing for the relevance of investigating lived experiences and events in the past.[37]

The "lived ancient religion" model is gradually making its way to the study of ancient Israel and early Judaism. Susan Niditch has conducted pioneering research on religion as lived in her book on personal religion in the Neo-Babylonian and Persian eras. As argued by Niditch, the approach enables scholars to reflect on the "variety, syncretisms, and synergies" of the ancient Israelite tradition. Furthermore, it helps scholars "to appreciate the interplay between individuals and communities, tradition and innovation, official and unofficial religion."[38] To take another example pertaining to Qumran studies, Jessica Keady has examined the embodied experiences and daily lives of ordinary men and women in ancient Judea. Analysing multiple writings concerned with (im)purity, she underlines how impurity made men vulnerable in the everyday life. These are questions of lived ancient religion without doubt, even though Keady does not explicitly associate her work with this stream of contemporary research but with the sociology of everyday life.[39]

Building on these developments in recent research, I will examine the topic of lived wisdom in Jewish antiquity, especially highlighting intersections of wisdom and behaviour or lived practices.[40] The latter include emulation of the sage and other exemplars, exercises and activities of wisdom teachers, and ideal ways of living in early Jewish communities. In so doing, I seek to approach wisdom from the perspective of lifestyle: What is a wise person like? How can one become wise or retain wisdom? What constitutes the erudite and exemplary lifestyle of the teacher? What does wisdom mean in the context of a group of people? Certain factors, however, may present potential problems for my aim to associate ancient Jewish wisdom with the study of "lived ancient religion," and some clarifying remarks on the frame and intention of my enquiry are thus in order.

First, as already discussed above, studies on lived religion typically stress the experiences and activities of "ordinary people," including the agency of women. Ancient Jewish texts on wisdom, however, tend to originate from the upper strata of society, as learned male teachers and thinkers with at least some monetary and social capital produced them.[41] Surely, these people did not belong to the highest strata of the society: they were not rulers, but financially dependent on those wealthier than and socially superior to them, which makes them a part of the "retainer class."[42] Yet, they obviously enjoyed a materially comfortable position and many privileges of which many other ancient Jews could not have dreamed, indicating that their world is one of privilege without doubt.

Second, as regards methodology, studies on lived religion tend to draw on interviews and ethnographic work, which enables scholars to hear and document the voices of ordinary people who do not hold positions of power in their respective communities. Such methods of research, however, are not available to scholars working on antiquity, which means that the study of lived religion will never be possible for us in the same sense that it is possible for those investigating contemporary forms of religion. The present investigation, as well, must rely on the evidence of ancient literary texts. Moreover, material culture does not come to my rescue, as the selected research question is rather conceptual. It does pertain to education in Jewish antiquity, but the archaeological evidence for that phenomenon is extremely limited.[43]

I have to consider all these factors as I embark on my study. While they might hamper it, I argue that they do not prevent the proposed analysis of lived wisdom in Jewish antiquity. In spite of obvious limitations, the extant literary sources may illuminate the phenomenon in question. In what sense, then, do Jewish texts on wisdom pertain to "lived (ancient) religion"? Most importantly, they describe and thus help one uncover the importance of human activities at the intersections of ancient wisdom and religion.[44] Furthermore, Jewish writings on wisdom, as I hope to demonstrate, illustrate more variegated social realities than one might expect, and they can be associated with both women and men, even if the role of the latter is more dominant in the extant textual evidence.

Unlike one might expect from a lived religion approach, most of the selected sources do not illuminate the everyday life of an "average" Jew in antiquity, for they originate from educated circles with many sorts of capital. While this capital was primarily intellectual and social in nature, these people also possessed a great deal of monetary capital in comparison with many other members of the society. Yet, as I will demonstrate in this book, wisdom is not only about privileged teachers and their wealthy pupils who are about to take important posts in society. Ancient Jewish sources illustrate the teaching of young men of privilege, but they also preserve accounts of communal and shared wisdom, which reveal that a life of wisdom and virtue does not only concern the upper strata of society and people with advanced education. The authors of such accounts specifically value daily life as a context of practising and performing wisdom and virtue, thus demonstrating that it also belongs to ordinary people who engage in mundane and manual labour or domestic life.

Regarding gender, the remaining evidence largely concerns the experiences of well-off men, as Jewish texts on wisdom, like other ancient intellectual cultures, originate from male-dominated circles. Even though the extant sources devote more attention to men than to women, I wish to emphasize that Jewish texts on wisdom contain some evidence on women's lived wisdom. In general, there are occasional glimpses of women's education in Jewish literature from the second temple period. In this book, I will address the topic of women's wisdom regarding the early Jewish movement known from the Qumran scrolls and the group of Jewish female philosophers depicted by Philo of Alexandria in his treatise *De vita contemplativa*.

Jewish texts on wisdom, therefore, communicate ideas of lived wisdom that apply to both sexes and to different strata of society, even if the agency of affluent males is overrepresented. Yet, the overall transition from text to life admittedly remains complicated. The literary and cultural representations of lived wisdom in ancient Jewish writings are idealized, and ideals are desirable states of affairs that may be difficult to realize, which means that one cannot read the ancient texts as directly shedding light on socio-historical realities in the lives of Jewish individuals and communities. I wish to stress, however, that ideals are not fully abstract or transcendent, but rooted in social reality.[45] Hence, while some of the accounts may tell more about the ideals of the ancient authors than about any real-life situations, I argue that these ideals, which provide one with access to ancient notions of how wisdom *ought* to be lived, are nevertheless rooted in social realities, even if they are covered with a rhetorical icing. This makes it likely that they at least echo practices of ancient Jews.

In summary, the selected approach underlines that ancient Israelite and early Jewish sources on wisdom illustrate a number of lived and embodied practices, which show that wisdom is not just about thinking but also about ways of living.[46] The extant sources highlight wisdom's social dimensions and interactions, thus illustrating that "religion arises at the intersection of inner experience and the outer world."[47] While the foci of the previous studies on lived religion have been different, they nonetheless help me draw attention to these hitherto largely ignored aspects of Jewish wisdom, as well as assisting me in the formulation of new research questions related to ancient texts and lived realities. A close reading of familiar writings from a new angle forces one to reimagine a phenomenon and may yield a fresh understanding of it.

Recent remarks on wisdom and formation

While my conception of lived wisdom opens up a new perspective on ancient Jewish culture, it builds on and is indebted to earlier observations on the formative aspect of the wisdom tradition. Character formation is here understood as denoting the training and shaping of a person, undertaken with the purpose that one would display qualities valued and privileged by the surrounding society. Several insightful analyses have already shown that in the Hebrew Bible and early Jewish writings, the pursuit of wisdom is not just about knowing, but it has the power to (trans)form the recipient.

William Brown's research on character formation in the books of Proverbs, Job, and Qoheleth has been pioneering.[48] Among a wealth of insights, he observes the significance of way imagery, which emerges in frequent references to the ways of the wise or the evil ones, denoting behaviour (cf. Deut 30:15–16). The assumption is that the pursuit of wisdom keeps the self in constant motion.[49] Wisdom is about a formative path, which Brown describes as "a rugged road of crisis and wonder."[50] The element of wonder is salient as Brown describes the three books as placing the reader on the "threshold of wonder," whether the question is about the son's silence before wisdom in Proverbs, about Job before the "alien world of brutal beauty," or about Qoheleth's encounter with death and life's elegance. By cultivating awe and amazement, the books evoke a desire to explore and encourage human growth, which is intellectual, moral, and aesthetic in nature.⁵¹ All of them engage with lived realities, thus attempting to make sense of life and its fullness.⁵²

Yet, scholars have not stressed the importance of character formation in biblical and cognate texts with one voice. It has also been argued that ideas of human development and moral formation, which are integral to virtue ethics, are secondary in biblical texts. John Barton states that in the wisdom literature of the Old Testament, "everyone is either good or bad, wise or foolish, and there is little idea of moral progress, at least beyond childhood."⁵³ He acknowledges that more nuanced ideas emerge at times, as is shown by complex protagonists of narrative materials. Even so, Barton argues that "there remains a lot of black-and-white thinking" and that "the quick categorization of people as either good or bad … dominates the impression."⁵⁴

The cited claims may not present Barton's final thoughts on the topic.⁵⁵ It is clear, however, that they simplify the evidence for ethical reflection in ancient Israel. Anne Stewart, for example, has demonstrated that Proverbs is concerned with "gradations, variations, and the particularity of moral decision making." The book's purpose is to cultivate the student who remains "on the path to wisdom, never having finally arrived."⁵⁶ In this book, too, I will discuss the value of aspiration in Jewish wisdom discourse. The search for wisdom involves an attempt to lead a life of virtue and even one of perfection.

In addition to Hebrew Bible studies, wisdom and formation have sparked interest in the study of early Judaism. During the past decades, Benjamin Wright has made pathbreaking observations on the formative purposes of compositions such as the book of Ben Sira, which aim at shaping the students' behaviour and "their manner of relation to the world."⁵⁷ In recent years, scholars have also begun to read Jewish texts in their wider ancient Mediterranean context. In this process, Jewish writings have been associated with the Greek concept of παιδεία, i.e., the educational and cultural formation of a person.⁵⁸ On the one hand, scholars have analysed the use of the concept in the Septuagint and in other Jewish sources written in Greek. On the other hand, they have evaluated the concept's interpretative potential in relation to Semitic wisdom discourses, tracing and analysing formative elements in them.⁵⁹ More broadly, scholars have explored ethical issues and instruction in Semitic materials, reflecting on the meaning and content of ethics for those Jews who lacked a specific category that would be a direct equivalent to the Greek term ἠθικός.⁶⁰

This trajectory, the growing interest in the formative purposes of wisdom-related materials, is a promising corrective. It complements and remedies the numerous previous studies, which have prioritized form and content, or mere form, as the key features of a Jewish wisdom text.[61] Form and content are certainly relevant for textual analysis and classification, but function is an equally salient aspect of a composition, and I argue that it should receive more explicit attention in the study of ancient wisdom than it has hitherto received. Wisdom texts, for one, do not aim at a neutral and objective presentation of information, but they constantly attempt to persuade, convince, and train their intended audiences, thus seeking to shape the thoughts, character, and actions of the addressees.[62]

In this book, I build on the previous research concerning wisdom and formation, as well as the aspirational nature of Jewish wisdom discourse. I am inspired by and indebted to the idea that the ancient authors who wrote on wisdom wished to have an effect on the audience, and I acknowledge that pedagogical concerns and character formation are part of the lifestyle aspect of wisdom. Yet, I will argue that wisdom is not just about the formation of one's thoughts and character. Moreover, the ancient seekers and lovers of wisdom were expected to engage with and perform wisdom through a range of lived exercises and practices. These activities are not detached from the formative process, but they constitute a part of the formation of an ethical subject.

Philosophy as a way of life

By means of this book on lived wisdom in Jewish antiquity, I seek to contribute to the ongoing scholarly conversations on lived ancient religion and wisdom's formative role in the ancient Jewish tradition. Moreover, the stress on lived wisdom is topical considering recent research on the aims and nature of Greco-Roman philosophy. Several scholars have argued that the aspect of lifestyle was integral to ancient philosophy in the Mediterranean region. This must also inform our reading of ancient Jewish materials on wisdom, which indicate some overlap with the phenomenon of philosophy.

To clarify, ancient Israelite and early Jewish wisdom is rooted in the ancient Near Eastern world. This means that it was never isolated from cross-cultural conversations but always carried a "cosmopolitan" flavour, as the authors knew and acknowledged that there exists an earnest quest for wisdom among other nations; they were also willing to engage with and learn from foreign traditions.[63] Hence, Jewish wisdom is not the same thing as Greek philosophy but has its own trajectory and multicultural roots. Meanwhile, it is striking that both neighbouring traditions focus on wisdom and share related questions of well-being and the good life. As such, the two phenomena are conceptually related and offer different perspectives on similar issues.[64]

Moreover, the distinction between Jewish wisdom and Greek philosophy becomes blurry in the Hellenistic period. In this era, the geographical, cultural, and social contexts of Jewish authors varied a great deal. First, Jewish authors writing in Semitic languages adopted philosophical ideas from the wider *Zeitgeist* of their time. In so doing, they took part in "philosophical" discussions broadly understood. Second, Greek was the mother tongue of many Jews, which means that the idiom of philosophy was native to them and they could actively operate within Greek philosophical discourse, producing new philosophical literature from their own loci. In fact, Greek Jewish authors explicitly identified Jews with philosophers.[65] These texts, too, are integral to our notion of ancient Jewish wisdom, even if biblical scholars have unfortunately tended to neglect them in their studies on "wisdom literature." In addition to illustrating the variety of Jewish wisdom, Greek Jewish texts contribute to our understanding of ancient philosophy as regards its breadth and cultural diversity.[66]

These factors urge one to analyse Jewish wisdom discourse over against a wider cross-cultural horizon and, in general, to explore the very concept of "philosophy." A contemporary Western person may think of a purely theoretical and academic discipline, whilst the term's connotations were much richer in the ancient Mediterranean world. First, philosophy was not radically separate from religion. Socrates, for example, valued religious commitments and Plato acknowledged the realm of divinity.[67] This speaks against the idea that religion and philosophy would have represented two "different realms of reality" in antiquity.[68] Second, philosophy was associated with phrases such as the art of living, lifestyle, or medicine for the soul. These expressions are rooted in Socrates' concern for taking care of one's soul, but the Stoics were the ones who fully developed the idea of philosophy as an art of living (τεχνὴ περὶ τὸν βίον).[69] The aspect of lifestyle was crucial to the extent that the Stoics, unlike Aristotle, made no distinction between the practical and theoretical parts of philosophy; the purpose of all philosophy was to live well and happily.[70]

The research of Pierre Hadot, in particular, has inspired scholars to explore the lived, pragmatic, and existential dimension of Greco-Roman philosophy. Hadot argued that philosophy was not limited to theoretical sophistication or the confines of thought and discussion, but it entailed a whole way of life.[71] Despite the emphasis on the power and use of reason, the question was not about a purely abstract subject to be studied in a social vacuum, but about the process of dedicating one's life to the cultivation of wisdom in the context of a specific school. Philosophy, therefore, provided the seeker of wisdom with instructions on how to be and act, as well as with a set of everyday practices.[72] This concern for lived wisdom is visible in the ancient synonyms for a "philosophical school": the authors frequently make use of terms such as αἵρεσις (school), *secta* (sect), ἀγωγή (way), ὁδός (path), ἄσκησις (discipline), and βίος (life), thus indicating that one's actions were regarded as being inseparable from one's beliefs.[73]

Several scholars have now argued that Greco-Roman philosophy involved a commitment to a certain type of behaviour.[74] Surely, one should not downplay the role of argumentation in ancient philosophy.[75] Yet, philosophy was not limited to developing one's argumentative skills, but the aim of philosophical discourse was to justify and motivate one's choice of lifestyle. Thereafter, various "spiritual exercises" – including diverse physical (e.g., bodily or dietary restrictions), discursive (e.g., dialogue), and intuitive (e.g., contemplation) practices – were undertaken in order to modify the self of the practising subject, preparing one to live and die well.[76] Alternatively, one could describe this aspect of philosophy as the mental training required for a philosophical life.[77] In any event, the assumption was that the soul's health presupposes training.[78] Apart from a mindset of theoretical reflection, philosophy was to provide the seekers of wisdom with ἄσκησις, "a lived exercise" involving discipline, training, and practice, and this act was not limited to the cognitive level.[79]

The remaining evidence for the techniques of spiritual exercise is scattered but adequate to prove the phenomenon. According to Diogenes Laertius, Diogenes of Sinope, one of the founders of cynic philosophy, distinguished between mental and bodily exercises (D.L. 6.70). He also reports that the early Stoics Herillus and Dionysus each wrote a work on ἄσκησις (D.L. 7.166–7). While these are not preserved, the Roman Stoic sources, which come from the first century CE but draw on an earlier tradition, document the conception of spiritual exercise. The latter include Musonius Rufus' *On Exercise*, which harks back to cynic views, and Epictetus' *Discourses* (3.12).[80] Seneca refers to a daily exercise of self-examination, which he learned from Quintus Sextius (*Ira* 3.36.1–3), but which is probably Pythagorean in origin (cf. *Aur. carm.* 40–4), and he comments on the cynic notion of daily meditation on "wholesome maxims" (*Ben.* 7.2.1). Moreover, Marcus Aurelius' *Meditations* materializes the conception of spiritual exercise by representing an extended form of such an exercise.[81]

Thus, whereas modern academia mostly separates philosophy from lifestyle commitments, the essential goal of Greco-Roman philosophy was neither neutral and objective thinking nor the achievement of a diploma. Philosophy was ultimately concerned with the formation of a wise person, it entailed a whole way of life, and it involved different types of practice (ἄσκησις). This sort of exercise and self-discipline was not just about "the *negative* denial of world," but it involved the wilful training of one's faculties in "the *positive* pursuit of moral and spiritual perfection."[82]

These observations on the intersections of philosophy and practice invite one to explore lived aspects of Jewish wisdom in a wider ancient Mediterranean context. What kinds of exercises are associated with a wise and learned lifestyle? How do Jewish authors situate their own practices in relation to philosophy?

An outline of the book

In what follows, I will move on to explore Jewish wisdom discourse from the viewpoint of lived ancient religion. I will analyse a number of Jewish portraits of ideal ways of living from three thematic angles, including the figure of the sage, the lifestyle of the teacher, and wisdom as a communal project. In so doing, I hope to demonstrate that wisdom counts as more than a mode of literature in the context of Jewish antiquity; it appears, as will be shown, as a lived and embodied phenomenon that entails constant exercise and performance.

In Chapter 2, titled "Living embodiments of wisdom: The sage as an exemplar," I will investigate the figure of the wise person in the ancient Jewish tradition and its immediate environs. The Hebrew Bible presents an array of wise and skilful people, including artisans, diviners, administrators, councillors, and kings. Jewish wisdom discourse changes in the Hellenistic period, however, as a specific concern for the sage as an intellectual emerges in the extant sources. Around the same time, Jewish authors begin to elucidate the import of emulation, i.e., the process of becoming identical to one's exemplar, and the ideal wise person becomes cast as a template to follow. The topic of ancestral perfection is also pertinent in this respect because many authors encourage emulation by immersing their audiences in the lives of biblical figures. In order to grasp the wider context of these changes in early Jewish discourse, I will also inspect Greek notions of the wise person, arguing that the wider Hellenistic *Zeitgeist* prompted Jewish authors to spell out the idea of an exemplary sage.

Chapter 3, "Learning and lifestyle: The everyday performance of wisdom teachers," explores how wisdom can be practised and performed in daily life, thus underlining the value of exercise and embodiment in the life of pedagogical professionals. I will make observations on biblical pedagogues in general, including Moses and Ezra, but my enquiry largely focuses on three major teachers from the Hellenistic and early Roman eras: the protagonist of the book of Qoheleth, the instructor featuring in the book of Ben Sira, and the figure of the maskil known from the Qumran scrolls. As I hope to demonstrate, it is possible to extract a number of lived practices from the literary portraits of these teachers. Based on them, an erudite lifestyle involves exercises such as reading, writing, observation, prayer, prophetic activity, liturgical performance, or reception of esoteric knowledge. In spite of certain parallels, the profiles of the pedagogues remain relatively distinct, thus illustrating the copious ways in which a Jewish teacher was imagined to execute his learned way of life; the wise lifestyle manifested itself variously in different local contexts.

In Chapter 4, "Shared wisdom: Ideal ways of living in Jewish communities," I will shift attention from wise individuals to clusters of people. My purpose is to explore desirable lifestyles attributed to early Jewish groups, including their motives and content, in order to comprehend what a life of wisdom and insight could mean in communal terms. My analysis will focus on three Jewish groups, including the *yaḥad* movement depicted in some of the Qumran scrolls, the classical sources on the Essenes by Philo of Alexandria and Josephus Flavius, and Philo's description of the Therapeutae in his *De vita contemplativa*. As I hope to show, these portraits of the good life serve to demonstrate that wisdom is more than a characteristic of an individual: wisdom and its pursuit characterize groups as well. The selected accounts of collective attempts to live virtuously document the idea of wisdom as a way of life. They also pertain to the question of Judaism as a type of philosophy in the ancient Mediterranean milieu.

My investigation into lived wisdom ends with a conclusion in Chapter 5, where I will summarize the key observations and arguments on the lived and embodied dimensions of Jewish wisdom in the second temple period. Furthermore, I will briefly address the afterlife of lived wisdom in late antiquity, including the early rabbinic tradition and the rise of early Christian practices.

2

Living embodiments of wisdom: The sage as an exemplar

In this chapter, I will approach the topic of lived wisdom by means of analysing the literary representation of wise people in the ancient Jewish tradition and its immediate environs. What is a wise person like? How do ancient authors depict and discuss the figure of the ideal sage? To clarify, the term "sage" (חכם in Hebrew; σοφός in Greek) can have multiple meanings depending on the context. While my survey will demonstrate this variety of connotations, I am primarily interested in the rise of the conception of the sage as a living embodiment of wisdom, i.e., as a wise person who serves as an exemplar to be followed by those who desire and pursue wisdom.

Scholars have previously undertaken many excellent analyses concerning social, historical, and literary aspects of ancient writings on sages, whether in the context of the ancient Near East, the biblical world, or the Greco-Roman tradition.[1] Nevertheless, there has been rather little reflection on the idealized nature of these wise figures. In what follows, I will specifically examine the emergence and manifestations of such a notion of the wise person, arguing that Jewish wisdom discourse indicates a major shift in the Hellenistic and early Roman periods. At this time, the extant sources begin to pay extensive attention to the model-sage, explicating his significance as an idealized figure and an object of emulation, whether the question is about promoting contemporary wise or about reimagining biblical figures of the past as templates to be followed.

After a survey of ancient Israelite and early Jewish compositions, I will contextualize the detected development in the portrayal of the wise person in relation to the wider Mediterranean context of these writings. As will be seen, a comparison with (non-Jewish) Greek[2] sources suggests that the Jewish discussion on the model-sage and the related process of emulation were moulded by the wider *Zeitgeist* of the Hellenistic period. Thus, while being rooted in the earlier Hebrew tradition, the figure of the ideal sage appears to be a product of cultural collaboration.

The rise of the ideal sage

The ancient Near Eastern tradition is familiar with a range of wise men and women: teacher-guides, scribes, advisors, diviners, and people with other esoteric skills. The mere fact that the Akkadian language does not have a single term denoting "wisdom" or a "wise person" shows that wisdom has many loci. Here one may consider a number of related terms such as *apkallu* denoting gods or legendary sages, *igigallu* meaning wisdom or a wise person, or *ummânu* referring to an expert or a skilled artisan.[3] At times, legendary wise figures are known by their proper names, as is the case with Adapa, the mythical and heroic scribe of the Sumero-Akkadian tradition, or Ahiqar, the wise scribe and counsellor of Assyria who is known from the Aramaic texts.[4] Mostly, however, the question is about various professional groups who held leadership positions in local communities and served them along with types of expertise and knowledge.

Traces of learned professionals date back to the third millennium BCE. The Sumerian tradition mentions *ummia*, the wise heads of the *edubba*, the "tablet-houses," from around 2500 BCE. These places of learning were crucial to the intellectual and cultural life of the time since they prepared students for taking up influential positions in society and for service in temple and palace settings.[5] Yet, kings came to be recognized as the wise *par excellence*, as the possessors of divine wisdom, in the ancient Near East. This is clear by the time of Hammurabi (1792–1750 BCE), although the evidence for the king's special knowledge may date back to the third millennium BCE. In spite of his exceptional aura, the ancient Near Eastern king relied on other experts in his daily life, and the performance of wisdom was not thus limited to the context of the royal court. A myriad of non-royal professionals displayed wisdom in many senses of the word, including skill, knowledge, and expertise. These "commoners" comprised artisans, architects, builders, soldiers, cult officials, diviners, exorcists, musicians, physicians, scribes, counsellors, and teachers.[6] It is worth highlighting that women, too, served as scribes, poets, performing artists, healers, mantic sages, and counsellors.[7]

Since ancient Israel belongs to this wider cultural milieu of the ancient Near East, it is hardly surprising that a myriad of wise figures appears in the Hebrew Bible. The term חכם refers to many sorts of people with special skills, insight, or intellectual abilities, ranging from artisans to humans with low cunning.[8] Meanwhile, some obviously exemplary people are not described by the term חכם

but by other desirable qualities. Job, for example, is introduced as a blameless and upright man who feared God and shunned away evil (Job 1:1, 8). The figure, undoubtedly a hero, rejected the conventional and conformist wisdom of his friends (e.g., 12:2, 12; 26:2–3).[9]

Several wise artisans, who are characterized as חכמים, perform their "wisdom" through crafts and designs. Some of them are named, including Bezalel, who is described as being filled "with a divine spirit of skill, ability, and knowledge (בחכמה ובתבונה ובדעת) in every kind of craft" (Exod 31:3–5), which makes him capable of working with precious metals, cutting stones, and carving wood (cf. 35:31–5).[10] Hiram, a son of a coppersmith from Tyre, is another named artisan, employed by Solomon to work on the temple of Jerusalem because of his חכמה. Similarly to Bezelel, he was filled "with skill, ability, and talent (את-החכמה ואת-התבונה ואת-הדעת) for executing all work in bronze" (1 Kgs 7:14, cf. 2 Chr 2:6). Other wise artisans of the Hebrew Bible remain anonymous, as is the case with those who prepare Aaron's priestly vestments (Exod 28:3) and the garments of the sanctuary (36:1, 4), or the women who spin (35:25–6); they demonstrate a distinctive skill, חכמת-לב, which literally denotes "wisdom of the heart."[11]

Even if any skilful men and women count as "wise" of some sort, the Hebrew Bible also refers to wise people in the sense of learned people and professionals, or remarkable leaders, who serve various social contexts and institutions.[12] Some texts surely doubt or challenge the presumed wisdom of the חכמים (e.g., Isa 29:14; 44:25; Jer 8:8–9), but many of them are rather confident about the capacities of human beings, although also warning against boast and stressing the value of humility (e.g., Isa 5:21; Jer 9:22–3; Prov 26:12).

While the spirit of wisdom is an attribute of the ideal king (Isa 11:2), only two kings, David and Solomon, are actually credited wisdom in the Hebrew Bible. David is described "as wise as an angel of God," knowing "all that goes on in the land" (2 Sam 14:20, cf. 14:17).[13] Solomon, however, is acclaimed as the wisest of all.[14] In a dream, the young king asks for an "understanding heart" (לב שמע) in order to be able to judge. God, impressed by Solomon's wish to acquire insight instead of longevity, riches, or the life of his enemies, grants him with a "wise and understanding heart" (לב חכם ונבון); God also assures wealth and honour for which Solomon had not asked (1 Kgs 3:5–15). A divine promise of exceptionality (3:12) follows the king, who exerts his wisdom in the execution of justice (3:16–28, esp. 3:28). Solomon's legendary wisdom is further clarified in the famous passage in 1 Kgs 5:9–14:

God endowed Solomon with wisdom and discernment in great measure, with understanding as vast as the sands on the seashore. Solomon's wisdom was greater than the wisdom of all the Kedemites and than all the wisdom of the Egyptians. He was the wisest of all men: [wiser] than Ethan the Ezrahite, and Heman, Chalkol, and Darda the sons of Mahol. His fame spread among all the surrounding nations. He composed three thousand proverbs, and his songs numbered on thousand and five. He discoursed about trees, from the cedar in Lebanon to the hyssop that grows out of the wall; and he discoursed about beasts, birds, creeping things, and fishes. Men of all peoples came to hear Solomon's wisdom, [sent] by all the kings of the earth who had heard of his wisdom.

This passage is informative beyond documenting the idea of Solomon's divine wisdom and understanding. First, it contextualizes the king's wisdom in a cross-cultural frame, signalling that the concern for wisdom knows no national boundaries. Second, it gestures at the lifestyle of the sage, explaining how Solomon composed (דבר) proverbs and songs, as well as discoursing (דבר) about the natural world. Third, the passage mentions educational travel, referring to people who journeyed in order to hear and learn from Solomon (cf. 2 Chr 9:22–3).[15] The travel motif also appears in the story of the Queen of Sheba who travelled to Jerusalem and tested the king with challenging questions, eventually acknowledging and praising his wisdom (1 Kgs 10:1–9).

In spite of Solomon's unmatched reputation, kings are not the only wise "professionals" of the Hebrew Bible. The latter include people with administrative and other leadership roles: the Pharaoh sets the wise and discerning Joseph over Egypt (Gen 41:39–40, cf. 41:33), and the tribal leaders set by Moses are described as חכמים (Deut 1:15). The wise are associated with counsel (Jer 18:18), and the advice of Ahitophel, for example, was esteemed to the extent that it was accepted like a "word of God" (2 Sam 16:23, cf. 17:23). Books such as Deuteronomy, Jeremiah, Proverbs, and Ezra-Nehemiah further attest to the intellectual efforts of scribal circles.[16]

A major proportion of the biblical material on wise figures concerns divinatory practices. The Hebrew Bible mentions Egyptian and Babylonian sages and magicians trained in divination and esoteric arts. The חכמים of Egypt, however, are not able to explain Pharaoh's dream (Gen 41:8), and Aaron's rod swallows the serpents that come out of the rods of the Egyptian חכמים and sorcerers (Exod 7:11, cf. 7:22; 8:3, 14).[17] Another group of foreign חכמים is mentioned in the book of Esther, which refers to the learned advisors whom the king of Persia consulted (Esth 1:13). The book of Daniel, in turn, juxtaposes the wisdom of four Judahite boys – Daniel, Hananiah, Mishael, and Azariah – with that of the Babylonians. God is said to have given them "knowledge and insight in all writings and wisdom" (מדע והשכל בכל-ספר וחכמה). Daniel also understands visions and dreams (Dan 1:17, cf. 1:4). In questions requiring wisdom, the heroic boys perform better than all the magicians and exorcists of the kingdom (1:20).

Intriguingly, the narrator mentions the boys' disciplined diet, explaining that Daniel had decided not to defile (געל) himself with the king's wine and food (1:8). The rigid diet of Daniel and his friends serves to bring about their success, including wisdom, well-being, and favour in the eyes of the king (1:15–17, 19–20). The diet motif alludes to a concern for purity, as is supported by the boys' willingness to eat vegetables instead of the king's menu (1:12, 16, cf. 10:2–3). This has led to an argument that the tale should be read in the context of national exclusiveness and not in that of "the disciplined withdrawal of the individual."[18] Yet, the either–or phrasing of a question seems misleading considering the Hellenistic context of the book: Daniel is surely presented as being dedicated to his ancestral laws, but I argue that such behaviour may simultaneously represent a form of spiritual exercise and an expression of lived and embodied wisdom.[19]

Daniel's mantic skills are another dimension of his wise persona. Nebuchadnezzar's dream agitates the king and makes him invite magicians, exorcists, sorcerers, and Chaldeans to explain it (2:2–3). When the Chaldeans confess the impossibility of the task, which would require divine powers, the king commands all the wise of Babylon (חכימי בבל) to be destroyed (2:10–12). This prompts Daniel to take up the interpretative task in order to avoid a sombre destiny that now threatens him and his friends (2:13–47). Daniel's divinatory skills are a salient aspect of his wisdom and exemplarity, as they reveal an intellectual and spiritual practice that counts as lived wisdom. Elements of lived religion also appear elsewhere in the book, for Daniel is presented as praying, fasting, and wearing sackcloth towards the end of it (9:3; 10:2–3).[20]

The aforementioned narratives acknowledge the cross-cultural nature of wisdom. At the same time, they downplay the wisdom of the other people and celebrate the wisdom of the Hebrews, which proves their excellence under challenging and unexpected circumstances. Furthermore, all these wise figures, apart from the spinning women mentioned in Exod 35:25–6, are males. This does not mean, however, that wisdom would be a gendered quality in the Hebrew Bible. On the contrary, several women manifest their wisdom through apt action and timely words.

The Song of Deborah refers to the wisest of the ladies of Sisera's mother (Judg 5:29), whereas Jer 9:16 mentions, likewise in passing, wise female lamenters. As for narratives, the story about the encounter between David and Nabal (1 Sam 25:2–43) juxtaposes Abigail with "good insight" (טובת-שכל) and Nabal the fool (1:23, 25). Abigail's considered words (1:23–31) affect the course of events as they make David refrain from violence and thus save David from himself.[21] Two anonymous women utter similarly measured responses. The wise woman of Tekoa (2 Sam 14:2) delivers a fictitious story in front of David, in order to enable Absalom's return to Jerusalem (14:1–24). Another אשה חכמה, the wise woman of Abel, speaks to Joab and agrees to hand the rebel Sheba to him for the sake of preventing an excessive destruction (20:16–22). Both women are eloquent and employ proverbs as they negotiate with powerful men (14:14; 20:18).[22]

The praise of the good wife (Prov 31:10–31) mentions the same capacity to speak well. This text celebrates the domestic virtues and household management skills of an industrious woman, but it also describes her mouth as being filled with wisdom (31:26). Women's words are further at stake elsewhere in the book of Proverbs. The words of Lemuel (31:1–9), which appear just before the praise of the good wife, present the king's mother as the teacher, thus underlining her erudition and influence (31:1–2). Moreover, the personified figure of wisdom has a voice of her own and serves to deliver teachings to a presumably male audience (1:20–33; 8:1–36; 9:1–12).

Thus, much of the intellectual vibrancy of ancient Israel is carried by a number of wise figures and their occasionally overlapping roles. The fluidity of the roles of the חכמים has resulted in critical comments on the very existence of such a professional class.[23] It clearly does not make sense to think of a fixed or well-defined category, but the idea of special wise people is plausible, as long as one acknowledges the variety of wisdoms that include both technical and cognitive skills and capacities. Some changes also took place over the course of time regarding the meaning of a wise person. The term חכמים came to describe learned intellectuals in the second temple era. The above references to the book of Daniel gesture at this development, whilst the books of Proverbs and Qoheleth explicate the concern for the sage as a prominent thinker.

The book of Proverbs consists of poems and sayings, setting a wise and virtuous life as the goal of its teaching (Prov 1:2–4). The book may have received its final form in the Hellenistic period if not before.[24] Regardless of the exact date, Proverbs signals seemingly small changes regarding the wise person, but these shifts have a profound impact on the notion of the sage. The opening of the collection of sayings, which begins in Prov 22:17, describes the content of instruction as דברי חכמים, "the words of the wise" (cf. 1:6), which gives an impression of a group of wise people involved in the teaching and transmission of literary materials.[25] While they remain anonymous, proper nouns designating specific sages occur elsewhere in the book. Prov 25:1 states that the following sayings are proverbs of Solomon, copied by the men of King Hezekiah of Judah. The references to the foreign Agur (30:1–4) and Lemuel (31:1–9) further underline individual sages, while also acknowledging wisdom that originates from outside Israel.

Other writings from the Hellenistic and Roman eras outline learned figures in more detail. The book of Qoheleth, which may hail from the late third century BCE, is essential in this respect.[26] The epilogue characterizes the book's protagonist as a חכם, stating that "[b]ecause Qoheleth was a sage, he continued to instruct the people" (Qoh 12:9), which points to the wise as a class of intellectuals and teachers.[27] Furthermore, the book contains reflections by and on this sage. The voice of the protagonist who takes the persona of Jerusalem's king is self-conscious: he is a critical thinker immersed in enquiry and investigation (e.g., 1:12–14; 2:3; 7:25). The epilogue of the book further mentions his scribal and noetic tasks (12:9–10). Qoheleth is not explicitly cast as an exemplar, but the address to the "son" (12:12) signals that the aim is to reach a pupil who seeks wisdom like him.

Another prominent sage from Hellenistic Judea appears in the book of Ben Sira, which was written in Jerusalem *c.* 180 BCE and translated into Greek later on in the same century.[28] According to the prologue to the Greek version, the anonymous grandson came to Egypt in the thirty-eighth year in the reign of Euergetes (i.e., Ptolemy VIII Euergetes II Physcon, who ruled in 170–116 BCE), which would permit the inference that he brought the text with him. The book is integral to our understanding of the sage as an admired figure. The wise person imagined in the book has a celebrated status in society and receives fame through afterlife remembrance (Sir 39:9–11). The search for wisdom requires time, and the sage has the privilege of leisure dedicated to study, teaching, and travels (34:9–13; 38:24–5; 39:4).[29] His idealized portrayal also absorbs features of teachers, counsellors, prophets, prayerful pious figures, and scribes (esp. 24:30–4; 38:34b–39:8). The many roles of the sage construct his vast expertise and exemplarity, and the figure holds a critical position in the transmission of wisdom to new generations.

The wise person invites students to come and learn in his "house of learning" or בית מדרש (51:23). This much-debated phrase implies a pedagogical setting of some sort, even if not an institutionalized school.[30] The Greek prologue indeed spells out that the instruction is intended for those who love learning (βουλομένοις φιλομαθεῖν), which associates Jewish students of wisdom with Greek philosophers, literally "lovers of wisdom."[31] What is more, the pupils have models to follow, and the exhortation in Sir 8:8 is worth considering in this respect: "Do not disregard a discourse of the wise, and turn to their proverbs, because from them you will learn instruction."[32] Hence, the wise form a chain that harks back to previous generations and continues to move forward. Similarly, the claim that the sage toils for all seekers of wisdom (24:34) implies that his wisdom is imagined to have an afterlife in the future generations.

Scholars have emphasized the importance of Ben Sira for cultural history and character formation. More than thirty years ago, Elias Bickerman argued that the Greek notion of παιδεία, "that education forms a man," was known in Jerusalem in the late third century BCE.[33] He observed that חכמה had acquired connotations that remind one of how the term "wisdom" is used in Hellenistic Greek.[34] More recently, Judith Newman has similarly described the book's intention with the concept of παιδεία. While many early Jewish texts invoke ancestral figures of the past, Ben Sira does not seek "to establish an ancient scribe of blessed memory, such as Shaphan or Baruch, Enoch or Ezra." Instead, the goal is, at least in the Greek version, to set up a contemporary person as an exemplar, i.e., "as an ideal type and practitioner of *paideia*." As Newman points out, certain aspects of the book underline its concern for the individual, including the grandson's autograph in the prologue and the poem in ch. 24, which implies that the "glorious robe" of wisdom (Sir 6:29, 31; 27:8) is accessible to any wise male.[35]

Specific literary techniques serve to construct the authority and exemplarity of the sage in the book. Benjamin Wright identifies three rhetorical strategies that are salient in this respect, including the father–son idiom, the first-person accounts of the wise person, and the section on scribal activity in Sir 38:34b–39:11.[36] The former signals parental authority, prompting the students to internalize the values of the instruction and limiting their ability to reject them.[37] The employment of first-person speech is another strategy that constructs the sage's exemplarity, whereas the meditation on the scribe illustrates the activities of an ideal wise person.[38]

The pedagogical ethos of Ben Sira suggests that the text is meant to activate processes of personal formation, and the sage imagined in the book provides a model to be emulated. Wright observes that the final invitation to seek wisdom (51:13–25) is pertinent in this respect, as it maps the search for wisdom and crystallizes how the sage establishes himself as the model. Regardless of whether the book harks back to the experience of a historical person or not, it motivates the pupil "not simply to abide by the sage's teaching, but to emulate and then become the sage who produced it."[39] The use of first-person language here, as well as elsewhere in the book, is pivotal regarding emulation: it evokes a wish in the pupil, who recites or meditates on the teaching, to adopt the persona of the ideal sage and to aspire to become one.

The Qumran scrolls further document the notion of the model-sage in the context of late second temple Judea. The remaining material preserves occasional references to wise teachers and their pupils, who are characterized by the term מבין or נבון, "an understanding one."[40] These anonymous figures are typically mentioned in passing and without any further specification. Yet, the motif of an exemplar to be emulated is obvious in a fragmentary text known as 4Q525. This composition contains a partially preserved section on the succession of a teacher and his students (frag. 14 ii 14–16):

> When you are swept away to eternal rest, they shall inherit ... and in your teaching all those who know you shall walk together ... together they shall mourn, but in your ways they shall remember you.

In other words, the students of an anonymous teacher commit to carry on his instruction, thus being inspired to imagine themselves as future sages.

The scrolls also illustrate a specific pedagogue, the pious and insightful figure of the maskil (משכיל), or literally the one who causes understanding or insight. This maskil appears in several pedagogical, rule, and liturgical texts.[41] The Hebrew term משכיל has many meanings to which I will return in Chapter 3 on the tasks and activities of the figure. At this point, it suffices to observe that this idealized wise person performs desirable acts (e.g., 1QS 9) and has a voice of his own (e.g., 1QS 10–11; 1QH^a 7, 20). The 1QS copy of the Community Rule is crucial regarding his exemplarity. As argued by Carol Newsom, its rhetorical shape points to a formative process: the compilation of materials is meant to form the maskil and to enact a transformative process in the audience.[42] The included sections recapitulate the stages of an ideal member from motivation to entry, admission, instruction, communal life, leadership, and spiritual perfection.[43]

The final part of 1QS (9:12–11:22) underlines the maskil's perfection. The section begins with a set of instructions (9:12–21a) related to his knowledge and responsibilities. As the opening lines state (9:12–14, par. 4Q259 frag. 3:7–10):

> These are the statutes (החוקים) by which the maskil shall walk with every living being, according to the norm of every time and the weight of every man. He

shall do God's will, according to everything, which has been revealed from time to time. He shall learn all the understanding (השכל) which has been found according to the times and the statute of the Endtime.⁴⁴

The figure, therefore, fulfils regulations, possesses perfect insight, and receives heavenly revelation. The second set of instructions (9:21–6, par. 4Q258 frag. 8:5–9; 4Q259 frag. 4:2–7) further elaborates on the maskil. Focusing on his desirable way of life, the author emphasizes the maskil's virtue, torah obedience, and devotion to God's will (9:21–4):

> These are the norms of the way (תכוני הדרך) for the maskil in these times with respect to his love and his hate. ... He shall be a man zealous for the statute and prepared for the day of vengeance. He shall perform (God's) will in every enterprise and in all his dominion, as he has commanded. And (in) all that befalls him he shall delight willingly and desire only God's will.

The final hymn at the very end of 1QS (10:5–11:22) offers yet another image of the maskil as an exemplar, depicting him as one filled with self-awareness and devotion. Lines 10:17–24 of the hymn, in particular, involve first-person claims on the figure's aspiration in order not to be revengeful, envious, violent, vain, or impure in heart.⁴⁵ The author also highlights the divine origin of his perfection (11:2–3). Considering the sum of these sections, the final part of 1QS seems to cast the maskil as a telos. The figure provides the audience with an object of emulation. As set out by Newsom: "If one is properly shaped by the teachings and disciplines of the community ... then this is the kind of voice with which one will speak."⁴⁶

Up until now, I have discussed the role of contemporary wise figures as templates to be followed. Furthermore, exemplarity was frequently associated with ancestral figures of the past in the late second temple era. Biblical traditions sparked new readings that sought to make them meaningful in new contexts. The so-called pseudepigrapha, early Jewish writings attributed to biblical characters, are relevant in this respect, as they show that powerful exemplars were unearthed from the Hebrew scriptures.

First, a pseudonymous attribution to a biblical figure may signal an act of emulation. As Hindy Najman has argued, this practice should not be understood as an act of forgery, as one might think from a modern perspective. Rather, the question is about a way to extend "a discourse attached to a founder of an earlier period." For the later writer, such an act could have served as "an attempt to recover an idealized or utopian past." Alternatively, it could have been "an attempt to work out the impossibility of recovering that past by grounding the present now in an idealized past."⁴⁷ Regardless of the exact motivation behind the practice, the pseudepigraphic attribution functioned as a means to follow and self-identify with the ancestral hero. As Najman describes, it was a "practice of effacing oneself in order to emulate an exemplary figure."⁴⁸

Second, the pseudepigrapha cast biblical figures as exemplars that provide the audience with models to follow.⁴⁹ The portrayal of Enoch, the enigmatic and mythical figure known from Gen 5:18–24, is conspicuous in this respect. In early Judaism, he became depicted as an exceptional scribe, which signals erudition (1 En 12:4; 15:1; 92:1; T. Abr. B 11:3).⁵⁰ Yet, Enoch is not an ordinary scribe concerned with mundane tasks but a visionary and revealer of divine secrets, thus serving as an apocalyptic seer and mantic sage.⁵¹ As for emulation, one should consider a passage that appears in the book of Parables (1 Enoch 37–71), originally composed in Aramaic around the turn of the era. The final chapters of this section describe Enoch's ascension to heaven and his activities there. In the very end of the section, Enoch reveals the words of the deity or an angel to him (1 En 71:16–17):

> And all will walk on your path since righteousness will never forsake you; with you will be their dwelling and with you, their lot, and from you they will not be separated forever and forever and ever. And thus there will be length of days with that son of man [Enoch], and there will be peace for the righteous, and the path of truth for the righteous, in the name of the Lord of Spirits forever and ever.⁵²

As this quote explicates, Enoch's followers are imagined to walk on the path of this ancestral figure, constantly remembering and even dwelling in him. The question is about more than mere imitation of the figure, as is suggested by the idiom of merging with the exemplar. The audience is motivated to take up an act of emulation that is promised to result in divine blessings.

Jewish voices from the diaspora

In the previous section, I commented on the figure of the sage in the Hebrew Bible and in other (originally) Semitic texts that hail from Judea. In the late second temple period, when the majority of Jews lived outside the ancestral land,⁵³ the production of Jewish literature also flourished in the diaspora. This is especially true of Alexandria, which was a major cultural centre of the time.⁵⁴ Importantly, Jewish texts written in Greek also outline the exemplary sage. In what follows, I will analyse the evidence of Wisdom of Solomon and of Philo of Alexandria's treatises.[55] The authors of these texts renewed Jewish wisdom discourse in new cultural contexts and thus made it accessible, at least in theory, to non-Jews as well.

Like the majority of Jewish wisdom texts, Wisdom of Solomon is difficult to pinpoint, although it may originate from the first-century BCE or the first-century CE Alexandria.[56] In any event, the text depicts, as is indicated by its title, an ideal sage who is associated with the fictitious king of the past. The identification of the protagonist is visible in the text's "autobiographical" accounts. In Wis 9:7–8, most importantly, the speaker refers to the divine decree that motivates his royal role: "You preferred me as king of your people … you said that I should build a shrine in your holy mountain."[57] Even if the sage is associated with the legendary wise king of Israel, the royal protagonist encountered in Wisdom of Solomon is not identical to the ancient ruler known from the book of Kings; he is transformed into an exemplar whose perfection rather than his human flaws are under scrutiny.[58] Such a development continues the trajectory of the Chronicler, who does not remark on Solomon's idolatry, caused by his attachment to his foreign wives and their gods (cf. 1 Kgs 11:1–13).[59]

The ancient king sets out to examine wisdom (σοφία), and the purpose of this enterprise is to benefit others (Wis 6:22–5). In fact, the book says more about wisdom, the teacher of all manners of knowledge and virtues (7:22; 8:7), than about the sage. Yet, there are essential materials on the wise person, including the king's eulogy in chs. 7–8 and his prayer in ch. 9, both of which demonstrate rich intellectual influences.[60] These speeches emphasize the devotion of the sage that enables him to receive a spirit of wisdom and knowledge (7:7, 15–22). The wise person appears as unerring in his knowledge, mastering secret things (7:17–22) and reaching immortality because of his wisdom (8:13, 17). Throughout chs. 7–9, the sage highlights that his wisdom is a divine gift and originates in prayerful life (esp. 7:7; 8:17–21; 9:1–18). Human perfection, after all, counts as nothing unless it is rooted in the divine realm (9:6).

The king figures as a living embodiment of wisdom, thus serving as a model. Yet, his royalty connotes hierarchy and makes one wonder about the book's audience. Does Wisdom of Solomon promote wisdom that is accessible to anyone? As observed by Newman, the author uses a royal motif, but he also reinterprets the idea of kingship and democratizes wisdom. Although the kingship language seems to be exclusive at first glance, the book actually implies a conception of "all human creatures as regents." Departing from the ancient Near Eastern tradition, the author argues that wisdom no longer belongs to kings alone. He rejects the idea of a Judahite monarch and democratizes kingship so that all pious Jews count as monarchs of some sort. "Everyman," as Newman argues, "can be a king, to the degree that it is possible for all to gain wisdom."[61] Thus, the aim of the author is to persuade his audience to desire and love wisdom who makes herself known to those worthy of her, eventually rewarding them with kingship (6:12–21).

As we have seen, Wisdom of Solomon stresses the wisdom and perfection of the sage, but the discussion on his emulation remains relatively suggestive. Another author who lived in the same Greek-speaking Roman milieu, Philo of Alexandria (c. 20 BCE–50 CE), explicated the process of emulation in a more sustained way. Philo's interest in the figure of the wise person is shown by the mere fact that the Greek term σοφός occurs 301 times in his vast corpus.[62]

Philo, a member of a wealthy Alexandrian family, was committed to Jewish scriptures and customs. At the same time, he was well read in the Greek curriculum, being acquainted with Homer, historians, poets, Attic law, mathematics, astronomy, rhetoric, and music.[63] Philo took part in the philosophical conversations of his time from a distinctly Jewish viewpoint, frequently recycling Platonic thought with Stoic, Aristotelian, and Pythagorean ideas, which has granted him the title of a Middle Platonist.[64] For the present purposes, it is worth highlighting that Philo regarded himself as a practiser of philosophy (φιλοσοφία) but barely as an actual sage (σοφός), for he calls himself imperfect (*Leg.* 2.91, 3.207; *Her.* 275). Philo's modest self-assessment aligns with the general difficulty of attaining wisdom in the Greek tradition; the philosopher only seeks and tends towards wisdom.[65] In a similar vein, Philo considers true sages to be rare (*Mut.* 34–8). The pursuit of wisdom remains a worthwhile project, however, and Philo maintains that wisdom never closes her school (*Prob.* 13).[66]

According to Philo, the rational nature of human beings inclines towards cultivation (*Somn.* 1.106–7), and parents wish to educate their children "so that they may have not only life, but a good life" (*Spec.* 2.229).[67] He promotes the importance of encyclical studies (ἐγκύκλιος παιδεία), which in Greek pedagogy denotes a cycle of subjects that prepare the pupil to take his or her place in society, even if the elementary studies are but the beginning of virtue (*Fug.* 183).[68] Some pupils continue to pursue wisdom through φιλοσοφία, which for Philo, like for the Greeks, represents the higher form of education that can elevate one's mind (*Spec.* 2.230).[69] Thus, "just as the school subjects contribute to ... philosophy, so does philosophy to the getting of wisdom" (*Congr.* 79).[70] As noted by Philo, even the perfect ones must strengthen their souls by undertaking constant study and exercise (*Agr.* 160).

Ultimately, a philosopher (φιλόσοφος) aims at becoming a sage (σοφός), an ideal wise person and an embodiment of virtue (*Congr.* 69–70), although the states of seeking and having wisdom intermingle at times (e.g., *Ebr.* 49). The calm mind of the wise person is connected to both God and other people: to God because of virtue and to other people because of humanity (*Somn.* 2.229–30). In *Sobr.* 56–7, Philo echoes the paradoxes attributed to the Stoic sage, commenting on the nobility, richness, high repute, kingship, and freedom of the sage.[71] Philo and the Stoics also share an emphasis on the emotional and ethical perfection of the wise person.[72] Such a person behaves virtuously without being commanded to do so (*Leg.* 3.144), does nothing against his intention (*Prob.* 97), is free because of right reason (*Prob.* 45–6), and is not attached to the mortal body (*QG* 4.74). The figure attains simplicity (*Migr.* 153), loves solitude (*Abr.* 23; *Spec.* 2.44), displays a harmony of words and deeds (*Post.* 88), and is prepared for whatever fortune might bring (*Spec.* 2.46). As such, the wise person fulfils the Stoic ideal of ἀπάθεια, i.e., a state of serenity where the mind is not disturbed with passions.[73]

Philo's ideas are Greek ideas, and he speaks of people with varying degrees of wisdom in a way that resembles Greek philosophy (e.g., *Agr.* 160–1; *Somn.* 2.235). Yet, Jewish scriptures are integral to his philosophy, which involves the task of allegorical interpretation; for Philo, "all or most of the law-book is an allegory" (*Ios.* 28).[74] As for exemplarity, Philo illustrates his claims on sages by invoking the precedents of biblical figures. Genesis, he argues, narrates lives of people that manifest both virtue and vice (*Abr.* 1). Explaining the difference between categories of humans, Philo refers to the earth-born hedonistic people who indulge in pleasures of the body, the heaven-born who progress towards perfection through study and learning, and the god-born who are sages by birth (*Gig.* 60–3). He presents Abraham as a prototype of a heaven-born person, whereas Isaac and especially Moses possess inborn wisdom and perfection.[75]

Moses has a distinctive status in Philo's scheme of exemplarity as "the greatest and most perfect man that ever lived," and as the one who left sacred books that testify to his excellence and serve as "marvellous memorials of his wisdom" (*Mos.* 1.1–3). Moses, Philo claims, "exhibited the doctrines of philosophy in all his daily actions, saying precisely what he thought, and performing such actions only as were consistent with his words" (*Mos.* 1.29).[76] In other words, Moses embodies the superior sage who reached the summit of philosophy (*Opif.* 8).[77]

Because of having reached the end goal, Moses was transformed into a mind (*Mos.* 2.288).[78] Philo regards him as being capable of perfect rationality to the extent that his bodily sensations did not produce lower impulses and desires.[79]

As such, Moses offers an example (παράδειγμα) to be emulated by those who aspire to achieve wisdom. Philo explains that Moses set before his subjects "the monument of his own life like an original design to be their beautiful model (παράδειγμα καλὸν)" (*Virt.* 51).[80] Philo also describes how this "god and king" of the nation established "a piece of work beautiful and godlike, a model (παράδειγμα) for those who are willing to copy it," and he motivates his audience to aspire to the same: "Happy are they who imprint, or strive to imprint, that image in their souls" (*Mos.* 1.158-9).[81]

Philo, therefore, goes so far as to state that Moses is "godlike" or "divine" (θεοειδής).[82] His perfection is distinct, but Philo also recognizes the value of the three patriarchs, Abraham, Isaac, and Jacob, as exemplars to be followed across time and place. This becomes evident, for example, in *Abr.* 3-4, which casts them as models of the good life:

> Let us postpone consideration of particular laws, which are, so to speak, copies (εἰκόνων), and examine first those which are more general and may be called the originals of those copies (ἀρχετύπους). These are such men as lived good and blameless lives, whose virtues stand permanently recorded in the most holy scriptures, not merely to sound their praises but for the instruction of the reader and as an inducement to him to aspire to the same (καὶ ἐπὶ τὸν ὅμοιον ζῆλον ἀγαγεῖν).[83]

For Philo, each of the patriarchs illustrates a specific method of acquiring virtue (*Abr.* 52-4; *Ios.* 1), including nature (Isaac), instruction (Abraham), or practice (Jacob).[84] The figure of Jacob is intriguing from the viewpoint of lived wisdom since he is associated with practice (ἄσκησις) instead of inborn wisdom or instruction.[85] On two occasions, Philo reads biblical narratives on Jacob as illustrating the practice of spiritual exercises that shape one's mind, attitude, and action, thus preparing for his transformation into Israel (*Leg.* 3.18-19; *Her.* 252-3).[86] Jacob, therefore, symbolizes a mindful attitude and readiness to exercise: he was not born as a flawless sage, but he proceeds towards wisdom through dedicated practice and cultivation of the mind, thus providing the seekers of wisdom with a rather human and easily identifiable model.

Philo outlines several male exemplars, but does he regard biblical female figures as wise models? Admittedly, Philo's notion of gender follows the Aristotelian model according to which women are inferior to men by nature.[87] He associates men with the rational mind or intellect (νοῦς), and women with the sense perception (αἴσθησις).[88] This categorization makes the base for the idea that males should rule over females like the superior mind rules over the inferior sense perception (*Leg.* 3.222).[89] In spite of this premise, which does not seem to leave much room for the positive portrayal of women, Philo's female characterization is more nuanced than one might anticipate. The figure of Sarah, in particular, is intrinsic to exemplarity.

To illustrate stages of education, Philo presents an allegorical treatment of the Hagar and Sarah story, which echoes the allegorical readings of Homer: Penelope's suitors could not win her and had to contend themselves with her maids (*Odyssey* 12).[90] For Philo, the foreign Hagar symbolizes encyclical studies, whereas Sarah represents wisdom (σοφία) and virtue (ἀρετή).[91] Abraham, the symbol of mind, had to take Hagar before he could conceive a child with his legitimate wife (*Congr.* 23–4). The implied claim is that Jews can attend encyclical training because it ultimately serves the practice of true philosophy, the union with Sarah (*Congr.* 22, 74–6, 80). Like Penelope's suitors, those who cannot attain the higher goal, whether Penelope or philosophy, should still undertake encyclical studies, the time of pregnancy preceding proper philosophy (*Congr.* 145).[92]

The fact that biblical women pinpoint ways to wisdom turns them into exemplars. Yet, while Philo's reading of Sarah is respectful, the symbolic figure transcends the human boundaries of sex and gender, nor is Sarah's female gender celebrated. She represents wisdom and virtue, but Philo considers these grammatically feminine terms to involve masculine powers (*Fug.* 51–2). Philo even removes Sarah from the realm of femininity by allegorically exposing the claim that she ceased to menstruate (*QG* 4.15, cf. Gen 18:11).[93]

Sarah's treatment is intelligible over against Philo's interpretative method, which aims at grasping the soul's migration from the material world towards the divine by means of analysing the biblical narrative. The selected method both grants Sarah an exceptional status and dissolves her into a quality of Abraham's character (e.g., *Cher.* 40). It is nevertheless striking that Philo singles out a woman in his discussion on wisdom. Sarah masters her emotions, thus filling the Hellenistic ideal of self-mastery (ἐγκράτεια).[94] She displays the spousal virtues of loyalty and love that were appreciated in Philo's Roman milieu.[95] Sarah even advises her husband, which indicates that her agency is not limited to that of a compliant spouse.[96]

In summary, early Jewish authors writing in Greek frequently invoke ancestral perfection in their discussion on the ideal sage. Instead of focusing on the wisdom and exemplary role of contemporary people, they reinterpret inherited traditions and cast biblical figures of the past as templates to be followed. In so doing, they equip old texts with new meanings and spell out the relevance of the biblical tradition in new settings of seeking wisdom and living a good life.

The Mediterranean milieu of Jewish sages

I will now turn to the wider context of ancient Jewish writers with an aim to comprehend the cultural milieu in which new types of claims on sages as exemplars and objects of emulation were made from the Hellenistic period onwards. As I hope to show, Greek sources on the wise person provide a meaningful and illuminating backdrop for reading Jewish notions of the sage.

To clarify, while I will compare Jewish texts to Greek ones, I do not suggest that ancient ideas of the sage would only, or most importantly, appear in Greek sources. Rather, wise figures occur in all cultures, as my previous remarks on the ancient Near East also indicate, and the Greeks were not the first ones to ask philosophical questions.[97] However, I have observed a major shift in Jewish wisdom discourse in the Hellenistic and early Roman periods, i.e., during an era when a mixture of Greek and local, or Western and Eastern, elements was intrinsic to the eastern Mediterranean region. Thus, all Judaism in this era can be characterized as Hellenistic in one way or another, even though the intermingling of ideas and practices took very different forms in different settings, as discussed in Chapter 1. The widespread evidence for cultural interaction between Jewish and Greek cultures also urges me to explore Jewish conceptions of the ideal sage in relation to Greek ideas of the wise person.

The intellectual tradition of ancient Greece cannot be limited to any single setting. It flourished in many social contexts such as poetry and myth telling, drama, prophecy and divination, or philosophical enquiry.[98] Three figures, however, are outstanding regarding wisdom: a sophist (σοφιστής), a philosopher (φιλόσοφος), and a sage (σοφός). Etymologically, all these terms pertain to "wisdom" (σοφία), which can mean cleverness, practical skilfulness in arts, prudence in public and political affairs, physical and theoretical knowledge, or poetical ability.[99] In spite of some famous early philosophers, the term "philosophy" (φιλοσοφία) is rarely used before Plato, and when it is employed, it simply means "intellectual cultivation."[100] The terms "sophist" (σοφιστής) and "sage" (σοφός) appear more frequently and often synonymously, designating an array of wise people – artisans, inventors, poets, prophets, political leaders, astronomers, and doctors – who possess symbolic capital in the form of power, status, and honour. Sophists and sages are typically linked with special talents, whether skills or knowledge.[101]

From the classical period onwards, the title "seven sages" (οἱ ἑπτὰ σοφοί) is given to seven philosophers, political leaders, and lawgivers from the seventh and early sixth centuries BCE. The oldest list in Plato's *Protagoras* (342e–343b) mentions Thales of Miletus, Pittacus of Mytilene, Bias of Priene, Solon of Athens, Cleobulus of Lindus, Myson of Chen, and Chilon of Sparta. Plato explains that the wisdom of these men can be recognized based on the memorable sayings linked with them, and they are further associated with practical inventions (*Republic* 600a). The seven sages differ from other similar figures because of their ability to perform wisdom through poetical and political activities.[102] Yet, the ancient sources disagree over which figures belong among the seven (cf. D.L. 1.13, 22, 41–2; Plutarch, *Septem sapientium convivium*). Likewise, the legitimacy of the maxims attributed to the wise is debated.[103]

As the variety of wise people shows, there is no clear conception of an ideal sage in the early period of Greek culture.[104] The situation changes in the classical era as the term "wisdom" develops the meaning of a "rationally worked out account of reality."[105] A philosopher comes to represent a person who loves wisdom and trains himself or herself accordingly, with the intention of becoming a sage who behaves ideally and masters the challenges of everyday life in an excellent manner.[106] In practice, the term "sage" is often used interchangeably with a good or virtuous person (ἀγαθός or σπουδαῖος), whereas the term "sophist" begins to denote itinerant instructors who teach rhetorical and argumentative skills that contribute to persuasive speech and are useful in public life.[107] The distinction between sophistry and philosophy is not always clear.[108] Sophists, however, typically differ from philosophers in that they are paid professionals, teaching for money in games, agoras, and private gatherings. Through their activities, which are not detached from business, sophists seek both material and symbolic capital.[109]

Both philosophers and sophists take part and assist others in the search for wisdom. Sages, who are discussed in the context of philosophical schools and their ideals of a virtuous life, differ from both in that the wise person manifests the object of such pursuits. There is no single notion of his nature agreed by all authors.[110] The sources, however, share the idea of the sage as "the ultimate objective for human aspiration."[111] Plato first links such a figure with tranquillity and calm, portraying him as self-sufficient (αὐτάρκης). The wise person is capable of being happy in spite of external conditions, and he does not rejoice or grieve as humans do.[112] As an embodiment of self-coherence, the sage does not fear death, is self-reliant with reference to living well, and mourns last in case a disaster befalls him (*Republic* 387d–e, 605c–606b). Plato further describes the sage as god-like, i.e., as "righteous and holy and wise" (*Theaetetus* 176b).[113]

While Plato's sage transcends the realm of everyday life, Aristotle describes him as staying within it and dealing with its questions. Despite the somewhat different foci, both figures are idealized and manifest wisdom and virtue to be emulated. According to Aristotle, "virtue and the virtuous man (ἡ ἀρετὴ καὶ ὁ σπουδαῖος) seem to be the standard in everything" (N.E. 1166a1–15).[114] The sage finds self-sufficiency (αὐτάρκεια) in contemplation (1177a27–35) and sees the truth in everything (1113a25–33, 1176a16–22). He is also free of contradictions and actively strives for the good. Furthermore, Aristotle speaks of a prudent person (φρόνιμος) with practical reason or wisdom, which enables one to make right moral judgements (e.g., 1141a9–1141b23).[115]

In addition to classical accounts, multiple conceptions of the sage can be extracted from Hellenistic philosophy. At times, the founding figure of the school counts as the wise person *par excellence*. The Epicureans, therefore, regard Epicurus as an embodiment of wisdom.[116] The Pythagoreans respectively honour the distant founder of the school and stress the practice of the whole range of Pythagorean philosophy.[117]

Other schools emphasized the value of practical wisdom. The Peripatetics were primarily concerned with the prudent person (φρόνιμος). Similarly, the Cynics, known for their commitment to a particular lifestyle, associated ideal wisdom with φρόνιμος. However, the very idea of the sage could be rejected, as in the case of the Pyrrhonian Skeptics, who denied the possibility of knowledge and thus also the existence of the wise person.[118]

In the Hellenistic period and beyond, the idea of the sage attained its greatest influence and broadest reach with the Stoics.[119] In this survey, I will primarily concentrate on the Greek sources. Thus, I will mostly exclude the sources of the Roman Stoics, as they go beyond the scope of my investigation, which aims at understanding the change in Jewish wisdom discourse in the Hellenistic period. Admittedly, however, early Stoic writings are virtually lost.[120] This hampers my enquiry, but there nonetheless remains a significant body of materials to be studied. Joannes Stobaeus' *Extracts, Sayings, and Advice* II.7, a text attributed to Arius Didymus who lived in the first-century BCE Alexandria, is especially relevant because the text concerns Stoic ethics and even a third of it discusses the wise person.[121] Other sources also contain much relevant material on Stoic thinking. These include but are not limited to the works of Plutarch (45–120 CE), Epictetus (55–135 CE), and Diogenes Laertius (third century CE).

According to Arius, Zeno of Citium (c. 334–262 BCE), who was the founder of Stoicism, and his followers maintained that there are two types of people: "The race of the worthwhile employ the virtues through all of their lives, while the race of the worthless employ the vices" (II.7.11g).[122] The figure of the sage obviously belongs to the former category, and three particular qualities characterize him and his conduct.

First, the wise person is neither omnipotent nor omniscient, but unfailingly able to act correctly in any life situation because of possessing truth.[123] The sage does well anything he undertakes (II.7.5b10–11), which means that he alone is capable of being a good prophet, poet, orator, dialectic, literary critic, priest, and king.[124]

Second, the sage has a harmonious inner life. Arius reports, while referring to early Stoics, that every good person is complete because of his virtue, thus leading "an absolute happy life" (II.7.11g).[125] In practical terms, this means that the sage shows equanimity and lacks passions (ἀπάθεια).[126] His perfect mental state further involves a capacity to regard indifferent things as indifferent, i.e., as neither good nor bad.[127]

Third, the Stoic sage is associated with the divine realm. Arius claims that the happiness of a wise person does not deviate from that of the gods (II.7.11g). Similarly, Diogenes Laertius (7.119) explains that the Stoics characterize the wise as godlike, for "they have something divine (οἱονεὶ θεόν) within them," whilst the bad are godless (ἄθεον). These exceptional people worship the gods through rituals, piety, sacrifices, and purity, and the gods respectively admire them.

Overall, the Stoic sage represents the culmination point of Stoic ethics.[128] The figure both aligns with and differs from the classical accounts. His happiness and god-like nature remind one of the wise persons outlined by Plato, but the Stoic sage, as Julia Annas points out, remains "*in* the world," being "the active force ordering the world, not something outside it."[129] Many authors even stress his participation in everyday affairs, whether the question is about family life, household managements, societal roles, or moneymaking.[130] Such an association between the sage and the material conditions of life is natural insofar as the Stoics generally promote the idea of virtue as a "skill in living." They assume that one should exercise and execute philosophy in daily life and actions, and not in removing oneself from them (e.g., Arius II.7.11k; Seneca, *Ep.* 20.2). The figure, in other words, serves to illustrate how to fill a practical or ethical role well.[131]

Although the Greek accounts on the sage vary considerably, Hadot has observed three central features that generally characterize the portrayal of the wise person in them: equanimity of soul, absence of need, and indifference to indifferent things. In other words, the sage remains happy in all external conditions and, as a self-sufficient (αὐτάρκης) person, finds happiness within himself. This is possible because external things do not disturb him.[132] All these features point to the ideal nature of the figure and the aspirational dimension of the process of becoming a sage. Annas clarifies: "It takes the form of aspiring to be more virtuous."[133] As an embodiment of wisdom, the nearly otherworldly figure of the sage provides the philosopher with an ideal rather than "a model incarnate in a living human being."[134] Hence, the wise person, as a "transcendent norm," serves to determine the way of life taken by the philosopher.[135]

The model function of the sage implies an idea of emulation (ζῆλος), which is an essential motif in several Greek writings and not limited to the context of philosophy. Young poets, for example, may emulate an older one (Aristophanes, *Test.* 1), or a younger brother may emulate an older brother (Plutarch, *De frat. amor.* 487B). Plato, for his part, mentions Pythagoras whose successors follow a Pythagorean way of life and depicts Homer as "a leading educator" who "passed on a kind of Homeric way of life to their successors" (*Republic* 600a).[136] Yet, the first philosophical discussion on the significance of emulation appears in Aristotle's *Rhetoric*, which states that "emulation ... is virtuous and characteristic of virtuous men" (11.1).[137] Valued goods such as virtues, as well as people possessing those goods, should be its object (11.4–7).

The topic of emulation can also be illustrated by considering the figure of Socrates. Socrates is already set as the model of a philosopher in Plato's *Symposium*, but he becomes widely celebrated in the later Greek tradition.[138] Epictetus, for example, writes on moral progress as follows (*Ench.* 51.3):

> Make up your mind ... remember that now is the contest ... and that it depends on a single day and a single action, whether progress is lost or saved. This is the way Socrates became what he was, by paying attention to nothing but his reason in everything that he encountered. And even if you are not yet a Socrates, still you ought to live as one who wishes to be a Socrates.[139]

As the quoted passage exhorts, the wisdom lover, regardless of one's current state on the path to wisdom, should seek to live as Socrates. In spite of Socrates' unmatched reputation, other philosophers are also cast as models to be followed. The portrayal of Zeno by Diogenes Laertius is another illuminating example in this respect (D.L. 7.10–11):

> Whereas Zeno of Citium, son of Mnaseas, has for many years been devoted to philosophy in the city and has continued to be a man of worth in all other respects, exhorting to virtue and temperance those of the youth who come to him to be taught, directing them to what is best, affording to all in his own conduct a pattern for imitation in perfect consistency with his teaching.[140]

Zeno, therefore, provides his followers with a "pattern for imitation" (παράδειγμα τὸν ἴδιον βίον).[141] Plutarch's writings are a treasure chest concerning such a process of emulation. According to *De profectibus in virtute* 84D–85B, the process begins when the virtue of a good person creates emulation in those who pursue virtue. One's love for the disposition of the exemplar is a symptom of true progress, and emulation results in an eagerness to join and cement oneself in the model figure. Accenting the relevance of historical exemplars, Plutarch argues that those admiring virtue "set before their eyes good men of the present or of the past" and ponder what figures such as Plato would have done or said in different situations.[142] Recollection leads into action as the student readjusts his or her habit, represses ignoble utterances, or resists emotions.

In summary, ancient Greek sources discuss the exemplary sage and the emulation of this figure starting from the classical period. The exact interpretations of the ideal wise person vary, but the figure is typically associated with equanimity and self-sufficiency, including the capacity to remain happy in all external conditions. These features turn him into an epitome of wisdom and an object of emulation. The perfect sage functions as a template to those with the bold intention of getting a grasp of wisdom, which means that the pursuit of wisdom is to be realized through one's dedication to the exemplar. Emulation also extends to exemplars who are not celebrated as actual sages, as is shown by pupils who model themselves after teachers and philosophers.

Reading Jewish sages in context

Ancient Jewish sources on sages are temporally, linguistically, geographically, and culturally diverse. The early Hebrew tradition displays a number of wise people, whilst the later sources document the rise of the sage as an intellectual, and the book of Qoheleth first outlines him as an erudite individual. Yet, exemplarity remains implicit in the latter, whereas several texts from the later Hellenistic and early Roman eras – the book of Ben Sira, the pseudepigrapha, and the Qumran scrolls – render the sage as an object of emulation. Greek Jewish texts similarly depict the ideal sage. Leaving societal issues aside, Wisdom of Solomon and Philo of Alexandria's treatises focus on his perfection, and Philo addresses the (Stoic) calmness and ἀπάθεια of the figure. Moreover, both sources underline the significance biblical characters as models.

Overall, several writings from the late second temple period cast the sage as a template to be followed by his students and/or later generations, but the authors tend to employ the figure to promote their own views instead of outlining a wise person that would suit the opinions of all Jews. The sage becomes a model to be emulated, but the features to be emulated vary markedly.

The shift in Jewish wisdom discourse raises the question of how to explain the new focus on individuals as exemplars and epitomes of wisdom. Such a conception does not appear in texts from the Persian period, but it becomes evident in those from the Hellenistic and Roman eras. When these accounts are read in their wider Mediterranean context, one may observe that similar ideas are presented in Greek writings slightly earlier and often more explicitly; the ideal sage to be emulated by wisdom lovers is attested in philosophical writings since the classical period.

Plato first outlines the wise person in the sense of a perfect exemplar and embodiment of wisdom. Yet, there is no single conception of the figure in the Greek tradition: Plato's sage is virtually transcendent, Aristotle casts him as the standard of everything, and the Stoics focus on his emotional and ethical perfection.[143] The sages described by Aristotle and the Stoics are rather active and linked with everyday life, dealing with its questions or taking part in its activities. In spite of such variation, all schools suggest that the status of a sage is nearly impossible to achieve. Mostly, they agree that the figure is self-sufficient (αὐτάρκης) and finds happiness in himself, regardless of external conditions. The sage, therefore, represents a paragon, even though students are also encouraged to emulate prominent philosophers and teachers.

As discussed in Chapter 1, the tendency to perceive of Judaism and Hellenism as two separate categories is misleading, and the debate of whether a form of early Judaism was Hellenistic or not is outdated. Since an intermingling of various cultural influences marked the eastern Mediterranean region at this time, it is more meaningful to map out processes of cultural interaction and manifestations of Hellenism that varied from place to place. Considering this backdrop, Jewish wisdom discourse appears as a multifarious project: it drew on the earlier Hebrew tradition while being simultaneously shaped by the spirit and questions of its time. Authors in the diaspora wrote in Greek and explicitly engaged with Greek ideas. Yet, Judea was not an island either. The Greek language, for example, was probably known in Jerusalem already by the time of Ben Sira.[144] This is a substantial indicator of cultural encounters, even though the adoption of new ideas or practices did not necessarily require access to Greek texts.

Ancient Israelite wisdom always interacted with surrounding traditions, as is shown by the parallels between the book of Proverbs and Egyptian texts or by the foreign setting of the book of Job. The inherent tendency to mix cultural elements supports the idea that scholars should not study early Jewish wisdom discourse in a vacuum. Based on my survey, the notion of an ideal model-sage, known from both Semitic and Greek Jewish sources, counts as one case of cultural collaboration. The authors who lived and wrote in the diaspora naturally had, along with their education, a direct access to and considerable acquaintance with (non-Jewish) Greek literature.

The explanation of the shift is not as straightforward as regards those authors who operated in Judea and wrote in Semitic languages. There is nothing to suggest that they would have directly borrowed the motif of an exemplary sage from Greek philosophical writings, but they clearly employed the motif in a number of contexts. This suggests that the Hellenistic context shaped the authors' concern for the model-sage, although the rather general nature of the detected parallel indicates that the change in the portrayal of the figure was most probably caused by the common *Zeitgeist* and not by deliberately copying from Greek literary sources.[145]

While the Hellenistic and early Roman sources posit a new focus on a model-sage, I also wish to acknowledge the prospect that the idea of emulating a sage already existed in the earlier Hebrew tradition, even if it the authors never bothered to explicate it. The mythical figure of Adapa, a scribal hero and a semi-human sage from the ancient Near East, is worth considering in this respect. A fragment of an incantation text found at Nippur states "I am [A]dapa," thus suggesting that Mesopotamian scribes and ritualists identified themselves with him.[146] Yet, such explicit identifications with past figures are absent from the Hebrew Bible; the wise intellectuals are rarely named and there is no indication that the pupil should adopt the persona of his teacher.

In spite of this general trend, I should consider two possible exceptions to it. First, the later Solomonic attributions of biblical books might count as the authors' attempts to identify with the wise king.[147] But then, Solomon is not portrayed as an exemplary teacher per se, nor is there evidence to suggest that the authors would have wished to imitate the life of the wise king, walking on and replicating his paths. Second, it is true that the familial idiom used in Hebrew wisdom texts seems to imply an exhortation to learn from the father. Wright argues as follows:

> With respect to the construction of the sage as an exemplar, father-son discourse contributes to that enterprise. The sage sets himself up as one who should be emulated. In other words, his goal is for students not only to do as he says, but to do as he does. Fathers expect their children to internalize their values in order to resist any external attempts to subvert them, and ultimately the children will be able to take their father's place and preserve their father's memory in

the community (see [Sir] 30:4–6). In this manner, the sage's adoption of the role of father is closely linked with the first-person passages in which Ben Sira constructs his ideal sage, an ideal that also serves as an exemplar.[148]

Thus, the idea of emulation may be incipient in the father–son discourse of Hebrew wisdom instruction. Yet, this feature alone does not explain *why* Jewish authors came to spell out the significance of emulation in the wise life in the late second temple period, nor does it explain the large scale of the authors' concern for the topic. Evidently, something in the wider Hellenistic environment – probably an external impetus of some sort – compelled Jewish authors to phrase the notion explicitly, stressing the role of the sage as an epitome of wisdom and the relevance of emulating one's teacher in the pursuit of wisdom. It seems plausible, however, that the father–son discourse prepared way for the idea of the sage as an exemplar, as people are likely to accept and adopt new ideas that resonate or can be reconciled with ones held by them previously.

Admittedly, the parallel between the (originally) Semitic writings from Judea and Greek sources on the exemplary sage is not very precise. The relative vagueness of the parallel does not mean, however, that it would be insignificant or secondary regarding our understanding of early Jewish wisdom discourse and its relation to the wider Hellenistic culture of its time. On the contrary, as Michael Fox has observed, "the most significant parallels may well be the least provable: affinities in attitude, epistemology, fields of inquiry, questions addressed, and the types of answers offered."[149] This may well be the case with the rise of the model-sage in Hellenistic Judaism, which primarily indicates a conceptual affinity with ancient Greek culture.

A negative criterion might further support my claim on the detected change in Jewish wisdom discourse. Many of the Jewish sources analysed above, starting from Qoheleth, allude to Greek materials.[150] Yet, there is nothing explicit to suggest that their authors would present themselves as models for emulation in the light of such Greek sources. Early Jewish authors do not build their arguments on the exemplary sage by quoting from, or alluding to, the Greek sources. This factor could favour the interpretation proposed here, i.e., that the type of influence or cultural collaboration is a matter of *Zeitgeist*. The significance of such interaction should not be downplayed, however, since the authors are operating in Hellenistic cultural terms instead of merely showing random influence, which occurs in, and is limited to, a single passage.

My thesis concerning the model-sage as a product of cultural collaboration may not be fashionable at a time when the comparison of cultures has been criticized because of different contextual meanings; some scholars posit the primacy of cultural difference over similarity, arguing that meaning is "lost in comparison."[151] In my view, however, it is intellectually rigorous to consider the cross-cultural horizon of Jewish ideas and to map related trajectories.[152] This applies to any era of time, as nothing in human cultures emerges in a vacuum, but here I am specifically thinking about the potpourri of the Hellenistic world, known for diverse mixtures of cultural elements.

Simplistic ideas of influence can obviously be harmful. Meanwhile, the extant sources from the late second temple period do attest to a cross-pollination of traditions in many different ways, which is only natural considering the hybrid nature of cultures. As Marshall Sahlins observes, cultures have never been "bounded, self-contained and self-sustaining." He continues: "No culture is *sui generis*, no people the sole or even the principal author of their own existence."[153] As I have demonstrated, the same applies to the ancient Jewish notion of an ideal model-sage, whilst the various ways in which the figure is portrayed remain distinctly local.[154]

I hope to have shown, therefore, that it is worthwhile to read early Jewish accounts of the sage in relation to both ancient Israelite and ancient Greek writings: they develop the earlier Hebrew tradition *and* count as Hellenistic representations of the wise person. While it is natural to expect parallels between Jewish and non-Jewish texts written in Greek because of the shared language and contexts in the Greek-speaking cities of the Mediterranean region, Jewish texts from Judea and non-Jewish texts also demonstrate a major parallel, the idea of the exemplary sage, despite the language gap. Even if this parallel is rather general, it reveals the importance of aspiration in wisdom discourse, pointing to the need of wisdom lovers to constantly (re)form themselves.[155] In addition, one may identify more specific (dis)similarities between Jewish and Greek sources on the sage, which help one observe distinctive aspects of the two wisdom traditions. These features perhaps would not be seen as readily if the sources were read in isolation from each other.[156]

Both Jewish and Greek sources tend to imagine the ideal sage as an ancestral figure; it seems easier to project wisdom and perfection to people back in time than to name contemporary sages. This tendency is not surprising, considering that both Greek and Jewish writings make use of past figures for rhetorical purposes, casting them as models of the good (or the bad) life.[157] The Greek tradition tends to celebrate the figure of Socrates, even if other philosophers are also remembered as models for their students and members of respective schools. As for Jewish texts written in Greek, Philo of Alexandria glorifies Moses and the patriarchs, whereas Wisdom of Solomon transforms the legendary king of the past into an ideal sage; the approach of these authors is philosophically generic yet religiously exclusive. The (originally) Semitic sources from Judea both imagine biblical characters of the past as exemplars and delineate contemporary sages, as is shown by the book of Ben Sira, the maskil materials, and the pseudepigrapha.

The concern for ancestral perfection indicates the importance of a "historical" example as an argumentative technique that conveys an effective demonstration. An example has evidential value: a claim seems more convincing and persuasive if the author can demonstrate that it has already happened.[158] Hence, an example bridges the past and the present, while also inspiring imitation that shapes the future.[159] Such acts of interpretation presuppose skilful application, and many ancient authors who discussed the sage could similarly transform their ancestral writings into vital educational resources. By creating links between the past and the present, they sought to experience the inherited tradition as topical and as their own. While their concern for past examples exposes a commitment to an ancestral tradition, it also indicates the production of "commentary" upon such a tradition; the invoking of biblical figures, in other words, serves to articulate an awareness of one's own literary culture.[160]

Another parallel between Greek and Jewish sources concerns the fluctuating interest in the societal matters: both sets of writings vary regarding the relationship between the sage and the surrounding society. In the Greek world, Plato shows little interest in practical matters of social life, whereas the Stoics discuss the everyday life of the wise person in more detail, meditating on his engagement with family, financial, and political affairs.

Jewish portraits of the sage are similarly diverse. The texts from the diaspora tend to leave everyday issues aside and to concentrate on the perfection of the solitary sage; this also concerns Philo's accounts that otherwise have close points of contact with the Stoic notion of the sage. The Judean accounts are different in that the sages depicted in them are closely rooted in their societies and communities. The book of Qoheleth hints at the wealth of the sage and presents him as meditating on government and justice (Qoh 8:1–17), although his ways of participating in the society remain unclear. The ideal wise person encountered in the book of Ben Sira is far from an isolationist, serving social roles and duties in the particular societal context in which he operates and thus providing one with glimpses of the tasks of an influential person in the second-century BCE Jerusalem. The figure of the maskil remains anonymous and somewhat enigmatic, but he also has specific functions in an early Jewish movement known from the Qumran scrolls.

Greek and Jewish accounts of the ideal sage share an aspirational ethos, a common interest in ancestral heroes, and a similarly fluctuating concern for the societal roles of the sage. In spite of these similarities, there are evident differences between the sources on the wise person.

As we have seen, (non-Jewish) Greek texts emphasize the difficulty of attaining wisdom. Only sages, who exist rarely if at all, have fully achieved wisdom, whereas other people – or, to be exact, those people who care for wisdom in the first place – strive to gain wisdom through their philosophical practice. The sage functions as a template directing one's search for wisdom instead of representing a real person to be encountered in this world.

Jewish texts on the sage also involve an aspirational element, but their attitude towards the human capacity to attain wisdom is generally more positive. The sources maintain that virtually anyone has potential to become a sage through an earnest search for wisdom.[161] Accordingly, sages appear as wisdom teachers who provide their pupils with models for living. Even if wisdom is regarded as relatively accessible, certain socioeconomical limitations remain valid: the pursuit of wisdom requires leisure time and dedication, and the sage-scribe's tasks and skills are contrasted with those of farmers and artisans (Sir 38:24–34).

Another difference concerns the naming of sages or the lack thereof. The Greek intellectual tradition names its wise people early on, beginning with a number of pre-Socratics. The situation is rather different in the Hebrew Bible. Apart from the exceptions of the foreign Agur (Prov 30:1–4) and Lemuel (Prov 31:1–9), the intellectuals who can be named are typically prophets, but they do not seem to be named for the purpose of emulation, although Elisha is portrayed as the follower of Elijah in 1 Kings (esp. 1 Kgs 19:21).

The situation begins to change in the later Hellenistic and Roman eras, as is shown by the protagonist of Ben Sira who seems to be happy to invite his pupils to emulate him. Even so, alongside the *Zeitgeist* of naming the wise teacher, there continues to exist a tradition that retains the anonymity of the earlier wisdom tradition known from Proverbs and even Qoheleth, as is suggested by the maskil of the Qumran scrolls. Likewise, several early Jewish authors project emulation back to ancient figures such as Solomon and Moses instead of naming a contemporary model.

Furthermore, the literary construction of exemplarity is rather different in Greek and Jewish sources from antiquity. As discussed above, Wright has aptly observed the use of first-person accounts as a literary strategy that contributes to the construction of the exemplary sage in the book of Ben Sira.[162] This observation actually applies to many texts from Jewish antiquity, ranging from the Hebrew sources of Qoheleth and the Qumran scrolls to the Greek Wisdom of Solomon. Greek philosophical sources that acclaim the sage, including Philo's texts, are rather different insofar as they tend to comment on the wise person in the third person. Such language seems to give a slightly more abstract flavour to the discussion on exemplarity and emulation.[163]

The relationship between the sage and the divine realm receives some attention in both Greek and Jewish sources. Yet, there are differences regarding this subject matter. The Greek accounts occasionally refer to the holy nature of the sage (e.g., Plato, *Theaetetus* 176b) or to cultic matters such as sacrifices and purity especially in Stoic contexts (D.L. 7.119). Jewish writings from the Hellenistic and early Roman eras describe the sage's engagement with the divine realm in a more emphatic way, although he is not yet depicted as a holy man.[164]

In early Jewish writings, the wise person prays for wisdom and knowledge (esp. Sir 39:5–8; Wis 9:1–18; 1QS 11; 1QH^a 5:12; 20:7). Engaging with the divine realm, he may praise God (e.g., Sir 42:15–43:33, 51:1–12; Shirot), receive esoteric revelation (esp. 1QS 9:13; 11:3–5), or create new inspired teaching (esp. Sir 24:23). A more sceptical attitude characterizes the book of Qoheleth, but its protagonist also has an established relation to God, irrespective of the fact that it appears to be more "formal and distant" than those of the other sages.[165]

In summary, the process of becoming wise involves an aspirational element: the sage offers a template to be followed by those who care for wisdom, regardless of whether the status of a wise person is deemed accessible or not. In the ancient Mediterranean context, Greek sources from the classical period are the first ones to depict the sage as the epitome of wisdom and an object of emulation. While ancient Hebrew literature refers to various wise people early on, the ideal sage in the sense of an exemplar or a model-teacher is not explicit until Hellenistic Judaism. The prospect of cultural interaction is likely, for the sources, starting from the book of Ben Sira, take the wise person for granted. Thus, a fundamental element of early Jewish discussion on wisdom is best understood as reflecting, adding to, and constituting a part of the wider Hellenistic discourse on the good life. Yet, as for texts from Judea, the Greek effect on Jewish construction of the wise person is a matter of *Zeitgeist* rather than one of deliberate copying.

Conclusions

The ideal sage is an essential aspect of lived wisdom because such a figure represents the epitome of wisdom, thus illustrating the type of character and behaviour at which the instruction on wisdom and the good life aim. The role of the sage as a model is equally relevant since it communicates the power of an example to shape and transform the lives of other people: the wise person invites seekers of wisdom to orient themselves according to a particular template, thus replicating a way of life that is celebrated as virtuous. The accounts of the sage are deeply aspirational, which reveals the formative and perfectionist purpose of wisdom discourse.

Ancient Israelite ideas of the wise person changed over time. Copious texts of the Hebrew Bible associate the figure with various skills, whereas texts from the second temple period develop an interest in the חכם as an intellectual. The book of Proverbs hints at the wise person as a learned figure, and the book of Qoheleth devotes much attention to his inner life. The instruction of Ben Sira and the Qumran scrolls further underline the exemplarity of the sage, while biblical figures feature as exemplars in the pseudepigrapha. In addition, ideal sages appear in Greek Jewish writings from the early Roman period. In Wisdom of Solomon, the prayerful protagonist is imagined in a way that echoes the ancient Israelite king, renowned for his exceptional wisdom (1 Kgs 5:9–14), but Solomon is transformed into a devout sage. For Philo of Alexandria, Moses personifies the perfect sage, whereas other biblical characters may also serve as exemplars. Philo stresses the prototype to the extent that he speaks of copying the model provided by the sage.

The occurrence of the model-sage in the (originally) Semitic texts is not to be taken for granted, for the idea fully emerges in the later Hellenistic era, i.e., at a time when Jewish texts frequently indicate an intermingling of cultural elements both "local" and "Greek." The Hebrew tradition displays a myriad of wise early on, but it is only in the Hellenistic period that the sources begin to describe the persona of the sage per se. In the later Hellenistic and early Roman eras, they further express the figure's role as an exemplar to be emulated by those who wish to become wise themselves. Since the Greek texts outline the ideal sage already in the classical period, this development probably resulted from cultural collaboration in the eastern Mediterranean region. The Hellenistic *Zeitgeist*, in other words, seems to have prompted Jewish authors to spell out the role of the sage as a living embodiment of wisdom. Despite the parallel, Jewish and Greek accounts of the sage are far from identical, as they vary regarding the amount of concreteness and the discursive strategies in which the figure's exemplarity is constructed. Hence, the wise person always hails from a specific context, serving the needs and agendas of local authors and communities.

3

Learning and lifestyle: The everyday performance of wisdom teachers

Copious writings from Jewish antiquity encourage one to search for wisdom and understanding, but what do they say about how one attains, retains, or manifests wisdom? What is actually known about the lived wisdom of pedagogical professionals in particular? What are the implications of the learned lifestyle for our understanding of Jewish wisdom as a cultural phenomenon?

As shown in Chapter 2, the ancient Israelite tradition is familiar with a range of wise people early on. Yet, a myriad of Jewish texts from the Hellenistic and early Roman periods outline the ideal sage, who serves as a template and an object of emulation, and the persona of the wise person is that of a contemporary wisdom teacher at times. In this chapter, I will argue that one way to comprehend the everyday practice and performance of wisdom in the ancient world is to examine the types of activities and exercises attributed to these pedagogues, who were erudite and rather privileged in terms of their socioeconomic status, thus illustrating life(style) in the upper strata of society. Such an analysis, as I hope to demonstrate, enables one to gain a more nuanced understanding of the repetitive and rhythmic actions that constituted both private and social life in at least some early Jewish circles.[1]

As we have already seen, two sets of texts originating from late second temple Judea, the book of Ben Sira and the Qumran scrolls, are integral to our notion of a wise exemplar in Jewish antiquity. They are also essential to our understanding of the teacher's lifestyle, for, unlike the diaspora texts, which primarily tend to focus on ancestral perfection,[2] these sources display the wise figure as a pedagogue modelling ideal ways of living and everyday patterns of practice. The contemporary wise persons from Judea are rooted in and serve their immediate communities through teaching and other duties.

In what follows, I will explore the topic of a learned lifestyle in more detail. I will begin my investigation with a review of the portrayal of teachers in the

Hebrew Bible, tracing a series of pedagogues from Moses to Qoheleth, in order to expose aspects of lived wisdom that apply to these figures. Thereafter, I will turn to analyse the evidence of Ben Sira and the Qumran scrolls, which underline the role of teachers, including their ways of life and their pedagogical programmes. Finally, I will address the issue of Jewish wisdom as a cultural phenomenon in antiquity and reflect on the Mediterranean locus of early Jewish wisdom teachers. I will argue that the emphasis on exercise and lifestyle probably enabled them to understand themselves as a type of philosophers.

Biblical pedagogues, from Moses to Qoheleth

Jewish texts from the late second temple era, especially the book of Ben Sira and the Qumran scrolls, are integral to my argument concerning the significance of lived and embodied acts in the lifestyle of a wisdom teacher. This does not mean, however, that materials predating the book of Ben Sira, which hails from the second century BCE, would be irrelevant in regard to the question of exercises that constitute the everyday life of the wisdom teacher. On the contrary, the texts of the Hebrew Bible feature several pedagogues that could be defined as wisdom teachers broadly understood, and these pedagogues undertake some acts as part of their learned lifestyles.

The Hebrew Bible is a pedagogical book in many ways, teaching the people of Israel what their God expects from them, and thus how to live. In fact, God is cast as Israel's educator in various contexts, from Moses' motivational speeches (e.g., Deut 4:36; 8:1–6) to prophetic proclamations (e.g., Isa 2:3; 48:17; 54:13; Jer 32:33; Mic 4:2), to liturgical poetry (e.g., Ps 32:8; 71:17; 94:10). Etymologically, the name of the first part of this collection, the Torah, also stands for "teaching," as the Hebrew term תורה derives from the verb ירה, "to teach."[3] The figure of Moses, to whom the five books of the Torah or the Pentateuch were attributed over time, is depicted as instructing the people of Israel through a series of speeches and poems; the book of Deuteronomy, in particular, contains his parenetic farewell speech to the people of Israel who is about to enter the promised land.[4] As is fit for a teacher, Moses urges his audience to listen to him and to obey his words (e.g., Deut 5:1–2; 11:8–31). Anticipating a future time, Moses urges the audience to transmit his teaching to the next generations (e.g., 6:4–8) and to be prepared for dialogical moments of teaching (e.g., 6:20–5).

Eventually, Moses became known as the first and foremost pedagogue of Israel, described as "Moses our teacher" (משה רבינו) in the rabbinic writings. He was also celebrated in numerous texts written in the second temple period, ranging from the book of Jubilees to the writings of Philo of Alexandria.⁵ In spite of this legacy, and the fact that the Bible credits Moses with a distinctive mediatory role between God and humans (e.g., Deut 34:10), Moses' pedagogical task and mission were far from effortless. In addition to saluting Israel's prime teacher, Deuteronomy meditates on the difficulty of learning and on the people's unwillingness to receive instruction.⁶ The book hints at the possibility of oversight early on (4:9, 23; 6:12), but these motifs are especially prominent in the final chapters. They tell how Moses, prior to his death, sets Joshua as his successor (31:1–8) and ensures the future of his teaching by writing it down so that the Levites and the elders could deliver the teaching to the people of Israel every seventh year during the Sukkot festival (31:9–13).⁷

God, however, is not optimistic about Israel's capacity to follow his teaching, predicting that they will forsake it (31:16–18, cf. 32:18). To mitigate the risks, God asks Moses to write down a song and teach it to the people (31:19–22). Even though Moses had earlier stressed the easiness of his teaching (30:11–14), he comes to doubt Israel's ability to walk on the assigned path (31:24–9, cf. 29:1–3). Moses nevertheless delivers his song (32:1–44), which he characterizes as an instruction (32:2),⁸ and he emphasizes its accessibility (32:45–7). Having completed his task, Moses dies and the people of Israel mourn for him (34:5–8). Their teacher-prophet is gone, but his teaching does not end: Joshua is then described as being filled with the "spirit of wisdom" (רוח חכמה), which makes the Israelites to obey him (34:9).

Moses, therefore, appears as a prime teacher who equips Israel with cross-generational instruction, despite the difficulty of his task. It is of interest that Deuteronomy, the book containing his teaching, entails a considerable amount of wisdom terminology and motifs.⁹ A nascent association of wisdom and torah is also made (4:5–6), which anticipates the later identification of these concepts (e.g., Sir 24:23; 4Q525 frag. 2 ii) and transforms Moses, a teacher of the torah, into a kind of wisdom teacher. All these features enhance the pedagogical flavour of the book, which provides Israel with a form of religion and culture that can be studied.¹⁰ The lifestyle of the teacher takes a backseat, however, as the narrative focuses on the content of Moses' teaching. Yet, it is striking that the pedagogue-leader integrates liturgical performance – i.e., acts of singing and blessing (31:20–32:44; 33:1–29) – into his teaching. It is also remarkable that Moses is followed by another teacher, Joshua, as this feature spells out the importance of a chain of transmission, although Joshua primarily appears as a military leader and offers related instruction in the book of Judges.

Moses has received unparalleled attention in the Jewish later tradition, but he is not the only biblical pedagogue. The Hebrew Bible refers to several instructors, although some of them are mentioned only in passing. A brief remark in 2 Kgs 12:3, for example, informs that King Jehoash was taught (ירה) by the priest Jehoiada, thus revealing the pedagogical responsibilities of priests. Another passage in 2 Chr 17:7–9 mentions itinerant teachers of Judah, Jehoshaphat's officials, who had "the book of the torah" and "went around through all the cities of Judah and instructed the people."[11] The Hebrew term for these professionals is שר, an official of the king, but their task is to teach (למד) the people of Judah about the torah. The Levites, too, are cast as instructors of the torah both here (2 Chr 17:8) and elsewhere in the Hebrew Bible (e.g., Deut 33:10; Neh 8:7; 2 Chr 35:3; Ps 78:1).[12]

More sustained discussion on a particular teacher arises concerning the figure of Ezra, who is cast as a priest, scribe, and expert in the torah of Moses (Ezra 7:1–11). The title "scribe" (ספר) applied to Ezra has given rise to various interpretations, as it may refer to his role as an official of the royal court, torah scholar, or scribe in the Achaemenid administration.[13] Leaving aside the exact meaning of Ezra's scribal identity, it is essential that the book of Ezra portrays the exceptional scribe as an itinerant teacher who comes from Babylon to Jerusalem with a group of other Israelites (7:6–10), including priests, Levites, singers, gatekeepers, and temple servants (7:7).[14] According to the narrative, King Artaxerxes had sent Ezra to investigate whether people in Jerusalem have followed the divine law (7:14). This gives an impression that missionary activity and spiritual judgement belong to the tasks of this teacher, who had dedicated himself to the torah of the Lord and wished "to teach the law and the regulation (חק ומשפט) to Israel" (7:10, cf. 7:11–12).

The timing of the trip from Babylon to Jerusalem (7:8–9; 8:31) is religiously motivated. The departure is said to have taken place in the first month like the exodus from Egypt (cf. Exod 12:2; Num 33:3). This creates an image of Ezra's trip as the second exodus, i.e., as a new beginning that eventually leads to another giving of the torah.[15] While the figure of Ezra is a literary construct, it is significant vis-à-vis learning and lifestyle that he is imagined to have partaken in a type of educational travel: Ezra's task is to spread and share his knowledge by instructing the precepts of the torah to Israel (Neh 8:1–12). Following his arrival in Jerusalem, people ask him to bring the torah of Moses, including the commandments given by God to Israel, to the square in front of the Water Gate (8:1). Ezra does as he is asked to do and then delivers his teaching to men and women in the city (8:2–5). The fact that the Levites are said to have helped him by explaining and translating the teaching to the people (8:7–8) reveals the communal nature of the pedagogical event, revealing that the act of teaching may have to be accompanied with an act of translation.

The story about Ezra describes another teacher of the torah who could also be seen as a type of wisdom teacher, considering that the text of Ezra-Nehemiah makes a move to associate wisdom and torah (Ezra 7:14, 25, cf. Neh 8:7–8).[16] In addition, the story points to a salient post-exilic development in ancient Judaism. The figure of Ezra is said to have "dedicated himself to study (לדרוש) the torah of the Lord so as to observe it, and to teach laws and rules to Israel" (Ezra 7:10). The use of the verb דרש regarding Ezra's investigation of the divine torah is striking, as it belongs to divination terminology and denotes oracular activity elsewhere in the Hebrew Bible (e.g., 1 Kgs 22:8), often referring to prophets who consult YHWH.[17] Yet, as Ezra 7:10 explicates, the root came to denote the search for divine knowledge from the torah. Ezra's "exegetical praxis," as Michael Fishbane describes the exercise undertaken by the figure, "functionally co-opted older mantic techniques of divine inquiry."[18] This development shows how textual interpretation became an explicit and integral part of the teacher's erudite lifestyle in the second temple period.

While the legacy of Moses and Ezra is striking, any study on pedagogy in ancient Israel is indebted to the book of Proverbs, which presents itself as delivering teaching on wisdom and virtues (Prov 1:1–7). The quality of wisdom is elevated and cast as "the precondition and guarantor of all virtues," as set out by Fox. In so doing, the author may develop "the ancient Hebrew tradition of ethical and practical maxims" in order to respond to "a vague awareness of the existence of Greek philosophical thinking."[19] Yet, as discussed in Chapter 2, the book's contribution to our notion of pedagogical professionals remains limited. There are only occasional references to the wise people (esp. 22:17), and the information on teachers is similarly sparse or at least scattered.

In lengthy sections of Proverbs, it is the personified and transcendent figure of female wisdom who instructs the audience (1:20–33; 8:1–36; 9:1–12), not any human being. Yet, there is some evidence for human teachers in the form of the parental figure, as much of the instruction is delivered by a "father" to a "son" (cf. Job 15:18). Overall, therefore, Proverbs seems to channel two authoritative voices, including the life-saving instructions of the father and the speech of wisdom herself. Fox compares the relation between the two voices to a counterpoint, the act of combining different melodies or voices that are independent in character. While the voices of the transcendent wisdom and the parental figure do not blend in Proverbs, the "down-to-earth teaching of the home" could be read as representing an instance of the "sublime power" of wisdom that permeates all creation.[20]

The father–son discourse communicates a vivid mental image of home-based learning, but one should remember that it does not primarily refer to any biological relations between the teacher and the pupils. Rather, the employment of familial idiom indicates that the book of Proverbs originates from learned circles, where the use of "paternal authority" had become an established literary device.[21] The language grants the speaker a type of power, aiming at helping the pupils to dodge destructive and shameful situations that one can avoid with the help of teachers (5:12–14).

In spite of the book's common focus on the father as the instructor, Prov 1:8 and 6:20 also acknowledge the pedagogical role of a mother. Moreover, the section titled as the words of Lemuel explicitly presents the king's mother as his teacher: "The words of Lemuel, king of Massa, with which his mother admonished him" (31:1–2). This is natural as much of the tuition and rearing typically takes place at home in societies that lack an institutionalised system of education, thus enabling women's role as educators (cf. Tob 1:8; Jub 25:1–3; Pseudo-Philo, LAB 33; 4 Macc 18:6–19).[22]

Proverbs, therefore, says little explicitly about wisdom teachers or their lifestyle. Yet, the idea of home as an educational setting lurks behind the text, which gestures towards the idea that wisdom and education could be embedded in daily life; the lifestyle of a teacher may include parenthood.

Overall, a great deal of discussion on learning in the Hebrew Bible revolves around the torah of Israel taught by Moses, Ezra, or other instructors who appear only incidentally. Parents, too, are credited with the task of teaching the torah in Prov 6:20, although it is far from clear whether the term pertains to Israel's divine revelation in this verse. All of these pedagogues differ from another biblical protagonist, Qoheleth, since the sources say more about the object of teaching than about the teacher.[23] The book of Qoheleth, which probably originates from the third century BCE,[24] marks a clear change in Jewish wisdom discourse by drawing attention to the inner life and lifestyle of the teacher, who takes the persona of Jerusalem's king (Qoh 1:1) and is designated as a חכם in the epilogue (12:9).[25] There is nothing to suggest that Qoheleth would be associated with public life, administration, or cult. Rather, the figure is wealthy to the extent that he can indulge in thinking about the meaning of life.[26]

The critical thinker encountered in the book explores the world and its transience; beginning with Qoh 1:2, all is characterized as הבל, a puff of wind.

Most of the book consists of reflections by this figure, who sets out "to study and to probe with wisdom all that happens under the sun." Such a task, "an unhappy business" (עִנְיַן רָע), is regarded as God-given (1:13). In what follows, the sage ponders a plethora of topics related to life and the world, including material prosperity, efforts, and pleasure (2:1–26), the benefits and joys of communal life (4:7–12), and the value of moderation (5:9–14). The figure tests himself in order to grasp the meaning of life (2:1–11) and prepares for his death (3:16–21; 12:1–7). Given his awareness of the history and the flow of time (1:10; 3:1–8), the speaker is capable of observing patterns in the repetitive cosmos and of conceiving of the present moment in a continuum of human experiences, as well as within a wider cosmic order. The tone is sceptical, but an aspect of wonder lurks in the background; the protagonist's quest for wisdom contains "a mixture of awe and disillusionment, bewilderment and resignation."[27]

The speaker in Qoheleth draws on his intellectual wherewithal and resources instead of speculating on divine revelation. The book refers to wisdom and knowledge that can be learned (1:16), but an innovation is implied in the idea that a person can make use of one's intellect independently in order to discover new knowledge, i.e., not only to absorb knowledge from one's predecessors. Overall, the idea that knowledge draws on experience and observations grants Qoheleth's approach an empirical flavour.[28]

Because of the book's concern for the "autonomy of individual reason," scholars have associated Qoheleth with Greek philosophy.[29] Similarly, it has been observed that the stress on individual experience and the devaluation of things that are out of one's control remind one of Hellenistic popular philosophy and its quest for individual happiness.[30] The shared attitudes between Qoheleth and contemporary Greek philosophy indicate an intermingling of cultural registers; any single school or tradition does not explain the evidence of Qoheleth.[31] While such a position appears eclectic, the term may create a misleading idea of thinkers who randomly picked things up from different places. Instead, it seems to be more helpful to think of Jewish wisdom lovers, including Qoheleth, as "absorbing" and incorporating various ideas that they claim to be their own.[32]

As can be gathered from above, the lifestyle of Qoheleth comprises enquiry, observation, contemplation, and judgement making. Some further points can be extracted from the epilogue of the book (12:9–14), which differs from the preceding first-person accounts insofar as it is delivered by a narrator. The narrator specifies activities in which the protagonist was engaged (12:9–10):

> Because Qoheleth was a sage, he continued to instruct the people. He listened to and tested the soundness of many maxims. Qoheleth sought to discover useful sayings and recorded genuinely truthful sayings.

This short passage asserts that the daily life of the teacher involves pedagogical efforts and anthological work, including the collection and writing down of משלים.[33] The teacher, therefore, actively looks for wisdom and documents insights in a written form.

The reference to Qoheleth's activity in the sphere of teaching (12:9) is essential because the book's pedagogical impulse is not as obvious as it is in the case of Proverbs, for example. Qoheleth's voice and accent are original, but the figure focuses on himself instead of communicating with his pupils.[34] Furthermore, there is little to suggest that the protagonist would explicitly serve as an exemplar. Yet, even if the book escapes the conventional wisdom of sayings and encourages independent enquiry, it is not devoid of instruction. The use of the first-person voice throughout the book is pertinent in this respect: it enables the reader to take part in the teacher's reflections and, presumably, to learn from them. This speaker, too, wishes to communicate his peculiar vision of the good life, exhorting the audience to enjoy the pleasures of eating, drinking, and working, which he includes in "realistic assessments of the human condition."[35] Moreover, the book clearly aims at reaching a pupil who seeks wisdom like the protagonist (12:12), although the speaker may also express some anxiety about the idea of his successor as the "inheritor" of his legacy.[36]

In summary, the Hebrew Bible exhibits several pedagogues who share their knowledge with the people of Israel. Their instruction is mostly anchored in Israel's divine instruction, as is shown by the two iconic teachers of the ancient Israelite narrative, Moses and Ezra. The book of Qoheleth is different insofar as it stresses both the importance of observation and the testing of the wisdom of the ancients; meanwhile, the book is attributed to the king of Jerusalem, which signals the inclusion of this original lesson within the ancient Israelite tradition.

As for wisdom and lifestyle, the literary representations of Moses and Ezra in Deuteronomy and Ezra-Nehemiah hint at liturgical performance, textual interpretation, and missionary activity as components of the teacher's way of life, while Qoheleth offers further hues of the learned lifestyle by underlining the tasks of enquiry and anthological work. Thus, the idea of exercising and performing one's wisdom through acts that constitute the lifestyle of a pedagogue is incipient in the Hebrew Bible. Yet, the teacher's lifestyle receives more sustained attention in Jewish texts from the late second temple period, including in the book of Ben Sira to which I will turn next.

The lifestyle of the teacher according to Ben Sira

The book of Ben Sira, similarly to Qoheleth, is a text that resists the idea of Judaism and Hellenism as mutually exclusive categories. In spite of this general parallel, these two writings from Hellenistic Jerusalem are distinctive in terms of their character and emphases. While Qoheleth offers a fascinating look at the inner life of one teacher, the evidence of Ben Sira illustrates a richer assortment of lived and embodied practices that were imagined to fill the life of a wisdom instructor in the later Hellenistic period. As discussed in Chapter 2, the book of Ben Sira underlines the exemplarity of the sage-teacher and brings wisdom's formative aspect to the forefront. Wright observes: "If a wisdom text like Ben Sira is meant to do anything at all, it is to 'construct paths for living.'"[37] Practices of the pedagogue are crucial in this respect, as they delineate how the ideal figure is expected to experience and embody wisdom in his daily life.

At the outset, I should clarify the presumed relation between this text and social history. The book of Ben Sira is attributed to a specific figure, and it is thus often described as the first Jewish book with a named author. In my investigation, however, I do not assume that the text would provide a direct access to socio-historical realities in Jerusalem in the second century BCE. The "author" of the book does not appear as an author in the modern sense of the word, including ideas of copyright and individual authorship, but as a collector and gatherer of ever-growing materials, as argued by Eva Mroczek. The outcome, the "book" of Ben Sira, is thus akin to a flowing and growing project.[38] Likewise, one should not expect that the text's statements on the wisdom teacher offer accurate information of a particular historical figure. Rather, the character encountered in the text indicates how an exemplary teacher was imagined, reflecting ideals of such a pedagogical professional. The text, in other words, illuminates conceptions of the lifestyle of a wisdom teacher in general.

The survey in Chapter 2 showed that wisdom is often associated with technical skills in the Hebrew Bible. Unlike these accounts, the book of Ben Sira promotes an exclusively noetic notion of wisdom: the section on trades and crafts in Sir 38:24–34 spells out that the pursuit of wisdom requires the luxury of leisure. The author presents sceptical remarks on the capacity of farmers, artisans, and potters to achieve wisdom. These groups of people master crucial skills that support the society; their work, in fact, sustains the world and can be compared to the offering of prayer (38:34). Yet, their expertise is of no use in public assemblies, courts, and the enterprise of ruling people. Although the author's attitude reveals an elitist notion of wisdom, it does not mean that the wisdom of an erudite person would be abstract or detached from his daily life in the world of Ben Sira. On the contrary, the wise teacher outlined in the book enacts his wisdom through various tasks and activities. In what follows, I seek to gather the book's sporadic evidence for the mental and spiritual exercises that he undertakes with an aim to attain, retain, or perform wisdom.[39]

Instruction obviously belongs to the life of any teacher, and some remarks on the portrayal of the pedagogical enterprise in Ben Sira are in order. The author makes use of "paternal authority" as a pedagogical tool, presenting the teacher as a father and the pupils figuratively as sons.[40] Thus, an element of intergenerational hierarchy between an elder, who delivers the lesson, and a junior, who receives the key to attaining wisdom, is implied. The teacher's agenda – his aim both to gain and spread wisdom – is underlined in Sir 24:30–4. The first-person account, which remains in Greek, begins with lush natural imagery pointing to the teacher's efforts (24:30–1):

> And I, like a canal from a river and a water channel, issued forth into an orchard. I said, "I will water my garden, and I will drench my flower bed." And look! The canal turned into a river for me, and my river turned into a sea.[41]

The speaker sees himself as one teacher among others, as a "canal" who first waters his own flowers, and the garden imagery echoes Genesis 2–3. Through the teacher, as Matthew Goff observes, the pupil has access to the fruits of Eden.[42] Moreover, the emphasis on water, which is used in connection with the divine torah just ahead of this passage (24:23–7), may signal that wisdom is to be found in the Jewish tradition.[43] Yet, the ethos does not suggest isolation of any kind. The next verses, where the sage describes his teaching, may even involve universal concerns (24:32–4):

> Still I will again make education (παιδείαν) enlighten like dawn, and I will shine them forth to far off. Still I will again pour out teaching (διδασκαλίαν) like prophecy, and I will leave it behind for generations of eternity. See that I have not toiled for myself alone but for all who seek it out.[44]

Here, the teacher's instruction is presented as παιδεία, the formation and socialization of a person through activities and discourses.[45] The light imagery applied to the teaching involves much metaphorical potential, for its connotations include creation, knowledge, and divine revelation in the Jewish tradition.[46] As such, the idiom must remain open to interpretation, but the claim that the speaker's teaching shines far off signals that his instruction is influential.[47] The comparison to prophecy further highlights its inspired nature (see more below), whereas the reference to future generations turns the audience to look for future. The final statement – that the teacher does not struggle just for himself but "for all who seek it out" – confirms the communal dimension of his endeavours: the instructor does not concentrate on his own progress and individual merit, but he makes a contribution that benefits other seekers of wisdom, including future generations.[48]

From a literary point of view, ch. 24 is located in the middle of the book, bringing its first half into a conclusion with an emphatic celebration of the teacher and his pedagogical efforts. Further reflection on the same topic occurs towards the end of the book in Sir 50:27–9. Referring to the instruction of "understanding and knowledge" provided ahead, the speaker explains how he has "poured forth wisdom from his heart" and then continues with an affirmative macarism directed at motivating the addressee: "Happy is he who is engaged in these things, and when he has placed them on his heart, he will be wise."[49] An immersion in the given instruction results in a fortunate state, so the promise goes, and eventually enables one to achieve wisdom.

Apart from teaching, the teacher is busy with the scribal tasks of composing, reading, and interpreting texts, as is spelled out in Sir 39:1–15 with a lengthy section that delineates the way of life of the ideal sage-scribe; this passage, too, remains only in Greek. Verses Sir 39:1–3 specify that the learned figure wishes to grasp the immaterial inheritance of the human past: he wants to comprehend the "wisdom of all the ancients" (σοφίαν πάντων ἀρχαίων), is concerned with "prophecies" (ἐν προφητείαις), and memorizes the "narrative of famous men" (διηγήσεις ἀνδρῶν ὀνομαστῶν). Generally, he is dedicated to the discovery of meaning as he explores "twists of illustrations" (ἐν στροφαῖς παραβολῶν), is absorbed in "obscurities of proverbs" (ἀπόκρυφα παροιμιῶν), and engages in "riddles of illustrations" (ἐν αἰνίγμασι παραβολῶν).[50]

The instructor, therefore, both masters and passes on inherited texts and traditions, including proverbs, narratives, and prophecies. A pertinent statement in the Greek prologue to Sirach clarifies that the author's grandfather wished both to understand old writings and make his own contribution to the body of texts that are worthy of study and consideration. He did not only study the torah, the prophets, and other ancestral books, but also wanted "to compose something pertaining to education and wisdom" (συγγράψαι τι τῶν εἰς παιδείαν καὶ σοφίαν ἀνηκόντων) in order to provide the "lovers of learning" (οἱ φιλομαθεῖς) with insights (Prologue, lines 10–14). This statement points to an ever-growing body of documented insights. The collection of valuable books, or the "canon" of authoritative writings, is not yet complete but continues to expand. Hence, the transmission of texts and the creation of new ones appear to be simultaneous processes.[51]

Since the wise teacher of Ben Sira is expected to know and meditate on the ancestral writings, it is worth appraising whether biblical figures of the past provide him and his pupils with models to imitate. The extensive survey of respected ancestors in Sir 44:1–49:24 outlines and praises lives of past heroes, including kings, rulers, leaders, legislators, advisers, prophets, heroes, sages, experts of scripture, and writers, depicting them as worthy of ongoing remembrance (44:1–15). The list begins with Enoch and reaches Simon the high priest, thus creating a continuum from primordial times to the author's own era (cf. 1 Clem 4:7–6:4). Notably, all the examples are selected from the Israelite tradition, even if the author was also familiar with and made use of some Greek texts.[52]

The author does not explicitly render the paragons as objects of emulation, i.e., the addressees are not expected to become them. Yet, it seems that he does not only praise the ancestors but also sets them as worthy models. The figures' occasional association with virtues favours such an interpretation of the account (e.g., 44:15, 17; 45:4; 46:1, 7; 47:14),[53] and the argument is further supported by the text's affinity with Greek encomia.[54] The latter places the hymn at the intersection of Hebrew and Greek literary cultures, showing that the author "read his own history paradigmatically," or as an analogue to texts that establish "the way and wisdom of the Greeks."[55] Importantly, the rhetorical effect of encomia entails imitation. As is clear from Pericles's funerary oration documented by Thucydides (*History* 2.43.1-4), an encomium seeks to praise virtuous people and, in doing so, to stir the audience to follow them.[56] Similarly, the author of Ben Sira offers to his audience an opportunity to learn from the positive examples of those who lived before.

Some of the teacher's activities explicitly orient towards his inner life. A life dedicated to wisdom involves contemplation, which takes many different forms. Considering the book's stress on inherited traditions, it is consistent that appropriate contemplation concerns the divine torah, Israel's foremost source of wisdom (24:23) and the "law of life" (17:11). Several passages throughout the book state that a person desiring wisdom should adhere to the torah and the commandments (e.g., 1:26; 6:18; 15:1; 19:20; 21:11; 33:2–3). As is specified in Sir 6:37, one's dedication to the divine statutes involves rumination on them: "Exercise your thoughts in the Lord's ordinances, and on his commandments continually meditate. It is he who will make your heart firm, and the desire for wisdom will be given to you."[57] Such devotion brings out about a state of happiness (14:20–1) and rewards: "Save for him who devotes his soul and thinks about the law of the Most High!" (38:34).[58]

Contemplation may also fall upon the created order, as is suggested by the extensive cosmological account in Sir 42:15–43:33, which portrays the teacher as meditating on the wonders of nature, including celestial bodies and weather phenomena.[59] He remembers and marvels at the elegance of God's creation, proclaiming that the universe mirrors the glory of the creator (42:17) and conceiving of the cosmos as a place where "each creature is preserved to meet a particular need" (42:23).[60] The speaker begins with praising God's omniscience, then proceeds to discuss the splendour of the created order, and finally concludes that "we could say more but could never say enough" (43:27).[61] Contemplation thus discloses a state of astonishment and wonder, which results in epistemic humility and in a belief in the meaningfulness of the cosmic order.[62]

Although a great deal of contemplation concerns divine revelation through either cosmos or the torah, human resources may also serve as objects of such an act. This is demonstrated by the aforementioned reference to the ideal sage-scribe who explores the "wisdom of all the ancients" (σοφίαν πάντων ἀρχαίων) (39:1). Likewise, the student should not disregard the "discourse of the wise" (שיחת חכמים/διήγημα σοφῶν) from which he can receive instruction (8:8), and there are remarks on one's devotion to wise words throughout the book (esp. 16:24; 21:15; 50:28). All these references suggest that engagement with texts is not about the acquisition of superficial knowledge but about a meditative exercise with potentially transformative outcomes.

Another practice that suggests sensitivity to and focus on inner life is self-mastery. While moderation is valued in the Hebrew tradition (e.g., Prov 25:16–17), it was integral to Greek philosophical traditions, and the *Zeitgeist* probably strengthened the author's concern for self-control. According to him, the wise person has self-control against sexual desires (Sir 23:6), appetite (18:30; 23:6; 37:29), and speech (19:6; 21:25; 32:8). The value of moderation emerges, for example, in Sir 18:30–3, which begins with advice not to follow one's desires in order to avoid disgrace. Speaking to someone with material comfort, the teacher exhorts his addressee not to rejoice "in great luxury" (ἐπὶ πολλῇ τρυφῇ) and to avoid poverty caused by the borrowing of money for feasts.[63] This signals that the addressee enjoys fine-dining and social life, and the instruction on how to behave in a symposium (31:12–32:13) further discusses good manners and the avoidance of excessive habits. It also communicates the book's participation in Hellenistic culture: the feast itself is taken for granted, and it simply serves as a framework for delineating good practice.[64]

The aforementioned exercise of torah devotion hints at engagement with God and the divine realm. The book of Ben Sira also presents prayer and prophetic activity as tasks of the wisdom teacher. Beginning with the former, the act of prayer has many functions: it may be undertaken for the sake of wisdom (51:13–14) or otherwise considerate life (23:1–6), and it can serve as a medium of thanksgiving (51:1–12), or purposes such as petition and healing (e.g., 3:5; 7:10, 14; 17:25; 36:1–19; 37:15; 38:9). In Sir 39:5–8, within a section that is only preserved in Greek, prayer and praise are further associated with the lifestyle of the wise person, who immerses himself in personal piety:

> He will devote his heart to rise early towards the Lord who made him, and he will petition in front of the Most High, and he will open his mouth in prayer, and concerning his sins he will petition. If the great Lord wants, he will be filled with a spirit of understanding. He will pour forth words of his wisdom, and in prayer he will acknowledge the Lord. He will direct counsel and knowledge, and on his hidden things he will think. He will illuminate the instruction of his teaching, and in the law of the Lord's covenant he will boast.[65]

The teacher, therefore, "petitions" (δεηθήσεται) because of his sins and speaks "in prayer" (ἐν προσευχῇ). There is a cosmological aspect to his prayerful life, for the instructor "devotes" (ἐπιδώσει) his heart towards the creator in the morning, perhaps pointing to prayer patterns. The text also elaborates on the consequences of prayer, stating that the wise person may be filled – God willing – with a "spirit of understanding" (πνεύματι συνέσεως) and express the "words of his wisdom" (ῥήματα σοφίας αὐτοῦ). Moreover, he contemplates "hidden things" (ἐν τοῖς ἀποκρύφοις), delivers enlightening instruction, and boasts in the divine torah.

The motif of prayer also closes the book. In this piece of liturgical poetry, the speaker expresses gratitude for divine deliverance from his enemies.[66] The humble tone of the prayer makes it a pledge, confirming that the author sought wisdom and was able to attain it with the help of God.

The sum of these statements means that wisdom cannot be attained with human efforts, but it requires prayer and petition.[67] Although prayer is an integral spiritual exercise, other forms of ritual activity are also valued, including sacrifices and gifts to God (7:9, 31; 14:11 LXX; 35:1–4, 10–12; 38:11). The overall picture created by the book may seem individualistic insofar as the wise teacher petitions for his own sins. Yet, the fruit of his prayer, wisdom, benefits other people. This is suggested by Sir 38:8, according to which the teacher shares the "instruction of his teaching" (παιδείαν διδασκαλίας αὐτοῦ), and by the general pedagogical ethos penetrating the book.

Another exercise of the teacher that involves communication with the divine realm is his prophetic activity. Scholars debate the existence of prophecy at the time of Ben Sira,[68] but a more nuanced understanding of the prophetic phenomenon in the second temple period has recently emerged. While the prophetic institution had ceased, claims on the end of prophecy (e.g., b. Sanh. 11a) simplify the evidence because prophecy persisted as a transformed phenomenon, even though it may be more productive to speak of ongoing modes of divine encounter.[69] The book of Ben Sira, too, expresses prophetic concerns, as can be gathered from the above citations. The wise teacher is "concerned with prophecies" (ἐν προφητείαις ἀσχοληθήσεται) (39:1) and meditates on God's secrets (39:7). A "spirit of understanding" (πνεύματι συνέσεως) may also fill the figure (39:6) who creates inspired teaching by pouring his teaching out "like prophecy" (ὡς προφητείαν) (24:33).[70]

The section on true and false visitations (34:1–8) is further relevant regarding prophecy since visitations often serve the mediation of divine knowledge. The author has some hesitations in this respect, stating that "dreams give wings to fools" (34:1), and he regards dreams, together with divinations and omens, as unreal (34:5). The audience should consider such an ambiguous message only if the Most High has sent it "by a visitation" (34:6).[71] Hence, the desirable divine–human communication is restricted to the reception of genuine revelation from the God of Israel. Yet, God seems to employ other agents in the transmission of divine knowledge, as is suggested by the portrayal of wisdom, who reveals secrets (4:17–18) and is cast as a prophetic mediatrix (24:1–22).[72]

The wise people, therefore, are presented as "recipients of heavenly revelation."[73] Study and human efforts are integral to the lifestyle of the teacher, but not at the expense of human–divine communication. In fact, one cannot separate the two because the instruction produced by the pedagogue is inspired in itself.[74] Considering the emphasis on the inspirational experience that results in the production of new teaching, the prophetic activity of the wisdom teacher seems to fall into the category of non-inductive divination. However, since the wise person also discovers wisdom from ancient writings (cf. 24:33; 38:1–3), the distinction between the two types of divinatory activity is not clear-cut in the book of Ben Sira. In fact, the evidence gestures at the idea that inductive means of divination may also be at stake.[75]

Up until now, I have discussed activities of the teacher that concern him and the pupils following his lifestyle. These circles are elitist, at least in relation to the majority of people in ancient Judea, but it should be remarked that their life is not fully isolated from that of the less privileged. The wise life, as Ben Sira sees it, is not a socially indifferent enterprise but involves prosocial concerns. Surely, the book presents neither sustained social critique nor attempts to change the unequal state of affairs. Yet, an educated person is expected to exercise conduct that affects the society beyond his immediate circles. He should feel compassion and respond to the pain of others by acts of assistance, i.e., by helping the poor, the oppressed, the sick, and those who mourn (4:1–10; 7:10, 32–5; 35:4). He should also give handouts and loans and serve as a guarantor according to his wealth (29:1–20).

The need to encounter human vulnerability with generosity (4:31) is based on the recognition of common humanity: anyone may encounter poverty and loss regardless of status (cf. 10:10; 18:25; 29:2), and "the kindness of something given is before everyone alive" (7:33).[76] As mentioned, however, there is no vision of an equal society. The care for the vulnerable takes place in a hierarchical context where acts of assistance accrue social rewards to the self (e.g., 4:7, 10; 12:1–2; 22:23; 29:12). As Françoise Mirguet observes, they serve to "enact the privilege of the giver and amplify the vulnerability of the recipient." Thus, prosocial deeds both alleviate the pain of another person and serve to institutionalise inequality.[77] While the social merits of care are obvious in the book, it should be noted that divine favour and blessings are also at display (4:10; 7:32).

As I hope to have shown, a close reading of Ben Sira shows that the book devotes thorough attention to the lifestyle of the teacher, who will have a long legacy after his death. While Qoheleth laments upon the disappearance of the memory of a wise person (2:16, cf. Wis 2:4), Ben Sira believes that many will continue to cherish his extraordinary memorial, including wisdom, understanding, and a great name (39:9–11). The teacher leaves the future generations with more than fame, however, as he leaves them with a model of a learned lifestyle. Such a way of life, as can be gathered from different parts of the book, entails teaching, scribal tasks, textual interpretation, imitation of exemplars, observation of the world, contemplation, self-mastery, prayer, prophecy, and prosocial deeds. The practice of moderation also makes wisdom visible in daily life, including in one's consumption habits, handling of money affairs, or conduct in the dining table.

In the book of Ben Sira, wisdom is associated with torah devotion, and the protagonist's final prayer crystallizes the merging of the two: "For I intended to practice her … My soul has grabbled with her, and in the performance of the law I was exacting" (51:18–19, cf. 24:23).[78] At the same time, the book participates in the Hellenistic culture, as is shown, for example, by its concern for the right conduct in symposia. Scholars have also observed that Ben Sira might echo ideas of Stoic philosophy.⁷⁹ For the present purposes, the striking likeness between the text and Greek philosophy does not concern specific ideas, however, but the conceptual parallel related to lifestyle and the performance of mental and spiritual exercises.⁸⁰ Such a notion of the pursuit of wisdom associates Ben Sira with the wider Mediterranean world, suggesting that the teachers and "lovers of learning" (cf. Sirach, Prologue, lines 10–14) who operated in Hellenistic Jerusalem could view themselves as being related to Greek philosophers. They could observe a resemblance between the Greek culture and their own tradition, which were perhaps perceived as rather separate in some other respects.

The worldly aspect of wisdom as a lifestyle resonates with the book's general ethos. Even though the author argues that wisdom settled into Jerusalem after her cosmic wanderings (24:1–12, cf. 1 En 42:1–3), he also maintains that wisdom belongs to and can be found among all peoples. The book states on the universal nature of wisdom as follows: "The Lord, he created her [wisdom], and he saw and enumerated her and poured her out upon all his works, among all flesh according to his giving" (1:9–10).⁸¹ Thus, traces of wisdom appear everywhere, and the claims that one may gain wisdom through travel (34:9–13; 39:4) express the same attitude of mental openness.⁸²

The figure of the maskil among the wisdom teachers

Another wisdom teacher whose portrayal prompts analysis from the viewpoint of a learned lifestyle is the figure of the maskil (משכיל) encountered in the Qumran scrolls. His audience is a particular early Jewish movement known for its dedication to the torah and its correct interpretation (e.g., 1QS 1:1–3; 5:1, 7–8; 8:15–16). While I will analyse wisdom's communal dimension in this movement in Chapter 4, I will focus on the persona and tasks of the maskil, whom I briefly introduced with respect to exemplarity in Chapter 2, in this section. As observed above, the figure of the maskil, especially as he is depicted in the 1QS copy of the Community Rule, offers an object of emulation, thus providing the audience with "the kind of voice with which one will speak" after being moulded by the group's instructions.⁸³ In order to better comprehend the maskil's lifestyle, I will now turn to his activities as they are described in the mostly fragmentary Qumran scrolls. How does the figure perform his wisdom? What does constitute the rhythm of his daily life?

I should begin by noting that general caution is needed in the identification and interpretation of the משכיל references because the term does not consistently appear in the sense of an "officer" in the Qumran corpus. Drawing on the translation of the phrase למשכיל in the Septuagint and in *targumim*, Robert Hawley in fact argues that the term משכיל can simply designate "insight" or "instruction," especially when it appears in headings, or stand for an adjective (e.g., 4Q421 frag. 1 ii 10, 12). This ambiguity concerning the meaning of the term leads him to conclude that the evidence for regarding the maskil as a profession in the *yaḥad* movement is weak.[84]

Hawley is correct in stating that the term משכיל does not always denote a particular officer; the term designates a prudent person with common sense or pragmatic wisdom in the book of Proverbs, and it frequently stands for the hymn's intended leader or head singer in Psalms.[85] The term also denotes the attribute "wise" in some texts from Qumran, but these cases tend to appear in wisdom instructions that may predate, at least in some form, the rise of the Jewish movement associated with the scrolls.[86] By contrast, several writings, specifically those originating from the early Jewish movement in question, imply that the term משכיל refers to a particular teacher and sage. As will be seen in the following survey, many of the extant references appear in superscriptions, which may have been added to the compositions over the course of their textual transmission.[87] It is likely, therefore, that the figure's authority developed over time.[88]

In what follows, I will proceed to read the maskil materials as illustrations of the life of one wisdom teacher from Judea. As regards embodiment and exercise, it is striking that the figure remains stupendously anonymous and is known for his functions instead. Admittedly, a great deal of the discussion in the extant sources may be glamorized, as in the case of all ancient portraits of sages. The idealized aspect of the maskil discourse does not rule out the present study, however, because my intention is not to detect the office of any historical figure, but to explore how the prototypical maskil and his exemplary way of life lived on in the literary imagination of the *yaḥad* movement.[89]

Beginning with the maskil's pedagogical profession, the Hebrew term משכיל can designate a teacher, as is natural of a *hiphil* participle of the root שכל, which can mean to teach, make someone prudent, or cause understanding (cf. Ps 32:8; Dan 9:22). Several texts from Qumran with an uncertain provenance imply the idea of the maskil as a teacher.[90] His pedagogical function is also marked in the writings of the *yaḥad* movement, including in Words of the Maskil to the Sons of Dawn (4Q298). This fragmentarily preserved text is written in a cryptic script, perhaps in order to conceal the esoteric wisdom it contains.[91] Following the title "[Word]s of the Maskil which he spoke to all the sons of dawn" (frag.

1–2 i 1), the speaker urges the audience, depicted as the "men of heart," "pursuers of justice," and "seekers of truth," to pay attention to his instruction. The tone is persuasive insofar as the search for these things involves a turn to the path of life (frag. 1–2 i 1–3). Another fragment of the same manuscript offers further insight into the maskil's teaching, exhorting the audience to listen, seek justice, practise humility, and know the appointed time (frag. 3–4 ii 4–10). These references point to the value of cultivating virtues and of understanding time.

The Community Rule is another text that illustrates the didactic role and curriculum of the maskil, regardless of whether the figure was the "primary reader" of the composition or whether it served as a "written extension" of his teaching function.[92] The lost beginning of the 1QS copy (1:1) may even have addressed the complete writing to the maskil.[93] While the option remains speculative, an adequate amount of material is preserved to demonstrate the text's deep interest in the ideal figure of the maskil. I will focus on the evidence of 1QS in the following discussion, but I wish to note that the S manuscripts from Cave 4 confirm the maskil's didactic role. They attribute the teaching found in 1QS 5:1–20 to the maskil, whereas 1QS 5:1 begins with the formula וזה הסרך לאנשי היחד, "this is the rule to the people of the *yaḥad*."[94]

The treatise on the two spirits in 1QS 3:13–4:26 is attributed to the maskil, beginning with the statement that "it is for the maskil (למשכיל) to instruct and teach (להבין וללמד) all the sons of light concerning the nature of all the sons of man" (3:13). The following text expands the content of this heading by covering issues of anthropology, pneumatology, and angelology, starting with a reference to ranks of people that are governed by the two spirits ruling the world (3:13–15). By way of discussing such a set of topics, the author delineates and clarifies God's creation plan, "the genealogy and teleology of human existence."[95] Scholars continue to debate the text's origin, but the content of the treatise clearly resonates with the core beliefs of the *yaḥad* movement, regardless of its exact date and place of composition. Ideas that connect the treatise with the ideology of the movement include a dualistic division of people, the agency and power of spirits, and the expectation of a final eschatological struggle. Immersing itself in the cosmic teaching, the intended audience may understand itself in relation to, and as partakers in, a larger divine plan.[96]

The didactic role of the figure of the maskil reappears in the end of 1QS with instructions to (9:12–21a, 9:21b–25) and a hymn of the maskil (9:26–11:22).[97] In the hymn, for example, the maskil contemplates his task to spread understanding, stating that he shall "strengthen the hands of the anx[ious, to cause to know] discernment to those erring of spirit, to teach understanding to those that grumble" (10:26–11:1). He also possesses divine knowledge and transmits divine mysteries; with the help of these, he can guide and instruct the addressees so that their walk would be perfect (9:18–19). Pedagogically, these statements imply that the maskil provides the group with an instrument through which "divine knowledge reaches and transforms" its members (cf. 4:22–3).[98]

Importantly, the maskil does not teach any kind of human wisdom to his audience, but he communicates a distinct notion of the cosmic order that claims to draw on a transcendent source. This intention shapes the figure's everyday performance of wisdom by granting him access to divine knowledge and the status of a spiritual authority within his community.

The instructions in 1QS 9:13–21a stress the maskil's fulfilment of regulations, correct attitude, and perfect insight. Another set of instructions emphasizes his virtuous torah obedience (9:21b–25), characterizing the figure as one who is "enthusiastic for the statute" and performs God's will "in every enterprise and in all his dominion" (9:23–4). The final hymn of 1QS, which portrays the maskil as speaking in the first person, attaches further esoteric colours to the maskil: "With the counsel of salvation I will conceal/recount knowledge, and with prudent knowledge I will hedge (it) with a firm boundary" (10:24–5).[99] Esotericism often pertains to power, and the maskil's secret knowledge also grants him an elevated status, although the figure stresses that he only mediates hidden wisdom and divine wonders that ultimately belong to God (11:3–5):

> For from the fountain of his knowledge he has released his light. My eye beheld his wonders, and the light of my heart beheld the mystery of existence and what shall occur forever. … From the fountain of his righteousness (is) my justice. A light (comes) into my heart from his wondrous mysteries.

Here, the maskil claims that his inner light emanates from God the celestial spring, which means that he has access to divine knowledge and is capable of transmitting heavenly mysteries. The use of light idiom may point to the modelling of the maskil after Moses. As argued by Samuel Thomas, the image of light is familiar from mystical and apocalyptic contexts, but it also reminds one of Moses' descent from the mountain after his encounter with God (cf. Exod 34:29).[100] Thus, the text might cast the maskil as a new Moses of some sort that experiences divine encounters.[101]

As for his lifestyle, it is startling that the maskil's knowledge of revealed things (9:13–14) affects his responsibilities beyond the duty of teaching about spirits (3:13–14) insofar as it makes him possess radical spiritual authority.[102]

The figure has an exquisite discrimination concerning the worth, weight, and substance of the community members (9:12–21). Such an administrative duty implies that he is responsible for the admission to, and the hierarchical ranking within, the group. In other words, the maskil marks boundaries between people, thus serving as a sort of "gateway" into the community or out of it.[103] His ability to evaluate people is depicted as follows (9:14–16):

> He shall separate and weigh the sons of righteousness according to their spirits. He shall keep hold of the chosen ones of the end time according to his will as he has commanded. And according to a man's spirit (is) justice to be done (to him), and according to the cleanness of a man's hands he may approach, and upon the authority of his insight he may draw near.

As this quote demonstrates, the maskil ranks people based on their spirits, i.e., their portions of light and darkness. This particular skill, as argued by Newman, results from the maskil having knowledge that originates from his "revelatory vision" and consequent "internal transformation" (cf. 11:3–4).[104] Owing to such a metamorphosis, the maskil appears as an enigmatic prophetic figure who comprehends and fulfils the divine expectations: "He shall do God's will, according to everything which has been revealed from time to time (לעת בעת ככול הנגלה)" (9:13). As the previous quote indicates, the author ties the maskil's knowledge and perfection to his sense of time and history.[105] Another passage in CD 13:22 (par. 4Q266 frag. 5 i 17; frag. 9 iii 15) similarly emphasizes that the figure acts during an ordained time when prophecies are being fulfilled.

The maskil's enigmatic roles resonate with mystical and prophetic traditions, alluding to the persistence of divine encounter in early Judaism and creating an esoteric aura around the figure. Regarding lived wisdom, it is crucial to observe the other side of the coin as well: the maskil's task of spiritual discernment has social effects in the movement served by him. Sociologically, it highlights the maskil's concrete political role as a person who somehow holds the group together. In the context of this movement, it is not up to the person himself or herself to evaluate his or her progress in the desired way of life. Rather, there are prominent leaders, including the wisdom teacher known as the maskil, whose task is to regulate the makeup of the group.[106]

In addition to teaching and spiritual judgement, the maskil enacts and performs his wisdom through worship and ritual tasks, including prayer, praise, and blessing. The 1QS copy of the Community Rule is again informative in this respect as it states that the maskil grasps divinely ordained time and observes the appointed times of praise (9:12; 10:1). The subsequent prayer calendar

(9:26–10:8) follows the rhythm of celestial bodies as heavenly luminaries that set out patterns of prayer.[107] The figure sings to God's glory and recites statutes (10:8–11), as well as confessing his sins and pleading (10:11–17). After commitments to self-discipline (10:18–11:2) and reflection on sinfulness and salvation (11:2–15), the maskil returns to bless God and asks for his guidance (11:15–20).[108]

The frequent use of the heading למשכיל in ritual contexts suggests that the figure of the maskil was considered to lead liturgical performance just as in the book of Psalms.[109] In the Rule of Blessings (1QSb), to begin with, three remaining headings are connected with words of blessings (דברי ברכה) uttered by the maskil (1:1; 3:22; 5:20). The figure strengthens and reinforces communal structures through such a deed, as his blessing activity is directed at the covenanters who fear God and keep his commandments (1:1–2). Furthermore, it should be noted that the audience of the text is identified as the priestly sons of Zadok (3:22) and the prince of the congregation (5:20), presumably referring to the leaders and members of the movement.[110]

Similarly, the 1QH[a] copy of the Hodayot illustrates the maskil's liturgical performance on several occasions, even if the evidence remains in a fragmentary form. The term משכיל is preserved five times in this collection of thanksgiving hymns (5:12; 7:21; 20:7, 14; 25:34). All the remaining cases, except for one, occur in superscriptions that attribute the hymn to the maskil.[111] First, the hymn in column five begins with the superscription "[A psalm for the ma]skil, that he may prostrate himself before God" (5:12).[112] The explicit mention of how the maskil prostrates reveals an embodied dimension of the spiritual exercise.[113] The liturgical act also serves didactic purposes, for the author next expresses its aim: "that the simple may understand" (5:13).[114] Second, the hymn in column seven discusses the maskil's devotion to God. In this case, the superscription "Bless[ed are you, God of mercy, with a]song, a psalm for the Mas[kil" (7:21) is followed by the maskil's confession that he loves God, contemplates God's creation, and comprehends the source of all light (7:23–37). This underlines the importance of divine–human interaction in the life of the figure.

The third and fourth references to the maskil occur in column twenty of 1QH[a] (par. 4Q427 frag. 8 ii 10, 17). The superscription "[For the maski]l, [th]anksgiving and prayer for prostrating oneself and supplicating continually at all times" (20:7) is followed by a list of ordained times of worship (20:7–12) and a claim of confidence in God as the establisher of all (20:12–14). The maskil speaks from line 20:14 onwards, acknowledging the operation of the divine spirit within him: "And I, maskil, I know you, my God, by the spirit that you have placed in me." The figure proclaims to have heeded God's secret counsel and reiterates the divine source of his gift: "By your holy spirit you have [o]pened up knowledge within me through the mystery of your wisdom and the fountainhead of [your] pow[er" (20:15–16). The last extant heading appears in line 25:34 within a partially reconstructed superscription "for the maskil, a melo[dy, a song for," but the following hymn is virtually lost. A few words remain, however, including the verbs "I shout" and "I] exalt myself" (25:36–7), which demonstrate the use of the first person speech in this section. In general, the passage witnesses to the musical duty and performance of the figure.

The maskil's liturgical practice has an emphatically mystical connotation in the Songs of the Sabbath Sacrifice, known through multiple fragmentary manuscripts from Qumran (4Q400-7; 11Q17) and one copy from Masada (MasShirot). The text contains a cycle of thirteen songs with several remaining למשכיל headings.[115] These songs of praise offer information about the heavenly realm and its beings. Crucially for the present purposes, they also constitute the wider body of literature on worship and instruction led by the maskil.[116] Based on the extant evidence, the songs are to be recited by the figure in the presence of a human community, but the people on earth may, through this act, experience a union with the angels who worship God in the celestial temple.[117] The songs thus offer the audience with a means to a mystical experience and point to the maskil's inner transformation, as the figure seems to ascend to heaven as the outcome of this mystical drama.[118]

In addition to mysticism, the activities of the maskil can be associated with magic. Such a quality of his performance is obvious in the Songs of the Maskil (4Q510-11), which contains pieces of liturgical poetry with a specific purpose: believed to contain ritual power, these songs are to be sung in the apotropaic quest to deter malignant forces. The maskil declares the splendour of God's radiance in order to frighten evils spirits, demons, and Lilith (4Q510 frag. 1:4–5). In his songs, the maskil also exhorts the audience to rejoice in God, proclaiming that the songs are "for the upright" (4Q510 frag. 1:8–9). Although the evidence is fragmentary, two למשכיל references in the extant headings (4Q511 frag. 2 i 1; frag. 8:4) further confirm the text's association with the maskil.

The figure of the maskil, elevated to a position among the angels (4Q511 frag. 8:6–10), speaks in fragmentary first-person accounts, and the function of his praise as a "weapon" against the evil is obvious in 4Q510 frag. 1:4–9. As observed by Joseph Angel, the prototypical nature of his voice enables the participants of the ritual to invest themselves with the first-person speech. By identifying themselves with the figure of the maskil, the worshippers, just as their exemplar, may become immune to demons.[119] This means that the maskil's words may have a sacrifice-like function, which grants them "cosmic cultic significance" (4Q511 frag. 63–4 ii 3–4).[120] In other words, the figure's ritual performance goes beyond the mere exercise of praise in that it is considered to have the effect of controlling demonic forces that cause trouble in this world.

Having outlined the lifestyle of the maskil, I will now turn to the figure's relevance for our understanding of early Judaism. Scholars have typically approached and analysed the maskil as an officer of the *yaḥad* movement, thus exploring his agency and activity in relation to a distinct group and its intentions. I argue, however, that the figure can also be situated in the context of ancient Jewish wisdom teachers: the maskil features as another pedagogue who does not only possess wisdom, but exercises and literally embodies her through a number of repetitive practices. The latter consist of edifying, devotional, and esoteric acts, including teaching, fulfilment of regulations, reception of esoteric knowledge, spiritual judgement, prayer, performance of hymns and mystical songs, and conduct of apotropaic rituals (esp. 1QS 3:3–4:26; 9:12–11:25; 1QSb; 1QH^a; 4Q298; 4Q510–11; Shirot). These roles and deeds emphasize that wisdom is expected to have practical implications insofar as it entails a whole way of life with an array of daily activities.

As we have seen in the previous survey, the authors and copyists of the Qumran scrolls present the maskil, who features as a wise pedagogue, in numerous writings of different literary genres. The figure serves the needs of the *yaḥad* movement, and the lack of explicit references to biblical figures in the contexts that discuss the maskil could be seen as stressing his distinctiveness. Yet, such an exclusive focus on the maskil does not mean that ancestral models would have been irrelevant to the movement. On the contrary, the maskil's association with light (1QS 11:3) signals that he is probably imagined as a new Moses of some sort. More broadly, many of the scrolls found at Qumran invoke biblical examples, thus encouraging one to learn about (un)desirable patterns of behaviour, including both perfection and utter failures, from ancestral figures.[121]

As noted vis-à-vis the book of Ben Sira, the emphasis on the significance of lifestyle and spiritual exercise constitutes a major parallel between Jewish wisdom and Greek philosophy. The same observation applies to the figure of the maskil, who models an ideal way of living and undertakes a range of pedagogical, liturgical, and esoteric acts that construct his perfection. This prompts one to re-evaluate the maskil's intellectual position in the Hellenistic world beyond the confines of the *yaḥad* movement from which the texts on the maskil hail.

While the authors of the Qumran scrolls promoted a particular notion of wisdom, they were well educated and could presumably observe conceptual (not necessarily textual) parallels between their own intellectual enquiries and similar efforts elsewhere in their wider habitat. In fact, some of the scrolls demonstrate "foreign knowledge,"[122] which warns against reading the Qumran collection in isolation from the rest of the Hellenistic world. Meanwhile, it seems accurate to conclude that instead of explicitly embracing other traditions, the members of this early Jewish movement turned to the figure of the maskil who provided them with a wisdom teacher of their own. In fact, implicit polemics might also be at play, as is suggested by the reclusive references to revelation hidden from others (1QS 9:16–19) and to wisdom hidden from humankind (1QS 11:5–7).

Jewish teachers and their Mediterranean habitat

The biblical narrative contains several wisdom teachers broadly understood if one counts Moses, Ezra, and other instructors of the torah as such. The book of Proverbs portrays teachers of both earthy and cosmic variety, displaying "parents" and female wisdom as instruments that offer understanding, and it documents the idea of the wise person (חכם) as a learned intellectual. The book of Qoheleth, however, is the first extant source to underline the role of a particular individual as the teacher, even if the text's pedagogical thrust is less dominant, being mostly preserved in the epilogue (12:9) and in the encouragement to exercise critical enquiry. The key sources on the lifestyle of the teacher are two texts from ancient Judea, the book of Ben Sira and the Qumran scrolls, which illustrate the topic in the context of later Hellenistic and early Roman periods.

Teaching and teachers are cross-cultural phenomena. At the same time, they are always tied to local contexts and conditions, thus varying across time and place. In the second temple period, Jewish sources, especially those hailing from the ancestral land, came to pay close attention to contemporary wise pedagogues and their learned ways of life, which prompts me to reflect on the contribution of the wisdom teacher to our notion of Jewish wisdom as a cultural phenomenon in antiquity. In this section, therefore, I will briefly offer some comparative remarks on Jewish teachers in order to demonstrate (dis)similarities between them. Thereafter, I will comment on the wisdom teachers and their pedagogical programmes from a wider Mediterranean perspective. I will argue that the focus on lifestyle, which became solid in the latter half of the second temple period, starting from the book of Qoheleth, suggests that Jewish teachers may have associated themselves with philosophers.

Let me begin with some comparative remarks on the extant sources. The books of Qoheleth and Ben Sira, as well as the maskil materials from Qumran, all illustrate aspects of lived wisdom, although the previous survey has demonstrated that the concern for exercising wisdom is even more emphatic in the latter two. This signals that the pursuit and possession of wisdom were expected to shape the teacher's personal and social life in various Hellenistic Jewish settings.

Overall, the texts' concern for a good conduct is not surprising in itself since wisdom instruction often concerns desirable behaviour; here one may consider, for example, the list of virtues in the prologue to the book of Proverbs (Prov 1:2–4). Yet, something different is at stake in the book of Ben Sira and the Qumran scrolls, and to some extent in the book of Qoheleth. While Proverbs illustrates ideals to which the audience should aspire, these slightly later sources from the Ptolemaic period onwards describe the lifestyles of teachers who enact their wisdom and invite others to do the same. As such, they signal that wisdom is not a technical skill that one can master after a short training period, but it requires a lifetime of dedicated reflection and committed practice.

In spite of the shared esteem for a wise and erudite lifestyle, as well as for pedagogical pursuits in general, the portraits of the three teachers in Qoheleth, Ben Sira, and the Qumran scrolls differ from each other. As shown above, the authors of these texts had various conceptions of the pedagogue, his exemplary way of living, and his performances of wisdom. The figure was moulded to suit multiple agendas and contexts, and the key literary sources on the teacher display distinctive emphases.

The maskil materials and the book of Ben Sira resemble each other – as well as differing from the book of Qoheleth – in that they display idealized teachers who lead and encourage others to lead a pious way of life filled with divine–human communication. The latter takes many forms, including torah-devotion, prayer practices, and prophetic tasks (esp. Sir 38:34b–39:11; 1QS 9:12–11:22).[123] Yet, the accounts are far from identical. While the book of Ben Sira is wary about the limits of human knowledge (Sir 3:21–4), the maskil is eager to speculate on the divine realm and has solid convictions about God and the elect, claiming that one may gain divine knowledge through esoteric revelation that is not available to all Israel (e.g., 1QS 10:24–5; 11:3–5). The maskil stresses God's role as the source of knowledge and perfection, and esoteric colours are present along with his skill of spiritual judgement and access to divine mysteries (e.g., 1QS 11:3–5).

Moreover, the book of Ben Sira is closer to Qoheleth than to the scrolls in two respects. First, the ethos of the maskil accounts is more exclusive than that of Ben Sira. The people behind the scrolls operated in the Hellenistic world, and their overall concern for the ideal sage is Hellenistic in nature, but the maskil restricts his activity to one movement within Judea. The teacher of Ben Sira, on the contrary, turns outwards and remains open to wisdom beyond his own setting, as is suggested by those passages that acknowledge the wisdom of other nations and the educational value of travel (Sir 1:9–10; 39:4). In this respect, the evidence of Ben Sira is closer to the inquisitive ethos of Qoheleth.

Second, another feature of Ben Sira that is absent from the maskil accounts is the teacher's scribal activity, including textual composition and interpretation. The pedagogue of Ben Sira engages with and produces texts, whereas the maskil is not explicitly associated with such tasks. In this respect, the pedagogue of Ben Sira is again closer to the protagonist of Qoheleth, who is said to have written down sayings (Qoh 12:10).[124] In addition to textual activity, the imitation of past figures counts as another mode of engaging with ancient Israelite traditions, and Ben Sira's emphatic interest in ancestral exemplarity and biblical afterlives (Sir 44:1–49:24) signals the value of following ancestral models. Similar accounts appear in neither Qoheleth nor the maskil materials, even though the figures of Solomon and Moses shape the portrayals of the teachers in them.

Even if the profiles of the three wisdom teachers vary, they all resist a division between "religious" and "secular" education. The book of Ben Sira and the maskil materials think highly of liturgical performance and prophetic activity, which implies that the teacher engages in divine–human communication and serves the needs of contemporary communities.[125] Moreover, the authors cast the divine torah as a source of study and meditation. Admittedly, the exact take on the Israelite narrative and tradition remains unclear in the case of Qoheleth, which concentrates on observing the peculiarities of human life. Meanwhile, a belief in and the attitude of fearing God are salient parts of the book's outlook (e.g., Qoh 3:10–14; 5:6; 7:18; 8:12–13; 12:13), although the author reminds his audience that it is better to have few words (4:17) and acknowledges that much in the world goes beyond one's understanding (8:17; 11:5). The epilogue, however, adds to the overall tone of the book by accenting the performance of divine commandments (12:13).[126]

Overall, the lifestyle of the wisdom teacher is a major concern in Qoheleth, Ben Sira, and the maskil materials. Yet, these sources from the Hellenistic and early Roman periods indicate diverse conceptions of the teacher, his pedagogical programme, and his daily activities; the exact role of the instructor varies across time and place. It is salient, however, that wisdom requires committed practice and performance according to each of these sources. What can one say about Jewish wisdom as a cultural phenomenon in the wider Mediterranean context based on them?

As a paragon of the learned lifestyle, the wisdom teacher signposts ways of living to those who search for wisdom, thus signalling that the respective pedagogical programmes have formative aims. Education is never disinterested but constitutes a form of socialisation; it involves the acquisition and internalization of values, attitudes, and manners that are appreciated and accepted by a given society. In a similar vein, early Jewish teachers from Hellenistic Judea sought to equip their pupils with skills and ideas that were esteemed by respective communities.

Surely, socialization remains in the background in the book of Qoheleth, which is less concerned with the creation of a productive and loyal member who would maintain the community.[127] Even so, Qoheleth, like the book of Ben Sira and the Qumran scrolls, promotes individual maturation in wisdom: all these texts cultivate erudite cultures that are to shape one's life and thought. Such a conception of pedagogy – that wisdom and learning are not about years of formal schooling or about the acquisition of technical skills – reminds one of the Greek notion of παιδεία, i.e., the process of forming and educating a person through activities and discourses.[128] Raffaella Cribiore has described the standard understanding of learning in the Hellenistic milieu as follows:

> On many levels, education was not a throw-away package ready to be discarded when school time was over; it became enmeshed in the lives of people, at least those able to reach its high levels. Though a glorification of ancient education would certainly be unrealistic, the important place it occupied in the lives of some individuals after schooling was over is notable. – *Paideia*, which originally meant "child rearing," was conceived almost as a slow vegetable growth that affected people through the course of their lives and embraced more than the purely intellectual. But with the same word, the Greeks defined "culture," that is, purely intellectual maturation and assimilation of the educational values acquired through schooling. Thus, individuals who were able to take advantage of higher training continued to draw on *paideia*. Life imitated school.[129]

Cribiore emphasizes the gradually unfolding and transformative effect of education in the ancient world. Jewish authors, too, wished to transmit educational values and effect their everyday implementation, thus assisting their students in processes of intellectual and moral maturation.

The parallel between Jewish pedagogy and Greek education is not only conceptual since the term παιδεία belongs to the vocabulary of Greek Sirach, denoting the instruction delivered in the book.¹³⁰ An ethos of παιδεία also characterizes the book of Qoheleth and the maskil materials, even if they are written in Hebrew and thus discuss learning and training in another cultural register. Qoheleth understands intellectual enquiry as a painful task (Qoh 1:13) that requires a lifetime of contemplation, further stressing the role of youth as a particularly sensitive and formative stage of one's life cycle (12:1–7). As for the Qumran scrolls, Karina Martin Hogan has noted the similarity between the Hebrew term מוסר and the Greek term παιδεία as they are used in the scrolls and in Philo of Alexandria's texts, respectively. She argues that the terms cover disciplinary and noetic nuances in both sets of early Jewish sources from different parts of the Mediterranean region.¹³¹ In fact, the double connotation is already present in the Septuagint version of Proverbs, where the term מוסר and its cognates are virtually always translated with the term παιδεία and its cognates, although the book's translation technique is generally free and flexible.¹³²

The formative and even transformative effect of education is not the only parallel between Jewish wisdom and pedagogical ideals cherished in the wider Hellenistic context. As mentioned above, Jewish teachers appear as akin, albeit not identical, to ancient philosophers if one looks at them from a wider Mediterranean point of view. In his pioneering book from 1988, Bickerman also made this association, describing the novel notion of wisdom in the instruction of Ben Sira as follows:

> *Hokmah* now meant culture, and Ben Sira was its prophet and teacher. This reevaluation of the meaning and essence of *hokmah* changed the social status of its servants. The *hokmah* that was sagacity was transmitted by leading men of practical experience, from the vizier Ptah-hotep and King Solomon to the vizier Ahikar and "the Convoker, the son of David, king in Jerusalem." But Ben Sira's sage, like a Greek philosopher, is an intellectual. ... for him, as it was for Plato, and as it is in every genuine civilization ... true education continued throughout one's life.¹³³

For Bickerman, the shift in Jewish wisdom discourse was an intensification of intellectual culture. He also stressed that the wisdom teacher, like a Greek philosopher, both gave and received knowledge as he spoke with people. The figure lacked an established institution, but he had followers to whom he transmitted "no technical skill, but the secret of happy and successful life."¹³⁴ Yet, the purpose was not to mimic Greek pedagogy but to promote a local counterpart. This is amply demonstrated by the wise teacher of Ben Sira, who assembles his own curriculum where the torah, rather than Homer's poems, constitutes the core of education; Moses provides the learned elite of Jerusalem with their own intellectual culture and heritage on which to draw.[135]

Bickerman's observations capture much of the spirit of Jewish wisdom in the late second temple era. While ancient Israel had a rich intellectual culture, including but not limited to scribal work, the extant literary sources from the Hellenistic and early Roman eras indicate a growing interest in particular teachers, their ways of life, and their pedagogical programmes. The surrounding Hellenistic context evidently shaped these concerns, but the authors simultaneously continued to engage with their own tradition, whether through praise and piety or creative reinterpretation.

Even though I generally agree with Bickerman's description of early Jewish wisdom, I would like to comment on his remark that the wisdom teacher, like a Greek philosopher, both gave and received knowledge as he conversed with people. The book of Ben Sira shows mental openness and there is no reason to think that its author would not have been willing to exchange knowledge or to learn from others, whether in Judea or elsewhere. Yet, the instruction of Ben Sira, like other texts from Judea, never spells out the dialogical aspect of Jewish education in the same way that the Greek writings do. In this respect, ancient Jewish instruction can also be contrasted with Šimâ Milka or the Instructions of Šūpê-amēli. This much earlier text from the ancient Near East, known from the late Bronze Age archives of Emar, Ḫattuša, and Ugarit, portrays the son as confidently responding to, challenging, and even rebutting his father's teaching. As such, it provides a striking contrast to Jewish teachings in which the son always remains silent.[136]

Furthermore, I wish to complement Bickerman's pioneering remarks by drawing attention to the significance of exercise in Jewish wisdom, for this feature, too, connects Jewish teachers with Greek philosophers. As discussed in Chapter 1, ancient philosophy entailed a whole way of life, including the practice and performance of spiritual and mental exercises.[137] Typically, the lived aspect of philosophy was characterized by the term ἄσκησις. Even though ἄσκησις was not the only term used to describe wisdom's performed aspects, it was a central concept and was advocated by nearly all schools. Philosophical schools promoted a plethora of exercises, but in all cases, the "I," the practising subject, distanced itself from its desires and gained awareness of its power to become detached from them.[138] Alternatively, to phrase the same slightly differently, the pupil engaged in "a process of transforming one's character (*ēthos*) and soul (*psykhē*), a transformation that would itself transform one's way of life (*bios*)."[139]

Philo of Alexandria promotes the importance of ἄσκησις, which, according to him, improves one's natural good qualities (*Prov.* 2.16), belongs to infants just as wisdom belongs to full-grown people (*Migr.* 46), and serves as a means to attain wisdom, virtue, and perfection.[140] As briefly mentioned in Chapter 2, Philo casts the figure of Jacob as a prototype of the practising subject. The training attributed to the patriarch involves common learning methods, such as listening and reading, as well as the generally philosophical exercises of investigation, examination, meditative exercises, and the remembrance of good things. A third group of exercises has a Stoic tone, including attention, indifference to indifferent things, accomplishment of duties, self-mastery, and therapies.[141]

The exercises of the three wisdom teachers surveyed in this chapter – Qoheleth, Ben Sira, and the maskil – overlap only partly with those outlined by Philo in Alexandria in the first century CE, but I argue that they, too, reveal an appreciation of mental and spiritual practice. As we have seen, the protagonist of Qoheleth is committed to critical investigation, pedagogical efforts, and scribal tasks, and the exercises that constitute a learned and virtuous way of life are even richer in the other two sources. The book of Ben Sira refers to teaching, textual work, imitation of exemplars, contemplation, self-mastery, prayer, prophetic acts, and prosocial deeds. The figure of the maskil, in turn, embodies and enacts his wisdom by teaching, receiving esoteric knowledge, undertaking spiritual judgement, performing songs, and participating in apotropaic rituals.

Early Jewish teachers from Judea did not cultivate wisdom in a vacuum, but they must have been aware of the search for wisdom elsewhere. After all, wisdom's international nature is already evident in the Hebrew Bible, the Greek language seems to have been known in Jerusalem by the time of Ben Sira, and even texts that have sometimes been seen as hostile to the Hellenistic culture display rich cross-cultural influences.[142] Significant thinkers also came from nearby areas, specifically from the coastal cities of Tyre and Sidon, as well as from the city of Gadara located southeast of the Sea of Galilee (see Strabo, *Geographica* 16.2.29).[143] Hence, Judean authors indisputably lived near Hellenistic learning centres, and one cannot exclude the possibility that they might even have gained some training in such centres. All these factors support the idea that Jewish teachers could observe conceptual parallels between their own pursuit of wisdom and similar pursuits elsewhere. It seems possible and even likely that they regarded themselves as similar to philosophers, or as representatives of local "philosophies" from the ancestral land of the Jews in the Hellenistic East.

The maskil materials discovered at the Qumran caves were the latest sources to be included in my previous survey. Yet, I would like to add a final note that one could also include Jesus, especially as he is portrayed in the gospels, in the cluster of early Jewish wisdom teachers from the late second temple period.[144] The gospels are now included in a Christian collection of texts, but Jesus was a Jew and the gospels originate from an era when the parting of the ways had not yet taken place.[145]

Markedly, the proper name of this pedagogue is known and whole biographies were written on his life(style). The gospel of Matthew, in particular, portrays Jesus as a wise teacher (esp. 11:19, 28; 12:42; 13:54; 23:10) who instructs his followers and does not hesitate to revisit the teachings of the torah (esp. 5:17–48). Jesus' teaching is aspirational, as he encourages his "pupils" to aim at perfection (5:48).[146] The distinct lifestyle of the teacher involves wandering and ascetic practices that Jesus' followers are encouraged to adopt (e.g., 10:9–10). In a similar vein, the gospel of Luke casts Jesus as teacher of a radically new way of life, portraying him as effective in both word and deed (e.g., 24:19). Jesus is listened to and consulted by others (e.g., 5:17; 17:20), he delivers a message with "a powerful ethical thrust" (e.g., 14:7–14), and he requires full dedication (9:57–62; 12:49–53; 14:26) as well as an ascetic way of life (e.g., 9:23–5; 12:33) from his followers.[147]

Conclusions

The Hebrew Bible is potentially a rich depository of wisdom teachers: one may count Moses, Ezra, and other instructors of the torah as such if the torah is understood as Israel's wisdom (cf. Deut 4:5–6). Yet, the literary evidence from the late second temple period deviates from the earlier sources on ancient Israelite pedagogues: three bodies of texts from Hellenistic and early Roman Judea – the books of Qoheleth and Ben Sira, as well as the Qumran scrolls – present sketches of contemporary teachers. While drawing on and renewing the ancient Hebrew tradition, each of them signals a new focus on the learned lifestyle of the teacher, as well as on the significance of lived and embodied practices that constitute such a lifestyle, and this development owes to the generally outward facing horizons of Jewish wisdom. The activities undertaken by the teacher range from scribal tasks and investigation of the torah and the cosmos to liturgical and prophetic performances. They all, however, promote a conception of wisdom as a way of life that requires dedication and constant exercise. Without a doubt, these accounts document ideal social realities, but there is no reason to think that they would not echo social life in the learned circles of ancient Judea.

Ancient Jewish teachers were part of the retainer class in terms of their socioeconomic position.[148] They were above the peasants but subordinate to the governing class. As noted by Mark Sneed, the world of wisdom writers, like any other layer or wing of a society, had its own preferences. The emphatic focus on piety and aesthetics in texts such as the book of Proverbs seems telling; it was in these realms where the teachers had an opportunity to excel. They lacked the economical capital of the society's most wealthy and privileged, but they had ways to compensate for this lack of money. In order to overcome the disparity, wisdom writers stressed the primacy of cultural capital, including educational skills and knowledge.[149] In a similar vein, Hellenistic Jewish wisdom teachers, even though privileged in many ways, excelled in their own particular niche of pedagogical pursuits and performed wisdom. Their focus on immaterial capital and a learned lifestyle was perhaps foreign to many other Jews, possibly including those with both more and less power and resources, although one should remember that the figure of the maskil, in particular, might have served communities that were socioeconomically diverse and included women.

I argue, however, that these wise pedagogues did not position themselves only in relation to other strata of Jewish society. They had wider horizons, for they knew that the search for wisdom and the good life was not limited to their own milieu in Judea. Surely, much concerning their self-understanding and notion of the Hellenistic world beyond the ancestral land remains unclear. Yet, there are major conceptual parallels between Jewish teachers and Greek philosophers. Education was seen as a slow and transformative phenomenon, which aimed at intellectual and moral maturation and involved a lifetime of practice. Importantly, mental and spiritual exercises were integral to both Jewish wisdom and Greek philosophy.[150] In other words, both traditions displayed a similar pattern of thought according to which the pursuit of wisdom presumes a commitment to an active lifestyle that embodies and conveys one's values. Thus, it is likely that Jewish authors could observe a parallel between their own search for wisdom and related pursuits elsewhere. The educated elite of Jerusalem and its environs probably saw themselves as akin to philosophers, or as local representatives of wisdom lovers who produced new forms of Hellenistic culture.

4

Shared wisdom: Ideal ways of living in Jewish communities

Up until now, I have discussed lived wisdom in relation to individual figures, first exploring the sage as an exemplar and then analysing the lifestyle of the wisdom teacher. In this chapter, I will move on to explore what a life of wisdom and insight was imagined to entail on a communal level, thus continuing the discussion on how wisdom may be lived and cultivated in everyday life, but approaching it from the viewpoint of ancient Jewish groups. My investigation into shared wisdom aims at highlighting that wisdom is not just a quality of an individual, nor is wisdom acquired and possessed by exceptional individuals alone. The process of becoming a good, wise, and virtuous person is not necessarily solitary, but it can take place in the context of a community. As such, the process involves an ideal way of living that is shared and agreed upon, or at least is imagined to be so.

As will be seen, early Jewish descriptions of communal endeavours to live in a virtuous way illustrate the pursuit, practice, and performance of wisdom in different parts of the ancient eastern Mediterranean, including in Judea and the environs of Alexandria. Surely, the book of Proverbs already emphasizes the communal dimension of well-being and happiness,[1] but several texts from the late second temple period – the writings of Philo of Alexandria and Flavius Josephus, as well as the Qumran scrolls – explicitly focus on describing the aims and activities of Jewish groups that were dedicated to a life of wisdom and virtue.[2] David Runia, for example, has described the portrayals of the Essenes and the Therapeutae as "the living embodiment of two ideal ways of life."[3] In this chapter, I will argue that the Qumran scrolls further compliment the picture by offering a myriad of Semitic materials from ancient Judea that outline another group, or a cluster of related groups, in search of wisdom and the good life.

I will begin my enquiry with some general remarks on the ancient identification of Judaism with a philosophy, as it is central to our understanding of how early Jewish authors conceived of their ancestral inheritance.[4] Thereafter, I will proceed to discuss the portrayal of three Jewish groups, including the Therapeutae described by Philo; the Essenes, known from Philo's and Josephus' writings; and the *yaḥad* movement associated with some of the Qumran scrolls. While the latter may be connected to the Essenes of the classical sources in one way or another,[5] I leave aside the question concerning the relationship between the two and proceed to read the extant writings – the Qumran scrolls and the classical sources – independently, in order to highlight the distinctive aims and contributions of each author.[6] The sources are written in different cultural registers, which means that they discuss wisdom and virtue from distinct angles and in diverse literary contexts. Yet, each of them points to the pursuit of a wise life as a communal effort that adds to the common good.

Judaism among philosophies

To understand the accounts of "shared wisdom" in early Jewish literature, it is necessary to begin with a brief reflection on the ancient conception of Judaism as a philosophy, for both Jewish and non-Jewish authors made such an identification. The extant evidence contains three (non-Jewish) Greek accounts from the third and fourth centuries BCE that describe Jews as philosophers, thus inviting one to imagine their place and pursuits in a wider cross-cultural milieu of learned efforts. Apart from "outsiders," who wished to map parallels between their own culture and other cultures, the identification was a native one. In the Hellenistic and Roman periods, several Jewish authors writing in Greek characterized Judaism as a philosophy or Jewish groups as philosophers.[7]

Let me begin with the earliest extant evidence. Non-Jewish accounts of Jews as philosophers include three relatively early texts by Theophrastus, Megasthenes, and Clearchus of Soli, who comment on the topic from slightly different positions. Two of them were Peripatetic philosophers, including Theophrastus (*c.* 371–287 BCE), who was Aristotle's successor at the Lyceum, and Clearchus of Soli (*c.* 4th–3rd century BCE), who was a student of Aristotle. Megasthenes (*c.* 350–290 BCE), in turn, was a historian and an explorer.[8] In spite of their different emphases, all three authors acknowledge Jewish wisdom, as well as recognizing certain lived practices of Jews as philosophical activities.

Beginning with Theophrastus, he writes that Jews, "being philosophers by race,"[9] think of the cosmos and its creator as they discuss the deity. They investigate the cosmos and undertake intellectual and spiritual exercise, observing the stars at night-time and praying to God.¹⁰ It is relevant vis-à-vis lived wisdom that Theophrastus recognizes such activities as philosophical. Another Peripatetic, Clearchus of Soli, reports an anecdote of an anonymous Jewish man from Coele-Syria who conversed with Aristotle and other scholars, having "the soul of a Greek."¹¹ Here one gets a glimpse of conversation as a means to display one's philosophical capacities. Finally, Megasthenes the explorer of Eastern cultures draws a comparison between (some) Jews and other groups of philosophers. He writes on the cross-cultural nature of philosophy as follows:

> All the opinions expressed by the ancients about nature are found also among the philosophers outside Greece, some among the Indian Brahmans and others in Syria among those called Jews.¹²

Hence, three relatively early non-Jewish writers establish a notion of Jews as philosophers who partake in the lettered culture of their time. Among Jewish authors, Philo and Josephus make such an identification frequently, arguing that Judaism is philosophical while retaining its biblical basis.

Philo, who wrote in Alexandria in the first half of the first century CE, depicts Judaism as a philosophy (e.g., *Legat.* 245). He specifically projects virtue onto the Essenes and the Therapeutae, claiming that they lead active and contemplative ways of life, respectively (*Contempl.* 1).¹³ While Philo extols forms of philosophical life within Judaism, he does not stress the existence of different parties or schools. Rather, Philo emphasizes the unity of Judaism as opposed to the divisions that characterize Greek philosophy.¹⁴ For him, Judaism counts as an "ancestral philosophy."¹⁵ Jews may gain from their own tradition, including its customs and laws, the same (i.e., knowledge concerning the divine) as other people gain from their philosophies (*Virt.* 64–5).

Josephus, a priest and historian from Jerusalem, wrote his works in Rome after the Jewish revolt in 70 CE. Unlike Philo, Josephus stresses the variety of Jewish philosophy and aligns the elite Jewish groups with philosophical schools, discussing the practices and beliefs of the Pharisees, the Sadducees, and the Essenes (*A.J.* 13.171–3; 18.11–25; *B.J.* 2.119–66).¹⁶ He also offers a brief and tendentious account of his experience among different philosophical schools (*Vita* 10–12).

In a similar vein, some other early Jewish authors either imply or explicate the idea of Judaism as a philosophical way of life. The Letter of Aristeas, known for its fictive account of the origins of the Septuagint, depicts Jewish legislation as philosophical (*Arist.* 31) and the translators of the Septuagint as philosophers (esp. 200, 235, 296). The author of the text known as 4 Maccabees focuses on the philosophical question of reason's capacity to master the passions (4 Macc 1:1), claiming that reason actively directs one towards virtues (1:30).[17] The author of 4 Maccabees also presents Judaism as a philosophy that equips its adherents with virtues (5:22–4; 7:6–7).

Moreover, two authors from Alexandria in the second and third centuries BCE argue for the primacy of Moses over against Greek philosophers. Artapanus maintains that Moses invented philosophy,[18] whereas Aristobulus argues that Pythagoras, Socrates, and Plato had investigated and imitated the legislation of Jews, borrowing from their ancestral books and Moses' wisdom while constructing their own systems of thought.[19] In addition, Aristobulus presents Judaism as a αἵρεσις that excels in a key aspect of philosophy, i.e., in having opinions of God, and he argues that the Jewish law "is arranged with reference to piety (εὐσέβεια) and justice (δικαιοσύνη) and temperance (ἐγκράτεια) and the rest of the things that are truly good."[20]

As the previous discussion shows, both non-Jewish Greek authors and Jewish authors recognized Judaism as a philosophy starting from the fourth century BCE.[21] Such a categorization is natural because the lexicon of classical Greek, like that of the ancient Hebrew language, has no word that would cover the modern term "religion." Steve Mason comments on the authors' choice of vocabulary as follows:

> Josephus has often been criticized for presenting his teacher Bannus as well as the Pharisees, Sadducees, and Essenes as *philosophical schools*, because of our modern assumption that they were obviously *religious* groups. But there was no such terminology available to Josephus that would be intelligible to his audiences. He *could* say that these groups or individuals were concerned with piety, simple living, contempt for suffering and death, and expectation of a certain afterlife, and that is what he does. But these were what philosophical schools did, and that is why he calls them philosophies. There was no genus called *religion*, of which any of these could be a *species*.[22]

Surely, the category of "cult" could describe aspects of Judaism, but as Mason points out, Jews (or Judeans, as he calls them) "seemed to behave as a philosophical school, not as a cult." In the second temple era, the cultic aspects of Judaism – i.e., temple, sacrifices, and priesthood – were visible in Jerusalem, whereas the study of sacred texts, moral exhortation, and a disciplined way of life would have been features associated with Judaism elsewhere.[23] Importantly, the erudite and ethical dimensions of Judaism were philosophical concerns in the conceptual world of the ancient authors. Schools had diverse ideas of how to behave, but the consensus view was that any philosophy would promote two "bedrock social values," piety towards the gods and justice or philanthropy towards humanity.[24] The realm of philosophy also encompassed piety, spirituality, and mysticism, which modern people have a propensity to associate these phenomena with the category of religion.[25]

The sum of these accounts forces one to think of early Judaism in terms other than "religion." In addition, it urges one to consider the nature of ancient cultural encounters. The sources offer, as Erich Gruen argues, "the reciprocal set of perceptions (or constructs) in which Greeks understood Jews as philosophers and Jews viewed Greek philosophers as dependent on Jewish lore." According to Gruen, such a "double lens" challenges the idea of otherness, which remains in the background.[26] In other words, the mutual appropriations do not underline difference and alterity between Jews and Greeks, but the shared concern for wisdom appears to be a uniting factor. Gruen phrases the positive force of cultural interaction as follows: "Jews and Greeks found a cross-cultural association to be not a diminution of their identity but an enchantment of it."[27] Competition and claims of superiority may certainly be at stake, as the maskil materials also suggest, but they do not exclude the idea of partaking in the same pursuit of wisdom.

In this section, I have shown that both Greek and Jewish authors portray Judaism as a philosophy, thus associating it with the love of wisdom in the Greek world. Non-Jewish Greek writers recognize aspects of Judaism as philosophical, including both ideas and lived practices in the form of intellectual and spiritual exercises. Jewish authors themselves present the idea of Judaism as an ancestral philosophy and discuss forms of philosophical life within Judaism. I will now continue to explore the latter in the light of the question of shared wisdom. I will begin my enquiry with the Therapeutae, a group of wisdom lovers from Roman Alexandria, after which I will proceed to discuss the evidence for the Essenes and the group of wisdom seekers known from the Qumran scrolls.

The lifestyle of the Therapeutae

Philo's treatise titled *De vita contemplativa* was probably the fourth part of a series of writings on virtues (περί αρετών). In this series, Philo sought to prove that Jews possess excellent virtue among them, as is suggested by the subheading ΠΕΡΙ ΑΡΕΤΩΝ ΤΟ ΤΕΤΑΡΤΟΝ found in most of the manuscripts.[28] In *De vita contemplativa*, Philo focuses on the distinction of the Therapeutae, and he characterizes these women and men as "the disciples of Moses" (οἱ Μωυσέως γνώριμοι) who follow his instructions (*Contempl.* 63–4), thus signalling devotion to a founding figure.[29] As I hope to demonstrate, the treatise offers a fascinating portrayal of shared wisdom in the life of an ancient Jewish group who had the desire as well as the resources to dedicate themselves to the pursuit of wisdom. An ideal lifestyle, in their understanding, involved strict routines and daily practice.

Philo calls the Therapeutae philosophers or describes their dedication to philosophy on several occasions throughout this treatise (2, 16, 26, 28, 30, 34, 67, 69, 89). These statements are relatively general in nature. According to Philo, the Therapeutae philosophize six days a week (30), utter the δόγματα of their philosophy even asleep (26), take their ancestral philosophy as an allegory (28), and continue to pursue philosophy after their nocturnal vigils (89). A slightly more specific claim is made when Philo explains that the branch of philosophy pursued by the Therapeutae is the contemplative one (67, cf. 1). He further associates the group with a life of beauty (1, 67, 88–9).[30]

Moreover, the issue of philosophy is explicitly at stake as Philo discusses the group designation: the vocation of these people is expressed by the titles "Therapeutae" and "Therapeutrides" that derive from the verb θεραπεύω, denoting either "to worship" or "to cure." The import of service is generally dominant in Philo's oeuvre,[31] but Philo obviously plays with the double meaning of the verb in *Contempl.* 2 (cf. Eusebius, *Hist. eccles.* 2.17.3). According to this passage, the group professes "an art of healing" that cures, in addition to bodily diseases, those of the soul caused by one's desires, pleasures, fears, and griefs. The sense of "worship" is also accurate, for, Philo explains, "nature and the sacred laws have schooled them to worship the Self-existent." In so doing, these people "keep the memory of God alive" (26).[32] As these claims indicate, the group of the Therapeutae is driven by a shared concern for the well-being of the soul.

Further illustrating the group's lifestyle, Philo writes that the Therapeutae give away their belongings for the sake of philosophy (16). They reject eating and drinking during the day because the place of philosophy is in the light and that of bodily needs in the darkness (34). Finally, they do not sit on couches, as one might expect from people trained in philosophy, but on wooden benches, thus demonstrating "a frugal contentment worthy of the free" (69). Such references gesture towards the idea that lifestyle is an essential component of the group's philosophy, but they do not imply any insignificance of "theoretical" philosophy. On the contrary, the Therapeutae pursue "the contemplative branch of philosophy, which indeed is the noblest and most god-like part" (67).

All the aforementioned references explicate the role of the Therapeutae as philosophers. David Hay, however, has been puzzled by the lack of information on their ideas, convictions, and teachings, pointing out that Philo praises the group's way of life instead of investigating their ideas.³³ Hay observes that Philo mentions the δόγματα and νοήματα of the group on several occasions (26, 31, 35, 68, 76, 78, 88), but he barely explains what those involve apart from describing the general ideal of self-mastery (ἐγκράτεια) and the task of allegorical interpretation. Hay calls this "a curious omission."³⁴ Philo's perceived vagueness leads him to suggest that the philosophy of the Therapeutae "may have little relation to Greco-Roman philosophical traditions."³⁵

Hay's conclusion may be incautious. Philo certainly had the knowledge to write about philosophical theories and ideas, had he wanted to do so, which suggests that he aimed at accomplishing something else in his treatise *De vita contemplativa*. I would like to propose, in fact, that the omission of theories and ideas does not seem so strange if Philo's treatise is read as a sort of *bios*, i.e., akin to ancient biographies. Most importantly, the present argument is supported by the fact that the given title – περὶ βίου θεωρητικοῦ in Greek or *De vita contemplativa* in Latin – contains, like the titles of ancient biographies, the preposition περί or *de* and the noun βίος or *vita*.³⁶

In addition, the lack of concern for ideas does not undermine the work's philosophical relevance insofar as ancient philosophy was not limited to thought; it was also about practice. As noted in Chapters 2 and 3, Philo specifically associates the concept of ἄσκησις with the figure of Jacob. In *De vita contemplativa*, he describes, instead of an ancestral model, a form of ἄσκησις in the life of some exemplary Alexandrian Jews. Concentrating on the lived dimension of their philosophy, Philo employs the term ἄσκησις and the cognate verb to describe the group of the Therapeutae who engage in spiritual exercise (28), practise simplicity (39), and train themselves in philosophy (69).³⁷

To clarify, my argument that *De vita contemplativa* could be read as a "biography" of the ἄσκησις of the Therapeutae does not mean that I would assume a *bios* in the sense of a biography of a remarkable individual.³⁸ Rather, I suggest that the treatise counts as a sort of *bios* on the lifestyle of a group of Alexandrian philosophers who demonstrate "the magnitude of virtue" (1), which aligns with the overall importance of lifestyle in Philo's comprehension of philosophy.³⁹ In fact, this idea resonates with John Sellars' observations on the nature of ancient philosophy. According to him, one may approach ancient philosophy as "a series of biographies of *philosophers* or examples of ideal philosophical lives" instead of "a collection of theoretical systems or *philosophies*."⁴⁰

Furthermore, my proposal to read *De vita contemplativa* as a biographical document does not mean that the work would exclusively represent the genre of biography. On the contrary, scholars have stressed that ancient biographies cover multiple literary forms, although a narrative element is generally prominent in them.[41] Even if such a manner of reading is not the only option, it is highly profitable, in my opinion, as it helps one understand Philo's intention and purpose. The ancient author is not primarily interested in the thought and convictions of the Therapeutae, but in the life(style) of these elite Jewish philosophers who dedicate themselves to a form of spiritual and mental training.

Before discussing the Therapeutae's daily performance of wisdom, I should finally note that scholars have both argued for and denied the historical value of *De vita contemplativa*. Some have read the treatise as reflecting historical reality while acknowledging the rhetorical nature of Philo's presentation.[42] Others have been more sceptical about the account's historical value, regarding it as simply fictional.[43] A third group of scholars has addressed the utopian nature of Philo's literary construction, but they have left the prospect of a historical background open, or even argued for it.[44]

For the present purposes, it suffices to remark that regardless of whether the group existed or not, the treatise illustrates Philo's conception of lived and shared wisdom. It is likely, however, that *De vita contemplativa* is based on some real group, especially since the Therapeutae are presented in parallel to the Essenes (*Contempl*. 1), who were a real group. In fact, a mixture of facts and fiction is to be expected considering the work's biographical character: it has been observed that Greco-Roman biographies do not aim at documenting historical truth per se, but they tend to combine factual information with fictional elements.[45] In the case of *De vita contemplativa*, however, the actual task of differentiating between Philo's rhetorical icing and the historical reality may remain virtually impossible without any external evidence to support one view or the other.

Having introduced the source text, I will now turn to the lifestyle of the Therapeutae. Philo explains that their longing for a happy life comes with a choice of abandoning one's property (13); the members' possessions are given away to those in need, which produces justice (16–17). The foundational decision is followed by leaving kinsfolk and friends because cities, "full of turmoils," are not suitable for those guided by wisdom.[46] Thereafter, these philosophers seek solitude in gardens and in isolated properties (18–20). Their settlement above the Mareotic Lake is safe and pleasant because of healthy breezes. The living conditions in the simple houses are modest (23–4), and their clothing lacks vanity (39).[47] The chosen lifestyle, therefore, serves the group's ideals of simplicity and equality. The latter extends to gender, as the elder women and men alike represent mothers and fathers to the junior members (72). The women, "mostly aged virgins," have chosen this way of life owing to their yearning for wisdom. Turning away bodily pleasures, they wish to have "immortal children" that can only be delivered by "the soul that is dear to God" (68).[48]

In all that they do, the Therapeutae manifest the virtue of self-mastery (ἐγκράτεια), the soul's foundation on which other virtues are built (34).[49] The members show strict self-control to the extent that they abstain from food and drink before sunset, for "philosophy finds its right place in the light, the needs of the body in the darkness" (34). On the seventh day, they eat and drink but only necessities of life, i.e., bread with salt and spring water (37).[50] Such regulation of food and drink counts as another way in which the pursuit of wisdom manifests itself in the group's everyday life.

As for the patterns of daily life, the Therapeutae pray at dawn, asking that a "heavenly light" would fill their minds, and at sunset in order to relieve the soul from the senses (27). They spend the interval between morning and evening in spiritual exercise (28). Markedly, the daily activities are both solitary and communal. For six days a week, the Therapeutae live in solitude (30) and withdraw into private chambers, taking with them only "laws and oracles delivered through the mouth of prophets, and psalms and anything else which fosters and perfects knowledge and piety" (25). They seek wisdom by reading scriptures, and they compose hymns and psalms (28–9). On the seventh day, they meet in the *semneion* where the senior member gives a discourse (31–2).[51] Notably, the women of the philosophical community come to *semneion* "with the same ardour and the same sense of their calling" (32–3).

According to Philo, the Therapeutae organize symposia, which lack the opulence of their Greek counterparts (66), every forty-ninth night. In their meetings, the members of the group sit on wooden benches, reminding one of the austerity of Sparta, and they practise "a frugal contentment worthy of the free" (69). No slaves are present, for the institution is against nature, and no wine is provided (70–4). The president solves questions that arise from the scripture (75–7), while the audience listens to his allegorical exposition attentively, denoting comprehension, praise, and difficulty by gestures and expressions.[52] The speech is followed by a hymn, a meal, and a nocturnal vigil. The latter involves a choral performance that is based on the songs delivered after the crossing of the Red Sea (cf. Exodus 15). At dawn, the Therapeutae finally stretch to heaven and pray before returning to practise philosophy on their own (80–9).

The way in which the ἄσκησις of the Therapeutae is described shows that Philo has internalized the conception of philosophy as a way of life. His concern for the communal search for and practice of wisdom forces one to rethink the argument that the group would have little to do with Greco-Roman philosophy.[53] It also prompts one to reconsider the argument that the Therapeutae's withdrawal would reflect a negative reaction to Hellenism.[54] A careful close reading of *De vita contemplativa* suggests quite the opposite: in this treatise, Philo forcefully promotes an ideal of lived wisdom. Instead of isolating the Mareotic group from the Hellenistic milieu, he casts them as Jewish exemplars of philosophical practice. Spiritual exercise and mental training, in the particular context of these philosophers, involve study, composition, liturgical performance, and pedagogical events.

In *De vita contemplativa*, Philo focuses on the virtuous lifestyle of a group of philosophers from Roman Alexandria. Yet, Philo acknowledges that excellent people who choose a contemplative way of life are not limited to any one place, but perfect goodness exists in both Greece and the world outside it (21). The universalistic claim, together with Philo's general concern for the significance of ἄσκησις, implies that he wishes to situate the Therapeutae in a wider context of seeking wisdom, which to his understanding flourishes within and beyond the Mediterranean region. This aim of Philo prompts me to further examine the dynamics of local and global in *De vita contemplativa*.

Philo contextualizes the group's lifestyle through specific examples. He states that the Therapeutae worship a God "who is better than the good, purer than the one and more primordial than the Monad" (2), thus trying to eclipse the Pythagoreans and the Platonists.[55] In another passage, the members' choice to abandon their property is compared to a similar choice made by two pre-Socratic philosophers; while Anaxagoras and Democritus gave their fields to the sheep, Philo commends how the Therapeutae benefitted both others and themselves by granting their belongings to family (13–17).[56] Philo further stresses that only two notable banquets were held in Greece, those in the houses of Callias and Agathon where Socrates was present (57–62).[57] Even these events seem ridiculous, however, if they are compared with the feast of Moses' disciples (58, cf. 63–5).

Apart from Greek philosophers, Philo contrasts the lifestyle of the Therapeutae with other worshippers of divine entities, ranging from the four elements and celestial bodies to demi-gods, sorts of wooden and stony images of gods, and Egyptian animal gods (3–9).[58] In his view, such practices are harmful because of forgetting the sight of the soul, which grants a person philosophical knowledge (10; cf. *Spec.* 3.185; *Abr.* 164). Hence, the Therapeutae should, in order to attain εὐδαιμονία, "desire the vision of the Existent and soar above the sun of our senses" (11). The group's association with seeing is also natural in that the Therapeutae embrace "the life of contemplation" (1), and the root behind the word for contemplation (θεωρία) means "to see."

Philo connects the Therapeutae's aspiration to gain a mystic vision with the task of textual interpretation. In order to find wisdom, he explains, the members read writings allegorically, for "they think that the words of the literal text are symbols of something whose hidden nature is revealed by studying the underlying meaning" (28). Philo also adds that these philosophers hold "writings of men of old" whose interpretative method they imitate and regard as "a kind of archetype" (29), and he refers to these men as the first leaders or founders of the αἵρεσις.[59]

As the previous quotes indicate, Philo projects the method of allegorical exegesis, popular among Alexandrian scholars both Jewish and non-Jewish, to the Mareotic group.[60] According to him, allegory serves as a means to find the texts' "inner meaning," and Philo compares the law book (ἡ νομοθεσία) to "a living creature" (78).[61] "Looking through the words as through a mirror," the rational soul (ἡ λογικὴ ψυχὴ) "removes the symbolic coverings," thus revealing and illuminating the hidden thoughts (78).

Elsewhere in his large oeuvre, Philo associates sight with allegory, described by him as the method that is dear to those with opened eyes (*Plant.* 36). The interpretative process, he claims, may even evoke a mystical ascent.[62] The same seems to apply to the Therapeutae, as is indicated by the following quote from the end of the treatise (*Contempl.* 90):

> So much then for the Therapeutae, who have taken to their hearts the contemplation of nature and what it has to teach, and have lived in the soul alone, citizens of heaven and the world, presented to the Father and Maker of all by their faithful sponsor Virtue, who has procured for them God's friendship and added a gift going hand in hand with it, true excellence of life, a boon better than all good fortune and rising to the very summit of felicity.

Philo spares no words as he acclaims the Therapeutae who live "in the soul alone" (ψυχῇ μόνῃ). Being citizens of both heaven and the world, they can gain access to εὐδαιμονία, the special state of felicity, happiness, and wellbeing, which Aristotle had defined as the end-goal of human life (*N.E.* 1176b, cf. Seneca, *Ep.* 15.1). As stressed by Runia, the concept of εὐδαιμονία here is "not just a state of mind, but a realised *way of life*."[63] While the group's exemplariness is clear from the outset, the reference to its double citizenship deserves more attention than it has hitherto received.

The idea of a heavenly citizenship echoes Philo's comments according to which the homeland of the sage is in virtue (*Virt.* 190) or in heaven (*Conf.* 77–8).[64] As for being a citizen of the world, Philo describes the wise person as a cosmopolitan (*Migr.* 59). In addition to the first human being (*Opif.* 142) and Moses (*Conf.* 106; *Mos.* 1.157), anyone serving the νόμος is said to count as a cosmopolitan (*Opif.* 3).[65] While Philo uses the term "cosmopolitan" as a philosophically coloured honorary title, he also presents critical remarks on citizenship, claiming that "God alone is in the true sense a citizen," whereas the wise are mere sojourners and the fools outcasts (*Cher.* 120–1).[66] Philo even argues that priests and prophets deny the citizenship of this world, thus rising above senses to the noetic cosmos, "the commonwealth of ideas" (*Gig.* 61).

In *Spec.* 2.43–5, Philo combines the ascension motif and the cosmopolitan nature of the philosophical life. He first notes that all who practise wisdom (ἀσκηταὶ σοφίας), "either in Grecian or barbarian lands," live an irreproachable life and observe forms of nature. Thereafter, Philo depicts a mystical process, which transforms them into cosmopolitans. He writes (2.45) that the bodies of philosophers remain on the land, but

> they provide their souls with wings, so that they may traverse the upper air and gain full contemplation of the powers which dwell there, as behoves true "cosmopolitans" who have recognized the world to be a city having for its citizens the associates of wisdom, registered as such by virtue to whom is entrusted the headship of the universal commonwealth.[67]

Granted, Philo does not directly mention the ascension of the Therapeutae. Yet, he explicitly writes, as cited above, that they live "in the soul alone" (ψυχῇ μόνῃ) and rise to εὐδαιμονία as the final outcome of their philosophical practice (*Contempl.* 90). Longing for immortality, the Therapeutae have a conviction that their mortal life, which typically denotes bodily life in Philo's texts,[68] has already ended (13). This makes them abandon their earthly belongings because those with "eyes to see should surrender the blind wealth to those who are still blind in mind" (13, cf. 10–11).

Cosmopolitanism, in turn, is a crucial motif in Hellenistic philosophy. It is prominent in Stoicism, although the theme of transcending political boundaries may hark back to Cynic philosophy.[69] As is well known, Zeno of Citium (334–262 BCE), the founder of Stoicism, is connected with the motif of an ideal community of sages.[70] The Roman Stoic sources, moreover, comment on the citizenship of the cosmos. Cicero, who lived just before Philo in the first century BCE, documents discussion on the idea of a commonwealth where everything belongs to all people (*Rep.* 3.33–7), as well as describing the universe as *una civitas communis* (*Leg.* 1.23). Seneca, who is roughly contemporary to Philo, writes about the commonwealth of all people (*Otio* 4.1), the world as one's country (*Ep.* 28.4), and the wise person whose country is in every place (*Helv.* 9.7).[71]

In *Gig.* 61, Philo maintains, as already mentioned, that priests and prophets deny the citizenship of this world and rise to the *politeia* of ideas. This implies that one may need to reject the citizenship of this world in order to rise to the noetic cosmos. At the same time, Philo claims, like the Stoics who imagine the sage in global terms, that philosophy brings one into a cosmopolitan realm (*Spec.* 2.43–5), also describing the Therapeutae as citizens of the world (*Contempl.* 90). This sort of cosmopolitanism is not this-worldly, however, but it entails philosophical perfection that may result from the soul's ascension: the Therapeutae are capable of rising above sense-perception (11) and living "in the soul alone," which makes them citizens of heaven as well (90).[72]

While the philosophy of the Mareotic group has a distinctly Jewish flavour, its outcome is strikingly inclusive: the philosophical process results in rising above the earthly divisions of people. Philo imagines the Therapeutae as attaining a state of existence in which ethnic and political boundaries cease to matter; they count as citizens of both heaven and the world. Intriguingly, the members become cosmopolitan by means of studying their ancestral literature, although they allegorize these texts and thus read Greek ideas into them; the particular and the universal merge as the Therapeutae remain dedicated to Moses as well as filling a cosmopolitan dream.

In summary, Philo's biographical narrative about the Therapeutae underlines the pursuit of wisdom as a communal project. While Philo does not say much about the theoretical content of their philosophy,[73] his treatise is of prime value for the study of lived wisdom. Doctrines and principles belonged to Hellenistic philosophy, but so did transformative training. In *De vita contemplativa*, Philo concentrates on the latter aspect of philosophy, which shapes the character and lifestyle of those who practise it.[74] The Therapeutae heal and cultivate the soul for the sake of wisdom, as well as professing piety and serving God (2, 12). Seeking a mystic vision of the divinity, they reject their belongings and dedicate themselves to daily exercise, including asceticism, study, liturgical acts, and communal gatherings in the form of Sabbath meetings (13–20, 25–39) and symposia (40–89).

Philo portrays these local philosophers as both remaining dedicated to an ancestral tradition and fulfilling a cosmopolitan dream. As the outcome of their dedicated practice, the Therapeutae are capable of transcending earthly boundaries, living in the soul alone, and becoming citizens of both heaven and the earth. Overall, Philo is clearly apologetic as he tries to demonstrate that Greek philosophers and Egyptian worshippers are but a shadow in comparison with the Therapeutae.[75] Yet, he is not an outsider who would borrow or weakly echo Greek ideas. Rather, Philo actively produces new Greek literature on the prospects of shared wisdom – or of a philosophical lifestyle cherished by a community of like-minded people – in the context of Roman Alexandria.

The Essenes, athletes of virtue

The evidence for the ancient Jewish group known as the Essenes is scattered: the classical sources contain rather extensive accounts by Philo and Josephus, as well as a series of brief remarks by several non-Jewish authors, including Pliny the Elder, Dio of Prusa, Hegesippus, and Hippolytus of Rome.[76] In this section, I will specifically explore Philo's and Josephus' descriptions of the group. My aim is to understand how these Jewish authors conceive of the communal dimension of virtue and how they project a desirable way of life onto the Essenes. As regards the practice of wisdom, both of them emphasize, as will be seen, the philosophical value of both the study of sacred texts and of mundane, manual labour.

The third early account of the Essenes from the first century CE also signals the value of lifestyle. Pliny the Elder observes the exceptionality of the Essenes, depicting the distinctive group as "admirable beyond all others in the whole world, without women and renouncing love entirely, without money, and having for company only the palm trees." Furthermore, he describes the group as attractive, stating that people "wearied by the fluctuations of fortune" adopt its customs.[77] These remarks by Pliny, a non-Jew who never visited Palestine, communicate the significance of a shared lifestyle and customs, whereas Philo and Josephus discuss the same topics in much more detail.

Both Philo and Josephus paint the group's lifestyle in idealizing and apparently somewhat apologetic strokes.[78] There are several parallels between the accounts, and scholars have explained them by assuming that either both authors used the same source or Josephus had access to Philo's writings.[79] Leaving aside this debate, I aim at examining the question of how Philo and Josephus conceived of the Essenes as a group committed to wisdom, or as people sharing the same concern for virtue. I will now begin my investigation with the writings of Philo, which offer the oldest extant source material on the Essenes, and Philo was in fact the group's contemporary.

Philo discusses the Essenes lengthily in his *Quod omnis probus liber sit* (75–91) and in another much shorter section included in his *Hypothetica* (11.1–8). He also seems to have written a whole treatise on them, as is suggested by *Contempl.* 1, where Philo refers to his earlier discussion on the Essenes, who are known for their adoption of an active and practical way of life, before proceeding to discuss the Therapeutae and their contemplative way of life.

In *Quod omnis probus liber sit*, Philo discusses the freedom of the good person; it is the second half of a larger work, which began with a now lost discussion on the slavery of the wicked person.[80] Unlike the majority of Philo's corpus, the treatise refers less to Jewish scriptures, primarily resonating with Greek and especially Stoic ideas.[81] As part of his discussion, Philo lists exemplary people, including Greek sages, Persian magi, Indian gymnosophists, and the Essenes in Syria-Palestine (*Prob.* 72–96), thus indicating that he understands philosophy as a "global" pursuit.[82]

By drawing attention to the Essenes (Ἐσσαῖοι), Philo seeks to show that Palestinian Syria is not barren of moral excellence. He speculates that the group designation may pertain to "holiness" (ὁσιότητος), as is appropriate of men devoted to the service of God (*Prob.* 75). The love of virtue brings about a lifestyle with a practical orientation, including a departure from the cities, a settlement in villages, and a choice to live without goods and property, thus celebrating "frugality and contentment" as "real superabundance." By investing their time in the beneficial tasks of agriculture and crafts, the Essenes consciously contribute to the common good. They reject slavery, which is against the law of nature, and they care for the old and the sick, who "are not neglected on the pretext that they can produce nothing" (75–9, 85–7).[83]

Hence, the Essenes live a life of virtue, demonstrating their exemplariness through mundane tasks and dedication to the group. Perhaps anticipating further questions about the type of philosophy practised by the Essenes, Philo explains that they reject logic, as it does not assist one in gaining virtue, and natural philosophy, which is mostly "beyond human nature." Instead, the Essenes practise ethics (80). The explicit primacy of ethics is notable, suggesting that Emmanuel Levinas was not the first Jewish philosopher to make such a claim.[84] Furthermore, Philo states that the Essenes draw on the divinely inspired "ancestral laws" in their ethics, studying them daily and especially on the seventh day in the synagogues (80–1). This suggests that sacred texts serve as resources for issues pertaining to character and a desirable way of life, and Philo in fact notes that the Essenes acquire knowledge of virtues, responsibilities, and priorities by studying them (83).

The shared lifestyle of the Essenes is not just about the cultivation of virtue in general, but it involves training in specific virtues that manifest the excellence of the group. The Essenes, Philo argues, are educated in the virtues of piety, holiness, and justice. They gain understanding of domestic and civic law, as well as becoming capable of making distinctions between good, bad, and indifferent things (83). The concern for piety and justice creates a link to ancient philosophy in general,[85] while the emphasis on holiness points to divine–human communication as an integral part of the good life. The attitude of indifference towards indifferent things further reveals the cultivation of a spiritual exercise with a Stoic outlook.[86] While the pursuit of desirable virtues and attitudes underlines the formation of an individual, the reference to domestic and civic conduct signals the significance of a community for the Essenes; the life of this group is not one of full isolation, but it is firmly rooted in a local context, in spite of the motif of withdrawing from the city.

Love is another motif that binds the group together as well as to God. Philo explains that three types of love orient the life of the Essenes, including those of God, virtue, and people, and they manifest themselves in the group's daily activities and attitudes. The love of God, for example, involves a concern for purity, whereas the love of virtue prompts a modest way of living, characterized by contentment, continence, and endurance. The love of people, in turn, produces good communal life in the spirit of kindness and equality (83–4). Love is embodied, therefore, as the members perform virtues with both horizontal and vertical dimensions. Purity indicates divine–human communication, as observed, whilst kindness and equality allude to harmony within the peer group. Finally, the choice to content oneself with a modest lifestyle underlines the autonomy of an individual. Thus, the group's ethics has several dimensions that include but are not limited to human relations.[87]

Philo ends his discussion on the Essenes by characterizing them as "athletes of virtue" (88), thus associating the group with the bodily imagery of training and competition.[88] A similar image appears in Philo's other account of the Essenes, preserved in *Hypothetica* (11.1–8), although the text's authorship remains open to debate.[89] Here (the assumed) Philo explains that the Essenes practise farming, shepherding, beekeeping, and artisanship tirelessly. Starting their tasks before the sunrise and continuing nearly until the sunset, the group gains similar joy from their daily toil as those training for gymnastic competition. Even if Philo employs the athletic metaphor, he now subverts it, arguing that the Essenes consider their training to be more helpful and lasting than that required for athletic games (11.6–9).[90]

In *Hypothetica*, Philo also mentions other aspects of the Essenes' lived wisdom, especially acclaiming their exceptional self-control, which includes their love of frugality and hate of luxury (11.11). He depicts the Essenes as "men of ripe years" who are no longer subject to bodily passions (11.3) and reject marriage for the sake of practising self-mastery (ἀσκεῖν ἐγκράτειαν).[91] To be exact, Philo does not claim that these men have never been married or never had children, and there even seems to be evidence of the opposite. As argued by Joan Taylor, *Hypoth.* 11.13 begins with the statement "Even if (κἂν εἰ) the older men, however, happen to be (τύχοιεν) childless" (trans. Taylor), and this particular formulation suggests that such childless people are exceptional.[92] However, Philo explains that women have their vices, and children, too, threaten the freedom of the man (11.14–17). These comments underline the all-male nature of the Essenes' communal enterprise, which is driven by their zeal for virtue and philanthropy (11.2).

On two occasions, therefore, Philo delineates the Essenes' dedication to the good life, explicitly presenting ethics as the prime branch of philosophy. Their pursuit of wisdom is depicted as a communal effort and a male project where the immanent and the transcendent intersect. In essence, it is about the superior performance of everyday tasks and duties, complemented by the study of ancestral books that provide a basis for the chosen lifestyle. Philo wishes to argue for the credibility of this group, as is demonstrated by the references to kings who admire and acknowledge its exceptionality (*Prob.* 88–91; *Hypoth.* 11.18). Markedly, he does so by spelling out the value of everyday life, i.e., by concentrating on the value of manual and mundane work instead of promoting a withdrawal from the world or neglecting the material conditions of the everyday life.

Towards the end of the first century CE, another Jewish author, Josephus, also commented on the Essenes. His texts offer further descriptions of their shared way of life, which manifests a marriage of thought and daily exercise.[93] The idea of Judaism as a superb embodiment of philosophical aspirations is already present in his earliest extant writing, *Bellum judaicum*.[94] In this work, Josephus portrays the elite Jewish groups – including the Pharisees, the Sadducees, and the Essenes – as philosophical schools.[95] While Josephus credits all three schools or societies (αἱρέσεις), he portrays the Essenes as the most exemplary of them all.[96]

Josephus' fullest account of the Essenes is found in B.J. 2.119-66.[97] A concern for virtue is clear from the outset: the group renounces evil pleasure and regards self-mastery (ἐγκράτεια) as a virtue (2.120). These claims align with Josephus' general emphasis on the "manliness and martial virtue" in the book: in the aftermath of the Jewish revolt, he aimed at rescuing the reputation of his defeated people.[98] Josephus' portrait of the Essenes may thus be an apology of some sort (cf. 2.152-3 on the bravery of the Essenes during the war). It is distinctive, however, that when Josephus apologizes, he does it by emphasizing the value of lived wisdom. Josephus also uses terms that bear relevance for the notion of wisdom as something shared by a community of like-minded people.

Despising riches, wearing white garments, and rejecting the sensual pleasure of oil,[99] the Essenes appear as equal, each receiving according to their needs, which results in the absence of both humiliating poverty and smug wealth (2.122-3, 127). The group leads a life of discipline, rigorous practice, and submission to hierarchies (2.143-6, 150-3). The process of entering this αἵρεσις requires a testing of one's character over several years and oaths (2.137-42), and the threat of expulsion lurks ever after (2.143-4). The daily practice of the Essenes begins with the recitation of ancestral prayers before the sunrise (2.128). Otherwise, the members carry out their own tasks apart from assembling for two communal meals; notably, the former is preceded by an embodied exercise, the act of bathing in cold water (2.129-33). Likewise, the Essenes keep Sabbaths rigorously (2.147), to the extent that they do not go to the stool on the seventh day (2.147-9). According to Josephus, the fact that the members of the group are long-lived is best explained as the consequence of their austere and regular way of life (2.151).

Although Josephus largely focuses on the shared lifestyle of the Essenes, he also addresses aspects of their thought. The group's veneration of the Lawgiver (2.145) hints at the role of Moses as the head of the school, and the Essenes are known for their learned efforts: they study the "works of the ancients" (2.136) with an extraordinary zeal, apparently deriving thoughts and ideas from those books. Their study also concerns the well-being of the body because it extends to medicine: Josephus describes the Essenes as caring for both the body and the soul, noting that they investigate how to heal diseases (2.136). Their doctrine includes beliefs in the corruptibility of the body and the immortality of the soul (2.154-8).[100] Finally, Josephus reports that some Essenes foretell the future (2.159), which alludes to prophecy as a spiritual exercise and another mode of performing one's wisdom.

Josephus' remarks on the Essenes imply a marriage of thought and everyday exercise. The *ora et labora* lifestyle of the group is generally ascetic and thus reminds one of Philo's remarks on the Essenes. A major difference is that the Essene way of life comes in two varieties according to Josephus. He notes that the Essenes do not abolish marriage but disdain it (2.120–1). He also observes the existence of another order of the Essenes who marry: they too embody virtue, showing a great concern for purity and stressing the primacy of procreation over sexual pleasure (2.160–1). These remarks are of interest regarding shared wisdom as they suggest that an ideal way of life does not only belong to celibate communities, but it can emerge in the context of the family life.

In his later writings, aimed at a non-Jewish audience (*A.J.* 1.5, 10–17; 20.262; *C. Ap.* 2.196), Josephus' philosophical agenda becomes more prominent.[101] He mentions the Essenes in *Antiquitates judaicae* and *Vita*. In *Antiquitates judaicae*, written some twenty years after *Bellum judaicum*, Josephus offers a few short accounts of the Essenes.[102] In *A.J.* 15.371–9, he compares the group's lifestyle to that of the Pythagoreans and mentions a man named Manaemus whose life witnessed to his goodness (καλοκαγαθία).[103] Josephus further illustrates the ideas and practices of the group in *A.J.* 18.18–22, explaining how the Essenes teach reliance on God, regard souls as immortal, and perform their own sacrifices. Rejecting private property, marriage, and slavery, they focus on serving each other. Nothing similar, Josephus claims, ever existed among either Greeks or the barbarians. These remarks are brief, but again, they underline the value of philosophy as a way of life, which involves some teachings and beliefs, but ultimately manifests itself in desirable action.

In his last work *Vita*, Josephus claims to have a personal relation to the Essenes. Following his education at home and his early conversations with priests and important men of the city, Josephus wished to try out different schools of thought, including the Pharisees, the Sadducees, and the Essenes, with the purpose of learning about each school before choosing the best one of them. Thereafter, Josephus continued his trial by living with a desert hermit called Bannus[104] before returning to the city and following the way of life of the Pharisees, whom he characterizes as akin to the Stoics, at the age of nineteen (*Vita* 8–12).[105]

The rhetorical nature of the account makes it arguable whether Josephus actually tried these lifestyles.[106] Even if he had some insider experience, it is remarkable that Josephus does not explicate the philosophical lifestyles of the groups. This suggests that he follows an established autobiographical pattern: the exposure to different philosophies is something that he needs as an elite person of the Roman society.[107] It is of interest, however, that Josephus underlines the value of socialization and lifestyle choice in the pursuit of wisdom. An individual has autonomy over what she or he chooses, but the formative process nevertheless takes place in the context of a school.

In summary, the Essenes pursue wisdom in a communal setting, sharing a vision of an ideal way of living that nurtures virtue and harmonious relations. Philo emphasizes the primacy of ethics and imagines any worthy deed, whether manual labour or textual study, as a valuable exercise that can demonstrate the excellence of its practiser. Josephus views the Essenes as akin to a Greek school with their system of discipleship, and he sketches out a lifestyle of exceptional self-mastery, even though also presenting occasional remarks on the group's thought and learned efforts. The Essenes' study of both ancestral books and medicine underlines the importance of holistic well-being. Overall, while both Philo and Josephus value the everyday exercise of virtue, Philo describes the Essenes' lifestyle as a homosocial project, whereas Josephus hints at family as a context of practising virtue.

The *yaḥad* movement as a wisdom body

In the previous sections, I have discussed how early Jewish authors writing in Greek formulated notions of shared wisdom by outlining ideal ways of living in Jewish communities. In order to bring another cultural register into the conversation, I will now draw attention to Jewish authors who wrote in Semitic languages and operated in Judea around the turn of the era. My aim is to grasp how they perceived of and promoted ideas of shared wisdom. This enquiry is enabled by the Qumran collection, which affords a plethora of materials illustrating Judaism in the late second temple period, including notions of a wise and virtuous life(style). The scrolls from Qumran serve as a means to reconstruct one specific movement from Judea, although they further hint at the generally strong influence of wisdom on early Judaism, considering that the corpus includes a great deal of wisdom-related literature that is relevant beyond the interests of the *yaḥad* movement.

As I argued in Chapter 3, it is necessary to re-evaluate the way in which one imagines, speaks of, and contextualizes the maskil materials from Qumran. The idealized figure can be analysed as the telos of the teachings of the movement associated with the collection and hiding of the Qumran scrolls. Yet, one may also examine the maskil materials as valuable evidence for another Hellenistic

Jewish pedagogue. In what follows, I will argue that wisdom is integral to the movement beyond its notion of the perfect sage and wisdom teacher, as the motif touches upon the very aims and aspirations of the group. Much of the previous scholarship has focused on the topics of revealed wisdom and esoteric knowledge (see more below). I will argue, however, that the type of wisdom cultivated by this movement is also about shared intellectual efforts and a virtuous way of living. These factors urge one to read the scrolls in relation to other early Jewish texts on shared wisdom.

In other words, I seek to communicate the value of communal wisdom as it is portrayed in the Qumran collection. The priestly Jewish group known via the scrolls was one of rituals, strict hierarchies, and rigorous discipline (esp. 1QS 1:18–2:19; 5:23–6:3; 6:8–7:25; 8:16–9:2).[108] As such, however, it endeavoured, in its own Judean milieu of the Hellenistic East, to fulfil a common vision of a perfect way of living. The members were united by a shared perception of the good life in which access to divine knowledge, processes of character formation, constant erudite efforts, and purity played major roles. The vision was seriously collective because it involved the idea of sharing both intellectual resources and a particular lifestyle. It also provided the members with a shared identity, to the extent that the group considered itself to constitute a temple.[109] Based on these factors, the *yaḥad* movement appears to be something akin to a "wisdom body."[110]

Yet, who were these people? It is now widely acknowledged that the activity of the movement was not limited to the settlement at Khirbet Qumran in the Judean wilderness, but it consisted of multiple communities living and operating around Judea.[111] Much remains unclear and open to debate, but the scrolls generally gesture towards an intricate web of related groups. The D and S traditions, which constitute the central rule texts of the movement, tend to use slightly divergent language of the group, preferring either the term עדה (D) or the term יחד (S). Their foci are also somewhat different. D addresses women and issues of family life, thus cancelling the notion of a celibate male group. It further draws a distinction between those walking in "holy perfectness" (בתמים קדש) and those living in camps, taking wives, and having children (CD 7:4–8, par. 19:3). At first sight, S may seem to speak of a single community, but a close reading of the text suggests that many small communities are in fact at stake (1QS 6:1–8, cf. CD 6:11–7:9; 12:19; 12:22–13:2).

To clarify, my aim here is not to write a social history of the movement associated with the scrolls, nor can I map all its intricacy in this brief survey.[112] The complex makeup of the movement should be kept in mind, however, since it suggests that the question is about a network of like-minded people who lived in different places; some of those who composed and/or transmitted the scrolls must also have spent time and studied, or perhaps even lived, in Jerusalem with rich intellectual and cultural resources. Although the exact organization of the movement remains obscure, the larger movement obviously consisted of (at least) two branches that are reflected in the D and S traditions.

Before moving on to analyse specific references to and attestations of shared wisdom in the extant primary sources, I should note that the Qumran scrolls create an overall impression of a group to whom learning and wisdom mattered a great deal. This is demonstrated by their appreciation of the enigmatic Teacher of Righteousness and other pedagogues, their collection of a wealth of wisdom-related compositions, and the frequent emphasis on revealed wisdom in their texts.

First, the mere importance of teachers in the movement's writings pertains to shared wisdom because it shows that the members appreciated and gave authority to pedagogues in particular. Apart from the maskil, the Teacher of Righteousness (מורה הצדק), or the "right teacher" (cf. Hos 10:12), features in some of the scrolls. Scholars debate his role in the history of the movement (cf. CD 1:10–11) and the timing of his dispute with the wicked priest.[113] For the present purposes, it suffices to emphasize that the group cherished the memory of a particular pedagogue, who is never personalized or named. Furthermore, virtually nothing is known about his life or the content of his teaching.[114] However, the teacher is presented as a priest (4Q171 3:15–16; 1QpHab 2:7–9) and as an expounder of the prophets (1QpHab 7:1–5). The term "interpreter of the torah" (דורש התורה) might also refer to him (CD 6:7), though this common assumption is not accepted by all scholars.[115]

Even if the technical terminology applied to classical prophets is never used to characterize the Teacher of Righteousness, his participation in inspired interpretative activity has a prophetic dimension to it.[116] The teacher transmits divine secrets and possesses an unusual understanding of time, as his interpretative task to unfold the mysteries of history is connected with a "calculable and predetermined historical sequence" (1QpHab 2:5–10; 7:3–5).[117] The underlying view that shapes his portrayal assumes that the meaning of prophecies is revealed through an "ongoing process."[118]

As is fit for such a mediatory figure, the legacy of the Teacher of Righteousness involves his voice (קול מורא צדק) to which the members of the movement should listen (CD 20:27–34). The use of the voice motif as an authority-conferring strategy suggests that the movement behind the scrolls regarded itself as a participant in the same revelatory process through which Israel's sacred texts had come to exist.[119] In fact, imagery of light and radiation probably marks the teacher, thus serving to cast him as a new Moses of some sort (1QH^a 12:6–7, cf. Exod 34:29).[120]

Second, the content of the Qumran collection is telling insofar as the movement collected, studied, and transmitted a large number of wisdom-related materials, which signals an emphatic concern for the topic. There are fragmentary remains of the majority of the "wisdom texts" that later ended up in the Jewish and Christian canons of scripture.[121] Moreover, and more intriguingly, the discovery of the scrolls exposed copious ancient Jewish wisdom writings that had been lost for millennia, but now prompt scholars to reconsider the place and significance of wisdom in early Jewish life and thought.[122]

The greater part of the newly discovered material remains fragmentarily, but the evidence remains more than sufficient to demonstrate that wisdom was not a side project for this movement. Its significance is indicated by the mere prevalence of wisdom motifs in numerous scrolls that represent different literary genres and are being rooted in diverse social contexts. Several texts have a pedagogical flavour and count as instructions, but as discussed in Chapter 1, one should not think that wisdom only belongs to the sphere of pedagogy. On the contrary, the Qumran scrolls clarify that wisdom permeates a range of texts, frequently intertwining with apocalyptic, liturgical, mantic, narrative, and other concerns.[123] There is, therefore, no doubt about the vitality of wisdom in the milieu from which the scrolls hail. Scholars, however, have rarely recognized wisdom's centrality in the movement. As George Brooke observes, the wisdom compositions from Qumran have often been studied as separate from the "core activity" of the group that preserved and disseminated them.[124]

Third, the Qumran corpus shows that the movement behind the scrolls cultivated esoteric wisdom and secret knowledge. In the late second temple era, Jewish authors generally stressed wisdom's divine sources and connected wisdom to divine revelation.[125] The members of this movement were also fascinated by and emphasized revealed wisdom, regarding themselves as an elect group with access to knowledge that is hidden from the rest of Israel (e.g., 1QS 8:11–12, 15–16; CD 3:12–14).[126] Such claims show that a wisdom motif – the desire to gain divine knowledge – lies in the very heart of their self-understanding. Particularly much ink has been spilled over the enigmatic concept of *raz nihyeh* (רז נהיה), which is typically translated as the "mystery of being" or the "mystery to come." Based on the remaining evidence, the question is about a form of divine revelation, exposed to the selected few, although *raz nihyeh* is not radically separate from the torah.[127] Furthermore, the Qumran scrolls contain traces of mantic wisdom in the form of divinatory texts and materials concerned with dream interpretation and the decoding of cryptic texts.[128]

As these preliminary observations indicate, the movement behind the Qumran corpus esteemed erudition and revealed wisdom. Yet, the references to the Teacher of Righteousness are relatively rare, which warns against putting too much emphasis on their relevance when it comes to the group's self-understanding, although at least some of its members saw themselves as followers of a particular teacher, whom they set in a continuum with Moses and the prophets, and shared memories of him. Furthermore, the previous focus on secret knowledge may have overshadowed other wisdom motifs of the scrolls, creating an idea of an esoteric and exceptional group that is radically different from the rest of the early Jewish society. The movement is peculiar, and the role of revealed wisdom in the scrolls is distinct, albeit not one of a kind.[129] A close reading shows, however, that the group's wisdom is also about shared intellectual efforts and a virtuous way of life, which encourages one to read the scrolls in relation to other ancient Jewish writings on the desirable lifestyle.

Having discussed the general importance of wisdom in the movement known from the Qumran scrolls, I will now turn to the aims and vision of the movement as they are documented in its own compositions and particularly in its rule texts. The idea of the *yaḥad* as a wisdom body is emphatic in the Community Rule, which sheds light on the values and activities of the group.[130]

In 1QS, which is the best-preserved copy of this writing, dated to *c.* 100–75 BCE, wisdom concerns are clear from the outset, although they are embedded in claims of general piety. The members of the *yaḥad* must "seek God" (לדרוש אל) and "do what is good and right before him" (לעשות הטוב והישר לפניו), (1:1–2) which signals that the good life involves cultivating vertical relationships with the divine.[131] Such a pursuit involves adherence to "all good works" (כול מעשי טוב) and, what is essential to the present purposes, a commitment to perform the virtues of truth, righteousness, and justice (1:5). The need to cultivate and display desirable qualities of character is repeated throughout the work (esp. 2:24; 5:3–4; 8:2). Most extensively, the topic is discussed in the so-called treatise on the two spirits (3:13–4:26), which delineates a set of virtues to be pursued and another set of vices to be avoided (4:2–11), thus charting ideal ways of living for the members of the movement.[132] This shows that the group, which seems to have cultivated deterministic beliefs (e.g., 1QS 3:15; 1QpHab 7:5–14), also valued human agency and individual choice.[133]

The promotion of virtues implies a concern for character formation and training, and perfection is indeed part of the movement's vision. Apart from representing "a most holy dwelling for Aaron" (8:8–9) and "the men of perfect holiness" (8:20), the members of the *yaḥad* constitute "a house of perfection and truth in Israel" (8:9), and they are attached with the aspirational label "the perfect of the way" (8:10, 18, 21; 9:5, 9). The community council must include twelve men and three priests, "perfect in everything that has been revealed from all the torah" (8:1),[134] and the figure of the maskil guides the members so that "they walk perfectly each one with his fellow" (9:18–19). The idiom of perfection is striking as it indicates a willingness to exceed a partial execution of virtue.[135] Despite the focus on the pursuit of human excellence, the capacity to perform "the perfection of the way" (תום דרך) is said to come from God (11:10–11). The celebration of humility is also indicated by the way in which 1QS ends: with praise and open questions that point to the smallness of people and underline God as the source of knowledge and perfection (11:15–20, cf. 10:12).

Another statement made in the beginning of 1QS concerns shared resources. All those who wish to dedicate themselves to God's truth are said to bring not just their property but also "all their knowledge and energies" (כול דעתם וכוחם) to the *yaḥad* of God (1:11–12). This claim explicitly states that the members of the group are expected to share, in addition to material belongings, their mental and intellectual capital. They have a vision of gaining understanding by means of a *communal* effort. Moreover, the possession and maintenance of both mental capital and good conduct are crucial: an officer (פקיד) examines the insight and deeds of every person wishing to join the community (6:13–14), and the candidate, after spending a year in the community, will be retested for these things (6:18).[136] Furthermore, all members of the *yaḥad* are examined every year, which results in the elevation of those showing insight and perfection (5:24).[137]

1QS underlines the desirability of perfection, as well as expressing that the acquisition of perfection takes place in a communal context. The voluntary group performs truth and other virtues "together" (יחד), as is specified in 5:3–4, and each member of the movement, resisting the stubbornness of his heart, is expected to circumcise the foreskin of his inclination in the community (ביחד), as is stated immediately thereafter (5:4–5). These claims allude to both agency and submission: the members choose to join the group voluntarily and then aim at fulfilling a shared vision. By committing themselves to a particular way of life, the members, as Steven Fraade argues, undertake collective ascetic practice and become "purified" through their participation in the group's discipline.[138]

Collective study is an essential part of the movement's way of life, and 1QS contains sections that illustrate the tasks of learning and enquiry as communal activities, which presumably aim at gaining wisdom, knowledge, and understanding. As is specified in 6:6–8 (par. 4Q258 frag. 2:10),

> where there are ten (members) there must not be lacking a person who studies (דורש) the torah day and night continually, one relieving another. The many shall spend the third part of every night of the year together, in order to read (לקרוא) the book, interpret (לדרוש) regulation, and bless (לברך) together.

Echoing the idiom of Josh 1:8 and Ps 1:2, this passage describes the *yaḥad* as being dedicated to the constant study of the torah.[139] Three types of related activities are mentioned, as the members are said to read (קרא), search (דרש), and bless (ברך) together in their gathering. The act of reading the book exposes an orientation to find wisdom from texts, whereas that of searching for or interpreting regulation signals that the movement seeks to discover the contemporary meaning of ancestral laws and to formulate its own legal outlook. The third act, blessing, probably took many forms, including prayers, thanksgivings, and blessings.[140] All these acts are relevant to the notion of lived wisdom, for they count as recurrent practices, but the act of blessing specifically alludes to liturgical performance as a core spiritual exercise. In the context of this movement, such acts of prayer and thanksgiving are not communal only in the sense that they join the members together because they also enable them to form a liturgical communion with the "holy ones," i.e., with angels in heaven with whom they praise God.[141] Thus, the line between the immanent and the transcendent is hazy.

Another pertinent statement on the value and intention of collective study is found in 8:12–16. Drawing on biblical idiom, the author describes the purpose of the group as follows:

> When these become the *yaḥad* in Israel, conforming to these arrangements, they shall separate themselves from the session of the men of injustice, in order to go to the wilderness, to prepare there the way of the Lord. As it is written: "In the wilderness prepare the way of the Lord, make straight in the desert a highway for our God." This means the study of the torah (מדרש התורה), wh[ic]h he commanded through Moses to do, according to everything which has been revealed (from) time to time, and according to that which the prophets have revealed by his holy spirit.

The passage begins with a statement on the group's aim to prepare a way in the wilderness (cf. Isa 40:3), and the same motif is repeated soon after in 9:19–20.

The claim in question does not necessarily express geographical and sociological isolation, even though it is likely that the movement contained at least one community living in the desert of Judea. Yet, the claim does signal a desire to withdraw for the sake of an ideal way of living, whatever that may mean in practice, and it connotes the idea of wilderness as a singular locus of purification and divine revelation.[142]

The following reference to study (מדרש) exposes a concern for the interpretation of Israel's divine instruction mediated by Moses and the prophets.[143] The nuances of the term מדרש vary in the scrolls.[144] Yet, this interpretative task of the *yaḥad* carries some revelatory power: it aims at the discovery of the divine will and thus pertains to revealed wisdom. The group's מדרש is set in a continuum with earlier moments of divine revelation, thus alluding to an idea of ongoing prophetic activity. The revelatory event at Sinai did not fulfil all needs of Israel, which means that revelatory experiences continue.[145] For this movement, therefore, divine revelation is interlocked with the study and interpretation of inherited ancestral texts. This implies that education and the esoteric intertwine in their self-understanding.

Based on the S tradition, the *yaḥad* movement considered an ideal way of living to comprise of communal training and study, which aimed at the perfection of character and behaviour. While the concern for shared wisdom is rather full-blown here, other rule texts of the movement further attest to ideas that count as manifestations of their pursuit of communal wisdom.

In the Damascus Document, the covenanters are associated with the wise and understanding ones (CD 6:2–3, cf. 1QSa 1:27–8; 2:16). Moreover, the faithful members are characterized as "the disciples of God" (למודי אל) and "the men of knowledge" (אנשי דעות) (20:4). As in S, they are to strive for perfection (2:15–16). On two occasions, the group receives the distinctive epithet בית התורה, or the "house of the torah" (20:10, 13), which only appears in this particular text.[146] The designation is relevant to the present purposes since it could also be understood as the "house of wisdom," considering the close relationship between wisdom and torah in the Qumran scrolls, to the extent that the concepts are equated with other in 4Q525 frag. 2 ii 3–4 (see also 4Q185 frag. 1–2 ii).[147] Be that as it may, the use of the term "house" in the aforementioned designation creates an image of a shared dwelling-place, or even an image of a family, where people come together in order to gain understanding of the torah/wisdom.

Like the Community Rule, the Damascus Document accents the value of a common way of life. The desired lifestyle involves the sharing of financial resources, which enables the group to take care of prosocial concerns (CD 14:12–16), and it underlines the significance of purity (10:10–13; 11:18–22; 12:1–20). Those who choose this particular way of living are guided by priests, who are expected to have expertise in the book of Hagi (ספר ההגי) and in the principles of the covenant (10:4–6; 13:2; 14:7–8; see also 1QSa 1:7), as well as by other personnel. Whereas the Community Rule stresses the pedagogical role of the maskil, the Damascus Document often mentions the figure of the mevaqqer (מבקר), or the examiner, who sometimes takes the role of a gentle and loving teacher (13:6–8; 15:14–15).[148] The didactic functions of the two figures resemble each other, but the emphasis on the maskil's pedagogical role is nevertheless distinctive.[149]

As briefly mentioned, the Damascus Document differentiates between those who walk in "holy perfectness" (בתמים קדש) and those who live in camps, take wives, and have children (CD 7:4–8, par. 19:3). The exact meaning of the former remains unsure, but it recapitulates the significance of perfection in the movement's thought. The latter, in turn, expresses the presence of women and children in the movement. It raises the question of whether women and children took part in education, which seems to have been an integral component of the movement's shared wisdom.

In antiquity, a great deal of teaching happened in the context of family, but the Qumran scrolls cast education as a communal responsibility.[150] Women and children, too, are expected to receive at least some tuition: the D manuscripts attest to the instruction of children (CD 13:17–18; 4Q266 frag. 9 iii 6–7) and preserve teaching on sexual relations of married people (4Q267 frag. 9 vi 4–5; 4Q270 frag. 7 i 12–13).[151] Furthermore, it is possible to interpret the masculine plural forms used in the text as including women (e.g., CD 1:1; 2:2), which would imply an idea of an inclusive albeit androcentric covenant, suggesting that women were also regarded as belonging to the text's addressees. However, as observed by Maxine Grossman, the Damascus Document allows for multiple gendered readings depending on the reference material, i.e., on the other scrolls in the light of which the text is read.[152]

Even though the evidence of the Damascus Document is open to different interpretations, the idea of women's involvement in education receives further support from another rule text, the Rule of the Congregation, which requires that all the precepts of the covenant and all the regulations are to be taught to women and children (1QSa 1:4–5). Admittedly, the question is about an eschatological vision concerning the congregation of Israel in the final days, but women and children are involved in education according to this ideal social reality, and the practices projected to a future time might mirror those of the movement.¹⁵³ Therefore, it seems safe to conclude that this group was barely committed to the provision of equal intellectual opportunities. Yet, women and children were informed, or at least they were supposed to be informed, concerning the basis of their common way of life.

Yet, were women regarded as active participants in the group's ideal way of living, or as active contributors to its shared wisdom? The Community Rule remains silent on women, which leaves the gendered aspect of the movement elusive, but the Damascus Document, as will be seen, enables one to reflect on the women's role in the communal enterprise. I will argue that the text even preserves evidence for women's active agency in a life of virtue.

In the Damascus Document, the references to women tend to revolve around sex or reproduction. They cluster around the issues of marriage and divorce (CD 13:16–17; 4Q266 frag. 9 iii 4–5; 4Q269 frag. 9:1–2); the ordeal of the *sotah* and the reputation of a new bride (4Q269 frag. 9:4–8; 4Q270 frag. 2 i 16–19; frag. 4:1–9; 4Q271 frag. 3:15); menstruation, birth, and post-partum purity (4Q266 frag. 6 ii 1–13; 4Q272 frag. 1 ii 7–10; 4Q273 frag. 5:4–5); and proper sexual practices within marriage (4Q267 frag. 9 vi 4–5; 4Q270 frag. 2 ii 15–17).¹⁵⁴ As the list of topics demonstrates, the passages on women largely pertain to marriage, including its preconditions and execution, as well as related purity regulations. Such a catalogue is barely surprising, considering that the people behind the scrolls were deeply committed to the cultivation of holiness that requires purity.¹⁵⁵

Women had a key role to play in the implementation of purity, as they needed to know related regulations in order to fulfil the movement's vision of an ideal way of life. Surely, the perspective of the texts is androcentric in that women receive attention in relation to an issue that directly affects the life of men.¹⁵⁶ As such, however, the references to purity reveal a core aspect of the movement's idea of shared wisdom. For its members, purity was a wisdom concern – it was about the good life and aspiration to strive for perfection – and not just a ritual issue. As Grossman observes, the marital life in this movement, along with its many constraints and high expectations, was grounded in an ideology of perfection.¹⁵⁷ Once the role of purity as a core virtue is recognized, women's agency turns out to be crucial in the fulfilment of the envisioned perfection.¹⁵⁸

The argument that a life of purity is essential to exemplarity may seem surprising since purity is often perceived as a ritual category. In the scrolls, however, purity is also an ethical category.¹⁵⁹ Virtue is not just about the mind, but also about the body, which signifies that purity is a component of an ideal lifestyle. The Testament of Qahat, for one, explains that the observance of Qahat's teaching means dedication to the inheritance left by ancestors, including the performance of seven desirable qualities: truth, justice, honesty, perfection, purity, holiness, and priesthood (4Q542 frag. 1 i 12–13). This list demonstrates that the author of this Aramaic text considered the virtues of purity and holiness to nurture an ideal order, which signals some overlap between the categories of ritual and ethical.[160]

Purity pertains to priestly thinking, but I wish to note that priestly thinking does not exclude wisdom and ethics, as notions of goodness and right order tend to intertwine in it.[161] It would be misleading, therefore, to think that women are of interest "only" regarding purity issues in the Qumran scrolls. Rather, one may conclude that they receive attention in relation to the issue of purity, which is integral to the movement's conception of virtue and the good life.

The complex social realities behind the scrolls remain open to debate. Clearly, however, the question is about a cluster of interlinked groups with peculiar ideological emphases. As I have demonstrated, these people were united by a vision of an ideal lifestyle and an aspiration to carry it out. The S tradition, in particular, spells out that their chosen way of life is supposed to be one of perfection. To achieve perfection, the members of the group share intellectual resources and seek a life of holiness and purity. They also cast learning as a communal effort and project. The D tradition imagines the group as a house of the torah, which could also be interpreted as the house of wisdom, and it explicitly recognizes the roles of women and children in the common enterprise. Many of the obligations that concern women revolve around purity, but I have argued that they are not radically separate from "wisdom concerns," as purity regulations, too, indicate a wish to cultivate a desirable order, thus suggesting some overlap between the ethical and ritual spheres.

Reading the Qumran scrolls as evidence for a group driven by a shared vision of the good life provides an alternative perspective on the corpus. Scholars have highlighted claims of separation, with the unfortunate outcome that non-specialists often know the scrolls as documentation for inner conflicts within early Judaism. My aim here is not to deny tensions between different groups, for such tensions existed, but I am concerned that the scholarly obsession in matters of dispute has overshadowed other crucial issues in the scrolls. In particular, scholars have not recognized their full potential for ancient intellectual cultures and discussions on ideal ways of living.[162] Thus, I hope that my brief investigation serves to map new lines of enquiry, inspiring one to read the scrolls as sources of wisdom and virtue discourses, and as sources of a group devoted to study and spiritual exercise. A concern for wisdom is something that the people behind the scrolls shared with each other, but it also connects them to many other ancient groups, whether Jewish or not.

My proposal that the movement's interest in wisdom highlights points of contact between it and other ancient groups resonates with the voices of those scholars who have argued for a need to deconstruct the idea of an isolationist movement. Such a need becomes obvious when one acknowledges that the content of the scrolls is a product of complex cultural collaboration. Levine, for example, observes that many of the group's beliefs and practices are rooted in the Hellenistic world, including its eastern parts. As examples, he lists such issues as determinism, dualism, the solar calendar, angelology, organizational patterns, communal property, and the desire to create a utopia.[163] Similarly, the inclusion of Greek manuscripts in the Qumran collection, as well as other traces of engagement with Greek literary culture, speaks for cultural interaction.[164]

Recently, Charlotte Hempel has challenged the "particularist paradigm" based on several factors. Revisiting the idea that the scrolls would originate from a separationist group, she argues that the people behind them "are emerging as less special and different from their ... contemporaries." In her opinion, many factors – textual pluriformity, the location of the site, ideas of the temple, elements shared with other Jews, and the earlier over-emphasis on the Teacher of Righteousness – suggest that the movement's intellectual, social, and cultural life was richer than previously expected.[165] I would add to Hempel's observations that the emphasis on wisdom is yet another feature that sets the movement known from the Qumran scrolls into a wider Jewish – and, in fact, ancient Mediterranean – context of cultivating a learned culture and a virtuous lifestyle.

In summary, the Qumran scrolls present an early Jewish group that seeks a life of wisdom and virtue through a communal effort, thus developing ancient Israelite traditions in a new Hellenistic context, even if wisdom takes its own shape in their understanding. In this enterprise, both study and everyday excellence are valued. Wisdom is lived and embodied through virtues, including holiness and purity, which implies that women, too, are active agents of the good life. These people mainly engaged with writings in Hebrew and Aramaic, which means that "philosophy" was not a native category to them. From a modern viewpoint, however, their activities look like practices that are called philosophical in Greek Jewish writings. This makes it likely that the learned members of the movement, who were aware of the world beyond Judea, could observe parallels between their own search for wisdom and the same search elsewhere. Instead of being indifferent to contemporary debates on wisdom, they focused on constructing their own take on the ideal way of life. The group did not hesitate to promote its superiority or to pose competing claims. Rather, it was eager to add another voice to the chorus of wise lifestyles in the eastern Mediterranean milieu.[166]

Conclusions

Philo's account of the Therapeutae, his and Josephus' writings on the Essenes, and the Qumran scrolls all shed light on ideas of shared wisdom in Jewish antiquity, inviting one to explore communal pursuits of wisdom and virtue. Philo's *De vita contemplativa* portrays a group of philosophers from Roman Alexandria who withdraw from the city in order to dedicate themselves to a life of intellectual and spiritual exercise. The sources on the Essenes express the value of mundane and manual labour, casting everyday life as the arena of philosophical practice in Syria-Palestine. Finally, the Qumran scrolls outline a group driven by a vision of an ideal way of life, which involves incessant study, character formation, and a life of purity. In each of these accounts, there is an aspirational element to the way in which the desirable lifestyle is imagined and outlined. They all indicate, albeit in different ways, that wisdom is not separate from behaviour, but it involves character formation and lived practices.

A commitment to virtuous conduct is essential to the aspirational projects of all three groups, and the extant portraits of the good life generally emphasize the importance of the ethical; Philo's remarks on the Essenes even elucidate the primacy of ethics.[167] As for the cultivation of specific virtues, the sources on all three groups promote moderation or even renunciation. There are ascetic tendencies, including the avoidance of extravagance and the stress on simplicity, whereas ancient Israelite wisdom books celebrate material prosperity as a (relative) good.[168] These values of contentment, which are sociologically relevant insofar as they imply a privileged status, are basic values of ancient philosophy and common tropes in related writings.[169] This does not mean, however, that they should be interpreted as uncommon foreign influence. Rather, ascetic practices belong to a morally and spiritually alert life according to multiple ancient Jewish texts.[170]

All the textual sources discussed in this chapter refer to communal practices, including education and liturgical performance. Study and interpretation of ancestral writings seem to be key exercises, which signals the value of inherited texts as a source of wisdom and insight, although Josephus' Essenes also explore medicine, which alludes to a holistic concern for the well-being of the body and the mind. The study of ancestral texts is further relevant in relation to ancient philosophy. According to Hadot, the spread of learning centres throughout the Mediterranean region changed the methods of instructing philosophy in the Roman period. The change meant easier access to the teachings of philosophical schools and enabled the blend of respective ideas. Meanwhile, a "living continuity" between many teachers and students as well as their "ancestors" was lost along with the rise of such learning centres. The significance of texts increased and commentary became a mode of philosophical practice, as well as a means to maintain the connection with the predecessors.[171]

The portraits of the three Jewish groups resist a distinction between religious and secular spheres. While education plays a key role in each case, the question is not about the mastery of technical skills, but about a holistic process in which noetic and spiritual concerns intertwine. Technical skills may be at stake, as in the case of the Essenes who embody virtue in their everyday efforts of agriculture and artisanship, but these pursuits, too, manifest forms of spiritual exercise and character training. Similarly, teachers serve as spiritual authorities in diverse contexts. The authors of the Qumran scrolls perhaps put more emphasis on contemporary pedagogues than Philo and Josephus, who stress the importance of Moses as the founding figure, teacher, and lawgiver. One should remember, however, that both the maskil and the Teacher of Righteousness might count as a new Moses of some sort. Hence, all the Jewish groups studied in this chapter associate themselves with Moses, whether directly or through a later mediatory figure.

In addition to parallels, there are differences between the portraits of shared wisdom. As for social isolation, the Therapeutae are committed to a strict withdrawal from the city, even if it happens in the context of a collective, whereas the Essenes contribute to the surrounding society through mundane labour. The Qumran scrolls send mixed signals in this respect: there are no explicit comments on the topic, but the movement's members live in different locations and probably work in local communities.

Moreover, there is some variation concerning the gendered aspect of the wise life. The Therapeutae consist of female and male philosophers, and women serve as elders within the group. Philo presents the Essenes as an all-male community, whilst Josephus' remarks on them signal that marriage and family life enable a life of virtue, albeit with restrictions. The Qumran scrolls leave many questions open, but they offer some limited evidence of women's education, and their frequent stress on purity transforms women into key agents of a virtuous lifestyle. Both sexes, therefore, add to the shared project of loving and cultivating wisdom, but not consistently throughout all the sources.

5

Conclusions

In the context of Jewish antiquity, wisdom is more than a body of texts or an abstract quality of character. A close look at the literary and cultural representations of wisdom in texts from the Persian, Hellenistic, and early Roman periods demonstrates the significance of a phenomenon that I have described as lived wisdom. Wisdom, in other words, involves a myriad of lived and bodily practices, thus including embodiment. Wisdom also counts as performative insofar as it has the effect of executing external actions. Importantly, wisdom is something to be exercised and executed at the level of both an individual and a community.

A modern reader of ancient texts may contextualize them in different ways. This study on lived wisdom can be associated with approaches that pose conceptual questions on Jewish texts. Traditionally, scholars working on biblical and cognate writings have primarily concentrated on issues of social, political, or religious history, but there are other questions to be addressed if one wishes to comprehend the richness of ancient Jewish culture and life. As argued by Najman, "we should not assume that political contextualisation or religious affiliation is the only way of doing history, or the most important." Mapping alternative modes of enquiry, Najman suggests that "intellectual, cultural and spiritual practices also constitute contexts within which texts can be rendered intelligible."[1] In her own study from which these quotations originate, Najman analyses ancient practices of authorship. In this book, I have sought to explore another intersection of intellectual, cultural, and spiritual practice in Jewish antiquity by drawing attention to the phenomenon of lived wisdom, which also touches upon questions of religious and social history.

In Chapter 1, I introduced the purpose and context of this book, which has been prompted by the observation that scholars continue to be obsessed with wisdom as a literary genre, even if they acknowledge that the evidence escapes any neat categorizations. I explained that I do not wish to close this conversation, which has its own value, but the exclusive focus on wisdom as a category of literature has had the unfortunate consequence of narrowing down research interests: scholars have come to ignore other relevant questions that apply to wisdom. With an aim to shake the current state of the art, I argue that alternative questions may help one reveal hitherto neglected aspects of wisdom in Jewish antiquity, specifically enabling a more holistic understanding of wisdom as a cultural phenomenon.

I also discussed the scholarly matrix of my study, which draws on the recent research on wisdom and education, in Chapter 1. In particular, this book is indebted to studies that highlight the formative intention and function of ancient Jewish texts on wisdom, i.e., that their authors wished to contribute to the moral, intellectual, and spiritual growth of their intended audiences. Building on these developments in scholarship, I proposed that it is worthwhile to approach wisdom as a phenomenon that covers lived and embodied practices. In so doing, it is necessary to deconstruct generic and canonical boundaries, as well as the artificial distinction between Judaism and Hellenism, in order to understand the variety of Jewish wisdom and its rootedness in the wider ancient eastern Mediterranean context.

An investigation into "lived wisdom" demonstrates that wisdom is not just about texts and thinking, but also about prudent behaviour, social commitments, and ideal ways of living. The transition from literary text to life is indeed complicated and remains difficult, as one must rely on literary representations of wisdom and a wise life(style), and one obviously cannot read these accounts as directly reflecting socio-historical realities. Despite these challenges, the extant texts enable an exploration of "lived wisdom" as they inform one about how ancient authors imagined and depicted desirable social realities and ways of life. Such accounts are idealized but not detached from life, for ideals are rooted in social practices.[2] Hence, the selected sources presumably echo real-life practices or, in the possible case of fictitious accounts, they illustrate how one *ought* to perform wisdom in everyday life. I argue, therefore, that an analysis of "lived wisdom" is not limited to the question of what actually happened in Jewish communities at particular moments of time, but it aims at examining the various agendas and aspirations sketched out by the ancient authors.

After outlining the aims of this book in Chapter 1, I provided three case studies on wisdom's lived dimensions in Jewish antiquity in the subsequent Chapters 2–4. These analyses concentrated on the figure of the sage, with a particular focus on the conception of the wise person as an object of emulation; the lifestyle of the wisdom teacher, including activities and exercises that constitute its daily rhythm; and the pursuit of wisdom as a communal enterprise that applies to groups of people. In all these cases, as I hope to have shown, wisdom pertains to ideal ways of living and is understood to shape the seeker or possessor of wisdom.

In Chapter 2, I examined literary and cultural representations of the wise person in the ancient Jewish tradition. In particular, I traced the development and rise of the notion of the ideal sage, i.e., the idea of the sage as an exemplar and a living embodiment of wisdom, thus showing how ancient Israelite ideas of the sage changed over time. The Hebrew Bible displays a number of wise figures early on, and it is worth highlighting that with regard to lived wisdom, חכמה is frequently associated with various physical and technical skills. Yet, Jewish texts from the second temple period, beginning with the book of Proverbs, suggest an increasing focus on the wise person (חכם) as a learned intellectual.

The persona and the inner life of the sage are first outlined in the book of Qoheleth. Soon after, in the later Hellenistic and early Roman periods, several authors elaborate on the importance of emulation, casting the sage as a template, whom his pupils should follow. These sources include both (originally) Semitic writings from Judea and Greek Jewish texts from the diaspora. Apart from describing contemporary sages, I observed that the authors devote attention to ancestral perfection, i.e., they display biblical figures of the past as prototypical exemplars. For example, Philo of Alexandria celebrates Moses as the superior sage and template to be followed, whereas the author of Wisdom of Solomon transforms the ancient king into a perfect and pious wise person.

The occurrence of the model-sage in Jewish writings should not be taken for granted because the authors make the motif explicit in the later Hellenistic era, i.e., during a time when Jewish texts generally indicate an intermingling of cultural elements, both "local" and "Greek." Markedly, Greek sources discuss the ideal sage and the significance of emulation in the pursuit of the good life already in the classical period. This suggests that the wider *Zeitgeist* of the Hellenistic era prompted early Jewish authors to spell out the conception of the model-sage, including his role as a living embodiment of wisdom and an object of emulation. In so doing, however, they built on the ancient Near Eastern and Hebrew traditions, specifically drawing on the distinctive father–son discourse used in these sources. Furthermore, even if the exemplary wise person is a product of cultural collaboration, Jewish and Greek accounts of the sage remain far from identical. This demonstrates that the figure of the sage always hails from a specific context, serving the needs and agendas of local communities.

The ideal sage is integral to the study of lived wisdom because the extant literary accounts of the figure display formative, aspirational, and even perfectionist propensities: the sage represents the epitome of wisdom and an object of emulation, thus illustrating the end-goal of instruction. As an exemplar, the wise person has the power to shape the lives of other people: those who desire and seek wisdom should orient themselves according to the template and replicate his virtuous way of life. In the ancient Mediterranean milieu, therefore, wisdom is not just about living one's own life, but also about renewing the life of someone else in doing so.

In Chapter 3, I explored the lifestyle of the wisdom teacher, including the types of practices that constitute the rhythm of his everyday life. By means of this examination, I wished to move beyond the question of what wisdom *is* and proceed to ask how a wise person *lives*. The Hebrew Bible, in fact, displays several wisdom teachers broadly understood, if one regards teachers of the torah (i.e., the divine wisdom of Israel) as such. At times, the portrayal of biblical pedagogues hints at lived practices such as liturgical performance or textual interpretation. It was shown, however, that the extant sources indicate a change starting from the Hellenistic period, when the teacher's daily exercises begin to receive more attention.

The book of Qoheleth underlines pedagogical and scribal tasks that belong to the life of the wise teacher, whereas the book of Ben Sira and the Qumran scrolls enumerate a plethora of exercises undertaken by two pedagogues from Judea. In the former case, the learned lifestyle of the ideal figure involves teaching, scribal tasks, textual interpretation, imitation of exemplars, observation of the world, contemplation, self-mastery, prayer, prophecy, and prosocial deeds. The figure of the maskil known from the scrolls, in turn, enacts and performs his wisdom by means of instruction, torah piety, reception of esoteric knowledge, spiritual judgement, prayer, performance of songs, and conduct of apotropaic rituals.

The term חכמה is associated with desirable behaviour already in the Hebrew Bible. Nevertheless, I have shown that the materials from the Hellenistic and early Roman periods demonstrate a new and striking interest in the erudite and virtuous lifestyle of a contemporary pedagogue, who enacts his wisdom and invites the audience to do the same. The practices attributed to the teachers such as scribal tasks or liturgical exercises vary a great deal, which signals slightly different foci or values of different Jewish groups, but each account points to a notion of wisdom as a way of life that requires dedication, cultivation, and constant exercise. Wisdom, in other words, is not a skill that one can master after a short and intensive period of training, but it involves the holistic formation and socialization of a person. This means that wisdom presumes aspiration, i.e., a willingness to pursue immaterial capital and a lifetime of committed practice.

I have argued that the value of exercise in early Jewish pedagogy is striking both in itself and vis-à-vis the wider Mediterranean context of Judean teachers. In particular, it raises the question of how Judean pedagogues comprehended their pursuit of wisdom in relation to contemporary Greek philosophy in which spiritual and mental exercise was essential. While Jewish teachers produced local educational programmes, they must have been aware of wisdom's inherently cross-cultural nature, which is already evident in the international content of the wisdom texts in the Hebrew Bible. The same assumption is supported by the occasional affinity of early Jewish texts with Greek ideas and practices and by their authors' geographical location near Hellenistic learning centres.

Conspicuously, both Jewish and Greek traditions posited that the pursuit of wisdom presumes a life that embodies and conveys one's values. This suggests that Jewish teachers and "lovers of learning" (cf. Sirach, Prologue, lines 10–14) could perceive of themselves as akin to philosophers, and intercultural communication perhaps facilitated the new focus on the lifestyle of the teacher. Simultaneously, Jews cultivated spiritual exercises flowing from their own tradition, including torah piety, prayer, liturgical performance, and prophetic activity. Their learned culture, in other words, resisted a distinction between sacred and secular.

In Chapter 4, I turned to shared wisdom in early Jewish communities, i.e., to the notion of wisdom as a communal enterprise, which excludes the idea that wisdom would only have been understood as the property of an individual in antiquity. I first discussed the ancient (both non-Jewish and Jewish) evidence for the identification of Judaism with a philosophy, for such claims are fundamental to the collective portraits of the wise life, which are written in Greek and hail from the diaspora. Thereafter, I examined the evidence for three early Jewish groups: the Therapeutae known from Philo's *De vita contemplativa*, the classical accounts of the Essenes by Philo and Josephus, and the movement that lurks behind the Qumran scrolls. The extant sources vary as they originate from disparate geographical and cultural contexts, ranging from Judea to Alexandria to Rome, but I have argued that they all communicate a form of the shared aspect of wisdom in one way or the other.

First, Philo's *De vita contemplativa* displays a group of female and male philosophers from Roman Alexandria who constitute a community of like-minded people. These disciples of Moses withdraw from the city to the Mareotic Lake in order to dedicate themselves to intellectual and spiritual exercise in the form of asceticism, liturgical acts, and communal gatherings. The chosen way of life, which involves the pursuit of a mystical vision of God, aims at transforming them into citizens of both heaven and earth. Hence, the local philosophers both remain dedicated to an ancestral tradition and seek to fulfil a cosmopolitan dream. The lack of details on their thought has puzzled scholars, but I argue that the extant evidence does not look odd if one reads the treatise as a communal "biography" of the lifestyle of the Therapeutae. In *De vita contemplativa*, Philo specifically focuses on transformative training and cultivation of the soul that were integral parts of Hellenistic philosophy. In so doing, he produces new Greek literature on the prospects of lived and shared wisdom.

Second, the sources on the Essenes stress the everyday life as an arena of philosophical practice, underlining that manual and mundane labour are not separate from the pursuit of wisdom. In his discussion on these "athletes of virtue," Philo even explicates the primacy of ethics, which elevates the pursuit of a good life. Josephus, in turn, attributes exceptional self-mastery to the Essenes while also observing their learned efforts and family life as a context of practising virtue. Moving beyond the frequently summoned binary construction that separates philosophy and religion, Philo's and Josephus' texts indicate that early Jewish wisdom involves both philosophical and religious convictions and practices, which – from the viewpoint of the ancients – comprise one entity.[3] These accounts should be understood neither as imperfect versions of Greek philosophy nor as dubious applications of Jewish tradition. Rather, they are voices that broaden our notion of ancient philosophy.

Third, the scrolls found at the caves in the vicinity of Khirbet Qumran sketch out another Jewish movement dedicated to wisdom, even if wisdom takes its own shape in their understanding. These people from Judea were not indifferent to contemporary conversations on the good life, but they concentrated on promoting their own notion of it. According to their vision, an ideal way of living involves study, performance of virtues, and divine–human communication. In particular, the group cultivated a life of holiness and stressed purity as an essential component of virtue, which points to the implementation of wisdom in the private sphere and to women's active role as agents of the good life. Scholars have often focused on tensions between this movement and other branches of early Judaism, but I argue that their emphatic concern for wisdom helps one map out parallels between the group and other contemporary groups. Surely, the term "philosophy" is not native to them, but their activities largely resemble practices that are named as philosophical in Greek Jewish writings from the same period.

Overall, the texts on shared wisdom promote values of contentment and communal practices, including but not being limited to study and interpretation of ancestral writings, liturgical performance, and cultivation of social virtues. They cast education as a process in which the noetic and the spiritual intertwine. Contemporary teachers are mentioned, but the groups also associate themselves with Moses, either directly or through a later mediatory figure. Philo describes the Therapeutae as the disciples of Moses, Josephus mentions the Essenes' veneration of the Lawgiver, and the authors of the Qumran scrolls cast the maskil as a new Moses of some sort. Yet, there are obvious differences between the accounts, especially regarding the amount of social isolation and gender. The idea of withdrawal is not uncommon, but the sources on the Essenes recognize the value of taking part in civic life. At times, the pursuit of wisdom appears to be an all-male project, but women are present and contribute to the collective effort according to *De vita contemplativa* and the Qumran scrolls.

Ancient Israelite wisdom, therefore, had lived and embodied dimensions early on, such as the idea that חכמה manifests itself in technical skills. Yet, Jewish wisdom became more closely associated with lifestyle in the second temple period; it came to constitute a way of life with an array of practices to be exercised and performed. In the Hellenistic and early Roman times, Jewish authors actively operated within wisdom discourse, producing new materials on pedagogical ideals and professionals, forms of spiritual and mental exercise, and desirable ways of living that apply to both individuals and groups of like-minded people. The sources document and promote local expressions of the wise and virtuous life that are rooted in their respective contexts, but they also make sense and can be read within a wider Mediterranean viewpoint, given their tendency to express the broader Hellenistic trends of their time.[4]

Considering the openness and cross-cultural resonances of wisdom in the Hebrew Bible, it is hardly surprising that a considerable amount of cultural interaction took place in the sphere of wisdom by the second temple period. As suggested by Burton Mack, wisdom enabled the Jewish culture to begin a conversation and exchange with the wider Hellenistic world, including constructive "translations" thereof. Wisdom, in other words, provided an "intellectual fabric" for cultural exchanges, as Mack describes the mediatory function of wisdom discourse.[5] As I hope to have shown over the course of this investigation, some of these exchanges took place in Semitic contexts where Jewish writers discussed wisdom and the good life in Hebrew and Aramaic. Other authors, for their part, produced texts that are Jewish as well as representing ancient Greek culture and literature.[6]

In this book, I have analysed early Jewish conceptions of wisdom in their immediate contexts, specifically observing the value of lifestyle and that of spiritual and mental practice in the ancient Mediterranean milieu. Yet, in order to anticipate future research, I finally wish to reflect on two possible trajectories of research that could flow from this study. It is worth considering the afterlife of lived wisdom beyond the second temple period, but one could also undertake cross-cultural comparative work instead of charting diachronic developments.

First, although this book on wisdom and lifestyle has largely focused on the Jewish tradition in the Persian, Hellenistic, and early Roman eras, the study of "lived wisdom" does not need to be limited to the context of second temple Judaism. On the contrary, the idea of living, exercising, and embodying wisdom could also be associated with other periods of the human past, and the idea indeed continued to flourish in new contexts in the Common Era.

For example, after the second temple era, the rabbis became major agents in Jewish intellectual life. Particularly Avot, a tractate of the Mishnah, illustrates processes of character formation in the rabbinic culture.[7] More broadly, the rabbis regarded themselves as חכמים and focused on חכמה, which for them meant the torah.[8] As such, the early rabbinic tradition aimed at cultivating "a culture and society of sages and their disciples by engaging them together in the … practice of Torah study."[9] In fact, the torah study of the rabbis can be seen as a mode of spiritual exercise in the world of late antiquity. Michael Satlow argues that it represents Greco-Roman spirituality expressed in Jewish idiom; it is a form of ascetic practice meant to heal and perfect one's self.[10] At times, ascetic tensions are also visible in the rabbinic literature. These tensions touch upon many issues, including fasting and mystical experience, but a great deal of the discussion results from the tension when the rabbis orient themselves between two major demands, the torah study and one's familial duties.[11]

Similarly, the emerging Christian tradition continued to focus on the cultivation of wisdom. Jesus in fact can be included among the wisdom teachers of the late second temple period who model ways of living, as briefly observed in Chapter 3. Likewise, many Christian teachers from late antiquity emphasized the importance of lifestyle in their instruction.[12] Moreover, it is pertinent that lived and embodied practices gained prevalence in Christian communities across time and place. Early Christian notions of the body, in particular, sparked a concern for regulating diet and sexuality for the sake of virtuous life.[13] Yet, spiritual exercise was not only about food and sex for these people. Rather, teachers and ascetics of late antiquity promoted numerous practices related to social life, matters of household, appearance, gestures and manners, eating and drinking, sleeping, laughter, bodily exercises, and the fighting of demons.[14] The sum of variegated exercises suggests that lived wisdom and virtue, for early Christians, was about dedicated practice and behaviour.

Second, while I have examined Judaism in its Mediterranean milieu, I would like to note that the appreciation of intellectual pursuits and forms of exercise was not limited to this geographical area in the ancient world. These phenomena could also be analysed in the context of the so-called Axial Age culture, which refers to processes of transition in Eurasian cultures that began in the middle of the first millennium BCE in China, India, Israel, and Greece. Scholars have observed that an intensification of theoretical cultures marks the period, including the capacity to undertake critical "second-order thinking."[15] Another feature of the Axial Age culture is even more salient for the present purposes: an increasing emphasis on training and self-exercises.[16] These developments inform one about wider trajectories across Eurasian cultures and may help one locate Jewish wisdom discourse (as well as Greek philosophy) in a broader cross-cultural framework: wisdom involves forms of training and repeated practice, which underlines its role as a type of self-exercise.[17] Thus, in order to expand the horizons of analysis, it will be worthwhile to examine Jewish sources on wisdom in an ever-widening cross-cultural paradigm in future.

To conclude, wisdom represents more than a mode of literature in Jewish antiquity. The question of wisdom as a literary genre is surely worth pondering, but it is not the only or necessarily the most significant question that one might pose to ancient texts on wisdom. As I have argued in this book, wisdom appears, based on the extant literary sources, as a phenomenon that encompasses both lifestyle and practice. While the texts on wisdom are often concerned with the knowledge one might need for right behaviour, the ultimate task and purpose of wisdom is not to inform, but to form the one who desires and seeks her.[18] The accounts invite one to pursue and perform ideal ways of living, whether through emulation of the ideal sage, forms of spiritual and mental exercise, or participation in the communal pursuit of wisdom.

Notes

Chapter 1

1. When I use the term "religion" to characterize ancient Judaism or to speak of ancient religious practices, I refer to a phenomenon and not to a concept. I do not claim that "religion" would have existed in the modern sense of the word in antiquity. Recently, see Carlin A. Barton and Daniel Boyarin, *Imagine No Religion: How Modern Abstractions Hide Ancient Realities* (New York: Fordham University Press, 2016). It is sometimes argued that the term Ἰουδαϊσμός, which first appears in 2 Maccabees (2:21; 8:1; 14:38), perhaps dating back to the second century BCE, refers to Judaism as a religion. Yet, the question is about a Judean way of life; see Brent Nongbri, *Before Religion: A History of a Modern Concept* (New Haven, CT: Yale University Press, 2013), 46–50. Similarly, scholars debate the terms "Judean" or "Jew." Steve Mason, in particular, has argued that the former is a more accurate rendering as it communicates the idea of an ethnic group with distinctive traditions; see Mason, "Jews, Judaeans, Judaizing, Judaism: Problems of Categorization in Ancient History," *Journal for the Study of Judaism* 38 (2007): 457–512. I agree that one should not think of Jews only as practisers of a specific religion (see more below on Jews as philosophers). In this book, however, I use the term "Jew" in order not to overemphasize the importance of a specific geographical location (Judea) at a time when Jews lived across the eastern Mediterranean region and beyond.
2. On the body as "a productive starting point for analyzing culture and self," see Thomas J. Csordas, "Embodiment as a Paradigm for Anthropology," *Ethos* 18 (1990): 5–47. The focus on embodiment means, as Csordas explains, that the body is regarded as "the subject of culture." In the context of biblical studies, Joan E. Taylor has described body as "an entity on which religious ideology is printed, both as a single artefact and in relation to other bodies." See Taylor, "Introduction," in *The Body in Biblical, Christian and Jewish Texts*, ed. Joan E. Taylor (London: Bloomsbury T&T Clark, 2014), xv–xxi, esp. xv.
3. With the term "performance," therefore, I simply refer to the execution of an action, task, or function. Importantly, performance is not something that would be confined to ritual alone; see Roy A. Rappaport, *Ritual and Religion in the Making of Humanity* (Cambridge: Cambridge University Press, 1999), 115.
4. Michael V. Fox, "Concepts of Wisdom in the Book of Proverbs," in *Birkat Shalom: Studies in the Bible, Ancient Near Eastern Literature, and Postbiblical Judaism*, ed. Chaim Cohen et al., 2 vols. (Winona Lake, IN: Eisenbrauns, 2008), 1:381–98, esp. 1:382.

5   Michael V. Fox, *Proverbs 1–9: A New Translation with Introduction and Commentary* (New York: Doubleday, 2000), 29. While particularly Proverbs insists that wisdom is ethical, the concept and its synonyms are not consistently such in the Hebrew Bible. At times, wisdom appears as ethically neutral or even immoral (2 Sam 13:3; Isa 19:11; 29:14; 47:10); see Fox, "Concepts," 382. Regarding the idea of wisdom as a virtue, I should clarify that the term "virtue" refers to desirable qualities throughout this book. On virtues as good qualities of character, see Christine Swanton, *Virtue Ethics: A Pluralistic View* (New York: Oxford University Press, 2003), 19. Such qualities can be either moral or epistemic/intellectual (cf. Aristotle, *N.E.* 1138b35–1139a1), although the distinction is not always clear-cut.

6   Mark R. Sneed, "Is the 'Wisdom Tradition' a Tradition?," *Catholic Biblical Quarterly* 73 (2011): 50–71.

7   John J. Collins, "Wisdom Reconsidered in Light of the Scrolls," *Dead Sea Discoveries* 4 (1997): 265–81, esp. 265–6.

8   On the wisdom texts from Qumran, see Daniel J. Harrington, *Wisdom Texts from Qumran* (London: Routledge, 1996); Matthew J. Goff, *Discerning Wisdom: The Sapiential Literature of the Dead Sea Scrolls* (Leiden: Brill, 2007); Armin Lange, "Wisdom Literature and Thought in the Dead Sea Scrolls," in *The Oxford Handbook of the Dead Sea Scrolls*, ed. Timothy H. Lim and John J. Collins (Oxford: Oxford University Press, 2010), 455–78; John I. Kampen, *Wisdom Literature* (Grand Rapids, MI: Eerdmans, 2011); Elisa Uusimäki, "Wisdom Texts from the Dead Sea Scrolls," in *The Wiley Blackwell Companion to Wisdom Literature*, ed. Samuel L. Adams and Matthew J. Goff (Hoboken, NJ: Wiley-Blackwell, 2020), 122–38.

9   See, e.g., Benjamin G. Wright and Lawrence M. Wills (ed.), *Conflicted Boundaries in Wisdom and Apocalypticism* (Atlanta, GA: Society of Biblical Literature, 2005); Bernd U. Schipper and D. Andrew Teeter (ed.), *Wisdom and Torah: The Reception of "Torah" in the Wisdom Literature of the Second Temple Period* (Leiden: Brill, 2013). Note that I do not capitalize the term "torah" because of its multiple meanings, which range from the etymological "instruction" to the more particular "Pentateuch" and "law." Carol A. Newsom describes תורה as "the site of intersecting accents." See Newsom, *The Self as Symbolic Space: Constructing Identity and Community at Qumran* (Leiden: Brill, 2004), 10–11. In the Jewish texts from the second temple period, the term "torah" often denotes divine instruction broadly understood.

10 See Will Kynes, "The 'Wisdom Literature' Category: An Obituary," *Journal of Theological Studies* 69 (2018): 1–24.

11 Matthew J. Goff, "Qumran Wisdom Literature and the Problem of Genre," *Dead Sea Discoveries* 17 (2010): 315–35, esp. 318.

12 So, John J. Collins, *Jewish Wisdom in the Hellenistic Age* (Edinburgh: T&T Clark, 1998), 1.

13 Mark R. Sneed writes on the identification of a wisdom text as follows: "As much as we might hate to admit it, basically you known it when you see it!" See Sneed,

"'Grasping after the Wind': The Elusive Attempt to Define and Delimit Wisdom," in *Was There a Wisdom Tradition? New Prospects in Israelite Wisdom Studies*, ed. Mark R. Sneed (Atlanta, GA: Society of Biblical Literature, 2015), 39–63, esp. 62.

14 See, e.g., Stuart Weeks, "Is 'Wisdom Literature' a Useful Category?" in *Tracing Sapiential Traditions in Ancient Judaism*, ed. Hindy Najman et al. (Leiden: Brill, 2016), 3–23.

15 See, e.g., Benjamin G. Wright, "Joining the Club: A Suggestion about Genre in Early Jewish Texts," *Dead Sea Discoveries* 17 (2010): 289–314.

16 See, e.g., Will Kynes, *An Obituary for "Wisdom Literature": The Birth, Death, and Intertextual Reintegration of a Biblical Corpus* (Oxford: Oxford University Press, 2019).

17 On the need to revive the relevance of biblical studies in contemporary academia, see Hindy Najman, "Ethical Reading: The Transformation of the Text and the Self," *Journal of Theological Studies* 68 (2017): 507–29.

18 Recently, see, e.g., Samuel L. Adams and Matthew J. Goff, "Editors' Introduction," in *The Wiley Blackwell Companion to Wisdom Literature*, 1–10, esp. 5: "Many of the texts that fall under the wisdom label are properly labeled instructions."

19 Hindy Najman has also indicated an interest in a wider "discourse of wisdom" in and beyond the Hellenistic era. She specifically addresses the overlap between wisdom, philosophical, and mystical traditions; see Najman, "Jewish Wisdom in the Hellenistic Period: Towards the Study of a Semantic Constellation," in *Is There a Text in This Cave? Studies in the Textuality of the Dead Sea Scrolls*, ed. Ariel Feldman et al. (Leiden: Brill, 2017), 459–72, esp. 461–2.

20 Robert A. Kraft, "Para-mania: Before, beside and beyond Biblical Studies," *Journal of Biblical Literature* 126 (2007): 5–27, esp. 10–18.

21 Hindy Najman, "The Vitality of Scripture within and beyond the 'Canon,'" *Journal for the Study of Judaism* 43 (2012): 497–518.

22 This is shown especially by the Qumran scrolls. See, e.g., Florentino García Martínez, "Rethinking the Bible: Sixty Years of Dead Sea Scrolls Research and Beyond," in *Authoritative Scriptures in Ancient Judaism*, ed. Mladen Popović (Leiden: Brill, 2010), 19–36.

23 See Timothy H. Lim, *The Formation of the Jewish Canon* (New Haven, CT: Yale University Press, 2013); Michael Satlow, *How the Bible Became Holy* (New Haven, CT: Yale University Press, 2014); Judith H. Newman, *Before the Bible: The Liturgical Body and the Formation of Scriptures in Early Judaism* (Oxford: Oxford University Press, 2018).

24 So, Philip S. Alexander, "Hellenism and Hellenization as Problematic Historiographical Categories," in *Paul beyond Judaism/Hellenism Divide*, ed. Troels Engberg-Pedersen (Louisville, KY: Westminster John Knox, 2001), 63–80, esp. 69.

25 See Erich S. Gruen, *Heritage and Hellenism: The Reinvention of Jewish Tradition* (Berkeley, CA: University of California Press, 1998); Lee I. Levine, *Judaism and Hellenism in Antiquity: Conflict or Confluence?* (Seattle, WA: University of

Washington Press, 1998); Peter Thonemann, *The Hellenistic Age* (Oxford: Oxford University Press, 2016). These studies build on the work of Martin Hengel, who observed nearly fifty years ago that all of Judaism from *c.* 250 BCE onwards is Hellenistic in one way or another; see Hengel, *Judaism and Hellenism: Studies in their Encounter in Palestine during the Early Hellenistic Period*, trans. John Bowden, 2 vols. (Philadelphia, PA: Fortress, 1974), 1:104.

26   Levine, *Judaism*, 19, 180–3.
27   Gruen, *Heritage*, xiv–xv.
28   The idea of Hellenism as a *Verschmelzung* of Eastern and Western elements goes back to Johann Gustav Droysen, *Geschichte des Hellenismus* (Gotha: Perthes, 1877–8). Although Droysen's work is illuminating regarding the nature of Hellenism, it problematically assumes Hellenism to serve as a link between classical Greece and the rise of Christianity. See, e.g., Arnaldo Momigliano, "J. G. Droysen between Greeks and Jews," *History and Theory* 9 (1970): 139–53; Ian S. Moyer, *Egypt and the Limits of Hellenism* (Cambridge: Cambridge University Press, 2011), 11–36.
29   Levine, *Judaism*, 19, 27–8.
30   On Hellenism in Judea, see John J. Collins and Gregory E. Sterling (ed.), *Hellenism in the Land of Israel* (Notre Dame, IN: Notre Dame University Press, 2001); Pieter B. Hartog and Jutta Jokiranta (ed.), *Dead Sea Discoveries* 24/3 (Leiden: Brill, 2017). On the Jewish diaspora, see Paul R. Trebilco, *Jewish Communities in Asia Minor* (Cambridge: Cambridge University Press, 1991); John M. G. Barclay, *Jews in the Mediterranean Diaspora from Alexander to Trajan (323 BCE – 117 CE)* (Edinburgh: T&T Clark, 1996); Mélèze Modrzejewski, *The Jews of Egypt from Rameses II to Emperor Hadrian Joseph*, trans. Robert Cornman (Princeton, NJ: Princeton University Press, 1997); Erich S. Gruen, *Diaspora: Jews amidst Greeks and Romans* (Cambridge, MA: Harvard University Press, 2002).
31   See David D. Hall (ed.), *Lived Religion in America: Toward a History of Practice* (Princeton, NJ: Princeton University Press, 1997); Robert A. Orsi, *The Madonna of 115th Street: Faith and Community in Italian Harlem, 1880–1950*, 3rd ed. (New Haven, CT: Yale University Press, 2010); Orsi, *Between Heaven and Earth: The Religious Worlds People Make and the Scholars Who Study Them* (Princeton, NJ: Princeton University Press, 2005); Meredith B. McGuire, *Lived Religion: Faith and Practice in Everyday Life* (Oxford: Oxford University Press, 2008).
32   Orsi, *Madonna*, xxxi.
33   Ibid., xxxvii.
34   McGuire, *Religion*, 12.
35   Ibid., 15.
36   See Rubina Raja and Jörg Rüpke, "Appropriating Religion: Methodological Issues in Testing the 'Lived Ancient Religion' Approach," *Religion in Roman Empire* 1 (2015): 11–19; Janico Albrecht et al., "Religion in the Making: The Lived Ancient Religion Approach," *Religion* 48 (2018): 568–93; Valentino Gasparini et al.

37 Albrecht et al., "Religion," 568–93.
38 Susan Niditch, *The Responsive Self: Personal Religion in Biblical Literature of the Neo-Babylonian and Persian Periods* (New Haven, CT: Yale University Press, 2015), 2.
39 Jessica M. Keady, *Vulnerability and Valour: A Gendered Analysis of Everyday Life in the Dead Sea Scrolls Communities* (London: Bloomsbury T&T Clark, 2017).
40 Although his approach is very different, aimed at understanding wisdom as "a program for human flourishing that is ordered to a holistic, authoritative account of reality in its metaphysical, cosmic, political, and ethical dimensions," Michael C. Legaspi, too, argues that wisdom refuses "to isolate knowledge from life." See Legaspi, *Wisdom in Classical and Biblical Tradition* (Oxford: Oxford University Press, 2018), esp. 11, 13.
41 On education in ancient Israel and in surrounding societies, see David M. Carr, *Writing on the Tablet of the Heart: Origins of Scripture and Literature* (Oxford: Oxford University Press, 2005).
42 So, Claudia V. Camp and Benjamin G. Wright, "'Who Has Been Tested by Gold and Found Perfect?' Ben Sira's Discourse of Riches and Poverty," *Henoch* 23 (2001): 153–74.
43 There is some evidence for pedagogical materials through ostraca and writing exercises. See André Lemaire, *Les écoles et la formation de la Bible dans l'ancien Israël* (Göttingen: Vanhenhoeck & Ruprecht, 1981), 7–33, on the pre-exilic epigraphic evidence of school exercises; and Joan E. Taylor, "4Q341: A Writing Exercise Remembered," in *Is There a Text in This Cave?*, 133–51, esp. 140–6, on writing exercises and abecedaries from the Dead Sea region.
44 On the significance of human activities in the lived religion approach, see Thomas A. Lewis, *Why Philosophy Matters for the Study of Religion – and Vice Versa* (Oxford: Oxford University Press, 2015), 3.
45 This makes it possible to characterize them as "values … embedded in social practices." See Sanne Taekema, "What Ideals Are: Ontological and Epistemological Issues," in *The Importance of Ideals: Debating their Relevance in Law, Morality, and Politics*, ed. Wibren van der Burg and Sanne Taekema (Brussels: Peter Lang, 2004), 39–57, esp. 39.
46 On the importance of embodied practice in the lived religion approach, see Orsi, *Madonna*, xxxix.
47 So, ibid., xl.
48 See William B. Brown, *Wisdom's Wonder: Character, Creation, and Crisis in the Bible's Wisdom* (Grand Rapids, MI: Eerdmans, 2014). Brown published an earlier version of the book under the title *Character in Crisis: A Fresh Approach to the Wisdom Literature of the Old Testament* (Grand Rapids, MI: Eerdmans, 1996).
49 Brown, *Wonder*, 189.

50 Ibid., 193.
51 Ibid., 184–6.
52 Ibid., 194.
53 John Barton, *Ethics in Ancient Israel* (Oxford: Oxford University Press, 2015), 159.
54 Ibid., 161.
55 Elsewhere, Barton has presented remarks that might enable a different conclusion, reflecting on the Hebrew Bible as "a text that can shape the reader in significant ways." See John Barton, "Old Testament Ethics: Story or Style?," in *Sibyls, Scriptures, and Scrolls*, ed. Joel Baden et al. (Leiden: Brill, 2016), 113–26, esp. 125.
56 Anne W. Stewart, *Poetic Ethics in Proverbs: Wisdom Literature and the Shaping of the Moral Self* (Cambridge: Cambridge University Press, 2015), 14–15. Note that Stewart responds to Barton's earlier book titled *Understanding Old Testament Ethics: Approaches and Explanations* (Louisville, KY: Westminster John Knox, 2003), esp. 65–74. Yet, the same argument appears in Barton's *Ethics in Ancient Israel*, as the previous quotes indicate. On ancient Israelite ideas of the moral self, see also Carol A. Newsom, "Models of the Moral Self: Hebrew Bible and Second Temple Judaism," *Journal of Biblical Literature* 131 (2012): 5–25.
57 See Benjamin G. Wright, "Wisdom, Instruction, and Social Location in Sirach and *1 Enoch*," in *Things Revealed: Studies in Early Jewish and Christian Literature*, ed. Esther G. Chazon et al. (Leiden: Brill, 2004), 105–21. I will return to Wright's contribution to our understanding of early Jewish wisdom in Chapter 2 on the sage.
58 See, e.g., Werner Jaeger, *Paideia: The Ideals of Greek Culture*, trans. Gilbert Highet, 3 vols., 2nd ed. (New York: Oxford University Press, 1962), 1:xxiii.
59 See Patrick Pouchelle, *Dieu éducateur: une novelle approche d'un concept de la théologie biblique entre Bible Hébraïque, Septante e littérature grecque classique* (Tübingen: Mohr Siebeck, 2015); Karina Martin Hogan et al. (ed.), *Pedagogy in Ancient Judaism and Early Christianity* (Atlanta, GA: Society of Biblical Literature, 2017); Jason M. Zurawski and Gabrielle Boccaccini (ed.), *Second Temple Jewish "Paideia" in Context* (Berlin: de Gruyter, 2017).
60 See esp. Marcus K. M. Tso, *Ethics in the Qumran Community: An Interdisciplinary Investigation* (Tübingen: Mohr Siebeck, 2010); Barton, *Ethics*; Patricia Vesely, *Friendship and Virtue Ethics in the Book of Job* (Cambridge: Cambridge University Press, 2019); Elisa Uusimäki, "Mapping Ideal Ways of Living: Virtue and Vice Lists in 1QS and 4Q286," *Journal for the Study of the Pseudepigrapha* 30 (2020): 35–45; Uusimäki, "In Search of Virtue: Ancestral Inheritance in the Testament of Qahat," *Biblical Interpretation* 29 (2021): in press.
61 See, e.g., James L. Crenshaw, *Old Testament Wisdom: An Introduction* (Atlanta, GA: Westminster John Knox, 1981), 19; John J. Collins, "Epilogue: Genre Analysis and the Dead Sea Scrolls," *Dead Sea Discoveries* 17 (2010): 418–30, esp. 429–30; Michael V. Fox, "Three Theses on Wisdom," in *Was There a Wisdom Tradition?*, 69–86, esp. 83.

62 On the persuasive aspect of wisdom teaching, see, e.g., Michael V. Fox, "Wisdom and the Self-Presentation of Wisdom Literature," in *Reading from Right to Left*, ed. J. Cheryl Exum and H. G. M. Williamson (London: T&T Clark, 2003), 153–72, esp. 154; Elisa Uusimäki, "Spiritual Formation in Hellenistic Jewish Wisdom Teaching," in *Tracing Sapiential Traditions in Ancient Judaism*, 57–70, esp. 58.

63 In the Hebrew Bible, the cross-cultural nature of wisdom is shown by the parallels between Prov 22:17–24:22 and the Egyptian Instruction of Amenemope, the materials attributed to foreigners in Prov 30:1–31:9, the foreign setting of the book of Job, and Qoheleth's affinity with Hellenistic philosophy. Aramaic, Egyptian, and Greek texts reflect similar awareness of wisdom as a cross-cultural project; see Miriam Lichtheim, *Late Egyptian Wisdom Literature in the International Context: A Study of Demotic Instructions* (Fribourg: Universitätsverlag, 1983), 106.

64 Legaspi has recently set the two into a dialogue with each other in his book *Wisdom in Classical and Biblical Tradition*. Legaspi, however, focuses on the concept of wisdom, whereas I concentrate on wisdom and lifestyle.

65 See the section "Judaism among philosophies" in Chapter 4.

66 On the need to include Greek Jewish texts into our notion of ancient Greek culture, see Tim Whitmarsh, *Beyond the Second Sophistic: Adventures in Greek Postclassicism* (Berkeley, CA: University of California Press, 2013), 2–7. For an insightful re-evaluation of what the category "philosophy" entails, see Bryan W. van Norden, *Taking Back Philosophy: A Multicultural Manifesto* (New York: Columbia University Press, 2017).

67 See Mark L. McPherran, "Platonic Religion," in *A Companion to Plato*, ed. Hugh H. Benson (Chichester: Wiley-Blackwell, 2007), 244–59. Socratic wisdom, in fact, is a type of theology along with its concern for piety. Consider, e.g., how Socrates includes holiness (ὁσιότης) in a list of virtues as he seeks convince Protagoras of their unity (*Protagoras* 349b); see Legaspi, *Wisdom*, 140–3.

68 Anders Klostergaard Petersen, "Dissolving the Philosophy–Religion Dichotomy in the Context of Jewish *Paideia*: Wisdom of Solomon, 4 Maccabees, and Philo," in *Second Temple Jewish "Paideia" in Context*, 185–204, esp. 185–6.

69 John Sellars, *The Art of Living: The Stoics on the Nature and Function of Philosophy* (Aldershot: Ashgate, 2003), 33–85, esp. 54. On the Stoic development of Socrates' analogy between medicine and philosophy, see Martha C. Nussbaum, *The Therapy of Desires: Theory and Practice in Hellenistic Ethics* (Princeton, NJ: Princeton University Press, 1994), 13–14.

70 John M. Cooper, *Pursuits of Wisdom: Six Ways of Life in Ancient Philosophy from Socrates to Plotinus* (Princeton, NJ: Princeton University Press, 2012), 218.

71 See Pierre Hadot, *Exercices spirituels et philosophie antique* (Paris: Études Augustiniennes, 1987); Hadot, *Qu'est-ce que la philosophie antique?* (Paris: Gallimard, 1995). In English, see Hadot, *Philosophy as a Way of Life: Spiritual Exercises from Socrates to Foucault*, ed. Arnold I. Davidson, trans. Michael Chase (Oxford: Blackwell, 1995); Hadot, *What Is Ancient Philosophy?*, trans. Michael Chase (Cambridge, MA: The Belknap Press of Harvard University Press, 2002).

72 Hadot, *Ancient Philosophy*, 220.
73 Steve Mason, "*Philosophiai*: Graeco-Roman, Judean and Christian," in *Voluntary Associations in the Graeco-Roman World*, ed. John S. Kloppenborg and Stephen G. Wilson (London: Routledge, 1996), 31–58, esp. 33.
74 See esp. Richard Sorabji, *Emotion and Peace of Mind: From Stoic Agitation to Christian Temptation* (Oxford: Oxford University Press, 2002); Sellars, *Art of Living*; Cooper, *Pursuits of Wisdom*; Xavier Pavie, *Exercices spirituels: leçons de la philosophie antique* (Paris: Les Belles Lettres, 2012).
75 John Sellars, "Review of P. Hadot, *What Is Ancient Philosophy?*," *Classical Review* 54 (2004): 69–70.
76 See Hadot, *Philosophy*, 83; Hadot, *Ancient Philosophy*, 6, 175, 177, 188–211, 220, 230.
77 So, John Sellars, "Review of J. Cooper, *Pursuits of Wisdom*," *Mind* 123 (2014): 1177–80.
78 Sellars, *Art*, 110.
79 Hadot, *Philosophy*, 82–3; Hadot, *Ancient Philosophy*, 220.
80 Musonius Rufus' lectures are not included in the Loeb Classical Library. For the text, see Cora E. Lutz, "Musonius Rufus, 'The Roman Socrates,'" *Yale Classical Studies* 10 (1947): 32–147.
81 Sellars, *Art*, 148.
82 Steven D. Fraade, "Ascetical Aspects of Ancient Judaism," in *Jewish Spirituality: From the Bible through the Middle Ages*, ed. Arthur Green (New York: Crossroad, 1986), 253–86, esp. 257.

Chapter 2

1 On the variety of the wise people in the ancient Near East and Greece, see George B. Kerferd, "The Image of the Wise Man in Greece in the Period before Plato," in *Images of Man in Ancient and Medieval Thought*, ed. F. Bossier et al. (Leuven: Leuven University Press, 1976), 17–28; John G. Gammie and Leo G. Perdue (ed.), *The Sage in Israel and the Ancient Near East* (Winona Lake, IN: Eisenbrauns, 1990); Joseph A. Blenkinsopp, *Sage, Priest, Prophet: Religious and Intellectual Leadership in Ancient Israel* (Louisville, KY: Westminster John Knox Press, 1995), esp. 9–65; Lester L. Grabbe, *Priests, Prophets, Diviners, Sages: A Socio-Historical Study of Religious Specialists in Ancient Israel* (Valley Forge, PA: Trinity Press International, 1995), esp. 152–80; Hadot, *Ancient Philosophy*, 220–33; Julia Annas, "The Sage in Ancient Philosophy," in *Anthropine Sophia*, ed. Francesca Alesse et al. (Naples: Bibliopolis, 2008), 11–27; Leo G. Perdue (ed.), *Scribes, Sages, and Seers: The Sage in the Eastern Mediterranean World* (Göttingen: Vandenhoeck & Ruprecht, 2008); Andrea Wilson Nightingale, "Sages, Sophists, and Philosophers: Greek Wisdom Literature," in *Literature in the Greek and Roman Worlds: A New*

Perspective, ed. Oliver Taplin (Oxford: Oxford University Press, 2009), 156–91; René Brouwer, *The Stoic Sage: The Early Stoics on Wisdom, Sagehood and Socrates* (Cambridge: Cambridge University Press, 2014).

2   When I use the term "Greek," I do not refer to authors from the Greek mainland alone, but to various people who wrote in Greek. In fact, many philosophers did not come from the mainland. The Presocratic philosophers, e.g., typically stemmed from islands and coastal cities in Asia Minor and southern Italy. Also later, as Greek was used around the Mediterranean region, Greek authors represented multiple tribes and cities, drawing on various traditions; see Stephen R. L. Clark, *Ancient Mediterranean Philosophy* (London: Bloomsbury, 2013), 8–9.

3   See the helpful terminological survey by Ronald F. G. Sweet, "The Sage in Akkadian Literature: A Philological Study," in *The Sage in Israel and the Ancient Near East*, 45–65, esp. 47–51.

4   See, e.g., Seth L. Sanders, *From Adapa to Enoch: Scribal Culture and Religious Vision in Judea and Babylon* (Tübingen: Mohr Siebeck, 2017); Seth A. Bledsoe, "Ahiqar and Other Legendary Sages," in *The Wiley Blackwell Companion to Wisdom Literature*, 289–309.

5   Samuel Noah Kramer, "The Sage in Sumerian Literature: A Composite Portrait," in *The Sage in Israel and the Ancient Near East*, 31–44.

6   Sweet, "Akkadian Literature," 51–65; Sweet, "The Sage in Mesopotamian Palaces and Royal Courts," in *The Sage in Israel and the Ancient Near East*, 99–107.

7   Rivkah Harris, "The Female 'Sage' in Mesopotamian Literature (with an Appendix on Egypt)," in *The Sage in Israel and the Ancient Near East*, 3–17, esp. 5–14.

8   Blenkinsopp, *Sage*, 11. On the variety of wise figures, see also ibid., 161. Apart from wise individuals, the Hebrew Bible contains the idea of Israel as a wise and understanding people (Deut 4:6, cf. 32:29).

9   On the wisdom features of the book, see Samuel Terrien, "Job as a Sage," in *The Sage in Israel and the Ancient Near East*, 231–42.

10 Throughout this book, the English translations of the Hebrew Bible are from JPS, slightly modified. See *JPS Hebrew-English Tanakh* (Philadelphia: The Jewish Publication Society, 2003).

11 Furthermore, the gods of foreign nations (Jer 10:9) and sculptures of divine beings (Isa 40:20) are recognized as the work of חכמים, even if the authors consider them as nothing in comparison with Israel's God. The lament over Tyre mentions how Tyre had its own חכמים as its pilots and Gebal's elders and חכמים as makings its repairs (Ezek 27:8–9); soon after, the wisdom of the prince of Tyre, which had helped him to gain riches and trade profitably, is condemned (28:1–10, 11–19). See also Isa 28:23–9 on the farmers' skills that come from God.

12 See Blenkinsopp, *Sage*, 11; Grabbe, *Priests*, 176, 179.

13 Roger Norman Whybray, "The Sage in the Israelite Royal Court," in *The Sage in Israel and the Ancient Near East*, 133–9, esp. 133.

14 In spite of their suspicious deeds, both kings were celebrated in early Jewish literature and beyond, prompting the creation of new writings that expand the lore around them. In the Dead Sea Scrolls, David, "a paradigmatic forgiven sinner," becomes an "unlikely ethical model." See Eva Mroczek, "Moses, David and Scribal Revelation: Preservation and Renewal in Second Temple Jewish Textual Traditions," in *The Significance of Sinai: Traditions about Sinai and Divine Revelation in Judaism and Christianity*, ed. George J. Brooke et al. (Leiden: Brill, 2008), 91–115, esp. 100–8. King Solomon, too, had a rich afterlife, even if his marriages to foreign women made his reception ambivalent (e.g., Sir 47:12–23; Josephus, *A.J.* 8.208). On Solomon's reception, see Joseph Verheyden (ed.), *The Figure of Solomon in Jewish, Christian and Islamic Tradition: King, Sage and Architect* (Leiden: Brill, 2013); Elisa Uusimäki, *Turning Proverbs towards Torah: An Analysis of 4Q525* (Leiden: Brill, 2016), 227–8.

15 On educational travel in ancient Greek and Jewish literature, see Silvia Montiglio, *Wandering in Ancient Greek Culture* (Chicago: The University of Chicago Press, 2005); Elisa Uusimäki, "Itinerant Sages: The Evidence of Sirach in Its Ancient Mediterranean Context," *Journal for the Study of the Old Testament* 44 (2020): 315–36.

16 Several individual scribes also appear in the Hebrew Bible (e.g., 1 Kgs 4:2–6; 2 Kgs 12:11; 22:8–10; 1 Chr 27:32; 2 Chr 24:11); see Grabbe, *Priests*, 153–5, 158, 160–1, 163.

17 Pharaoh's wise advisors are also condemned in the pronouncement on Egypt in Isa 19:11–15, which mocks their attempts to offer advice on the future. Further, see Isa 47:10 on the hybris of Babylonian wisdom.

18 So, David Satran, "Daniel: Seer, Philosopher, Holy Man," in *Ideal Figures in Ancient Judaism: Profiles and Paradigms*, ed. George W. E. Nickelsburg and John J. Collins (Chico, CA: Scholars Press, 1980), 33–48, esp. 33–4.

19 On the text's concern for physical and mental training, see Josephus, *A.J.* 10.190 and Satran, "Daniel," 36–9.

20 Such acts are a typical response to calamity in the Hebrew Bible (e.g., 1 Kgs 21:27; Jonah 3:5; Esth 4:3). Scholars debate whether they are connected to the following visionary activity, as is typical of apocalyptic literature; see Satran, "Daniel," 35–6. Here, it suffices to remark that the practices represent modes of spiritual exercise that involve communication with the divine.

21 Ultimately, they illustrate Abigail's excellence, indicating that she became David's wife because of her virtue and intellect – not by accident or because of David's wrongdoing; see P. Kyle McCarter, *1 Samuel: A New Translation with Introduction, Notes and Commentary* (Garden City, NY: Doubleday, 1980), 400–1.

22 Notably, the authors use the designation "wise woman" without any clarifying remarks, which suggests that the audiences understood its meaning; Claudia V. Camp, "The Female Sage in Ancient Israel and in the Biblical Wisdom Literature," in *The Sage in Israel and the Ancient Near East*, 185–203, esp. 187–8.

23 See, e.g., Roger Norman Whybray, *The Intellectual Tradition in the Old Testament* (Berlin: de Gruyter, 1974), esp. 54, 70.
24 On the date of Proverbs, see Fox, *Proverbs*, 6. As argued by Fox, some sayings in chs. 10–29 are older, but the final form of the book is post-exilic and perhaps even Hellenistic.
25 Admittedly, the definite article is not missing, but one should not deduct too much from its absence (cf., e.g., the title פרקי אבות in the Mishna); so, Blenkinsopp, *Sage*, 11.
26 Thomas Krüger argues for a date at the Ptolemaic period; see Krüger, *Kohelet (Prediger)* (Neukirchen-Vluyn: Neukirchener Verlag, 2000), 39.
27 Blenkinsopp, *Sage*, 11.
28 For the historical context, see, e.g., Leo G. Perdue, *The Sword and the Stylus: An Introduction to Wisdom in the Age of Empires* (Grand Rapids, MI: Eerdmans, 2008), 259–63.
29 The sage-scribe might have owned land (Sir 7:3, 15, 22) and slaves (7:20–1; 33:25–32; 42:5). He also had the opportunity to travel (34:9–13; 39:4). On the latter, see Uusimäki, "Sages," 315–36.
30 This is barely surprising, considering that ancient education was typically informal. The biblical evidence for educational settings is also indirect; see André Lemaire, "The Sage in School and Temple," in *The Sage in Israel and the Ancient Near East*, 165–81. Similarly, Greek schools were informally institutional at the most; see Troels Engberg-Pedersen, "The Hellenistic Öffentlichkeit: Philosophy as a Social Force in the Greco-Roman World," in *Recruitment, Conquest, and Conflict: Strategies in Judaism, Early Christianity and the Greco-Roman World*, ed. Peder Borgen et al. (Atlanta, GA: Scholars Press, 1998), 15–38, esp. 18–19.
31 Note that there is a contrast between the elegant style of the Greek prologue and that of the actual Greek translation, which tends to be isomorphic and often mirrors the Hebrew *Vorlage*; see Benjamin G. Wright, *No Small Difference: Sirach's Relationship to Its Hebrew Parent Text* (Atlanta, GA: Scholars Press, 1989).
32 Trans. Benjamin G. Wright, NETS.
33 Elias J. Bickerman, *The Jews in the Greek Age* (Cambridge, MA: Harvard University Press, 1988), 171.
34 Ibid., 166.
35 Judith H. Newman, "Liturgical Imagination in the Composition of Ben Sira," in *Prayer and Poetry in the Dead Sea Scrolls and Related Literature*, ed. Jeremy Penner et al. (Leiden: Brill, 2011), 311–26, esp. 325–6.
36 Benjamin G. Wright, "Ben Sira on the Sage as Exemplar," in idem, *Praise Israel for Wisdom and Instruction: Essays on Ben Sira and Wisdom, the Letter of Aristeas and the Septuagint* (Leiden: Brill, 2008), 165–82.
37 Ibid., 169–71.
38 Ibid., 171–81. The first-person accounts include Sir 22:25–23:6; 24:30–4; 25–6; 33:16–19; 34:9–13; 39:12–13, 32–5; 42:15; 43:32; 50:25–6; 51; ibid., 169–81.

39   Ibid., 178.
40   See the survey of Armin Lange, "Sages and Scribes in the Qumran Literature," in *Scribes, Sages, and Seers*, 271–93, esp. 274–8. On the use of the term חכם, see ibid., 272–3, 284–6.
41   These include the Community Rule, Rule of Blessing, War Scroll, Hodayot, Songs of the Sabbath Sacrifice, Songs of the Maskil, Instruction, Ways of Righteousness, and Words of the Maskil to the Sons of Dawn. See, e.g., Hans Kosmala, "Maskil," *The Journal of the Ancient Near Eastern Society of Columbia University* 5 (1973): 235–41, esp. 240–1; Lange, "Sages and Scribes," 277–8, 286–91.
42   Newsom, *Self*, 154, 165–6, 187.
43   Ibid., 107.
44   The English translations of 1QS throughout this book are, with minor modifications, from James H. Charlesworth et al. (ed.), *The Dead Sea Scrolls: Hebrew, Aramaic, and Greek Texts with English Translations, Vol. 1: Rule of the Community and Related Documents* (Tübingen: Mohr Siebeck; Louisville, KY: Westminster John Knox Press, 1994), 6–51.
45   Newsom, *Self*, 103, 167–9, 172.
46   Ibid., 107, 153, 167. However, note that not all six copies of the Community Rule are the same: 4QS^e ends with a calendrical teaching (Otot) instead of the maskil's hymn.
47   Hindy Najman, "How Should We Contextualize Pseudepigrapha? Imitation and Emulation in *4 Ezra*," in *Flores Florentino*, ed. Anthony Hillhorst et al. (Leiden: Brill, 2007), 529–36, esp. 532.
48   Ibid., 535–6.
49   Consider, e.g., how Enoch, Noah, Abraham, and Levi exemplify "how to be worthy of receiving the heavenly tablets" in the book of Jubilees. So, Hindy Najman, "Reconsidering *Jubilees*: Prophecy and Exemplarity," in *Enoch and the Mosaic Torah*, ed. Gabriele Boccaccini and Giovanni Ibba (Grand Rapids, MI: Eerdmans, 2009), 229–43. Torah devotion is an integral aspect of the patriarchs' exemplarity in Jubilees, which depicts them as celebrating festivals and undertaking practices that only later become commandments of the torah; see James L. Kugel, "The Figure of Moses in *Jubilees*," *Hebrew Bible and Ancient Israel* 1 (2012): 77–92, esp. 82–7.
50   This characterization is confirmed by two fragmentary scrolls from Qumran, which refer to Enoch as the "noted scribe" (ספר פרשא). See 4Q203 frag. 8:4 and 4Q503 frag. 2 ii 14. Furthermore, Enoch records the deeds of people in Jub 4:21–4 and 2 En 53:2, but he is not named as a scribe in these passages; see Christine Schams, *Jewish Scribes in the Second-Temple Period* (Sheffield: Sheffield Academic Press, 1998), 207–8.
51   John J. Collins, "The Sage in Apocalyptic and Pseudepigraphic Literature," in *The Sage in Israel and the Ancient Near East*, 343–54, esp. 344–7. Although wisdom did not find a place on earth and returned to heaven according to 1 En 42:1, "the apocalyptic sage is not at a loss." See ibid., 353.

52 The English translation is from George W. E. Nickelsburg and James C. VanderKam, *1 Enoch: A New Translation Based on the Hermeneia Commentary* (Minneapolis: Fortress, 2004), 95.

53 Gruen, *Diaspora*, 7. On the breadth of Jewish settlement, see 1 Macc 15:22–3; Philo, *Legat.* 281–4; Acts 2:5–11; and the comments of Tessa Rajak, *Translation and Survival: The Greek Bible of the Ancient Jewish Diaspora* (Oxford: Oxford University Press, 2009), 105.

54 The city had gymnasia as well as the mouseion and the library, which gathered intelligentsia; see Peter M. Fraser, *Ptolemaic Alexandria*, 3 vols. (Oxford: Clarendon, 1972), 1: 312–35.

55 Wise figures also appear in other Greek Jewish writings. Consider the Letter of Aristeas with a fictitious account of the origins of the Septuagint. The seventy-two translators who travel from Jerusalem to Alexandria in order to undertake the translation project are not called sages, but they are nevertheless portrayed as excellent, well-educated, and virtuous men who know how to interpret the Jewish *nomos* (Arist. 32, 39, 46, 121–2); see Schams, *Scribes*, 263.

56 While there is little to support any specific location, the idea of Alexandria as the place of composition relies on the topic of exodus and the polemical attitude towards animal worship and idolatry; see Perdue, *Sword*, 292–3.

57 Trans. Michael A. Knibb, NETS.

58 See Devorah Dimant, "Pseudonymity in the Wisdom of Solomon," in *La Septuaginta en la Investigacion Contemporanea*, ed. Natalio Fernández Marcos (Madrid: Instituto Arias Montano, 1985), 243–55; Nathalie LaCoste, "Solomon the Exemplary Sage: The Convergence of Hellenistic and Jewish Traditions in the Wisdom of Solomon," *The University of Toronto Journal of Jewish Thought* 1 (2010). Online: http://cjs.utoronto.ca/tjjt/node/18.

59 See Benjamin G. Wright, "Solomon in Chronicles and Ben Sira: A Study in Contrasts," in *Rewriting Biblical History: Essays on Chronicles and Ben Sira*, ed. Jeremy Corley and Harm van Grol (Berlin: de Gruyter, 2011), 139–57.

60 The section makes use of Solomon's nocturnal prayers (1 Kgs 3:1–15; 2 Chr 1:7–12), as well as drawing on the knowledge of Aristotelian science (Wis 7:17–20). The list of wisdom's qualities in Wis 7:22–3 is shaped by Stoic thought, whereas Wis 8:7 refers to cardinal virtues (cf. Plato, *Phaedo* 69c; *Laws* 631c); see Michael Kolarcik, S.J., "The Sage behind the Wisdom of Solomon," in *Scribes, Sages, and Seers*, 245–57, esp. 253.

61 Judith H. Newman, "The Democratization of Kingship in Wisdom of Solomon," in *The Idea of Biblical Interpretation*, ed. Hindy Najman and Judith H. Newman (Leiden: Brill, 2004), 309–28, esp. 327. The recasting of the motif is meaningful in both cultural contexts of the text. First, Wisdom of Solomon shows knowledge of Greek philosophy, which is pertinent in that the Stoic tradition portrays the wise person as a king; see Sellars, *Art*, 60. Second, the development might well draw on biblical ideas. In Gen 1:26–8, God gives the first humans dominion over the earth,

thus gesturing at the idea of all people as rulers. Deut 17:18–19 also limits the power and privileges of the sole monarch by making the king subordinate to the laws and regulations ordered by God; see Uusimäki, *Proverbs*, 230.

62 See Peder Borgen, *The Philo Index* (Grand Rapids, MI: Eerdmans; Leiden: Brill, 2000), 311.
63 On Philo's education, see Erkki Koskenniemi, *Greek Writers and Philosophers in Philo and Josephus: A Study of Their Secular Education and Educational Ideals* (Leiden: Brill, 2019).
64 On Philo's intellectual position, see, e.g., John M. Dillon, *The Middle Platonists 80 B.C. to A.D. 220* (Ithaca, NY: Cornell University Press, 1977), 139–83; Jaap Mansfeld, "Philosophy in the Service of Scripture: Philo's Exegetical Strategies," in *The Question of "Eclecticism": Studies in Later Greek Philosophy*, ed. John M. Dillon and Anthony A. Long (Berkeley, CA: University of California Press, 1988), 70–102; Francesca Alesse (ed.), *Philo of Alexandria and Post-Aristotelian Philosophy* (Leiden: Brill, 2008); Cristina Termini, "Philo's Thought within the Context of Middle Judaism," in *The Cambridge Companion to Philo*, ed. Adam Kamesar (Cambridge: Cambridge University Press, 2009), 95–123.
65 Hadot, *Ancient Philosophy*, 4.
66 The latter statement contains a retort to Aristophanes who presents the door of Socrates' school as locked (*Clouds* 132–83); see Sami Yli-Karjanmaa, "Philo of Alexandria," in *Brill's Companion to the Reception of Plato in Antiquity*, ed. Harold Tarrant et al. (Leiden: Brill, 2018), 115–29, esp. 119n27.
67 Trans. F. H. Colson, LCL 320.
68 Yet, elementary studies have "inherent spiritual value" for Philo as he tries to make them compatible with the divine; see Alan Mendelson, *Secular Education in Philo of Alexandria* (Cincinnati, OH: Hebrew Union College Press, 1982), xxiv, 83.
69 For Philo, philosophy involves the study of logic, ethics, and physics, and it aims at a life of virtue (*Leg.* 1.57-8). The idea that virtue is both practical and theoretical draws on the Platonic idea of the unity of virtue (cf. Plato, *Republic* 443E), often addressed by the Stoics. Like the Stoics, Philo understands philosophy as involving the knowledge of things divine, human, and their causes; see Gregory E. Sterling, "Philosophy as the Handmaid of Wisdom: Philosophy in the Exegetical Traditions of Alexandrian Jews," in *Religiöse Philosophie und philosophische Religion der frühen Kaiserzeit: Literaturgeschichtliche Perspektiven*, ed. Rainer Hirsch-Luipold et al. (Tübingen: Mohr Siebeck, 2009), 67–98, esp. 95.
70 Trans. F. H. Colson and G. H. Whitaker, LCL 261.
71 David Winston, "Sage and Super-Sage in Philo of Alexandria," in *The Ancestral Philosophy: Hellenistic Philosophy in Second Temple Judaism*, ed. Gregory E. Sterling (Providence, RI: Brown University Press, 2001), 171–80, esp. 171.
72 On the perfection of the sage, see, e.g., *Prob.* 43; *Migr.* 128-9. Yet, Philo also notes that perfection belongs to God alone; so, *Her.* 121, *Fug.* 172, *Mut.* 181-5.

73 See, e.g., Margaret R. Graver, *Stoicism and Emotion* (Chicago: The University of Chicago Press, 2007), 35, 81, 210. Regarding ἀπάθεια in Philo's texts, see esp. *Leg.* 2:99–102, 3:129–32; *Plant.* 98; *Abr.* 256–7. Yet, Philo also refers to the Aristotelian moderation (μετριοπάθεια) of passions (*Virt.* 195); see Winston, "Sage," 171–7.
74 Trans. F. H. Colson, LCL 289. Philo is known for his allegorizing (Platonic) interpretation of the Pentateuch, but he also uses literal (Aristotelian) interpretative techniques; see Maren R. Niehoff, *Jewish Exegesis and Homeric Scholarship in Alexandria* (Cambridge: Cambridge University Press, 2012).
75 Mendelson, *Education*, 50–9.
76 Trans. F. H. Colson and G. H. Whitaker, LCL 261.
77 See Wayne A. Meeks, "Moses as God and King," in *Religions in Antiquity*, ed. Jacob Neusner (Leiden: Brill, 1968), 354–71; Erkki Koskenniemi, "Moses – A Well-Educated Man: A Look at the Educational Idea in Early Judaism," *Journal for the Study of the Pseudepigrapha* 17 (2008): 281–96.
78 For Philo, the "mind alone" denotes the state of the first human creation (*Leg.* 1.92); see Hindy Najman, "Text and Figure in Jewish *Paideia*," in *Authoritative Scriptures in Ancient Judaism*, 253–65, esp. 256–7.
79 See *Leg.* 3.129; *Sacr.* 8; *Migr.* 67; *Mos.* 1.155–6, 158. Here Philo even transcends the Stoic view, which is unfamiliar with the idea of the passion's complete absence; see Winston, "Sage," 177–80.
80 Trans. F. H. Colson, LCL 341.
81 Trans. F. H. Colson and G. H. Whitaker, LCL 261.
82 These claims are conspicuous, considering that Philo stresses God's distinctiveness (*Leg.* 2.1; *Sacr.* 92) and attacks against polytheism (*Decal.* 65; *Spec.* 1.28). At times, the question is about metaphorical language: Moses' divinity refers to his kingship, which is a central motif in Philo's oeuvre. Some of the claims are ontological, however, which suggest that Philo considers divinity to constitute a "chain of existence." In this chain, the human and the divine realms intertwine. God represents the fundamental divinity, i.e., God is divine in himself. Other creatures – like Moses – may take part in the Divinity and, in so doing, represent indirect divinity. In the heavenly hierarchy, the divinity of Moses seems to correspond to the nature of angelic beings as Philo describes Moses like them (*Mos.* 2.288); see M. David Litwa, "The Deification of Moses in Philo of Alexandria," *Studia Philonica Annual* 26 (2014): 1–27, esp. 1, 5–7, 9, 24–7.
83 Trans. F. H. Colson, LCL 289. On the model of the patriarchs, see also *Gig.* 62; *Mut.* 12; *Somn.* 1.168; *Abr.* 52–4.
84 The idea of a triad is known from the Greek pedagogical tradition. Plutarch mentions how it is perfectly united in the souls of Pythagoras, Socrates, and Plato (*De lib.* 2A–C); see Peder Borgen, *Philo of Alexandria: An Exegete for His Time* (Leiden: Brill, 1997), 70.
85 See, e.g., *Sobr.* 65; *Conf.* 69–70; *Congr.* 35–6; *Mut.* 12, 88; *Somn.* 1.120–6, 168–71; *Abr.* 52–3; *Ios.* 26. Josephus also enhances Jacob's virtuous qualities of wisdom,

courage, temperance, justice, and piety; see Louis H. Feldman, "Josephus' Portrait of Jacob," *Jewish Quarterly Review* 79 (1988–9): 101–51, esp. 109–13, 148.

86 Elisa Uusimäki, "A Mind in Training: Philo of Alexandria on Jacob's Spiritual Exercises," *Journal for the Study of the Pseudepigrapha* 27 (2018): 265–88.

87 See *Spec.* 2.124; 4.223; *QE* 1.7 and the comments of Yehoshua Amir and Maren R. Niehoff, "Philo Judaeus," in *Encyclopaedia Judaica*, ed. Fred Skolnik and Michael Berenbaum, 2nd ed., 22 vols. (Detroit: Thomson Gale, 2007), 16:59–64, esp. 16:63–4.

88 *Opif.* 165; *Spec.* 1.201; *Leg.* 2.38; *QG* 1.25. See also Sharon Lea Mattila, "Wisdom, Sense Perception, and Philo's Gender Gradient," *Harvard Theological Review* 89 (1996): 103–29.

89 Joan E. Taylor, *Jewish Women Philosophers of First-Century Alexandria: Philo's "Therapeutae" Reconsidered* (Oxford: Oxford University Press, 2003), 231.

90 See esp. Gorgias of Leontini's interpretation, which can be found in Kathleen Freeman, *Ancilla to the Pre-Socratic Philosophers: A Complete Translation of the Fragments in Diels Fragmente der Vorsokratiker* (Cambridge, MA: Harvard University Press, 1957), 139. See also Plutarch, *De lib.* 7D.

91 On Sarah and wisdom, see *Cher.* 10; *Leg.* 2.82; and on Sarah and virtue, see *Leg.* 3.217–18, 3.244; *Abr.* 206; *Sacr.* 59; *Fug.* 128; *Det.* 59; *Post.* 62; *Her.* 62. The attribute "wise" is never applied to Sarah in the Hebrew Bible, but she is capable of effecting results through her knowledge and related action; see Tikva Frymer-Kensky, "The Sage in the Pentateuch: Soundings," in *The Sage in Israel and the Ancient Near East*, 275–87, esp. 275–8.

92 See, e.g., Borgen, *Philo*, 163–4; Justin M. Rogers, "The Philonic and the Pauline: Hagar and Sarah in the Exegesis of Didymus the Blind," *Studia Philonica Annual* 26 (2014): 57–77.

93 Judith Romney Wegner, "Philo's Portrayal of Women: Hebraic or Hellenic?" in *"Women Like This": New Perspectives on Jewish Women in the Greco-Roman World*, ed. Amy-Jill Levine (Atlanta, GA: Scholars Press, 1991), 41–66, esp. 55–6.

94 See Maren R. Niehoff, "Mother and Maiden, Sister and Spouse: Sarah in Philonic Midrash," *Harvard Theological Review* 97 (2004): 413–44, esp. 420–1, on *Abr.* 248–50. This passage narrates how Sarah overcame her jealousy and attachment to Abraham, exhorting her husband to have a child with Hagar.

95 Atar Livneh, "Jewish Traditions and Familial Roman Values in Philo's *De Abrahamo* 245–254," *Harvard Theological Review* 109 (2016): 536–49.

96 See esp. *Leg.* 3.244–5 (cf. *Genesis Rabbah* 47:1) and the analysis of Hanna Tervanotko and Elisa Uusimäki, "Sarah the Princess: Tracing the Hellenistic Afterlife of a Pentateuchal Female Figure," *Scandinavian Journal of the Old Testament* 32 (2018): 271–90, esp. 274–6.

97 See Marc van de Mieroop, *Philosophy before the Greeks: The Pursuit of Truth in Ancient Babylonia* (Princeton, NJ: Princeton University Press, 2015).

98 See, e.g., Richard Buxton, *Imaginary Greece: The Contexts of Mythology* (Cambridge: Cambridge University Press, 1994); Richard Stoneman, *The Ancient Oracles: Making the Gods Speak* (New Haven, CT: Yale University Press, 2011).
99 Kerferd, "Image," 17, 22–3.
100 Nightingale, "Sages," 156.
101 George B. Kerferd, "The Sage in Hellenistic Philosophical Literature (399 B.C.E.–199 C.E.)," in *The Sage in Israel and the Ancient Near East*, 319–28, esp. 319. The superior role of any single group of professionals should not be taken for granted since early philosophical and historical thinkers were seen as competing for intellectual authority with poets; see Nightingale, "Sages," 157–8, 167.
102 Nightingale, "Sages," 159.
103 See, e.g., Aude Busine, *Le Sept Sages de la Grèce antique* (Paris: de Boccard, 2002).
104 Kerferd, "Image," 27.
105 Cooper, *Pursuits*, 30.
106 See Hadot, *Ancient Philosophy*, 220–33; Annas, "Sage," 11–27. The logic of this distinction is found in Plato's *Symposium* where Socrates discusses the nature of love (esp. 199c–201c, 203e–204b), but it is less clear in Stoic philosophy; see Sellars, *Art*, 82.
107 Well-known sophists include Protagoras of Abdera, Gorgias of Leontiti, Antiphon, Hippias, Prodicus of Leos, and Thrasymachus. The term carried a polemical flavour from the classical period to the Roman era. See, e.g., Beatrice Wyss et al. (ed.), *Sophisten in Hellenismus und Kaiserzeit* (Tübingen: Mohr Siebeck, 2017).
108 This is shown, e.g., by Socrates' portrayal as a sophist or the praise for Prodicus' wisdom in Aristophanes' *Clouds* (line 361); see Rachel Barney, "The Sophistic Movement," in *A Companion to Ancient Philosophy*, ed. Mary Louise Gill and Pierre Pellegrin (Oxford: Blackwell, 2006), 77–97. In spite of his association, Socrates does not act like most of the sophists; see Nightingale, "Sages," 172.
109 Cf. Plato, *Apology* 19E; see ibid., 168–9.
110 Annas, "Sage," 13–14.
111 Kerferd, "Image," 320.
112 Annas, "Sage," 14.
113 Trans. Harold North Fowler, LCL 123.
114 Trans. H. Rackham, LCL 731.
115 See Julia Annas, *The Morality of Happiness* (Oxford: Oxford University Press, 1995), 73; Rachana Kamtekar, "Ancient Virtue Ethics: An Overview with an Emphasis on Practical Wisdom," in *The Cambridge Companion to Virtue Ethics*, ed. Daniel C. Russell (Cambridge: Cambridge University Press, 2013), 29–48, esp. 34–7.
116 See Kerferd, "Sage," 323; Brouwer, *Sage*, 169–70.
117 Kerferd, "Sage," 325–6.
118 Kerferd, "Image," 322–8; Kerferd, "Sage," 324–8.

119 So, e.g., Kerferd, "Image," 320; Benjamin Fiore, "The Sage in Select Hellenistic and Roman Literary Genres (Philosophical Epistles, Political Discourses, History, Comedy, and Romances)," in *The Sage in Israel and the Ancient Near East*, 329–41, esp. 330. There is no sustainable evidence that the earliest Stoics (Zeno, Persaeus, Sphraerus, Cleanthes, Chrysippus) would have declared themselves to be sages; see Brouwer, *Sage*, 92–135. Yet, they may have considered Socrates to have acquired wisdom late in his life; ibid., 163–6. The Roman Stoics are somewhat more optimistic; ibid., 110–12.

120 See Robert W. Sharples, "The Problem of Sources," in *A Companion to Ancient Philosophy*, 430–47.

121 The citations are from Arthur J. Pomeroy (trans. and ed.), *Arius Didymus: Epitome of Stoic Ethics* (Atlanta, GA: Society of Biblical Literature, 1999).

122 Underlying this claim is an idea of the universe as a product of the active intelligence/reason and the passive/material principle; see Kerferd, "Image," 321. Nevertheless, the Stoics maintain that there are people (προκόπτοντες) who are advancing on the path to virtue, but yet inferior to sages (e.g., Seneca, *Ep.* 94.50–1). Plutarch associates discussion on them with Zeno (*Prog. in Virt.* 82F); see Ian G. Kidd, "Stoic Intermediates and the End for Man," in *Problems in Stoicism*, ed. Anthony A. Long (London: Athlone, 1971), 150–72, esp. 164–5, 172.

123 Anthony A. Long, "Language and Thought in Stoicism," in *Problems in Stoicism*, 75–113, esp. 101; Long, *Hellenistic Philosophy: Stoics, Epicureans, Sceptics* (New York: Charles Scribner's Sons, 1974), 205.

124 Arius II.7.5b12, 11m, 11s. See also Plutarch, *De tranq. anim.* 472A; Lucian, *Vit. auct.* 20.

125 Epictetus' claim (*Frag.* 2) that the one who bears his or her fortune deserves to be called a good person (ἀνὴρ ἀγαθὸς) also indicates the irrelevance of external conditions. On Roman Stoics, see esp. Cicero, *Fin.* III.75–6; Seneca, *Ep.* 41.4.

126 Cf. D.L. 7.117–18. See Long, *Philosophy*, 206; Graver, *Stoicism*, 35, 210.

127 D.L. 7.102 reports that Chrysippus (*c.* 279–206 BCE), Apollodorus (*c.* 150 BCE), and Hecato (*c.* 100 BCE) regarded most things as morally indifferent, i.e., as neither beneficial nor harmful.

128 Kerferd, "Image," 321.

129 Annas, "Sage," 17–18.

130 On marriage and family life, see Arius II.7.11m and D.L. 7.121 (cf. Seneca, *Ep.* 116.5); on household management, see Arius II.7.11d; on politics and societal activities, see Arius II.7.11m, Plutarch's *De Stoic repugn.* 1043b–e, and D.L. 7.121; and on moneymaking, see Arius II.7.11d. According to a quotation preserved in Plutarch, *De Stoic repugn.* 1033c–d, Chrysippus even seems to have rejected the life of study as being "no different from the life of pleasure." See Annas, "Sage," 18–19.

131 Ibid., 21, 24.

132 The quality of self-coherence, the capability of being happy in spite of external conditions, is associated with Socrates in particular (on his pupil Aristippus, see

also D.L. 2.66). As for self-sufficiency, Plato documents Socrates saying that "such a man [a good person] is particularly self-sufficient with regard to living well, and is different from others in having the least need of someone else" (*Republic* 387d12, trans. Chris Emlyn-Jones and William Preddy, LCL 237); see Hadot, *Ancient Philosophy*, 221–2, 313.

133 Annas, "Sage," 13.
134 Hadot, *Ancient Philosophy*, 224.
135 Ibid., 220.
136 Trans. Christopher Emlyn-Jones and William Preddy, LCL 276. The positive role attributed to Homer is notable because Plato also rejected Homer's importance as an educator and preferred to banish him from his own ideal state. See, e.g., Elizabeth S. Belfiore, "Plato's Greatest Accusation against Poetry," *Canadian Journal of Philosophy* 9 (1983): 39–62; Ramona A. Nadaff, *Exiling the Poets: The Production of Censorship in Plato's Republic* (Chicago: The University of Chicago Press, 2002).
137 Trans. J. H. Freese, LCL 193.
138 Note that Socrates' portrayal as a contemplative philosopher in *Symposium* is a novelty in comparison with Plato's earlier dialogues; see Nightingale, "Sages," 181. The secondary literature on Socrates' reception in Greco-Roman thinking is extensive; see, e.g., Anthony A. Long, "Socrates in Later Greek Philosophy," in *The Cambridge Companion to Socrates*, ed. Donald R. Morrison (Cambridge: Cambridge University Press, 2010), 355–79.
139 Trans. W. A. Oldfather, LCL 218.
140 Trans. R. D. Hicks, LCL 185.
141 On Zeno's school, see Hadot, *Ancient Philosophy*, 100–1, 126–39. The significance of emulating one's teacher is also apparent in a humorous fictional letter of Alciphron, the ancient Greek sophist and epistolographer, who perhaps lived in the second or third century CE. Alciphron tells about Crito who had sent his son to a philosophical school in order to be instructed in logic and speaking skills. Instead, "the boy modelled himself after his teacher to the smallest detail; he preferred to study, not doctrines, but his way of life and his behaviour" (*Letters* 3.64, trans. A. R. Benner and F. H. Fobes, LCL 383).
142 Trans. Frank Cole Babbitt, LCL 197. Lucian of Samosata, the rhetorician and satirist from the second century CE, crystallizes the same idea of learning from the ancients as follows: "Two things can be acquired from the ancients, the ability to speak and to act as one ought, by emulating the best models (ζήλῳ τῶν ἀρίστων) and shunning the worst" (*Ind.* 17, trans. A. M. Harmon, LCL 130).
143 This is not say that the Stoics would have regarded the sage's epistemological perfection as less important. On the contrary, the Stoic sage has true knowledge lacked by the rest of the people.
144 See the recent assessment of Benjamin G. Wright, "Ben Sira and Hellenistic Literature in Greek," in *Tracing Sapiential Traditions in Ancient Judaism*, 71–88.

Considering various factors – our knowledge of educational institutions in Palestine, the discovery of Greek inscriptions and of the Qumran scrolls, the composition of Jewish texts in Greek in Palestine, the knowledge of Greek literature shown by Jewish authors writing in Semitic languages, and aspects of Ben Sira's instruction that align with Hellenistic thought – Wright concludes (ibid., 86): "It is difficult for me not to think that Ben Sira knew Greek and that he knew more than simply how to get along when he traveled." On the authors who probably operated in Palestine and wrote in Greek (Theodotus, Philo the Epic Poet, Eupolemus), thus indicating that they had received "a level of Greek education well beyond the *enkyklios paideia*," see ibid., 76–7, 79. The fact that more than half of the discovered public inscriptions are in Greek also indicates a widespread knowledge of Greek; see Pieter van der Horst, "Greek in Jewish Palestine in Light of Jewish Epigraphy," in *Hellenism in the Land of Israel*, ed. John J. Collins and Gregory E. Sterling (Notre Dame, IN: Notre Dame University Press, 2001), 154–74.

145 Another example of the *Zeitgeist* type of influence could be the emergence of voluntary associations. See, e.g., Yonder M. Gillihan, *Civic Ideology, Organization, and Law in the Rule Scrolls: A Comparative Study of the Covenanters' Sect and Contemporary Voluntary Associations in Political Context* (Leiden: Brill, 2012).

146 Sanders, *Adapa*, 71–101. The English translation of the text is from ibid., 76.

147 On pseudepigraphic attribution as a means to self-identify with an ancestral figure, see Najman, "Pseudepigrapha," 535–6.

148 Wright, "Exemplar," 170–1. On the "cultural reproduction of the parent," see also Carr, *Writing*, 130.

149 Michael V. Fox, *A Time to Tear Down and a Time to Build Up: A Rereading of Ecclesiastes* (Grand Rapids, MI: Eerdmans, 1999), 8.

150 See, e.g., Theophil Middendorp, *Die Stellung Jesu Ben Siras zwischen Judentum und Hellenismus* (Leiden: Brill, 1973); Ludger Schwienhorst-Schönberg, "*Nicht im Menschen gründet das Glück*" (Koh 2,24): *Kohelet im Spannungsfeld jüdischer Weisheit und hellenistischer Philosophie* (Freiburg: Herder, 1994), 232–332. Philo does not only allude to, but he often cites from Greek poets, historians, and philosophers; see Erkki Koskenniemi, "Philo and Classical Drama," in *Ancient Israel, Judaism, and Christianity in Contemporary Perspective*, ed. Jacob Neusner et al. (Lanham, MD: University Press of America, 2006), 137–52; Koskenniemi, "Philo and Greek Poets," *Journal for the Study of Judaism* 41 (2010): 301–22; Katell Berthelot, "Philon d'Alexandrie, lecteur d'Homère: quelques éléments de réflexion," in *Prolongements et renouvellements de la tradition classique*, ed. Anne Balansard et al. (Aix-en-Provence: Université de Provence, 2011), 145–57; David Lincicum, "A Preliminary Index to Philo's Non-Biblical Citations and Allusions," *Studia Philonica Annual* 25 (2013): 139–67.

151 See Amar Annus, Review of "Seth L. Sanders, From Adapa to Enoch: Scribal Culture and Religious Vision in Judea and Babylon," *Bibliotheca Orientalis* 75

(2018): 159–65, esp. 159–60. On the postmodern focus on difference, see also Wendy Doniger, "Post-modern and -colonial -structural Comparisons," in *A Magic Still Dwells: Comparative Religion in Postmodern Age*, ed. Kimberley C. Patton and Benjamin C. Ray (Berkeley, CA: University of California Press, 2000), 63–74, esp. 69.

152 Cf. John J. Collins' remarks on the intellectual profit of reading the treatise on the two spirits (1QS 3:13–4:26) in the light of Persian ideas; see Collins, "The Two Spirits and the Origin of Evil," presented at Enoch Seminar Online, July 2020.

153 Marshall Sahlins, "Two or Three Things That I Know about Culture," *The Journal of the Royal Anthropological Institute* 5 (1999): 399–421, esp. 412.

154 Cf. ibid., 412, who describes cultures as "largely foreign in origin, but distinctively local in pattern."

155 On the aspirational nature of the human self, see Stanley Cavell, *Cities of Words: Pedagogical Letters on a Register of the Moral Life* (Cambridge, MA: The Belknap Press of Harvard University Press, 2004), esp. 13, 26.

156 On the comparative method, see, e.g., Brent A. Strawn, "Comparative Approaches: History, Theory, and the Image of God," in *Method Matters: Essays on the Interpretation of the Hebrew Bible*, ed. Joel M. LeMon and Kent H. Richards (Atlanta, GA: Society of Biblical Literature, 2009), 117–42, esp. 117.

157 On the use of exempla in Greco-Roman antiquity, see, e.g., Michael R. Cosby, *The Rhetorical Composition and Function of Hebrews 11 in Light of Example Lists in Antiquity* (Macon, GA: Mercer University Press, 1988), 93–105; Teresa Morgan, *Popular Morality in the Early Roman Empire* (Cambridge: Cambridge University Press, 2007), 122–3. On the early reception of biblical figures, see, e.g., Collins and Nickelsburg (ed.), *Ideal Figures in Ancient Judaism*; Gruen, *Heritage*, 110–88; Michael E. Stone and Theodore A. Bergren (ed.), *Biblical Figures outside the Bible* (Harrisburg, PA: Trinity Press International, 1998); Diana V. Edelman and Ehud Ben Zvi (ed.), *Remembering Biblical Figures in the Late Persian and Early Hellenistic Periods: Social Memory and Imagination* (Oxford: Oxford University Press, 2013).

158 Aristotle, in fact, divides examples into historical and fictive types. He specifically credits the historical ones, stating that "while the lessons conveyed by fables are easier to provide, those derived from facts are more useful for deliberative oratory, because as a rule the future resembles the past" (*Rhetoric* 2.20, trans. J. H. Freese, LCL 193).

159 Anna-Liisa Tolonen and Elisa Uusimäki, "Managing the Ancestral Way of Life in the Roman Diaspora: The Mélange of Philosophical and Scriptural Practice in 4 Maccabees," *Journal for the Study of Judaism* 48 (2017): 113–41, esp. 123.

160 Ibid., 128–9. In the case of early Judaism, ancestral exemplarity shows the veneration of inherited textual traditions, thus signalling the gradual formation of Jewish scripture. However, the distinction between scriptural texts and their commentary was not clear-cut in the late second temple era, when the

boundaries of the canon were in flux and the text forms of authoritative writings could fluctuate. See, e.g., Eugene Ulrich, "The Jewish Scriptures: Texts, Versions, Canons," in *Early Judaism: A Comprehensive Overview*, ed. John J. Collins and Daniel C. Harlow (Grand Rapids, MI: Eerdmans, 2012), 121–50, esp. 140–8. Yet, an elevated status of certain texts was in the making. The act of reinterpretation added further authority to the biblical tradition by demonstrating its ongoing relevance; see, e.g., George J. Brooke, "Between Authority and Canon: The Significance of Reworking the Bible for Understanding the Canonical Process," in *Reworking the Bible: Apocryphal and Related Texts at Qumran*, ed. Esther G. Chazon et al. (Leiden: Brill, 2005), 85–104.

161 There are some exceptions to this general trend, the most famous being the book of Job (see Job 28; 38:4). In Proverbs, the speech attributed to Agur (Prov 30:1–33) complicates the ethos of the book, which generally displays human beings as capable of pursuing and achieving wisdom, by meditating on the limits of human knowledge.

162 Wright, "Exemplar," 171–8.

163 Note, however, that Socrates is portrayed as speaking in Plato's dialogues. It is questionable whether Plato presents him as a true sage, for the idea of Socrates as an exemplar probably comes from a later date. In any event, the use of the dialogue form is worth highlighting since Jewish sources do not document dialogues between the sage-teacher and his students, even though such probably took place in one form or another.

164 Cf. Peter Brown, "The Rise and Function of the Holy Man in Late Antiquity," *Journal of Roman Studies* 61 (1971): 80–101; Brown, "The Saint as Exemplar in Late Antiquity," *Representations* 2 (1983): 1–25.

165 On the nature of this relation, see John Rogerson, *A Theology of the Old Testament: Cultural Memory, Communication, and Being Human*, 1st Fortress Press ed. (Minneapolis, MN: Fortress, 2010), 54.

Chapter 3

1 On this aim of researching everyday life, see Susie Scott, *Making Sense of Everyday Life* (Cambridge: Polity, 2009), 2. My interest in exercise is indebted to the work of Hindy Najman, who has previously applied Pierre Hadot's idea of spiritual exercise to the practice of pseudepigraphical attribution in ancient Jewish writings; see Najman, *Past Renewals: Interpretative Authority, Renewed Revelation and the Quest for Perfection in Jewish Antiquity* (Leiden: Brill, 2010), xxi and chs. 13–14.

2 The same concerns Philo of Alexandria, who otherwise depicts the sage in a manner that reminds one of the Stoic wise persons, known for his societal engagement. Yet, this does not mean that the rewritten portraits of biblical figures could not shed light on contemporary practices in ancient Jewish communities.

Consider, e.g., the figure of Jacob whom Philo of Alexandria portrays as undertaking a series of exercises on his way to virtue (*Leg.* 3.18–19; *Her.* 252–3). See the section "Jewish teachers and their Mediterranean habitat" below.

3   On the idea of the torah/law as a teacher, see, e.g., Psalms 19 and 119; 4 Macc 5:34; Gal 3:24.

4   On the educational vision of Deuteronomy, see Carr, *Writing*, 134–9. As Carr observes, the rest of the Deuteronomistic history indicates some pedagogical concerns (e.g., Josh 1:7–8), but they are less dominant than in Deuteronomy.

5   See, e.g., Hindy Najman, *Seconding Sinai: The Development of Mosaic Discourse in Second Temple Judaism* (Leiden: Brill, 2003).

6   On this anxiety, see Steven Weitzman, "Was Moses our Teacher a Good Teacher?," n.p. [cited 9 July 2020]. Online: https://www.thetorah.com/article/was-moses-our-teacher-a-good-teacher.

7   The motif of writing down is already introduced ahead, as Moses and the elders exhort the people of Israel to keep the given regulations and to inscribe them to stones in the promised land (Deut 27:1–8); they are motivated to do so by the threat of curses and the reward of blessings (27:9–30:20).

8   In fact, Moses' song was apparently used for pedagogical purposes in the late second temple era. It is copied separately in 4QDeuteronomy^q from Qumran, suggesting that the song was read on specific didactic or liturgical occasions; see Jeffrey H. Tigay, *Deuteronomy: Devarim* (Philadelphia, PA: Jewish Publication Society, 1996), 31. On the use of the song, see also Uusimäki, *Proverbs*, 118–21. Furthermore, note David's lament over Saul and Jonathan in 2 Sam 1:19–27. According to the text itself, David's song was taught to the people of Judah.

9   See Moshe Weinfeld, *Deuteronomy and the Deuteronomistic School* (Oxford: Clarendon, 1972). Especially the late Deuteronomistic circles seem to have stressed the concern for learning and teaching since the root למד only occurs in the late section of Deuteronomy within the Pentateuch; see Timo Veijola, *Leben nach der Weisung: Exegetisch-historische Studien zum Alten Testament*, ed. Walter Dietrich and Marko Marttila (Göttingen: Vandenhoeck & Ruprecht, 2008), 323–42, esp. 148.

10   See, e.g., Joseph Blenkinsopp, *Wisdom and Law in the Old Testament: The Ordering of Life in Israel and Early Judaism*, rev. ed. (Oxford: Oxford University Press, 1995), 100.

11   According to Sara Japhet, it is impossible to say whether the Chronicler's reference to folk education has any historical basis; see Japhet, *I & II Chronicles: A Commentary* (Louisville, KY: Westminster John Knox Press, 1993), 750. Yet, there seems to be some evidence to support the historical reliability of the idea of itinerant teachers, for scribes are sent to teach in Sargon II's Dûr-Sharrukîn Cylinder inscription; see William M. Schniedewind, *A Social History of Hebrew: Its Origins through the Rabbinic Period* (New Haven, CT: Yale University Press, 2013), 85.

12 On the Levites as teachers, see Line Søgaard Christensen, "Homo Repetitivus and Anthropotechnics: Exercise Systems, Elite Practitioners, and Teaching Missions in the Hebrew Bible," in *"What Is Human?": Theological Encounters with Anthropology*, ed. Eve-Marie Becker et al. (Göttingen: Vandenhoeck & Ruprecht, 2017), 45–64, esp. 60–2.

13 Schams, *Scribes*, 53–4.

14 To be exact, Ezra 7:7 does not mention Ezra, but the literary context of the verse supports the idea that the aforementioned people accompanied him. The content of the group is logical since the mission aimed at restoring the temple worship; see Joseph Blenkinsopp, *Ezra-Nehemiah: A Commentary* (London: SCM Press, 1989), 138.

15 Blenkinsopp, *Ezra-Nehemiah*, 138–9.

16 In his letter, King Artaxerxes advises Ezra to act according to both the law and the wisdom of his God (Ezra 7:14, 25). Note, however, that the Aramaic word דת used of law here has many meanings such as "decree" and "religion."

17 The term דרש is used of divination in Deut 18:11; 1 Sam 9:9; 28:7; 1 Kgs 22:5–8; 2 Kgs 1:2; 3:11; 8:8; 22:13, 18; Isa 8:19; 19:3; Jer 8:2; 21:2; 37:7; Ezek 14:3, 7; 20:3, 31; 1 Chr 10:13–14; 13:3; 2 Chr 17:3–4; 25:20; see Esther J. Hamori, *Women's Divination in Biblical Literature: Prophecy, Necromancy, and Other Arts of Knowledge* (New Haven, CT: Yale University Press, 2015), 28.

18 Michael Fishbane, "From Scribalism to Rabbinism: Perspectives on the Emergence of Classical Judaism," in *The Sage in Israel and the Ancient Near East*, 439–56, esp. 441.

19 Michael V. Fox, "What the Book of Proverbs Is about," in *Congress Volume: Cambridge 1995*, ed. John A. Emerton (Leiden: Brill, 1997), 153–67, esp. 166.

20 Michael V. Fox, "Ideas of Wisdom in Proverbs 1–9," *Journal of Biblical Literature* 116 (1997): 613–33, esp. 633.

21 See Benjamin G. Wright, "From Generation to Generation: The Sage as Father in Early Jewish Literature," in *Biblical Traditions in Transmission*, ed. Charlotte Hempel and Judith M. Lieu (Leiden: Brill, 2006), 309–32.

22 On the family as a setting for learning in the ancient world, see Carole R. Fontaine, "The Sage in Family and Tribe," in *The Sage in Israel and the Ancient Near East*, 155–64; Carr, *Writing*, 129–30. Camp proposes that the pedagogical role of mothers decreased by the Hellenistic and Roman times, when the teaching of the torah became more organized and school-like. The book of Ben Sira, e.g., does not mention the mother's role; see Camp, "Sage," 199. Yet, one should be careful not to make an argument from silence, as hardly anything concrete is known about the context(s) of torah study. Consider also the evidence of 4 Macc 18:10–19, where a mother delivers instruction on ancestral writings; see, e.g., Tessa Rajak, "The Maccabean Mother between Pagans, Jews, and Christians," in *Being Christian in Late Antiquity*, ed. Carol Harrison et al. (Oxford: Oxford University Press, 2014), 39–56.

23 As Legaspi observes, Qoheleth differs from other biblical books because of "the attention that the narrator, Qohelet, constantly draws to himself: his background, his experience, his observations, his reflections, even his emotional states." See Legaspi, *Wisdom*, 65.

24 For an argument that the book of Qoheleth comes from the Ptolemaic period, see Krüger, *Kohelet*, 39.

25 There has been much discussion on the identity of the speaker. The book is attributed to Solomon, but the associations of the name קהלת also include other royal figures since several kings summon assemblies in the Hebrew Bible. Thus, Jennie Barbour characterizes the figure of Qoheleth as "everyking." See Barbour, *The Story of Israel in the Book of Qohelet: Ecclesiastes as Cultural Memory* (Oxford: Oxford University Press, 2013), 26.

26 Grabbe, *Priests*, 170.

27 So, Brown, *Wonder*, 167.

28 Fox, *Time*, 71–3, 75–7, 82.

29 Ibid., 81.

30 Ibid., 7–8.

31 As Fox argues, the display of concerns and attitudes of various Hellenistic philosophies does not require that the book of Qoheleth would "have had an immediate 'source' in Greek philosophy." See ibid., 8.

32 So, Troels Engberg-Pedersen, "Setting the Scene: Stoicism and Platonism in the Transitional Period in Ancient Philosophy," in *Stoicism in Early Christianity*, ed. Tuomas Rasimus et al. (Grand Rapids, MI: Baker Academic, 2010), 1–14, esp. 9–10. Engberg-Pedersen makes the claim regarding Paul's thought and its connections to Greek philosophy, but one could say the same of Hellenistic Jewish thinkers in general.

33 On the ancient Israelite interest in the collection of written material, see James L. Kugel, "Wisdom and the Anthological Temper," *Prooftexts* 17 (1997): 9–32.

34 In fact, Brown describes Qoheleth as a selfish sage, arguing that his quest for wisdom cannot be detached from his desire to enhance the self; see Brown, *Wonder*, 188.

35 Ibid., 167.

36 See Qoh 2:18–23 where the speaker doubts the usefulness of his efforts: he has to leave the results of his עמל (trouble, labour, toil) to his successor, who may be either wise or foolish, ruling everything with this undeserved "inheritance." Fox writes: "It is not the thought of losing wealth that pains Qohelet so much as the affront to his sense of propriety and justice. The crisscrossing of effort and result is unfair and absurd, and it is God's doing." See Fox, *Time*, 37.

37 Wright, "Exemplar," 168. On wisdom and behaviour, see also James L. Crenshaw, "The Primacy of Listening in Ben Sira's Pedagogy," in *Wisdom, You Are My Sister*, ed. Michael L. Barré (Washington, DC: Catholic Biblical Association of America, 1997), 172–87, esp. 183: "The true scribe is the one who hears, which means that his actions embody the teachings."

38 Eva Mroczek, *The Literary Imagination in Jewish Antiquity* (New York: Oxford University Press, 2016), 87–113.

39 Previously, the question of spiritual exercise in the book of Ben Sira has been addressed by Daniel J. Harrington, *Jesus ben Sira of Jerusalem: A Biblical Guide to Living Wisely* (Collegeville, MN: Liturgical Press, 2005), 100–32. Yet, Harrington's approach to spiritual exercise is fundamentally different from mine. He employs the term as referring to "a method for reading Ben Sira's book" and its key topics (ibid., 131). By listing spiritual exercises, Harrington aims at imagining and thus reproducing what took place in Ben Sira's school (ibid., 102). He identifies ten thematic categories, including the origin and nature of wisdom; the fear of the Lord; the quest for wisdom; cultivation of virtues and avoidance of vices; friendship; sin; the problem of evil; mourning, death, and afterlife; the manifestation of God's glory in creation; and the manifestation of God's glory in Israel's history. While Harrington's observations on the book are insightful, he does not consider the lived aspect of wisdom, as I aim at doing in my reading of the text.

40 Wright, "Generation," 309–32.

41 Trans. Benjamin G. Wright, NETS.

42 Matthew J. Goff, "Gardens of Knowledge: Teachers in Ben Sira, 4QInstruction, and the Hodayot," in *Pedagogy in Ancient Judaism and Early Christianity*, 171–93, esp. 176.

43 Alexander A. Di Lella proposes that the author imagines his teaching to be seen in the diaspora; see Di Lella, *The Wisdom of Ben Sira: A New Translation with Notes by Patrick W. Skehan. Introduction and Commentary by Alexander A. Di Lella* (New York: Doubleday, 1987), 336–8.

44 Trans. Benjamin G. Wright, NETS.

45 See Yun Lee Too, "Introduction: Writing the History of Ancient Education," in *Education in Greek and Roman Antiquity*, ed. Yun Lee Too (Leiden: Brill, 2001), 1–21, esp. 11.

46 The maskil describes his light with a divine origin in 1QS 11:3. Light is also associated with wisdom or virtue (Wis 6:12; 7:10, 26, 29; Philo, *Leg.* 1.43–6) or with the torah (Ps 119:105; Wis 18:4; Jub. 24:18–20; CD 6). Ps 19:5–6 connects it with creation, whereas light pertains to the future vanquishing of injustice in 1Q27 frag. 1 i 5–6.

47 So, Di Lella, *Wisdom*, 338.

48 As argued by Newman, the sage is expected to create "an eternal dynasty through generations of future students." See Newman, "Imagination," 325–6.

49 Trans. Benjamin G. Wright, NETS. The macarism is also preserved in the Hebrew MS B, though it refers to a person who meditates (יהגה) on "these things." All the Hebrew texts of Ben Sira are from Pancratius C. Beentjes, *The Book of Ben Sira in Hebrew: A Text Edition of All Extant Hebrew Manuscripts and a Synopsis of All Parallel Hebrew Ben Sira Texts* (Leiden: Brill, 1997).

50 Trans. Benjamin G. Wright, NETS.

51 On the inclusion of the book of Ben Sira in the corpus of revered texts, see Francis Borchardt, "Prologue of Sirach (Ben Sira) and the Question of Canon," in *Sacra Scriptura: How "Non-Canonical" Texts Functioned in Early Judaism and Early Christianity*, ed. James H. Charlesworth et al. (London: Bloomsbury T&T Clark, 2014), 64–71, esp. 69.

52 Scholars debate the extent to which the author used (non-Jewish) Greek sources. See Middendorp, *Stellung*, 7–34, who detects innumerable parallels. Yet, many of them remain contested. See the critique of Jack T. Sanders, *Ben Sira and Demotic Wisdom* (Chico, CA: Scholars Press, 1983) and that of Hans Volker Kieweler, *Ben Sira zwischen Judentum und Hellenismus: Eine Auseinandersetzung mit Th. Middendorp* (Frankfurt: Peter Lang, 1992). See also the more cautious survey of Wright, "Literature," 80–6. The most likely dependence on Greek literature concerns Theognis's gnomic poetry on the theme of friendship (Sir 6:5–17); ibid., 83–5. Most recently, see James E. Harding, "Ben Sira on Friendship: Notes on Intertextuality and Method," in *Perspectives on Israelite Wisdom*, ed. John Jarick (London: Bloomsbury T&T Clark, 2016), 439–62, esp. 445n15, 447–8, 452.

53 Similarly, other sequences of virtuous examples in early Jewish and Christian texts do not necessarily use the idiom of imitation, but the audience is nonetheless expected to learn from the past figures. See Wisdom of Solomon 10–19; 1 Macc 2:49–64; 4 Macc 16:20–3 (cf. 1:30–3:18); Apoc. Zeph. 9:4; 4 Ezra 7:106–10; Heb 11:2–39; 1 Clem 4:7–6:4, 9:2–12:8.

54 See, e.g., Burton L. Mack, *Wisdom and the Hebrew Epic: Ben Sira's Hymn in Praise of the Fathers* (Chicago: The University of Chicago Press, 1985), 128–37; David A. deSilva, "The Wisdom of Ben Sira: Honor, Shame, and the Maintenance of the Values of a Minority Culture," *Catholic Biblical Quarterly* 58 (1996): 433–55.

55 Mack, *Wisdom*, 136, 158.

56 DeSilva, "Wisdom," 433–55. On Pericles' speech, see David A. deSilva, *Despising Shame: Honor Discourse and Community Maintenance in the Epistle to the Hebrews*, rev. ed. (Atlanta, GA: Society of Biblical Literature, 2008), 50–3.

57 Trans. Benjamin G. Wright, NETS. According to the Hebrew version of the text, the first hemistich refers to "the fear of the Most High" (יראת עליון) instead of "Lord's ordinances" (MS A).

58 Trans. Benjamin G. Wright, NETS. The verse is not preserved in Hebrew.

59 See also Sir 13:15–19 on the roles of animals and humans in the world, as well as on the related question of whether a harmonious co-existence is possible.

60 Trans. Benjamin G. Wright, NETS. Parts of the Hebrew text are preserved in MS B and SirMas.

61 Similarly the Hebrew version: עוד כאלה לא נוסף (MS B).

62 On epistemic humility, see also Sir 3:21–4, which reminds one of understanding the limits of one's knowledge.

63 Only Sir 18:32–3 (and the last word of verse 18:31) remain in Hebrew. The Greek translation develops the content of the Hebrew text, which simply exhorts the

reader not to rejoice of vain things (the exact meaning of שמץ is unclear), or behave like a glutton or drinker, in order not to make himself poor.

64 So, James K. Aitken, "Ben Sira's Table Manners and the Social Setting of His Book," in *Perspectives on Israelite Wisdom*, 418–38.

65 Trans. Benjamin G. Wright, NETS.

66 Only two of the prayers embedded in the composition (Sir 22:27–23:6; 51:1–12) are presented as first-person speeches; see Wright, "Exemplar," 171. To clarify my use of the term "liturgical," I wish to emphasize, drawing on the work of Newman, that liturgy is not limited to temple rites or fixed prayers, but it covers "a constellations of actions" reflecting "a covenantal response to Israel's God." This means that the study of sacred texts, fasting, prayers, and benedictions all belong to the sphere of liturgy. So, Newman, "Imagination," 325.

67 For the view that sins prevent wisdom, see Ps 51:8–9; Wis 1:4–5. The passage in Wis 7:1–22 depicts another praying wise person, the fictitious Solomon (cf. 1 Kgs 3:6–9; Psalm 72).

68 See, e.g., Benjamin D. Sommer, "Did Prophecy Cease? Evaluating a Reevaluation," *Journal of Biblical Literature* 115 (1996): 31–47.

69 So, Hindy Najman, *Losing the Temple and Recovering the Future: An Analysis of 4 Ezra* (Cambridge: Cambridge University Press, 2014), 5–6.

70 Trans. Benjamin G. Wright, NETS. The phrase ὡς προφητείαν could be translated as either "like prophecy" or "as prophecy." Even though the translation "like prophecy" seems natural, the question is about the reception and transmission of divine wisdom; see Benjamin G. Wright, "Conflicted Boundaries: Ben Sira, Sage and Seer," in *Congress Volume Helsinki 2010*, ed. Martti Nissinen (Leiden: Brill, 2012), 229–53, esp. 236.

71 Trans. Benjamin G. Wright, NETS.

72 On wisdom in Sir 4:17–18, see Wright, "Boundaries," 236–7. On wisdom in Sir 24:1–22, see Martti Nissinen, "Wisdom as Mediatrix in Sirach 24: Ben Sira, Love Lyrics, and Prophecy," in *Of God(s), Trees, Kings, and Scholars*, ed. Mikko Luukko et al. (Helsinki: The Finnish Oriental Society, 2009), 377–90.

73 Wright, "Boundaries," 230.

74 Newman even argues that "the role of the sage in Ben Sira has usurped the role of the ancient Israelite prophet." Yet, the question is not about delivering prophecy "simply for an immediate situation ... but as an inheritance for future generations who seek wisdom." See Newman, "Imagination," 318–19.

75 See Elisa Uusimäki, "Sages as Mediators of Divine Knowledge in Jewish Antiquity," in *The Textualization of Revelation*, ed. Jonathan Stökl and Hanna Tervanotko (London: Bloomsbury T&T Clark, forthcoming).

76 Trans. Benjamin G. Wright, NETS. The quotation follows the Greek text. The Hebrew text exhorts one to give a gift to all living beings (MS A).

77 Françoise Mirguet, *An Early History of Compassion: Emotion and Imagination in Hellenistic Judaism* (Cambridge: Cambridge University Press, 2017), 111–19, esp. 118–19.

78 Trans. Benjamin G. Wright, NETS. The Hebrew text has the same meaning apart from not referring to the precise performance of the torah/law (MS B).

79 See, e.g., David Winston, "Theodicy in Ben Sira and Stoic Philosophy," in *Of Scholars, Savants, and Their Texts: Studies in Philosophy and Religious Thought*, ed. Ruth Link-Salinger et al. (New York: Lang, 1989), 239–49. For a critique of the idea that the text would include Stoic ideas, see Sharon Lea Mattila, "Ben Sira and the Stoics: A Reexamination of the Evidence," *Journal of Biblical Literature* 119 (2000): 473–501.

80 On conceptual parallels or comparisons between Jewish and Greco-Roman texts, see also Hindy Najman and Tobias Reinhardt, "Exemplarity and Its Discontents: Hellenistic Jewish Wisdom Texts and Greco-Roman Didactic Poetry," *Journal for the Study of Judaism* 50 (2019): 460–96.

81 Trans. Benjamin G. Wright, NETS.

82 Uusimäki, "Sages," 315–36.

83 Newsom, *Self*, 167.

84 Robert Hawley, "On Maskil in the Judean Desert Texts," *Henoch* 28 (2006): 43–77.

85 See Prov 10:5, 19; 14:35; 15:24; 16:20; 17:2; 19:14; 21:12; Pss 32:1; 42:1; 44:1; 45:1; 52:1; 53:1; 54:1; 55:1; 74:1; 78:1; 88:1; 89:1; 142:1. Elsewhere in biblical texts, see 1 Sam 18:14, 15; Amos 5:13; Pss 14:2; 41:2; 47:8; 53:3; Job 22:2; 2 Chr 30:22; Dan 1:4; 11:33, 35; 12:3, 10; Sir 7:21; 10:23; 13:22; 47:12.

86 See, e.g., 4Q416 frag. 2 ii 15 and the comments of Charlotte Hempel, "The Qumran Sapiential Texts and the Rule Books," in *The Wisdom Texts from Qumran and the Development of Sapiential Thought*, ed. Charlotte Hempel et al. (Leuven: Peeters, 2002), 277–95, esp. 295.

87 So, Charlotte Hempel, "The Treatise of the Two Spirits and the Literary History of the Rule of the Community," in *Dualism in Qumran*, ed. Géza G. Xeravits (London: T&T Clark, 2010), 102–20, esp. 116.

88 The increasing emphasis on the maskil was rooted in earlier traditions, as the use of the term draws on the משכילים of Dan 11:33–5; 12:3, 10. Matthias Henze argues that the language of Daniel "became the language of the covenanters themselves." See Henze, *The Madness of King Nebuchadnezzar: The Ancient Near Eastern Origins and Early History of Interpretation of Daniel 4* (Leiden: Brill, 1999), 241. Charlotte Hempel concludes that they did not only adapt Daniel's language, but, "to some extent, it *was* their own." According to her, "the shared roots of these movements" might explain the overlap. See Hempel, "*Maskil(im)* and *Rabbim*: From Daniel to Qumran," in *Biblical Traditions in Transmission*, 133–56, esp. 156. Either way, the motif's integration into new literary contexts demonstrates more continuity between "pre-sectarian" and "sectarian" texts than scholars have often recognized. So, George J. Brooke, "The Place of Wisdom in the Formation of the Movement behind the Dead Sea Scrolls," in *Goochem in Mokum, Wisdom in Amsterdam: Papers on Biblical and Related Wisdom*, ed. Bob Becking (Leiden: Brill, 2016), 20–33, esp. 28–9.

89 Cf. Carol A. Newsom, "The Sage in the Literature of Qumran: The Functions of the Maśkîl," in *The Sage in Israel and the Ancient Near East*, 373–82, esp. 374n4: "I interpret all of the references to the *maśkîl* in the Qumran literature as referring to the one who performs the official function of instruction in the community. … Even if some of the occurrences should be read in the nontechnical sense … the values and accomplishments associated with the wise person form part of the ideal that would pertain especially to the leaders of the community."

90 In Instruction, the phrase "all your maskilim" (כול משכילכה) refers to the people (i.e., not to an institution held by one person) from whom the addressee, designated as an "understanding one" (מבין), receives understanding (4Q418 frag. 81:17). Another copy of the same composition addresses the pupil as a "son of maskil" (בן משכיל), who should acquire understanding about mysteries (4Q417 frag. 2 i 25). Finally, according to Ways of Righteousness[b], the maskil may express reproofs, which implies an authoritative position in relation to his students (4Q421 frag. 1 ii 11–12). These cases demonstrate that there are many maskils, i.e., the term can designate wisdom teachers in general.

91 See Harrington, *Wisdom*, 65–6; Kampen, *Wisdom*, 270–9.

92 For further remarks on these options, see Newsom, *Self*, 102–3.

93 See Dominique Barthélemy and Józef T. Milik, *Qumran Cave 1*, DJD 1 (Oxford: Clarendon, 1955), 121; Jean Carmignac, "Conjecture sur la première ligne de la Règle de la Communauté," *Revue de Qumran* 2 (1959): 85–7, esp. 85; Sarianna Metso, *The Textual Development of the Qumran Community Rule* (Leiden: Brill, 1997), 111–12.

94 See also 4Q256 frag. 9:1 (par. 4Q258 frag. 1:1), which begins with the title "midrash for the maskil (מדרש למשכיל)."

95 Newsom, *Self*, 79.

96 Newsom, "Sage," 377. Apart from 1QS, the War Scroll may attest to the maskil's task of teaching about cosmic and eschatological matters. See the reconstructed heading in 1QM 1:1, "For the ma[skil(מ]שכיל): the rule of] the war," which is followed by a reference to the attack of the sons of light against the sons of darkness.

97 Some of this material appears in the Cave 4 manuscripts of S. Six S manuscripts in total preserve material from the end of the work, including 1QS, 4QS[b], 4QS[d], 4QS[e], 4QS[f], and 4QS[j]. Each of them seems to have contained the third-person instructions attached to the maskil. Yet, they are followed by a calendrical teaching (Otot) in 4QS[e], whereas the maskil hymn occurs in 4QS[b], 4QS[d], 4QS[f], and 4QS[j]. The difference in content has some rhetorical consequences. The ending with Otot emphasizes the content of the maskil's teaching, whilst the hymn grants the maskil with a voice of his own, stressing the work's rhetorical structure and providing it with "a genuine conclusion." So, Newsom, *Self*, 104n22, 166. The hymn may have been added to one line of the S tradition later; see Metso, *Development*, 146–7.

98 So, Joseph L. Angel, "Maskil, Community, and Religious Experience in the Songs of the Sage (4Q510–511)," *Dead Sea Discoveries* 19 (2012): 1–27, esp. 10.
99 The verb אסתר ("I conceal") has been edited by the scribe into אספר ("I recount").
100 Samuel I. Thomas, *The "Mysteries" of Qumran: Mystery, Secrecy, and Esotericism in the Dead Sea Scrolls* (Atlanta, GA: Society of Biblical Literature, 2009), 217.
101 Furthermore, note that both figures are associated with the virtue of meekness. Num 12:3 characterizes Moses as the humblest man on earth, whilst the maskil's humility is stressed later in the hymn of 1QS, which continues with God's plan of salvation (11:6–9), the maskil's confession (11:9–11), and his proclamation of trust in God's mercy and justice (11:11–15).
102 The Community Rule has been described as a "manual to guide the Maskil in his duties as the spiritual head of the Community." So, Philip S. Alexander and Geza Vermes, *Qumran Cave 4.XIX: 4QSerekh Ha-Yaḥad and Two Related Texts*, DJD 26 (Oxford: Clarendon, 1998), 10.
103 Newsom, "Sage," 376; Newsom, *Self*, 82, 169–70.
104 In addition to 1QS, the Hodayot is an important source concerning the maskil's inspired role, for these thanksgiving hymns associate him with a divine and holy spirit (1QH^a 20:14–17, see also 7:21–8:41). For discussion, see Judith H. Newman, "Speech and Spirit: Paul and the Maskil as Inspired Interpreters of Scripture," in *The Holy Spirit, Inspiration, and the Cultures of Antiquity: Multidisciplinary Perspectives*, ed. Jörg Frey and Jon R. Levison (Berlin: de Gruyter, 2014), 243–64, esp. 245, 249.
105 On the concern for and the construction of time in 1QS, see Newsom, *Self*, 81, 174–86.
106 On authoritative figures in the movement, see the section "The *yaḥad* movement as a wisdom body" in Chapter 4.
107 This calendar, like the one in 1QH^a 20:7–14, may set out four times of prayer within one day/night cycle (sunrise, midday, sunset, midnight); see Jeremy Penner, *Patters of Daily Prayer in Second Temple Period Judaism* (Leiden: Brill, 2012), 137–64. It has been suggested that the calendar in 1QS 9:26–10:8 is a later addition; see Sarianna Metso, *The Serekh Texts* (London: T&T Clark, 2007), 14.
108 On the structure of the hymn, see Newsom, *Self*, 168–9.
109 Although the ל preposition could be interpreted in many ways, such as "for the maskil" or "of the maskil," the phrase למשכיל allows for an understanding of the figure as a liturgical master. Similarly Torleif Elgvin, "Maskil," in *Theologisches Wörterbuch zu den Qumrantexten: Band II*, ed. Heinz-Josef Fabry et al. (Stuttgart: Kolhammer, 2013), 802–6, esp. 806.
110 Newsom, "Sage," 375.
111 Another superscription without a context occurs in a Hodayot copy from Cave 4 (4Q428 frag. 12 ii 3). The same applies to the Hodayot-like text 4Q433a frag. 2:2. Some other hymns of 1QH^a may also have been associated with the maskil. First, the editors reconstruct a superscription referring to the figure in 1QH^a 1:1; see

Hartmut Stegemann and Eileen M. Schuller, *Qumran Cave 1.III: 1QHodayot*ᵃ, *with Incorporation of 4QHodayot*ᵃ⁻ᶠ *and 1QHodayot*ᵇ, DJD 40 (Oxford: Clarendon, 2009), 13–53. Second, the hymn in column four, which shares motifs and language with 1QS 10–11, was perhaps attributed to the maskil; see Daniel K. Falk, "Petition and Ideology in the Dead Sea Scrolls," in *Prayer and Poetry in the Dead Sea Scrolls and Related Literature*, 135–59, esp. 140–2. Third, even if the formula למשכיל does not appear in 1QHᵃ 6:8–12, the speaker might be the maskil as he establishes the community's hierarchical order (cf. 1QS 9:14–16). The first-person prayers also serve to highlight his authority; see Newsom, *Self*, 277–9.

112 The English translations of the Hodayot are by Carol A. Newsom, with occasional modifications, and taken from Stegemann and Schuller, DJD 40.

113 See Judith H. Newman, "Embodied Techniques: The Communal Formation of the Maskil's Self," *Dead Sea Discoveries* 22 (2015): 249–66.

114 The rest of the song praises God who teaches the maskil through his mysteries and has revealed to him "the ways of truth and the works of evil, wisdom and folly" (1QHᵃ 5:19–20). The maskil also (re)confesses the divine source of his knowledge (5:35–6).

115 See 4Q400 frag. 1 i 1; frag. 3 ii 8; 4Q401 frag. 1–2:1; 4Q403 frag. 1 i 30; frag. 1 ii 18; 4Q405 frag. 20 ii 6; 4Q406 frag. 1:4; 11Q17 frag. 7:9.

116 Newsom, "Sage," 380.

117 Philip S. Alexander, *Mystical Texts* (London: T&T Clark, 2006), 44; see also pp. 48–9.

118 The Self-Glorification Hymn (4Q491c; 4Q471b; 4Q427 frag. 7 i–9; 1QHᵃ 26:6–16) preserves other evidence for the ascent-to-heaven traditions in the scrolls; see Alexander, *Texts*, 85–91. See also Judith H. Newman, "Priestly Prophets at Qumran: Summoning Sinai through the *Songs of the Sabbath Sacrifice*," in *The Significance of Sinai*, 29–72, esp. 39. Newman argues that the final song, where the maskil serves as the head of the angel-like priests, culminates the series, thus signifying the "transformation of the mystic."

119 Angel, "Maskil," 2, 4, 11, 13, 16.

120 Ibid., 12–13.

121 Consider both brief references to exemplary patriarchs (e.g., 4Q185 frag. 1–2 ii 4; 4Q542 frag. 1 i 7–10) and more extended accounts of ancestral perfection. The latter include the portrait of David in 11Q5 27, which ignores any misdoings of the figure and celebrates his wisdom, understanding, and perfection; David, "a light like the light of the sun," spoke through "prophecy," leaving behind him an exceptional inheritance of thousands of songs. The scrolls also display cases of ancestral failure. Reviewing mistakes of the patriarchs, CD 3:1–16 warns the audience against deeds that provoke divine wrath. Furthermore, consider the list of seven virtues in 4Q542 frag. 1 i 10–13. These virtues might stand for seven patriarchs, ranging from Abraham to Aaron (on Aaron as the seventh man, see 4Q545 frag. 4:18–19). Yet, the deeds of each figure seem to manifest the reversal

of the virtue attached to him, which suggests that the author perhaps transformed the ancestors' mistakes into lessons on virtues; see Uusimäki, "Virtue."

122 Consider, e.g., the Persian flavour of the treatise on the two spirits (1QS 3:13–4:26) or the inclusion of astrological texts in the Qumran corpus. See Mladen Popović, *Reading the Human Body: Physiognomics and Astrology in the Dead Sea Scrolls and Hellenistic-Early Roman Period Judaism* (Leiden: Brill, 2007); Albert de Jong, "Iranian Connections in the Dead Sea Scrolls," in *The Oxford Handbook of the Dead Sea Scrolls*, 479–500, esp. 490–5; Jonathan Ben-Dov and Seth L. Sanders (ed.), *Ancient Jewish Sciences and the History of Knowledge in Second Temple Literature* (New York: New York University Press, 2014).

123 Note that the exact connotations of the term "torah" remain unclear, for the authors of these texts tend to abstract torah piety to a conceptual level, thus painting it with rather impressionistic strokes. Yet, both Ben Sira and the texts on the maskil stress the value of the torah in the sense of Israel's (growing) divine instruction. On the torah discourse of early Jewish wisdom texts, see, e.g., George J. Brooke, "Biblical Interpretation in the Wisdom Texts from Qumran," in *The Wisdom Texts from Qumran and the Development of Sapiential Thought*, 201–20; Lawrence H. Schiffman, "Halakhic Elements in the Sapiential Texts from Qumran," in *Sapiential Perspectives: Wisdom Literature in Light of the Dead Sea Scrolls*, ed. John J. Collins et al. (Leiden: Brill, 2004), 89–100; Uusimäki, *Proverbs*, 246–7.

124 On philosophers and pedagogues as text-brokers, see H. Gregory Snyder, *Teachers and Texts in the Ancient World: Philosophers, Jews and Christians* (London: Routledge, 2000).

125 Compare *b. B. Bathra* 12a on the rabbinic discussion concerning the contemporary relevance of the wise. According to the text, prophecy was taken away from the prophets and given to the sages after the destruction of the temple. A wise person is superior to a prophet, for his task is to take care of "the urgent intellectual and spiritual needs of the present," whereas the prophet appears as "the hero of a time-hallowed tradition." The sages, as successors of the prophets, indicate "a victory of the moderns over the ancients." So, Guy G. Stroumsa, "From Master of Wisdom to Spiritual Master in Late Antiquity," in *Religion and the Self in Antiquity*, ed. David Brakke et al. (Bloomington, IN: Indiana University Press, 2005), 183–96, esp. 185–6.

126 On this debated passage, see, e.g., Stuart Weeks, "'Fear God and Keep His Commandments': Could Qohelet Have Said This?," in *Wisdom and Torah*, 101–18. According to Weeks, it is unlikely that the author "would have used these terms," but Qoh 12:13–14 also contains "nothing with which he would strictly have disagreed" (ibid., 117).

127 On the aim of socialization is ancient education; see Too, "Introduction," 13.

128 Ibid., 11. See also Jaeger, *Paideia*, 1:xxiii: "the process of educating man into his true form, the real and genuine human nature." Jaeger's definition of παιδεία captures the aspirational nature of the enterprise.

129 Raffaella Cribiore, *Gymnastics of the Mind: Greek Education in Hellenistic and Roman Egypt* (Princeton, NJ: Princeton University Press, 2001), 243–5.
130 The occurrence of the term was noted above regarding Sir 24:32. It appears thirty-six times in Sirach; see Edward Hatch et al., *A Concordance to the Septuagint*, 2nd ed. (Grand Rapids, MI: Baker Academic, 1998), 1046–7.
131 Karina Martin Hogan, "Would Philo Have Recognized Qumran *Musar* as Paideia?," in *Pedagogy in Ancient Judaism and Early Christianity*, 81–100.
132 On the connotations of מוסר/παιδεία in the LXX Proverbs, see ibid., 83–6.
133 Bickerman, *Jews*, 166.
134 Ibid., 167–8.
135 Ibid., 170–1. On the centrality of Homer's poems in the Greek tradition, see Margalit Finkelberg, "Homer as a Foundation Text," in *Homer, the Bible and Beyond: Literary and Religious Canons in the Ancient World*, ed. Margalit Finkelberg and Guy G. Stroumsa (Leiden: Brill 2003), 75–96. Yet, one should understand neither "torah" nor "Homer" narrowly because both Jewish scriptures and Homeric texts were transmitted with an interpretative tradition in the Hellenistic and early Roman periods. See, e.g., Niehoff, *Exegesis*.
136 For the son's reply in Šimâ Milka, see Yoram Cohen and Andrew R. George, *Wisdom from the Late Bronze Age* (Atlanta, GA: Society of Biblical Literature, 2013), 96–101.
137 See, e.g., Hadot, *Philosophy*; Hadot, *Ancient Philosophy*; Sellars, *Art*.
138 In Platonism and Neopythagoreanism, e.g., ἄσκησις involved the rejection of bodily pleasures, while the Cynics even advocated hunger and cold. The Epicureans limited desires for the sake of attaining pure pleasure, the Pyrrhonians trained themselves to regard everything as indifferent, and the Stoics practised non-attachment to indifferent things; see Hadot, *Ancient Philosophy*, 189–90. On ancient therapeutic exercises, see also Sorabji, *Emotion*, 211–25.
139 Sellars, *Art*, 23.
140 See *Praem.* 51 on wisdom; *Leg.* 3.135, *Det.* 10, *Congr.* 35, *Somn.* 1.167–9, *Abr.* 52–4, and *Ios.* 1 on virtue; and *Gig.* 26, *Conf.* 181, and *Praem.* 65 on perfection.
141 See Philo, *Leg.* 3.18–19; *Her.* 252–3. The lists were first observed by Hadot, *Philosophy*, 83–4. I have analysed them in detail in my article "Mind," 265–88.
142 On the movement associated with the Qumran scrolls, see the section "The *yaḥad* movement as a wisdom body" in Chapter 4. Moreover, consider the evidence of the book of Jubilees, which some scholars have regarded as anti-Hellenistic. Pieter B. Hartog, however, defines it as "glocal." As Hartog shows, Jubilees displays "encyclopedic" tendencies, including a rhetoric of presenting knowledge of the entire course of history, a concern for types of knowledge (astronomical, textual, geographical, medicinal, agricultural), and a bookish outlook stressing the value of the written text. As such, the text manifests "intricate interactions between global and local trends in the Hellenistic period." The author was "at home within the global intellectual culture," as is shown by the parallels between Jubilees and other

scholarly texts. Yet, he promotes "a local message," stressing the distinctiveness of Jewish culture to which the audience should remain faithful. The local agenda, in other words, does preclude wider cultural interaction; see Hartog, "Jubilees and Hellenistic Encyclopaedism," *Journal for the Study of Judaism* 50 (2019): 1–25, esp. 19–20.

143 Wright, "Literature," 74, 86. On the intellectual life in Hellenistic Palestine and Phoenicia, see also Hengel, *Judaism*, 83–8.

144 See, e.g., Bernard Brandon Scott, "Jesus as Sage: An Innovative Voice in Common Wisdom," in *The Sage in Israel and the Ancient Near East*, 399–415; Ben Witherington, *Jesus the Sage: The Pilgrimage of Wisdom* (Edinburgh: T&T Clark, 1994). On Jesus as a wandering cynic preacher, see, e.g., Francis Gerald Downing, *Cynics and Christian Origins* (Edinburgh: T&T Clark, 1992). While the gospels shed much light on Jesus the teacher, other texts of the New Testament gesture towards the same. The First Letter to the Corinthians creates an impression that Jesus had early followers who esteemed him "primarily as a teacher of *knowledge*," i.e., as one who instructs about a wise life that leads to happiness; see Mason, "*Philosophiai*," 48. On philosophical motifs in the pastoral epistles, see ibid., 48–9.

145 In fact, the parting of the ways of Judaism and Christianity is complex much beyond the end of the second temple period. See, e.g., Adam H. Becker and Annette Yoshiko Reed (ed.), *The Ways That Never Parted: Jews and Christians in Late Antiquity and the Early Middle Ages* (Tübingen: Mohr Siebeck, 2003).

146 On Jesus' instructions, see Matt 5:1–7:29; 10:1–11:1; 13:1–53; 18:1–19:2; 24:1–26:1.

147 See Mason, "*Philosophiai*," 49–50. Luke also comments on Jesus' formative period, which prepares him for his ministry: at the age of twelve, the boy discussed with teachers in the temple, listening, posing questions, and delivering astonishing replies (Luke 2:46–47).

148 See, e.g., Camp and Wright, "Riches," 153–74.

149 Mark R. Sneed, "A Taste for Wisdom: Aesthetics, Moral Discernment, and Social Class in Proverbs," in *Imagined World and Constructed Differences in the Hebrew Bible*, ed. Jeremiah W. Cataldo (London: T&T Clark, 2016), 111–26.

150 The same applies to early Christian schools; see Judith L. Kovacs, "Divine Pedagogy and the Gnostic Teacher According to Clement of Alexandria," *Journal of Early Christian Studies* 9 (2001): 3–25; Ismo Dunderberg, *Beyond Gnosticism: Myth, Lifestyle, and Society in the School of Valentinus* (New York: Columbia University Press, 2008).

Chapter 4

1 See Carol A. Newsom, "Positive Psychology and Ancient Israelite Wisdom," in *The Bible and the Pursuit of Happiness: What the Old and New Testaments Teach Us about the Good Life?*, ed. Brent A. Strawn (Oxford: Oxford University Press, 2012),

117–36, esp. 134; Elisa Uusimäki, "Virtues and Practical Wisdom in the Book of Proverbs," *Journal for the Study of Diaconia* 2 (2017): 62–79 (in Finnish).

2 On virtue and ideal ways of living, see Daniel C. Russell, "Introduction: Virtue Ethics in Modern Moral Philosophy," in *The Cambridge Companion to Virtue Ethics*, ed. Daniel C. Russell (Cambridge: Cambridge University Press, 2013), 1–6, esp. 2.

3 So, David T. Runia, "Eudaimonism in Hellenistic-Jewish Literature," in *Shem in the Tents of Japhet: Essays on the Encounter of Judaism and Hellenism*, ed. James L. Kugel (Leiden: Brill, 2002), 131–57, esp. 139.

4 While Judaism's association with philosophy is crucial for my present purposes, I do not make a claim that early Jewish authors only would have understood Judaism as a philosophy. On the contrary, there are alternative ways to perceive the place of Judaism in the Greco-Roman world, such as the model according to which Jewish communities were akin to private or voluntary associations. Recently, see esp. Eckhardt Benedikt (ed.), *Private Associations and Jewish Communities in the Hellenistic and Roman Cities* (Leiden: Brill, 2019).

5 See, e.g., Jodi Magness, *The Archaeology of Qumran and the Dead Sea Scrolls* (Grand Rapids, MI: Eerdmans, 2002), esp. 39–43; Joan E. Taylor, *The Essenes, the Scrolls, and the Dead Sea* (Oxford: Oxford University Press, 2012).

6 The need to read Josephus' account in its own right has been addressed by Steve Mason, "Essenes and Lurking Spartans in Josephus' Judean War: From Story to History," in *Making History: Josephus and Historical Method*, ed. Zuleika Rodgers et al. (Leiden: Brill, 2007), 219–61.

7 See, e.g., Mason, "*Philosophiai*," 31–58; Taylor, *Women*, 105–25.

8 The primary sources can be found in Menahem Stern, *Greek and Latin Authors on Jews and Judaism*, 2 vols. (Jerusalem: The Israel Academy of Sciences and Humanities, 1974). See ibid., 1:10 on Theophrastus, p. 1:46 on Megasthenes, and p. 1:50 on Clearchus of Soli. Additional non-Jewish evidence on the Jewish people is provided by Hecateus of Abdera's *Aegyptica*. This text is partly preserved in Diodorus of Sicily's *Bibliotheca historica* and cited by Josephus in his *Contra Apionem*; see Legaspi, *Wisdom*, 160–3.

9 The Greek term used for "race" (γένος) has multiple meanings (e.g., sort, category, or lineage). It came to denote social groups who used a collective plural name in self-identification. Such names could be geographical, occupational, or patronymic; see John K. Davies, "genos," in *Oxford Classical Dictionary*, ed. Simon Hornblower and Anthony Spawforth, 3rd ed. (Oxford: Oxford University Press, 2005), 630.

10 Trans. Stern, *Authors*, 1:10.

11 Ibid., 1:50. Josephus discusses Clearchus of Soli in *C. Ap.* 1.176–82.

12 Trans. Stern, *Authors*, 1:46. On parallels and interaction between Hellenistic philosophy and ancient Indian traditions, see John Sellars, *Hellenistic Philosophy* (Oxford: Oxford University Press, 2018), 209–13.

13 Along with this association, Philo evokes Aristotle's topos of the theoretical and practical ways of life (*N.E.* 1177a–b); see Cooper, *Pursuits*, 70–143. Other pre-Hellenistic authors were also interested in the motif of a philosophical way of life. Consider especially Plato's portrayal of Socrates; ibid., 29, 59–60.
14 David T. Runia, "Philo of Alexandria and the Greek *Hairesis*-Model," *Vigiliae Christianae* 53 (1999): 117–47, esp. 140.
15 See Philo, *Somn.* 2.127; *Mos.* 2.216; *Contempl.* 28; *Legat.* 156.
16 In *A.J.* 18.23–5, Josephus also notes the "fourth philosophy," i.e., the Zealots. See, e.g., Albert I. Baumgarten, "Josephus and the Jewish Sects," in *A Companion to Josephus*, ed. Honora Howell Chapman and Zuleika Rodgers (Chichester: John Wiley & Sons, 2016), 261–72.
17 See, e.g., Tolonen and Uusimäki, "Mélange," 117, 121.
18 Artapanus, frag. 3, preserved in Eusebius, *Praep. ev.* 9.27.4. For the text, see John J. Collins, "Artapanus," in *The Old Testament Pseudepigrapha*, ed. James H. Charlesworth, 2 vols., 5th Hendrickson Edition (Peabody, MA: Hendrickson, 2016), 2:889–903, esp. 2:898.
19 Aristobulus, frags. 2–4, preserved in Eusebius, *Praep. ev.* 8.10.3–4; 13.12–13. For the text, see Adela Yarbro Collins, "Aristobulus," in *The Old Testament Pseudepigrapha*, ed. James H. Charlesworth, 2 vols., 5th Hendrickson Edition (Peabody, MA: Hendrickson, 2016), 2:831–42, esp. 2:838–40.
20 Aristobulus, frag. 4, preserved in Eusebius, *Praep. ev.* 13.13.8. Trans. Collins, "Aristobulus," 2:841.
21 The same applies to early Christianity. The author of Luke-Acts, e.g., may depict the emerging church as another Jewish school of philosophy; see Mason, "Philosophiai," 46–55, esp. 49–51. See also Loveday Alexander, "Paul and the Hellenistic Schools: The Evidence of Galen," in *Paul in His Hellenistic Context*, ed. Troels Engberg-Pedersen (Minneapolis, MN: Fortress, 1995), 60–83; George H. van Kooten, "Is Early Christianity a Religion or a Philosophy? Reflections on the Importance of 'Knowledge' and 'Truth' in the Letters of Paul and Peter," in *Myths, Martyrs, and Modernity: Studies in the History of Religions*, ed. Jitse H. F. Dijkstra et al. (Leiden: Brill, 2010), 393–408; Christopher Kavin Rowe, *One True Life: The Stoics and Early Christians as Rival Traditions* (New Haven, CT: Yale University Press, 2016).
22 Steve Mason, *Orientation to the History of Roman Judaea* (Eugene, OR: Wipf and Stock, 2016), 165.
23 Mason, "*Philosophiai*," 42.
24 For example, Plato, *Gorgias* 507b; Diodorus of Sicily 1.92.5; Xenophon, *Memorabilia* 4.8.11. See ibid., 33.
25 Taylor, *Women*, 106–11.
26 Erich S. Gruen, *Rethinking the Other in Antiquity* (Princeton, PA: Princeton University Press, 2010), 309.
27 Ibid., 325.

28 Yet, the sub-headings are not mentioned by Eusebius, *Hist. Eccles.* 2.17.3; 2.18.7. On the partially unclear content of the five-part work, see Taylor, *Women*, 34–9.
29 On Moses as a teacher (διδάσκαλος), see also *Gig.* 54 and *Spec.* 1.59.
30 Cf. Plato, *Symposium* 204c; David M. Hay, "Things Philo Said and Did Not Say about the Therapeutae," *Society of Biblical Literature Symposium Papers* 31 (1992): 673–83, esp. 679.
31 So, Joan E. Taylor and Philip R. Davies, "The So-Called Therapeutae of '*De vita contemplativa*': Identity and Character," *Harvard Theological Review* 91 (1998): 3–24.
32 Trans. F. H. Colson, LCL 363. The same applies to all the English translations of *De vita contemplativa* below.
33 See Hay, "Things," 683; Hay, "The Veiled Thoughts of the Therapeutae," in *Mediators of the Divine: Horizons of Prophecy, Divination, Dreams and Theurgy in Mediterranean Antiquity*, ed. Robert M. Berchman (Atlanta, GA: Scholars Press, 1998), 167–84.
34 Hay, "Thoughts," 178–84.
35 Ibid., 176n31.
36 See Tomas Hägg, *The Art of Biography in Antiquity* (Cambridge: Cambridge University Press, 2012), 7. Eusebius' documentation of the title supports its authenticity (*Hist. eccles.* 2.17.3; 2.18.7). On biography in Greco-Roman antiquity, see also Arnaldo Momigliano, *The Development of Greek Biography*, 2nd ed. (Cambridge, MA: Harvard University Press, 1993); Koen de Temmerman and Kristoffel Demoen (ed.), *Writing Biography in Greece and Rome: Narrative Technique and Fictionalization* (Cambridge: Cambridge University Press, 2016).
37 Taylor has previously addressed the importance of asceticism in the life of the Therapeutae. She briefly explores its context in ancient philosophy both Eastern and Western, including variegated sources that range from the Vedic *Aranyakas* to Plato (*Timaeus* 90a–d; *Phaedo* 81c), Musonius Rufus' *On Training*, and Martial's *Epigram* 11.56. See Taylor, *Women*, 146–7. I agree with Taylor that an ascetic attitude and behaviour – i.e., the renouncement of material comfort – is central to the life of the Therapeutae. Yet, I wish to emphasize that the content of their ἄσκησις is not limited to bodily asceticism; rather, it designates an inclusive understanding of the group's spiritual training.
38 Philo also wrote biographies of remarkable individuals; see Maren R. Niehoff, "Philo and Plutarch as Biographers: Parallel Responses to Roman Stoicism," *Greek, Roman, and Byzantine Studies* 52 (2012): 361–92.
39 For example, *Plant.* 151; *Prob.* 121–31. On sophists, who speak well but neglect action, see *Post.* 86; *Congr.* 67; *Det.* 72.
40 Sellars, *Art*, 23. On the concern for "the *way* in which an individual lived," see also ibid., 22.
41 So, Hägg, *Biography*, 2, 4. Hägg argues (ibid., ix–xi) for analysing the "art of biography" in all its variety rather than limiting his interest in the study of "biographical genre."

42 Hay, "Things," 673–83; Holger Szesnat, "'Mostly Aged Virgins': Philo and the Presence of the Therapeutrides at Lake Mareotis," *Neotestamentica* 32 (1998): 191–201; Taylor, *Women*, 8–10, 21–54, esp. 52–3.
43 Jean Riaud, "Les Thérapeutes d'Alexandrie dans la tradition et dans la recherche critique jusqu'aux découvertes de Qumran," *Aufstieg und Niedergang der römischen Welt* 2 (1987): 1189–295; Troels Engberg-Pedersen, "Philo's *De Vita Contemplativa* as a Philosopher's Dream," *Journal for the Study of Judaism* 30 (1999): 40–64.
44 Mary Ann Beavis, "Philo's Therapeutae: Philosopher's Dream or Utopian Construction?" *Journal for the Study of the Pseudepigrapha* 14 (2004): 30–42; Ross Shepard Kraemer, *Unreliable Witnesses: Religion, Gender, and History in the Greco-Roman Mediterranean* (Oxford: Oxford University Press, 2011), 57–116, esp. 66. In the latter book, Kraemer revises the more optimistic views she had earlier presented in her article "Monastic Jewish Women in Greco-Roman Egypt: Philo Judaeus on the Therapeutrides," *Signs* 14 (1989): 342–70.
45 See Hägg, *Biography*, 3–4; Koen de Temmerman, "Ancient Biography and Formalities of Fiction," in *Writing Biography in Greece and Rome*, 3–25, esp. 6.
46 On Philo's criticisms of the city, see David T. Runia, "The Idea and the Reality of the City in the Thought of Philo of Alexandria," *Journal of the History of Ideas* 61 (2000): 361–79, esp. 370–2. On the Therapeutae, see ibid., 373–5.
47 On the ideal of modesty, cf. Musonius Rufus' *On Clothing and Shelter* and his *On Furnishings*.
48 See Szesnat, "Virgins," 191–201; Taylor, *Women*, 173–226; Shari Goldberg, "The Two Choruses Become One: The Absence/Presence of Women in Philo's *On the Contemplative Life*," *Journal for the Study of Judaism* 39 (2008): 459–70.
49 Although ἐγκράτεια was presented as a virtue since the classical period (e.g., Aristotle, *N.E.* 1145b8), it was emphasized by the Stoics from Zeno onwards (D.L. 7.92). In Philo's thought, the concept denotes the victory of rational over non-rational forces, the control of excessive impulse, and the dominance of rational motivation over against an urge towards pleasure; see Hans Svebakken, *Philo of Alexandria's Exposition of the Tenth Commandment* (Atlanta, GA: Society of Biblical Literature, 2012), 81–97.
50 Cf. Musonius Rufus' *On Food* on the ideal of simple vegetarian food.
51 On the Sabbath "schools" and the task of philosophizing on the Sabbath, see Philo, *Opif.* 128; *Mos.* 2.216; *Spec.* 2.62.
52 On Roman reading communities, see Matthew D. Larsen, "Listening with the Body, Seeing through the Ears: Contextualizing Philo's Lecture Event in *On the Contemplative Life*," *Journal for the Study of Judaism* 47 (2016): 1–28.
53 Cf. Hay, "Thoughts," 176n31.
54 See Barclay, *Jews*, 399–400. Barclay argues that "the spectrum of social responses spreads all the way from total assimilation to near total isolation: at one end, a Tiberius Julius Alexander wholly integrated into the social life of the Roman world, at the other, one of the 'Therapeutae' meditating on the law in the monastic

conditions described by Philo." Barclay's language of assimilation and isolation creates a misleading "either–or" impression, which does not get hold of Philo's creative and inherently cross-cultural project.

55 So, Taylor, *Women*, 229.
56 Classical sources differ as to whether Anaxagoras and Democritus gave away or lost their properties. See Horace, *Ep.* I.12.12; Plato, *Hippias Major* 283a; Cicero, *Tusc. disp.* 5.114; Plutarch, *Pericles* 16; D.L. 2.3.6.
57 See Plato's *Symposium* and Xenophon's *Symposium*. Maren R. Niehoff argues that Philo's account reflects a "Roman orientation." By contrasting Jewish frugality with Greek excessiveness, Philo constructs the Greek other (esp. *Contempl.* 40, 58–64, 68, 73–4); see Niehoff, "The Symposium of Philo's Therapeutae: Displaying Jewish Identity in an Increasingly Roman World," *Greek, Roman, and Byzantine Studies* 50 (2010): 95–117.
58 See Joan E. Taylor, with David Hay, "Astrology in Philo of Alexandria's *De vita contemplativa*," *ARAM Periodical* 24 (2012): 293–309. Taylor and Hay show the great value of astronomical knowledge for Philo. Yet, if regarded as a cult, ἀστρονομία becomes "a distortion of true religiosity, a vehicle for promoting pantheism and fatalism."
59 See Runia, "*Hairesis*-Model," 125, 139–40.
60 On the intellectual context of Philo's allegorical project, see David Dawson, *Allegorical Readers and Cultural Revision in Ancient Alexandria* (Berkeley, CA: University of California Press, 1992).
61 Apart from Jewish scriptures, Philo applies the allegorical method to Homer in *Contempl.* 17 (cf. *Iliad* 13:5, 6). On the metaphor of the law book as a living being (cf. *Migr.* 93; Plato, *Phaedrus* 264c), see Taylor, *Women*, 145.
62 So, Scott D. Mackie, "Seeing God in Philo of Alexandria: Means, Methods, and Mysticism," *Journal for the Study of Judaism* 43 (2012): 147–79. On the Therapeutae, see ibid., 162, 167–8.
63 David T. Runia, "The Reward for Goodness: Philo, *De Vita Contemplativa* 90," *Studia Philonica Annual* 9 (1997): 3–18, esp. 14.
64 Philo also describes the soul of the sage as an "imitation of heaven" (*Her.* 88). In *Virt.* 190, the bad person is said to be driven away from his proper country, virtue. See also *Leg.* 3.1 on the hiding of Adam and Eve.
65 In *Opif.* 3, Philo underlines the law of nature, which he connects with the law of Moses. See, e.g., Hindy Najman, "A Written Copy of the Law of Nature: An Unthinkable Paradox?," *Studia Philonica Annual* 15 (2003): 54–63.
66 Trans. F. H. Colson and G. H. Whitaker, LCL 227.
67 Trans. F. H. Colson, LCL 320. On the ascension motif, see Plato, *Phaedrus* 245b–249d; Seneca, *Ep.* 92.30–3; *Nat. quaest.* 1.7–8; cf. *Helv.* 9.1–2. On the connection to Seneca, see Sarit Kattan Gribetz, "The Festival of Every Day: Philo and Seneca on Quotidian Time," *Harvard Theological Review* 111 (2018): 357–81, esp. 374.

68 Sami Yli-Karjanmaa, *Reincarnation in Philo of Alexandria* (Atlanta, GA: Society of Biblical Literature, 2015), 47.

69 If Diogenes Laertius (6.63, 72) preserves correct information, the use of the term goes back to Diogenes the Cynic (412–323 BCE), thus predating Alexander's conquests; see John Sellars, "Stoic Cosmopolitanism and Zeno's Republic," *History of Political Thought* 28 (2007): 1–29, esp. 4–8. Sellars argues that the Cynics did not reject the city as a geographical entity. This separates them from the Stoics who rejected the existence of any real cities. For the Stoics, a *polis* is a community of virtuous people, but such a community does not exist on earth (ibid., 10). Socrates, too, identifies himself as a citizen of the world according to Cicero (*Tusc. disp.* 5.108), but the tale's historical accuracy has been denied; see Eric Brown, "Hellenistic Cosmopolitanism," in *A Companion to Ancient Philosophy*, ed. Mary Louise Gill and Pierre Pellegrin (Oxford: Blackwell, 2006), 549–58.

70 While Zeno's *Republic*, the first work of Stoic political philosophy, has not survived, some of his ideas are preserved. See Plutarch, *De Alex. fort.* 329a–d, on all people as one community and D.L. 7.33 on good people as citizens.

71 On the citizens of the world-city, see also Plutarch, *De Alex. fort.* 329a–d; Epictetus, *Disc.* 1.9.1–2; 2.10.3; Marcus Aurelius, *Med.* 2.16; 3.11; 4.4; 4.32; 10.15. The development of the Stoic ideas remains uncertain. Sellars is critical of such an interpretation that associates Zeno with "the ideal of an isolated community of sages" and the later Stoics (e.g., Seneca) with "a cosmopolitan utopia transcending all traditional States." Rather, Sellars examines the Cynic background of both Zeno's *Republic* and the cosmopolitan tradition, arguing that the two are not as far away from each other as has been suggested; see Sellars, "Cosmopolitanism," 1–29.

72 On the heavenly city of the wise people, see *Conf.* 77–88. Cf. the Stoic emphasis on the ideal nature of the *polis*, to the extent that such a *polis* does not exist on earth; see Sellars, "Cosmopolitanism," 10.

73 See Hay, "Thoughts," 168, 178, 184.

74 Cf. Sellars, *Art*, 23, 78.

75 On Philo as an advocate of Judaism in *De vita contemplativa*, see James R. Royse, "The Works of Philo," in *The Cambridge Companion to Philo*, 32–64, esp. 50.

76 For the sources, see Geza Vermes and Martin D. Goodman, *The Essenes: According to the Classical Sources* (Sheffield: Sheffield Academic Press, 1989). All the English translations of the classical sources quoted in this chapter are by Vermes and Goodman, unless otherwise indicated.

77 Pliny the Elder, *Nat. hist.* 5.17.4. Interestingly, Pliny does not explicitly refer to the Essenes as Jews; see Robert A. Kraft, "Pliny on Essenes, Pliny on Jews," *Dead Sea Discoveries* 8 (2001): 255–61. Regarding the later sources, Hippolytus of Rome offers a lengthy account on their way of life in his *Refutatio omnium haeresium* (9.18–28), but Hippolytus' text is close to Josephus' account; see Vermes and Goodman, *Essenes*, 62–3.

78 See, e.g., Doron Mendels, "Hellenistic Utopia and the Essenes," *Harvard Theological Review* 72 (1979): 207–22; Gregory E. Sterling, "'Athletes of Virtue': An Analysis of the Summaries in Acts (2:41–47; 4:32–35; 5:12–16)," *Journal of Biblical Literature* 113 (1994): 679–96, esp. 695–6.
79 See, e.g., the helpful summary of (dis)continuities by John J. Collins, *Beyond the Qumran Community: The Sectarian Movement of the Dead Sea Scrolls* (Grand Rapids, MI: Eerdmans, 2010), 131–3.
80 Although Philo's discussion on the Essenes in *Quod omnis probus liber sit* concerns men, women and children are presented as lovers of freedom elsewhere in the same treatise (see *Prob.* 115–17).
81 See, e.g., Taylor, *Essenes*, 23–4.
82 On Philo's conception of non-Greek wisdom, see Mireille Hadas-Lebel, *Philo of Alexandria: A Thinker in the Jewish Diaspora* (Leiden: Brill, 2012), 171–3. It is unclear whether Philo understood himself as a Greek or a barbarian. In *Mos.* 2.27, he states that Jewish laws were only accessible to the barbarians prior to the Septuagint. On the other hand, he characterizes Greek as "our language (διάλεκτος)" in *Congr.* 44. In any event, the invoking of philosophical excellence among the "barbarians" is a common literary trope in Greco-Roman literature. Consider several lost works, including Aristotle's *Magicus*, Sotion's *Succession of the Philosophers* (cf. D.L. 1.1–11; Clement of Alexandria, *Strom.* 1), and Megasthenes' *Indica* (cf. Strabo, *Geographica* 15.1.59–60). Furthermore, Porphyry's *Abst.* 4 discusses Egyptian and Indian ascetics, also mentioning the Essenes. For discussion, see Taylor, *Essenes*, 24–5.
83 The ideal of the "pooling of possessions" can be compared to Plato's *Republic* 416d, 462c and Iamblichus' *Vita Pythagorae*; see Taylor, *Essenes*, 35. Importantly, Philo presents the lack of wealth as "a matter of choice," as observed by Runia, "City," 373.
84 See, e.g., Wes Avram, "On the Priority of 'Ethics' in the Work of Levinas," *The Journal of Religious Ethics* 24 (1996): 261–84.
85 Cf. Mason, "*Philosophiai*," 33.
86 According to Diogenes Laertius (7.102), Zeno argues that virtues include goods and vices respectively evils, whereas the ἀδιάφορα are morally neutral objects of pursuit (e.g., life, health, pleasure, beauty, strength, wealth, fame; as well as their opposites). Philo notes that philosophers are trained to regard indifferent things as indifferent (*Spec.* 2.46), but his notion of the ἀδιάφορα remains unclear. Unlike Zeno, Philo admits that health, wealth, and fame are somewhat good things (*Leg.* 3.86). The passage in *QG* 3.16 also echoes Aristotle's idea of spiritual, corporeal, and external goods.
87 Drawing on the work of cultural anthropologists, one may observe traces of the ethics of autonomy, community, and divinity in the account, even though the former is not prominent. On these types of ethics, see Richard A. Shweder et al., "The 'Big Three' of Morality (Autonomy, Community, Divinity) and the 'Big Three'

Explanations of Suffering," in *Morality and Health*, ed. Allan Brandt and Paul Rozin (New York: Routledge, 1997), 119–69.

88 The earliest reference to an "athlete of virtue" seems to be found in Diodorus of Sicily 9.1, which concerns Solon. As for Jewish texts, see 4 Macc 9:8; 17:12, 16; Philo, *Somn.* 1.131; *Migr.* 167; *Praem.* 5. See also Clare Poliakoff and Michael Poliakoff, "Jacob, Job, and Other Wrestlers: Reception of Greek Athletics by Jews and Christians in Antiquity," *Journal of Sport History* 11 (1984): 48–65.

89 The text is preserved in Eusebius, *Praep. ev.* 8.6–7. Its accuracy cannot be guaranteed, as Eusebius may adjust the views of Jewish authors to fit his Christian apologetic perspective; see Sabrina Inowlocki, *Eusebius and the Jewish Authors: His Citation Technique in an Apologetic Context* (Leiden: Brill, 2006), 290. For an argument against Philo's authorship, see John M. G. Barclay, *Flavius Josephus: Translation and Commentary, Vol. 10: Against Apion* (Leiden: Brill, 2007), 353–5.

90 On the defensive tone of *Hypothetica*, see, e.g., Taylor, *Essenes*, 39.

91 The focus on an old age aligns with Philo's suspicion of ascetic life at an early age (*Fug.* 30–40; see also *Det.* 19–21). For discussion, see Fraade, "Aspects," 265–6; Taylor, *Essenes*, 41.

92 The idea that the men had children before their commitment to celibacy would align with Philo's belief in the divine order to multiply (*Det.* 147–8; *Praem.* 108–9). Philo's interest in the promotion of celibacy may pertain to the fact that it was advocated in Stoic (e.g., Musonius Rufus, *On Exercise*) and Pythagorean (e.g., D.L. 8.1) circles. It may also signal that the Essenes do not have an ideal of a "community of wives." The latter motif is found in Greek philosophical systems (see D.L. 7.131; Diod. Sic. 2.58.1) and based on Plato's notion of the philosophical city where wives and children are held in common (e.g., *Republic* 457d); see Taylor, *Essenes*, 43–4.

93 In fact, Josephus makes use of two designations, "Essene" and "Essaean." They are, however, simply variants of the same designation; see Steve Mason, "What Josephus Says about Essenes in His Judean War," in *Text and Artifact in the Religions of Mediterranean Antiquity*, ed. Stephen G. Wisdom and Michael Desjardins (Waterloo, ON: Wilfrid Laurier University Press, 2000), 423–55, esp. 426–7. Thus, I will use the English translation "Essene" in my analysis. On the enigmatic origin and etymology of the name, see Collins, *Qumran*, 156–60.

94 Josephus began his literary career by writing a version of *Bellum judaicum* in Aramaic, but he translated the work into Greek. Later on, Josephus composed in Greek, working hard to master it (see *A.J.* 20.263).

95 Even so, philosophical themes seem to be subordinate to Josephus' "cultic apologetic" in *Bellum judaicum*. He uses cultic apologetic "to the effect that lassitude in the observance of temple ritual led to its destruction." So, Mason, "*Philosophiai*," 44.

96 Josephus' technical focus on the three schools is remarkable, for he also discusses other Jewish groups without defining them as αἱρέσεις. In this respect, Josephus differs from Philo who uses the term αἵρεσις in a loose way as referring to "varieties of thought." See Taylor, *Essenes*, 56.
97 In addition, Josephus makes five incidental references to the Essenes in *Bellum judaicum*. Four of them concern individuals (1.78–80; 2.113, 567; 3.11), whereas the fifth one mentions a gate of the Essenes in Jerusalem (5.145).
98 Steve Mason, *Flavius Josephus: Translation and Commentary. Vol. 1b, Judean War 2* (Leiden: Brill, 2008), 85–6.
99 The avoidance of oil does not pertain to impurity, but to asceticism; see ibid., 101–2.
100 On the Essenes' concern for medicine, see Taylor, *Essenes*, 76, 306–8.
101 Josephus presents Judaism as a way of life (*C. Ap.* 2.258) and seeks to demonstrate the philosophical and ethical nature of Moses' laws (*A.J.* 1.14, 19, 25; *C. Ap.* 2.171–5). Likewise, some biblical figures feature as intellectuals that possess exquisite wisdom and knowledge (e.g., *A.J.* 1.154–7; 8.42–4); see Mason, "Philosophiai," 44.
102 In addition to the sections discussed below, note *A.J.* 13.171–2, where Josephus mentions the three schools within Judaism, also remarking that the Essenes consider the fate or destiny to govern all things.
103 The Greek term may denote both aristocratic status and morally excellent character, but the meaning of "moral nobility" is predominant from the classical era onwards (cf. Socrates' portrayal as an exemplar of καλοκαγαθία). For discussion, see John B. Weaver, "The Noble and Good Heart: καλοκαγαθία in Luke's Parable of the Sower," in *Scripture and Traditions*, ed. Patrick Gray and Gail R. O'Day (Leiden: Brill, 2008), 151–72, esp. 152–64.
104 Note that Bannus has also been associated with the Essenes, but Josephus' narrative speaks against such an identification; see Steve Mason, *Flavius Josephus: Translation and Commentary. Vol. 9, Life of Josephus* (Leiden: Brill, 2001), 18.
105 It is unclear whether Josephus actually was a Pharisee or not; see Steve Mason, "Was Josephus a Pharisee? A Reconsideration of Life 10–12," *Journal of Jewish Studies* 40 (1989): 31–45; Taylor, *Essenes*, 54–5.
106 For different interpretations of the evidence, see, e.g., Collins, *Qumran*, 128; Taylor, *Essenes*, 102.
107 The section reminds one of Cicero's experience in different philosophical schools (*Brutus* 307–10, 315–16). Consider also Justin Martyr's remarks on his wandering from one philosophy to another (*Dial.* 1–9); see Maren R. Niehoff, "Parodies of Educational Journeys in Josephus, Justin Martyr, and Lucian," in *Journeys in the Roman East: Imagined and Real*, ed. Maren R. Niehoff (Tübingen: Mohr Siebeck, 2017), 203–24.
108 The explicit use of the idiom of discipline (יסר and its derivatives) is worth highlighting here. As observed by Hogan, such language is not "terribly frequent"

in the scrolls, but it is consistently used to refer to "the process of indoctrination or enculturation" into the group's "regulated life" (e.g., 1QS 2:25–3:1; 3:5–6; 6:13–15; 9:3–11; CD 4:6–10; 20:27–34; 1QSa 1:6–8); see Hogan, "*Musar*," 86–9.

109 For the members as a "sanctuary of man," see 4Q174 frag. 1 i 6–7. In 1QS 9:3, their "offering of the lips" is compared to a pleasant aroma, and the perfection of their way to an acceptable offering.

110 Steven D. Fraade has previously characterized the group as "a studying body." See Fraade, "Interpretive Authority in the Studying Community at Qumran," *Journal of Jewish Studies* 44 (1993): 46–69. As I hope to show next, study is integral to the life of the group, but its notion of shared wisdom also covers other concerns and lived practices.

111 See, e.g., Torleif Elgvin, "The *Yaḥad* Is More than Qumran," in *Enoch and Qumran Origins: New Light on a Forgotten Connection*, ed. Gabrielle Boccaccini (Grand Rapids, MI: Eerdmans, 2005), 273–9; Alison Schofield, *From Qumran to the Yaḥad: A New Paradigm of Textual Development for the Community Rule* (Leiden: Brill, 2009); Collins, *Qumran*; George J. Brooke, "Crisis without, Crisis within: Changes and Developments in the Dead Sea Scrolls Movement," in *Judaism and Crisis: Crisis as a Catalyst in Jewish Cultural History*, ed. Armin Lange et al. (Göttingen: Vandenhoeck & Ruprecht, 2011), 89–107.

112 On the history of the movement, see, e.g., Collins, *Qumran*, 2–121.

113 For the position that this dispute happened in the first century BCE, i.e., not in the second century BCE as has typically been assumed, see Collins, *Qumran*, 8–9.

114 On the memory of the teacher, see Loren T. Stuckenbruck, "The Legacy of the Teacher of Righteousness in the Dead Sea Scrolls," in *New Perspectives on Old Texts*, ed. Esther G. Chazon et al. (Leiden: Brill, 2010), 23–49; Travis B. Williams, *History and Memory in the Dead Sea Scrolls: Remembering the Teacher of Righteousness* (Cambridge: Cambridge University Press, 2019).

115 For counter-arguments, see Fraade, "Authority," 62.

116 George J. Brooke, "Was the Teacher of Righteousness Considered to Be a Prophet?" in *Prophecy after the Prophets? The Contribution of the Dead Sea Scrolls to the Understanding of Biblical and Extra-Biblical Prophecy*, ed. Kristin de Troyer and Armin Lange (Leuven: Peeters, 2009), 77–97.

117 Devorah Dimant, *History, Ideology and Bible Interpretation in the Dead Sea Scrolls* (Tübingen: Mohr Siebeck, 2014), 315–32, esp. 316–17, 320.

118 Ibid., 318.

119 Florentino García Martínez, "Beyond the Sectarian Divide: The 'Voice of the Teacher' as an Authority-Conferring Strategy in Some Qumran Texts," in *The Dead Sea Scrolls: Transmission of Traditions and Production of Texts*, ed. Sarianna Metso et al. (Leiden: Brill, 2010), 227–44, esp. 243. According to García Martínez, the teacher's voice is as strong a claim as the voices of Moses and the prophets. In a way, however, the teacher's voice surpasses that of the earlier prophets; see Pieter B. Hartog, "Pesher as Commentary," in *The Dead Sea Scrolls and the Study of the*

Humanities: Method, Theory, Meaning, ed. Pieter B. Hartog et al. (Leiden: Brill, 2018), 92–116, esp. 109.

120 This interpretation naturally depends on whether the hymn is regarded as representing the teacher's self-understanding; see George J. Brooke, "The 'Apocalyptic' Community, The Matrix of the Teacher and Rewriting Scripture," in *Authoritative Scriptures in Ancient Judaism*, 37–54, esp. 48. The Mosaic association connects the teacher to the maskil, but is not the only parallel between their personae. Both figures transmit divine secrets (1QS 9:13, 18; 1QpHab 2:5–10; 7:3–5), but the maskil is not connected to certain interpretative tasks that are essential to the teacher; he neither participates in halakhic debates nor engages in the pesharim type of explicit commentary. Yet, note the use of the root פתר (a cognate of פשר) in 4Q298 frag. 3–4 ii 9, as this text is attributed to the maskil. On this passage, see Shani Tzoref, "*Pesher* and Periodiziation," *Dead Sea Discoveries* 18 (2011): 129–54, esp. 149–52. Another difference concerns priesthood: such an identification is not made regarding the maskil, though he serves as the head of the angelic priests in the Songs of the Sabbath Sacrifice. On the latter, see Newman, "Prophets," 39.

121 See the remaining materials of the books of Job (2Q15; 4Q99–101; 4Q157; 11Q10), Proverbs (4Q102–3, 103a; 6Q30, or 6QpapProv?), Qoheleth (4Q109–10), and Ben Sira (2Q18; 11Q5 21:11–17, 22:1; MasSir).

122 See esp. Instruction (1Q26; 4Q415–18, 418a, 418c, 423), Mysteries (1Q27; 4Q299–301), Wiles of the Wicked Woman (4Q184), Sapiential Admonitions B (4Q185), Ways of Righteousness[a–b] (4Q420–1), and Beatitudes (4Q525). Consider also several manuscripts with mostly a single fragment, including 4Q298, 4Q302, 4Q303–305, 4Q411, 4Q412, 4Q413, 4Q419, 4Q424, 4Q425, 4Q426, 4Q473, and 4Q528.

123 Consider, e.g., the Community Rule (esp. 1QS 3:13–4:26; 9:12–11:22), the Hodayot, and the Songs of the Sage[a–b] (4Q510–11). Wisdom also pertains to the didactic tale in 1QapGen 18:24–21:4, the Admonition based on the Flood (4Q370), the Aramaic Levi Document (ALD), and the body of Enochic literature; see Lange, "Wisdom," 469–70.

124 Brooke, "Wisdom," 25.

125 See, e.g., Uusimäki, "Formation," 60.

126 The idea of an elect group is distinct, but it also occurs elsewhere, including in the books of Enoch, the book of Jubilees, and the Temple Scroll. For an overview, see Collins, *Qumran*, 40–6.

127 In fact, the torah seems to function as one manifestation of *raz nihyeh*. The mystery has several functions, as it is associated with creation, history, end-times, and ethics. Furthermore, it "articulates itself in the shape of the Torah." See Lange, "Wisdom," 459.

128 The key divinatory texts include 4Q186, 4Q561, 4Q318, and perhaps 4Q534; see James C. VanderKam, "Mantic Wisdom in the Dead Sea Scrolls," *Dead Sea Discoveries* 4 (1997): 336–53.

129 For early Jewish ideas of revealed wisdom, see, e.g., Grant Macaskill, *Revealed Wisdom and Inaugurated Eschatology in Ancient Judaism and Early Christianity* (Leiden: Brill, 2007).
130 On the sections of 1QS as samples that shed light on the community's ethos, values, and life, see Newsom, *Self*, 135.
131 Cf. Tso's argument that instead of enquiring how the group's members imagined an ideal way of life on a personal level, it may be better to ask the following question: "How should I (or *we*) respond to the presence of the (human or divine) Other?" So, Tso, *Ethics*, 56. On the prophetic connotation of the verb "seek" (דרש), see Hamori, *Divination*, 28.
132 Uusimäki, "Lists."
133 For an overview of deterministic ideas in the scrolls, see Jean Duhaime, "Determinism," in *Encyclopedia of the Dead Sea Scrolls*, ed. Lawrence H. Schiffman and James C. VanderKam, 2 vols. (New York: Oxford University Press, 2000), 1:194–8.
134 It is unclear whether this core group of twelve men and three priests constitutes an elite group within the *yaḥad* (cf. 1QS 8:10–11). Even if that is the case, as argued by Collins, all members are equally expected "to walk in perfection of the way" and "to pursue a life of holiness." See Collins, *Qumran*, 70–3.
135 *Pace* Barton, who argues that there are no "gradations or variations" or "half-measures" in virtue ethics of the Hebrew Bible or the Qumran scrolls. See Barton, *Ethics*, 159–60. For the *yaḥad* movement, perfection (תמים) was to be realized in the present, but it also carried eschatological relevance; see George J. Brooke, "Some Issues behind the Ethics in the Qumran Scrolls and Their Implications for New Testament Ethics," in *Early Christian Ethics in Interaction with Jewish and Greco-Roman Contexts*, ed. Jan Willem van Henten (Leiden: Brill, 2013), 83–106, esp. 103.
136 The entrance to the community is potentially relevant regarding ancient philosophy, for Philip S. Alexander argues that both the Pythagoreans and the *yaḥad* used physiognomy as a test of admission; see Alexander, "Physiognomy, Initiation, and Rank in the Qumran Community," in *Geschichte – Tradition – Reflexion*, ed. Hubert Cancik et al., 3 vols. (Tübingen: Mohr, 1996), 1:385–94, esp. 1:392. Although the Qumran scrolls include physiognomic material (4Q186), 1QS does not mention people's physical characteristics and it is unclear whether the term "signs" (אתות) mentioned in 1QS 3:14 could include physiognomic criteria; see Popović, *Body*, 188–9.
137 See, e.g., Fraade, "Authority," 53–4.
138 Fraade, "Aspects," 268.
139 Yet, while Josh 1:8 stresses the utterance of or the meditation on the torah, the focus here is on the study of the torah; see Fraade, "Authority," 56.
140 So, George J. Brooke, "Reading, Searching and Blessing: A Functional Approach to Scriptural Interpretation in the *yaḥad*," in *The Temple in Text and Tradition*, ed.

R. Timothy McLay (London: Bloomsbury, 2015), 140–56, esp. 151–5. Many of the maskil's duties discussed in Chapter 3 correspond with the third community action listed in 1QS 6:8.

141 See Esther G. Chazon, "Liturgical Communion with the Angels at Qumran," in *Sapiential, Liturgical and Poetical Texts*, ed. Daniel K. Falk et al. (Leiden: Brill, 2000), 95–105.

142 See Hindy Najman, "Towards a Study of the Uses of the Concept of Wilderness in Ancient Judaism," *Dead Sea Discoveries* 13 (2006): 99–113.

143 On Moses' mediatory role, consider the evidence of the book of Jubilees, which narrates how the Angel of Presence dictated the divine revelation to Moses, who then transmitted the contents of the heavenly tablets in a written form.

144 See George J. Brooke, "Pešer and Midraš in Qumran Literature: Issues for Lexicography," *Revue de Qumran* 24 (2009): 79–95, esp. 87–91.

145 On prophecy and progressive revelation in this passage, see Alex P. Jassen, *Mediating the Divine: Prophecy and Revelation in the Dead Sea Scrolls and Second Temple Judaism* (Leiden: Brill, 2007), 49–52, esp. 52. For prophecy as a "contemporaneous and ongoing phenomenon" in the *yaḥad* movement, see also Newman, "Speech," 245.

146 On the house/home idiom, see also CD 3:18–20. Familial language applies to relations within the group in CD 13:9.

147 See Elisa Uusimäki, "'Happy Is the Person to Whom She Has Been Given': The Continuum of Wisdom and Torah in *4QSapiential Admonitions B* (4Q185) and *4QBeatitudes* (4Q525)," *Revue de Qumran* 26 (2014): 345–59. The same association occurs in many texts beyond the Qumran scrolls; see, e.g., Eckhard J. Schnabel, *Law and Wisdom from Ben Sira to Paul* (Tübingen: Mohr, 1985); Schipper and Teeter (ed.), *Wisdom and Torah*.

148 Cecilia Wassen, "On the Education of Children in the Dead Sea Scrolls," *Studies in Religion/Sciences Religieuses* 41 (2012): 350–63, esp. 356–7. Despite the general distribution of the terms, note CD 12:21; 13:22 on the maskil and 1QS 6:12, 20 on the mevaqqer. The mevaqqer references may have eventually overshadowed those to the maskil in the Damascus Document because of the merging of traditions; see Charlotte Hempel, *The Laws of the Damascus Document: Sources, Tradition and Redaction* (Leiden: Brill, 1998), 105–6, 118–21, 123–5, 150, 189.

149 For a balanced discussion on these figures, see Arjen Bakker, "The Figure of the Sage in Musar le-Mevin and Serek Ha-Yahad," Ph.D. diss. (KU Leuven, 2015), 44–52.

150 Wassen, "Education," 355.

151 Although Instruction may originate from outside this movement, note that 4Q415 frag. 2 ii may also contain marital advice to a woman. As for CD 13:17–18, this passage seems to describe the situation of teaching children whose father is divorced; see Matthew J. Goff, "Students of God in the House of Torah: Education in the Dead Sea Scrolls," in *Second Temple Jewish 'Paideia' in Context*, 71–89, esp. 85.

152 Maxine L. Grossman, "Reading for Gender in the Damascus Document," *Dead Sea Discoveries* 11 (2004): 212–39, esp. 218. The group seems more egalitarian if the Damascus Document is read in the light of 4Q502, which refers to a "daughter of truth" (frag. 1–3:6) and mentions a collective assembly with gendered pairs (frag. 14:6; 19:2–3). Respectively, the outcome is more exclusive and misogynist if the text is read in the light of 4Q184, which casts the wicked woman as a threat to men (frag. 1); see ibid., 212–39.

153 Fraade, "Authority," 55. 1QSa 1:4–5 may pertain to an annual covenant renewal ceremony. The following remarks on the education of children in 1:6–8 may apply to both sexes and not just to boys; see Wassen, "Education," 352, 356.

154 Grossman, "Gender," 218–19.

155 On the ideology of purity and holiness, as well as the partially overlapping relationship between the two, see Hannah K. Harrington, "The Halakah and Religion of Qumran," in *Religion in the Dead Sea Scrolls*, ed. John J. Collins and Robert A. Kugler (Grand Rapids, MI: Eerdmans, 2000), 74–89.

156 Cecilia Wassen, *Women in the Damascus Document* (Atlanta, GA: Society of Biblical Literature, 2005), 102–3.

157 Maxine L. Grossman, "Sectarian Marital Practice: Rethinking the Role of Sexuality in the Dead Sea Scrolls," *Dead Sea Discoveries* 26 (2019): 339–61.

158 Here I build on Keady's work on the gendered implications of purity within the movement; see Keady, *Vulnerability and Valour*. As Keady argues, the focus on purity can be interpreted as a democratizing factor in the life of these men and women, for the uncontrollable aspects of male impurity made men vulnerable.

159 See John I. Kampen, "Ethics," in *Encyclopedia of the Dead Sea Scrolls*, ed. Lawrence H. Schiffman and James C. VanderKam, 2 vols. (New York: Oxford University Press, 2000), 1: 272–6, esp. 1:273–4; Tso, *Ethics*, 37.

160 Uusimäki, "Virtue."

161 See Mary Douglas, *Leviticus as Literature* (New York: Oxford University Press, 1999), 44–5. Building on Douglas, Barton argues that impurity signals the violation of the right order; see Barton, *Ethics*, 204. On the merging of wisdom and holiness in the scrolls, see Arjen Bakker, "Sages and Saints: Continuous Study and Transformation in *Musar le-Mevin* and *Serek ha-Yaḥad*," in *Tracing Sapiential Traditions in Ancient Judaism*, 106–18, esp. 107–8, 118.

162 Martin Hengel's brief remarks are a major exception. He observed an "intellectualization of piety" in the scrolls, arguing that aspects of the group's thought can be associated with the *Zeitgeist* of the era. "For the first in Jewish history," Hengel writes, "a group developed a system of universal wisdom with a theocratic character, a system that encompassed God and creation, heaven and earth, humankind and history." He also noted early traces of the same process in Deutero-Isaiah, the priestly code, and the book of Job; see Hengel, "Qumran and Hellenism," in *Religion in the Dead Sea Scrolls*, 46–56, esp. 51.

163 Levine, *Judaism*, 20.

164 While the number of Greek manuscripts found at Qumran is sparse, they show that Greek was "sufficiently widely used and accepted to make its presence felt." So, James C. VanderKam, "Greek at Qumran," in *Hellenism in the Land of Israel*, ed. John J. Collins and Gregory E. Sterling (Notre Dame, IN: Notre Dame University Press, 2001), 175–81, esp. 179. As for other engagement with Greek literary culture, Pieter B. Hartog argues that the commentary writing of the pesharim bears resemblance to the hypomnemata of Alexandrian textual scholarship, suggesting that there were intellectual networks between Alexandria and Jerusalem; see Hartog, *Pesher and Hypomnema: A Comparison of Two Commentary Traditions from the Hellenistic-Roman Period* (Leiden: Brill, 2017).

165 Charlotte Hempel, "The Dead Sea Scrolls: Challenging the Particularist Paradigm," in *Torah, Temple and Land: Ancient Judaism(s) in Context*, ed. Verena Lepper et al. (Tübingen: Mohr Siebeck, forthcoming).

166 Cf. Hempel on how "debates presuppose concern and engagement with the same issues on both sides." See Hempel, "Particularist."

167 While the aspect of lifestyle was integral to ancient philosophy from the Hellenistic era onwards, such claims could also be subject to criticism. In fact, Diogenes Laertius (6.103), after having discussed the lives of several Cynics, reflects on the question of whether Cynicism is a real philosophy or just a way of life. These people, he reports, are happy to reject logic and physics so that they can fully focus on ethics (cf. Philo, *Prob.* 80 on the Essenes).

168 See, e.g., Newsom, "Psychology," 122–3.

169 See Mason, "*Philosophiai*," 34.

170 For an overview of apocryphal and pseudepigraphical writings, see Fraade, "Aspects," 261–3, 280–1.

171 Hadot, *Ancient Philosophy*, 147–8.

Chapter 5

1 Najman, "Pseudepigrapha," 529.
2 On the intimate link between ideals or values and social practices, see Taekema, "Ideals," 39.
3 Cf. Tolonen and Uusimäki, "Mélange," 116.
4 On the intricate interaction between a local agenda and global intellectual culture, see Hartog, "Jubilees," 20.
5 Mack, *Wisdom*, 156.
6 Cf. Whitmarsh, *Sophistic*, 2–7.
7 Amram D. Tropper, *Wisdom, Politics, and Historiography: Tractate Avot in the Context of the Graeco-Roman Near East* (Oxford: Oxford University Press, 2004), 51–87.

8   Ishay Rosen-Zvi, "The Wisdom Tradition in Rabbinic Literature and Mishnah *Avot*," in *Tracing Sapiential Traditions in Ancient Judaism*, 172–90.
9   Steven D. Fraade, "The Early Rabbinic Sage," in *The Sage in Israel and the Ancient Near East*, 417–36, esp. 436.
10 Michael L. Satlow, "'And on the Earth You Shall Sleep': 'Talmud Torah' and Rabbinic Asceticism," *The Journal of Religion* 83 (2003): 204–25.
11 Fraade, "Aspects," 275.
12 See, e.g., Kovacs, "Pedagogy," 3–25; Dunderberg, *Gnosticism*, 25, 77–8.
13 Teresa M. Shaw, *The Burden of the Flesh: Fasting and Sexuality in Early Christianity* (Minneapolis, MN: Fortress, 1998).
14 For a helpful table that summarizes the evidence of Clement, Athanasius, and Evagrius, see Joona Salminen, "Asceticism and Early Christian Lifestyle," Ph.D. diss. (University of Helsinki, 2017), 47–8.
15 See, e.g., Robert N. Pellah, "What Is Axial about the Axial Age?" *European Journal of Sociology* 46 (2005): 69–89, esp. 71, 88; Pellah, *Religion in Human Evolution: From the Paleolithic to the Axial Age* (Cambridge, MA: Belknap Press of Harvard University Press, 2011), esp. xix, 14.
16 Christensen, "Repetitivus," 46; Petersen, "Dichotomy," 192.
17 On the idea of humans as practising beings who seek to shape, create, and transform themselves through repeated exercise, whether the question is about sport, religious rituals, education, art, or labour, see Peter Sloterdijk, *You Must Change Your Life: On Anthropotechnics*, trans. Wieland Hoban (Cambridge: Polity, 2013).
18 On ancient philosophy and transformation, cf. Hadot, *Ancient Philosophy*, 6.

Bibliography

Adams, Samuel L. and Matthew J. Goff. "Editors' Introduction." In *The Wiley Blackwell Companion to Wisdom Literature*. Edited by Samuel L. Adams and Matthew J. Goff, 1–10. Hoboken, NJ: Wiley-Blackwell, 2020.

Aitken, James K. "Ben Sira's Table Manners and the Social Setting of His Book." In *Perspectives on Israelite Wisdom*. Edited by John Jarick, 418–38. London: Bloomsbury T&T Clark, 2016.

Albrecht, Janico et al. "Religion in the Making: The Lived Ancient Religion Approach." *Religion* 48 (2018): 568–93.

Alesse, Francesca, ed. *Philo of Alexandria and Post-Aristotelian Philosophy*. Leiden: Brill, 2008.

Alexander, Loveday. "Paul and the Hellenistic Schools: The Evidence of Galen." In *Paul in His Hellenistic Context*. Edited by Troels Engberg-Pedersen, 60–83. Minneapolis, MN: Fortress, 1995.

Alexander, Philip S. "Hellenism and Hellenization as Problematic Historiographical Categories." In *Paul beyond Judaism/Hellenism Divide*. Edited by Troels Engberg-Pedersen, 63–80. Louisville, KY: Westminster John Knox, 2001.

Alexander, Philip S. *Mystical Texts*. London: T&T Clark, 2006.

Alexander, Philip S. "Physiognomy, Initiation, and Rank in the Qumran Community." In *Geschichte – Tradition – Reflexion*. Edited by Hubert Cancik et al., 1: 385–94. 3 vols. Tübingen: Mohr, 1996.

Alexander, Philip S. and Geza Vermes. *Qumran Cave 4.XIX: 4QSerekh Ha-Yaḥad and Two Related Texts. Discoveries in the Judaean Desert 26*. Oxford: Clarendon, 1998.

Amir, Yehoshua and Maren Niehoff. "Philo Judaeus." In *Encyclopaedia Judaica*. Edited by Fred Skolnik and Michael Berenbaum, 16:59–64. 22 vols. 2nd ed. Detroit, MI: Thomson Gale, 2007.

Angel, Joseph L. "Maskil, Community, and Religious Experience in the Songs of the Sage (4Q510–511)." *Dead Sea Discoveries* 19 (2012): 1–27.

Annas, Julia. *The Morality of Happiness*. Oxford: Oxford University Press, 1995.

Annas, Julia. "The Sage in Ancient Philosophy." In *Anthropine Sophia*. Edited by Francesca Alesse et al., 11–27. Naples: Bibliopolis, 2008.

Annus, Amar. Review of "Seth L. Sanders, *From Adapa to Enoch: Scribal Culture and Religious Vision in Judea and Babylon*." *Bibliotheca Orientalis* 75 (2018): 159–65.

Avram, Wes. "On the Priority of 'Ethics' in the Work of Levinas." *The Journal of Religious Ethics* 24 (1996): 261–84.

Bakker, Arjen. "The Figure of the Sage in Musar le-Mevin and Serek Ha-Yahad." Ph.D. dissertation. KU Leuven, 2015.

Bakker, Arjen. "Sages and Saints: Continuous Study and Transformation in *Musar le-Mevin* and *Serek ha-Yaḥad*." In *Tracing Sapiential Traditions in Ancient Judaism*. Edited by Hindy Najman et al., 106–18. Leiden: Brill, 2016.

Barbour, Jennie. *The Story of Israel in the Book of Qohelet: Ecclesiastes as Cultural Memory*. Oxford: Oxford University Press, 2013.

Barclay, John M. G. *Flavius Josephus: Translation and Commentary, Vol. 10: Against Apion*. Leiden: Brill, 2007.

Barclay, John M. G. *Jews in the Mediterranean Diaspora from Alexander to Trajan (323 BCE–117 CE)*. Edinburgh: T&T Clark, 1996.

Barney, Rachel. "The Sophistic Movement." In *A Companion to Ancient Philosophy*. Edited by Mary Louise Gill and Pierre Pellegrin, 77–97. Oxford: Blackwell, 2006.

Barthélemy, Dominique and Józef T. Milik. *Qumran Cave 1*. Discoveries in the Judaean Desert 1. Oxford: Clarendon, 1955.

Barton, Carlin A. and Daniel Boyarin. *Imagine No Religion: How Modern Abstractions Hide Ancient Realities*. New York: Fordham University Press, 2016.

Barton, John. *Ethics in Ancient Israel*. Oxford: Oxford University Press, 2015.

Barton, John. "Old Testament Ethics: Story or Style?" In *Sibyls, Scriptures, and Scrolls*. Edited by Joel Baden et al., 113–26. Leiden: Brill, 2016.

Barton, John. *Understanding Old Testament Ethics: Approaches and Explanations*. Louisville, KY: Westminster John Knox, 2003.

Baumgarten, Albert I. "Josephus and the Jewish Sects." In *A Companion to Josephus*. Edited by Honora Howell Chapman and Zuleika Rodgers, 261–72. Chichester: John Wiley & Sons, 2016.

Beavis, Mary Ann. "Philo's Therapeutae: Philosopher's Dream or Utopian Construction?" *Journal for the Study of the Pseudepigrapha* 14 (2004): 30–42.

Becker, Adam H. and Annette Yoshiko Reed, eds. *The Ways That Never Parted: Jews and Christians in Late Antiquity and the Early Middle Ages*. Tübingen: Mohr Siebeck, 2003.

Beentjes, Pancratius C. *The Book of Ben Sira in Hebrew: A Text Edition of All Extant Hebrew Manuscripts and a Synopsis of All Parallel Hebrew Ben Sira Texts*. Leiden: Brill, 1997.

Belfiore, Elizabeth S. "Plato's Greatest Accusation against Poetry." *Canadian Journal of Philosophy* 9 (1983): 39–62.

Ben-Dov, Jonathan and Seth L. Sanders, eds. *Ancient Jewish Sciences and the History of Knowledge in Second Temple Literature*. New York: New York University Press, 2014.

Benedikt, Eckhardt, ed. *Private Associations and Jewish Communities in the Hellenistic and Roman Cities*. Leiden: Brill, 2019.

Berthelot, Katell. "Philon d'Alexandrie, lecteur d'Homère: quelques éléments de reflexion." In *Prolongements et renouvellements de la tradition classique*. Edited by Anne Balansard et al., 145–57. Aix-en-Provence: Université de Provence, 2011.

Bickerman, Elias J. *The Jews in the Greek Age*. Cambridge, MA: Harvard University Press, 1988.

Bledsoe, Seth A. "Ahiqar and Other Legendary Sages." In *The Wiley Blackwell Companion to Wisdom Literature*. Edited by Samuel L. Adams and Matthew J. Goff, 289–309. Hoboken, NJ: Wiley-Blackwell, 2020.

Blenkinsopp, Joseph A. *Ezra-Nehemiah: A Commentary*. London: SCM Press, 1989.

Blenkinsopp, Joseph A. *Sage, Priest, Prophet: Religious and Intellectual Leadership in Ancient Israel*. Louisville, KY: Westminster John Knox Press, 1995.

Blenkinsopp, Joseph A. *Wisdom and Law in the Old Testament: The Ordering of Life in Israel and Early Judaism*. Rev. ed. Oxford: Oxford University Press, 1995.

Borchardt, Francis. "Prologue of Sirach (Ben Sira) and the Question of Canon." In *Sacra Scriptura: How "Non-Canonical" Texts Functioned in Early Judaism and Early Christianity*. Edited by James H. Charlesworth et al., 64–71. London: Bloomsbury T&T Clark, 2014.

Borgen, Peder. *The Philo Index. Grand Rapids, MI: Eerdmans*. Leiden: Brill, 2000.

Borgen, Peder. *Philo of Alexandria: An Exegete for His Time*. Leiden: Brill, 1997.

Brooke, George J. "The 'Apocalyptic' Community, The Matrix of the Teacher and Rewriting Scripture." In *Authoritative Scriptures in Ancient Judaism*. Edited by Mladen Popović, 37–54. Leiden: Brill, 2010.

Brooke, George J. "Between Authority and Canon: The Significance of Reworking the Bible for Understanding the Canonical Process." In *Reworking the Bible: Apocryphal and Related Texts at Qumran*. Edited by Esther G. Chazon et al., 85–104. Leiden: Brill, 2005.

Brooke, George J. "Biblical Interpretation in the Wisdom Texts from Qumran." In *The Wisdom Texts from Qumran and the Development of Sapiential Thought*. Edited by Charlotte Hempel et al., 201–20. Leuven: Peeters, 2002.

Brooke, George J. "Crisis without, Crisis within: Changes and Developments in the Dead Sea Scrolls Movement." In *Judaism and Crisis: Crisis as a Catalyst in Jewish Cultural History*. Edited by Armin Lange et al., 89–107. Göttingen: Vandenhoeck & Ruprecht, 2011.

Brooke, George J. "Pešer and Midraš in Qumran Literature: Issues for Lexicography." *Revue de Qumran* 24 (2009): 79–95.

Brooke, George J. "The Place of Wisdom in the Formation of the Movement behind the Dead Sea Scrolls." In *Goochem in Mokum, Wisdom in Amsterdam: Papers on Biblical and Related Wisdom*. Edited by Bob Becking, 20–33. Leiden: Brill, 2016.

Brooke, George J. "Reading, Searching and Blessing: A Functional Approach to Scriptural Interpretation in the *yaḥad*." In *The Temple in Text and Tradition*. Edited by R. Timothy McLay, 140–56. London: Bloomsbury, 2015.

Brooke, George J. "Some Issues behind the Ethics in the Qumran Scrolls and Their Implications for New Testament Ethics." In *Early Christian Ethics in Interaction with Jewish and Greco-Roman Contexts*. Edited by Jan Willem van Henten, 83–106. Leiden: Brill, 2013.

Brooke, George J. "Was the Teacher of Righteousness Considered to Be a Prophet?" In *Prophecy after the Prophets? The Contribution of the Dead Sea Scrolls to the*

Understanding of Biblical and Extra-Biblical Prophecy. Edited by Kristin de Troyer and Armin Lange, 77–97. Leuven: Peeters, 2009.

Brouwer, René. *The Stoic Sage: The Early Stoics on Wisdom, Sagehood and Socrates*. Cambridge: Cambridge University Press, 2014.

Brown, Eric. "Hellenistic Cosmopolitanism." In *A Companion to Ancient Philosophy*. Edited by Mary Louise Gill and Pierre Pellegrin, 549–58. Oxford: Blackwell, 2006.

Brown, Peter. "The Rise and Function of the Holy Man in Late Antiquity." *Journal of Roman Studies* 61 (1971): 80–101.

Brown, Peter. "The Saint as Exemplar in Late Antiquity." *Representations* 2 (1983): 1–25.

Brown, William P. *Character in Crisis: A Fresh Approach to the Wisdom Literature of the Old Testament*. Grand Rapids, MI: Eerdmans, 1996.

Brown, William P. *Wisdom's Wonder: Character, Creation, and Crisis in the Bible's Wisdom*. Grand Rapids, MI: Eerdmans, 2014.

Busine, Aude. *Le Sept Sages de la Grèce antique*. Paris: de Boccard, 2002.

Buxton, Richard. *Imaginary Greece: The Contexts of Mythology*. Cambridge: Cambridge University Press, 1994.

Camp, Claudia V. "The Female Sage in Ancient Israel and in the Biblical Wisdom Literature." In *The Sage in Israel and the Ancient Near East*. Edited by John G. Gammie and Leo G. Perdue, 185–203. Winona Lake, IN: Eisenbrauns, 1990.

Camp, Claudia V. and Benjamin G. Wright III. "'Who Has Been Tested by Gold and Found Perfect?' Ben Sira's Discourse of Riches and Poverty." *Henoch* 23 (2001): 153–74.

Carmignac, Jean. "Conjecture sur la première ligne de la Règle de la Communauté." *Revue de Qumran* 2 (1959): 85–7.

Carr, David M. *Writing on the Tablet of the Heart: Origins of Scripture and Literature*. Oxford: Oxford University Press, 2005.

Cavell, Stanley. *Cities of Words: Pedagogical Letters on a Register of the Moral Life*. Cambridge, MA: The Belknap Press of Harvard University Press, 2004.

Charlesworth, James H. et al., eds. *The Dead Sea Scrolls: Hebrew, Aramaic, and Greek Texts with English Translations, Vol. 1: Rule of the Community and Related Documents*. Tübingen: Mohr Siebeck. Louisville, KY: Westminster John Knox Press, 1994.

Chazon, Esther G. "Liturgical Communion with the Angels at Qumran." In *Sapiential, Liturgical and Poetical Texts*. Edited by Daniel K. Falk et al., 95–105. Leiden: Brill, 2000.

Christensen, Line Søgaard. "Homo Repetitivus and Anthropotechnics: Exercise Systems, Elite Practitioners, and Teaching Missions in the Hebrew Bible." In *"What Is Human?": Theological Encounters with Anthropology*. Edited by Eve-Marie Becker et al., 45–64. Göttingen: Vandenhoeck & Ruprecht, 2017.

Clark, Stephen R. L. *Ancient Mediterranean Philosophy*. London: Bloomsbury, 2013.

Cohen, Yoram and Andrew R. George. *Wisdom from the Late Bronze Age*. Atlanta, GA: Society of Biblical Literature, 2013.

Collins, Adela Yarbro. "Aristobulus." In *The Old Testament Pseudepigrapha*. Edited by James H. Charlesworth, 2:831–42. 2 vols. 5th Hendrickson Edition. Peabody, MA: Hendrickson, 2016.

Collins, John J. "Artapanus." In *The Old Testament Pseudepigrapha*. Edited by James H. Charlesworth, 2:889–903. 2 vols. 5th Hendrickson Edition. Peabody, MA: Hendrickson, 2016.

Collins, John J. *Beyond the Qumran Community: The Sectarian Movement of the Dead Sea Scrolls*. Grand Rapids, MI: Eerdmans, 2010.

Collins, John J. "Epilogue: Genre Analysis and the Dead Sea Scrolls." *Dead Sea Discoveries* 17 (2010): 418–30.

Collins, John J. *Jewish Wisdom in the Hellenistic Age*. Edinburgh: T&T Clark, 1998.

Collins, John J. "The Sage in Apocalyptic and Pseudepigraphic Literature." In *The Sage in Israel and the Ancient Near East*. Edited by John G. Gammie and Leo G. Perdue, 343–54. Winona Lake, IN: Eisenbrauns, 1990.

Collins, John J. "The Two Spirits and the Origin of Evil." Presented at Enoch Seminar Online, July 2020.

Collins, John J. "Wisdom Reconsidered in Light of the Scrolls." *Dead Sea Discoveries* 4 (1997): 265–81.

Collins, John J. and George W. E. Nickelsburg, eds. *Ideal Figures in Ancient Judaism: Profiles and Paradigms*. Chico, CA: Scholars Press, 1980.

Collins, John J. and Gregory E. Sterling, eds. *Hellenism in the Land of Israel*. Notre Dame, IN: Notre Dame University Press, 2001.

Cooper, John M. *Pursuits of Wisdom: Six Ways of Life in Ancient Philosophy from Socrates to Plotinus*. Princeton, NJ: Princeton University Press, 2012.

Cosby, Michael R. *The Rhetorical Composition and Function of Hebrews 11 in Light of Example Lists in Antiquity*. Macon, GA: Mercer University Press, 1988.

Crenshaw, James L. *Old Testament Wisdom: An Introduction*. Atlanta, GA: Westminster John Knox, 1981.

Crenshaw, James L. "The Primacy of Listening in Ben Sira's Pedagogy." In *Wisdom, You Are My Sister*. Edited by Michael L. Barré, 172–87. Washington, DC: Catholic Biblical Association of America, 1997.

Cribiore, Raffaella. *Gymnastics of the Mind: Greek Education in Hellenistic and Roman Egypt*. Princeton, NJ: Princeton University Press, 2001.

Csordas, Thomas J. "Embodiment as a Paradigm for Anthropology." *Ethos* 18 (1990): 5–47.

Davies, John K. *Oxford Classical Dictionary*. Edited by Simon Hornblower and Anthony Spawforth. 3rd ed. Oxford: Oxford University Press, 2005.

Dawson, David. *Allegorical Readers and Cultural Revision in Ancient Alexandria*. Berkeley, CA: University of California Press, 1992.

deSilva, David A. *Despising Shame: Honor Discourse and Community Maintenance in the Epistle to the Hebrews*. Rev. ed. Atlanta, GA: Society of Biblical Literature, 2008.

deSilva, David A. "The Wisdom of Ben Sira: Honor, Shame, and the Maintenance of the Values of a Minority Culture." *Catholic Biblical Quarterly* 58 (1996): 433–55.

Di Lella, Alexander A. *The Wisdom of Ben Sira: A New Translation with Notes by Patrick W. Skehan. Introduction and Commentary by Alexander A. Di Lella.* New York: Doubleday, 1987.
Dillon, John M. *The Middle Platonists 80 B.C. to A.D. 220.* Ithaca, NY: Cornell University Press, 1977.
Dimant, Devorah. *History, Ideology and Bible Interpretation in the Dead Sea Scrolls.* Tübingen: Mohr Siebeck, 2014.
Dimant, Devorah. "Pseudonymity in the Wisdom of Solomon." In *La Septuaginta en la Investigacion Contemporanea.* Edited by Natalio Fernández Marcos, 243–55. Madrid: Instituto Arias Montano, 1985.
Doniger, Wendy. "Post-modern and -colonial -structural Comparisons." In *A Magic Still Dwells: Comparative Religion in Postmodern Age.* Edited by Kimberley C. Patton and Benjamin C. Ray, 63–74. Berkeley, CA: University of California Press, 2000.
Douglas, Mary. *Leviticus as Literature.* New York: Oxford University Press, 1999.
Downing, Francis Gerald. *Cynics and Christian Origins.* Edinburgh: T&T Clark, 1992.
Droysen, Johann Gustav. *Geschichte des Hellenismus.* Gotha: Perthes, 1877–8.
Duhaime, Jean. "Determinism." In *Encyclopedia of the Dead Sea Scrolls.* Edited by Lawrence H. Schiffman and James C. VanderKam, 1:194–8. 2 vols. New York: Oxford University Press, 2000.
Dunderberg, Ismo. *Beyond Gnosticism: Myth, Lifestyle, and Society in the School of Valentinus.* New York: Columbia University Press, 2008.
Edelman, Diana V. and Ehud Ben Zvi, eds. *Remembering Biblical Figures in the Late Persian and Early Hellenistic Periods: Social Memory and Imagination.* Oxford: Oxford University Press, 2013.
Elgvin, Torleif. "Maskil." In *Theologisches Wörterbuch zu den Qumrantexten: Band II.* Edited by Heinz-Josef Fabry et al., 802–6. Stuttgart: Kolhammer, 2013.
Elgvin, Torleif. "The Yaḥad Is More than Qumran." In *Enoch and Qumran Origins: New Light on a Forgotten Connection.* Edited by Gabrielle Boccaccini, 273–9. Grand Rapids, MI: Eerdmans, 2005.
Engberg-Pedersen, Troels. "The Hellenistic Öffentlichkeit: Philosophy as a Social Force in the Greco-Roman World." In *Recruitment, Conquest, and Conflict: Strategies in Judaism, Early Christianity and the Greco-Roman World.* Edited by Peder Borgen et al., 15–38. Atlanta, GA: Scholars Press, 1998.
Engberg-Pedersen, Troels. "Philo's *De Vita Contemplativa* as a Philosopher's Dream." *Journal for the Study of Judaism* 30 (1999): 40–64.
Engberg-Pedersen, Troels. "Setting the Scene: Stoicism and Platonism in the Transitional Period in Ancient Philosophy." In *Stoicism in Early Christianity.* Edited by Tuomas Rasimus et al., 1–14. Grand Rapids, MI: Baker Academic, 2010.
Falk, Daniel K. "Petition and Ideology in the Dead Sea Scrolls." In *Prayer and Poetry in the Dead Sea Scrolls and Related Literature.* Edited by Jeremy Penner et al., 135–59. Leiden: Brill, 2011.

Feldman, Louis H. "Josephus' Portrait of Jacob." *Jewish Quarterly Review* 79 (1988–9): 101–51.

Finkelberg, Margalit. "Homer as a Foundation Text." In *Homer, the Bible and Beyond: Literary and Religious Canons in the Ancient World*. Edited by Margalit Finkelberg and Guy G. Stroumsa, 75–96. Leiden: Brill, 2003.

Fiore, Benjamin. "The Sage in Select Hellenistic and Roman Literary Genres (Philosophical Epistles, Political Discourses, History, Comedy, and Romances)." In *The Sage in Israel and the Ancient Near East*. Edited by John G. Gammie and Leo G. Perdue, 329–41. Winona Lake, IN: Eisenbrauns, 1990.

Fishbane, Michael. "From Scribalism to Rabbinism: Perspectives on the Emergence of Classical Judaism." In *The Sage in Israel and the Ancient Near East*. Edited by John G. Gammie and Leo G. Perdue, 439–56. Winona lake, IN: Eisenbrauns, 1990.

Fontaine, Carole R. "The Sage in Family and Tribe." In *The Sage in Israel and the Ancient Near East*. Edited by John G. Gammie and Leo G. Perdue, 155–64. Winona lake, IN: Eisenbrauns, 1990.

Fox, Michael V. "Concepts of Wisdom in the Book of Proverbs." In *Birkat Shalom: Studies in the Bible, Ancient Near Eastern Literature, and Postbiblical Judaism*. Edited by Chaim Cohen et al., 1: 381–8. 2 vols. Winona Lake, IN: Eisenbrauns, 2008.

Fox, Michael V. "Ideas of Wisdom in Proverbs 1–9." *Journal of Biblical Literature* 116 (1997): 613–33.

Fox, Michael V. *Proverbs 1–9: A New Translation with Introduction and Commentary*. New York: Doubleday, 2000.

Fox, Michael V. "Three Theses on Wisdom." In *Was There a Wisdom Tradition? New Prospects in Israelite Wisdom Studies*. Edited by Mark R. Sneed, 69–86. Atlanta, GA: Society of Biblical Literature, 2015.

Fox, Michael V. *A Time to Tear Down and a Time to Build Up: A Rereading of Ecclesiastes*. Grand Rapids, MI: Eerdmans, 1999.

Fox, Michael V. "What the Book of Proverbs Is about." In *Congress Volume: Cambridge 1995*. Edited by John A. Emerton, 153–67. Leiden: Brill, 1997.

Fox, Michael V. "Wisdom and the Self-Presentation of Wisdom Literature." In *Reading from Right to Left*. Edited by J. Cheryl Exum and H. G. M. Williamson, 153–72. London: T&T Clark, 2003.

Fraade, Steven D. "Ascetical Aspects of Ancient Judaism." In *Jewish Spirituality: From the Bible through the Middle Ages*. Edited by Arthur Green, 253–86. New York: Crossroad, 1986.

Fraade, Steven D. "The Early Rabbinic Sage." In *The Sage in Israel and the Ancient Near East*. Edited by John G. Gammie and Leo G. Perdue, 417–36. Winona Lake, IN: Eisenbrauns, 1990.

Fraade, Steven D. "Interpretive Authority in the Studying Community at Qumran." *Journal of Jewish Studies* 44 (1993): 46–69.

Fraser, Peter M. *Ptolemaic Alexandria*. 3 vols. Oxford: Clarendon, 1972.

Freeman, Kathleen. *Ancilla to the Pre-Socratic Philosophers: A Complete Translation of the Fragments in Diels Fragmente der Vorsokratiker*. Cambridge, MA: Harvard University Press, 1957.

Frymer-Kensky, Tikva. "The Sage in the Pentateuch: Soundings." In *The Sage in Israel and the Ancient Near East*. Edited by John G. Gammie and Leo G. Perdue, 275–87. Winona Lake, IN: Eisenbrauns, 1990.

Gammie, John G. and Leo G. Perdue, eds. *The Sage in Israel and the Ancient Near East*. Winona Lake, IN: Eisenbrauns, 1990.

García Martínez, Florentino. "Beyond the Sectarian Divide: The 'Voice of the Teacher' as an Authority-Conferring Strategy in Some Qumran Texts." In *The Dead Sea Scrolls: Transmission of Traditions and Production of Texts*. Edited by Sarianna Metso et al., 227–44. Leiden: Brill, 2010.

García Martínez, Florentino. "Rethinking the Bible: Sixty Years of Dead Sea Scrolls Research and Beyond." In *Authoritative Scriptures in Ancient Judaism*. Edited by Mladen Popović, 19–36. Leiden: Brill, 2010.

Gasparini, Valentino et al., eds. *Lived Religion in the Ancient Mediterranean World: Approaching Religious Transformations from Archaeology, History and Classics*. Berlin: de Gruyter, 2020.

Gillihan, Yonder M. *Civic Ideology, Organization, and Law in the Rule Scrolls: A Comparative Study of the Covenanters' Sect and Contemporary Voluntary Associations in Political Context*. Leiden: Brill, 2012.

Goff, Matthew J. *Discerning Wisdom: The Sapiential Literature of the Dead Sea Scrolls*. Leiden: Brill, 2007.

Goff, Matthew J. "Gardens of Knowledge: Teachers in Ben Sira, 4QInstruction, and the Hodayot." In *Pedagogy in Ancient Judaism and Early Christianity*. Edited by Karina Martin Hogan et al., 171–93. Atlanta, GA: Society of Biblical Literature, 2017.

Goff, Matthew J. "Qumran Wisdom Literature and the Problem of Genre." *Dead Sea Discoveries* 17 (2010): 315–35.

Goff, Matthew J. "Students of God in the House of Torah: Education in the Dead Sea Scrolls." In *Second Temple Jewish "Paideia" in Context*. Edited by Jason M. Zurawski and Gabrielle Boccaccini, 71–89. Berlin: de Gruyter, 2017.

Goldberg, Shari. "The Two Choruses Become One: The Absence/Presence of Women in Philo's *On the Contemplative Life*." *Journal for the Study of Judaism* 39 (2008): 459–70.

Grabbe, Lester L. *Priests, Prophets, Diviners, Sages: A Socio-Historical Study of Religious Specialists in Ancient Israel*. Valley Forge, PA: Trinity Press International, 1995.

Graver, Margaret R. *Stoicism and Emotion*. Chicago: The University of Chicago Press, 2007.

Gribetz, Sarit Kattan. "The Festival of Every Day: Philo and Seneca on Quotidian Time." *Harvard Theological Review* 111 (2018): 357–81.

Grossman, Maxine L. "Reading for Gender in the Damascus Document." *Dead Sea Discoveries* 11 (2004): 212–39.

Grossman, Maxine L. "Sectarian Marital Practice: Rethinking the Role of Sexuality in the Dead Sea Scrolls." *Dead Sea Discoveries* 26 (2019): 339–61.
Gruen, Erich S. *Diaspora: Jews amidst Greeks and Romans*. Cambridge, MA: Harvard University Press, 2002.
Gruen, Erich S. *Heritage and Hellenism: The Reinvention of Jewish Tradition*. Berkeley, CA: University of California Press, 1998.
Gruen, Erich S. *Rethinking the Other in Antiquity*. Princeton, PA: Princeton University Press, 2010.
Hadas-Lebel, Mireille. *Philo of Alexandria: A Thinker in the Jewish Diaspora*. Leiden: Brill, 2012.
Hadot, Pierre. *Exercices spirituels et philosophie antique*. Paris: Études Augustiniennes, 1987.
Hadot, Pierre. *Philosophy as a Way of Life: Spiritual Exercises from Socrates to Foucault*. Edited by Arnold I. Davidson. Translated by Michael Chase. Oxford: Blackwell, 1995.
Hadot, Pierre. *Qu'est-ce que la philosophie antique?* Paris: Gallimard, 1995.
Hadot, Pierre. *What Is Ancient Philosophy?* Translated by Michael Chase. Cambridge, MA: The Belknap Press of Harvard University Press, 2002.
Hägg, Tomas. *The Art of Biography in Antiquity*. Cambridge: Cambridge University Press, 2012.
Hall, David D., ed. *Lived Religion in America: Toward a History of Practice*. Princeton, NJ: Princeton University Press, 1997.
Hamori, Esther J. *Women's Divination in Biblical Literature: Prophecy, Necromancy, and Other Arts of Knowledge*. New Haven, CT: Yale University Press, 2015.
Harding, James E. "Ben Sira on Friendship: Notes on Intertextuality and Method." In *Perspectives on Israelite Wisdom*. Edited by John Jarick, 439–62. London: Bloomsbury T&T Clark, 2016.
Harrington, Daniel J. *Jesus ben Sira of Jerusalem: A Biblical Guide to Living Wisely*. Collegeville, MN: Liturgical Press, 2005.
Harrington, Daniel J. *Wisdom Texts from Qumran*. London: Routledge, 1996.
Harrington, Hannah K. "The Halakah and Religion of Qumran." In *Religion in the Dead Sea Scrolls*. Edited by John J. Collins and Robert A. Kugler, 74–89. Grand Rapids, MI: Eerdmans, 2000.
Harris, Rivkah. "The Female 'Sage' in Mesopotamian Literature (with an Appendix on Egypt)." In *The Sage in Israel and the Ancient Near East*. Edited by John G. Gammie and Leo G. Perdue, 3–17. Winona Lake, IN: Eisenbrauns, 1990.
Hartog, Pieter B. "Jubilees and Hellenistic Encyclopaedism." *Journal for the Study of Judaism* 50 (2019): 1–25.
Hartog, Pieter B. *Pesher and Hypomnema: A Comparison of Two Commentary Traditions from the Hellenistic-Roman Period*. Leiden: Brill, 2017.
Hartog, Pieter B. "Pesher as Commentary." In *The Dead Sea Scrolls and the Study of the Humanities: Method, Theory, Meaning*. Edited by Pieter B. Hartog et al., 92–116. Leiden: Brill, 2018.

Hartog, Pieter B. and Jutta Jokiranta, eds. *Dead Sea Discoveries* 24/3. Leiden: Brill, 2017.

Hatch, Edward et al. *A Concordance to the Septuagint*. 2nd ed. Grand Rapids, MI: Baker Academic, 1998.

Hawley, Robert. "On Maskil in the Judean Desert Texts." *Henoch* 28 (2006): 43–77.

Hay, David M. "Things Philo Said and Did Not Say about the Therapeutae." *Society of Biblical Literature Symposium Papers* 31 (1992): 673–83.

Hay, David M. "The Veiled Thoughts of the Therapeutae." In *Mediators of the Divine: Horizons of Prophecy, Divination, Dreams and Theurgy in Mediterranean Antiquity*. Edited by Robert M. Berchman, 167–84. Atlanta, GA: Scholars Press, 1998.

Hempel, Charlotte. "The Dead Sea Scrolls: Challenging the Particularist Paradigm." In *Torah, Temple and Land: Ancient Judaism(s) in Context*. Edited by Verena Lepper et al. Tübingen: Mohr Siebeck, forthcoming.

Hempel, Charlotte. *The Laws of the Damascus Document: Sources, Tradition and Redaction*. Leiden: Brill, 1998.

Hempel, Charlotte. "*Maskil(im)* and *Rabbim*: From Daniel to Qumran." In *Biblical Traditions in Transmission*. Edited by Charlotte Hempel and Judith M. Lieu, 133–56. Leiden: Brill, 2006.

Hempel, Charlotte. "The Qumran Sapiential Texts and the Rule Books." In *The Wisdom Texts from Qumran and the Development of Sapiential Thought*. Edited by Charlotte Hempel et al., 277–95. Leuven: Peeters, 2002.

Hempel, Charlotte. "The Treatise of the Two Spirits and the Literary History of the Rule of the Community." In *Dualism in Qumran*. Edited by Géza G. Xeravits, 102–20. London: T&T Clark, 2010.

Hengel, Martin. *Judaism and Hellenism: Studies in Their Encounter in Palestine during the Early Hellenistic Period*. Translated by John Bowden. 2 vols. Philadelphia, PA: Fortress, 1974.

Hengel, Martin. "Qumran and Hellenism." In *Religion in the Dead Sea Scrolls*. Edited by John J. Collins and Robert A. Kugler, 46–56. Grand Rapids, MI: Eerdmans, 2000.

Henze, Matthias. *The Madness of King Nebuchadnezzar: The Ancient Near Eastern Origins and Early History of Interpretation of Daniel 4*. Leiden: Brill, 1999.

Hogan, Karina Martin. "Would Philo Have Recognized Qumran *Musar* as Paideia?" In *Pedagogy in Ancient Judaism and Early Christianity*. Edited by Karina Martin Hogan et al., 81–100. Atlanta, GA: Society of Biblical Literature, 2017.

Hogan, Karina Martin et al., eds. *Pedagogy in Ancient Judaism and Early Christianity*. Atlanta, GA: Society of Biblical Literature, 2017.

Horst, Pieter van der. "Greek in Jewish Palestine in Light of Jewish Epigraphy." In *Hellenism in the Land of Israel*. Edited by John J. Collins and Gregory E. Sterling, 154–74. Notre Dame, IN: Notre Dame University Press, 2001.

Inowlocki, Sabrina. *Eusebius and the Jewish Authors: His Citation Technique in an Apologetic Context*. Leiden: Brill, 2006.

Jaeger, Werner. *Paideia: The Ideals of Greek Culture*. Translated by Gilbert Highet. 3 vols. 2nd ed. New York: Oxford University Press, 1962.

Japhet, Sara. *I & II Chronicles: A Commentary*. Louisville, KY: Westminster John Knox Press, 1993.
Jassen, Alex P. *Mediating the Divine: Prophecy and Revelation in the Dead Sea Scrolls and Second Temple Judaism*. Leiden: Brill, 2007.
Jong, Albert de. "Iranian Connections in the Dead Sea Scrolls." In *The Oxford Handbook of the Dead Sea Scrolls*. Edited by Timothy H. Lim and John J. Collins, 479–500. Oxford: Oxford University Press, 2010.
JPS Hebrew-English Tanakh. Philadelphia, PA: The Jewish Publication Society, 2003.
Kampen, John I. "Ethics." In *Encyclopedia of the Dead Sea Scrolls*. Edited by Lawrence H. Schiffman and James C. VanderKam, 1: 272–6. 2 vols. New York: Oxford University Press, 2000.
Kampen, John I. *Wisdom Literature*. Grand Rapids, MI: Eerdmans, 2011.
Kamtekar, Rachana. "Ancient Virtue Ethics: An Overview with an Emphasis on Practical Wisdom." In *The Cambridge Companion to Virtue Ethics*. Edited by Daniel C. Russell, 29–48. Cambridge: Cambridge University Press, 2013.
Keady, Jessica M. *Vulnerability and Valour: A Gendered Analysis of Everyday Life in the Dead Sea Scrolls Communities*. London: Bloomsbury T&T Clark, 2017.
Kerferd, George B. "The Image of the Wise Man in Greece in the Period before Plato." In *Images of Man in Ancient and Medieval Thought*. Edited by F. Bossier et al., 17–28. Leuven: Leuven University Press, 1976.
Kerferd, George B. "The Sage in Hellenistic Philosophical Literature (399 B.C.E.–199 C.E.)." In *The Sage in Israel and the Ancient Near East*. Edited by John G. Gammie and Leo G. Perdue, 319–28. Winona Lake, IN: Eisenbrauns, 1990.
Kidd, Ian G. "Stoic Intermediates and the End for Man." In *Problems in Stoicism*. Edited by Anthony A. Long, 150–72. London: Athlone, 1971.
Kieweler, Hans Volker. *Ben Sira zwischen Judentum und Hellenismus: Eine Auseinandersetzung mit Th. Middendorp*. Frankfurt: Peter Lang, 1992.
Kolarcik, Michael, S.J. "The Sage behind the Wisdom of Solomon." In *Scribes, Sages, and Seers: The Sage in the Eastern Mediterranean World*. Edited by Leo G. Perdue, 245–57. Göttingen: Vandenhoeck & Ruprecht, 2008.
Kooten, George H. van. "Is Early Christianity a Religion or a Philosophy? Reflections on the Importance of 'Knowledge' and 'Truth' in the Letters of Paul and Peter." In *Myths, Martyrs, and Modernity: Studies in the History of Religions*. Edited by Jitse H. F. Dijkstra et al., 393–408. Leiden: Brill, 2010.
Koskenniemi, Erkki. *Greek Writers and Philosophers in Philo and Josephus: A Study of Their Secular Education and Educational Ideals*. Leiden: Brill, 2019.
Koskenniemi, Erkki. "Moses – A Well-Educated Man: A Look at the Educational Idea in Early Judaism." *Journal for the Study of the Pseudepigrapha* 17 (2008): 281–96.
Koskenniemi, Erkki. "Philo and Classical Drama." In *Ancient Israel, Judaism, and Christianity in Contemporary Perspective*. Edited by Jacob Neusner et al., 137–52. Lanham, MD: University Press of America, 2006.

Koskenniemi, Erkki. "Philo and Greek Poets." *Journal for the Study of Judaism* 41 (2010): 301–22.

Kosmala, Hans. "Maskil." *The Journal of the Ancient Near Eastern Society of Columbia University* 5 (1973): 235–41.

Kovacs, Judith L. "Divine Pedagogy and the Gnostic Teacher According to Clement of Alexandria." *Journal of Early Christian Studies* 9 (2001): 3–25.

Kraemer, Ross Shepard. "Monastic Jewish Women in Greco-Roman Egypt: Philo Judaeus on the Therapeutrides." *Signs* 14 (1989): 342–70.

Kraemer, Ross Shepard. *Unreliable Witnesses: Religion, Gender, and History in the Greco-Roman Mediterranean*. Oxford: Oxford University Press, 2011.

Kraft, Robert A. "Para-mania: Before, beside and beyond Biblical Studies." *Journal of Biblical Literature* 126 (2007): 5–27.

Kraft, Robert A. "Pliny on Essenes, Pliny on Jews." *Dead Sea Discoveries* 8 (2001): 255–61.

Kramer, Noah. "The Sage in Sumerian Literature: A Composite Portrait." In *The Sage in Israel and the Ancient Near East*. Edited by John G. Gammie and Leo G. Perdue, 31–44. Winona Lake, IN: Eisenbrauns, 1990.

Krüger, Thomas. *Kohelet (Prediger)*. Neukirchen-Vluyn: Neukirchener Verlag, 2000.

Kugel, James L. "The Figure of Moses in *Jubilees*." *Hebrew Bible and Ancient Israel* 1 (2012): 77–92.

Kugel, James L. "Wisdom and the Anthological Temper." *Prooftexts* 17 (1997): 9–32.

Kynes, Will. *An Obituary for "Wisdom Literature": The Birth, Death, and Intertextual Reintegration of a Biblical Corpus*. Oxford: Oxford University Press, 2019.

Kynes, Will. "The 'Wisdom Literature' Category: An Obituary." *Journal of Theological Studies* 69 (2018): 1–24.

LaCoste, Nathalie. "Solomon the Exemplary Sage: The Convergence of Hellenistic and Jewish Traditions in the Wisdom of Solomon." *The University of Toronto Journal of Jewish Thought* 1 (2010). Online: http://cjs.utoronto.ca/tjjt/node/18.

Lange, Armin. "Sages and Scribes in the Qumran Literature." In *Scribes, Sages, and Seers: The Sage in the Eastern Mediterranean World*. Edited by Leo G. Perdue, 271–93. Göttingen: Vandenhoeck & Ruprecht, 2008.

Lange, Armin. "Wisdom Literature and Thought in the Dead Sea Scrolls." In *The Oxford Handbook of the Dead Sea Scrolls*. Edited by Timothy H. Lim and John J. Collins, 455–78. Oxford: Oxford University Press, 2010.

Larsen, Matthew D. "Listening with the Body, Seeing through the Ears: Contextualizing Philo's Lecture Event in *On the Contemplative Life*." *Journal for the Study of Judaism* 47 (2016): 1–28.

Legaspi, Michael C. *Wisdom in Classical and Biblical Tradition*. Oxford: Oxford University Press, 2018.

Lemaire, André. *Les écoles et la formation de la Bible dans l'ancien Israël*. Göttingen: Vanhenhoeck & Ruprecht, 1981.

Lemaire, André. "The Sage in School and Temple." In *The Sage in Israel and the Ancient Near East*. Edited by John G. Gammie and Leo G. Perdue, 165–81. Winona Lake, IN: Eisenbrauns, 1990.

Levine, Lee I. *Judaism and Hellenism in Antiquity: Conflict or Confluence?* Seattle, WA: University of Washington Press, 1998.

Lewis, Thomas A. *Why Philosophy Matters for the Study of Religion – and Vice Versa*. Oxford: Oxford University Press, 2015.

Lichtheim, Miriam. *Late Egyptian Wisdom Literature in the International Context: A Study of Demotic Instructions*. Fribourg: Universitätsverlag, 1983.

Lim, Timothy H. *The Formation of the Jewish Canon*. New Haven, CT: Yale University Press, 2013.

Lincicum, David. "A Preliminary Index to Philo's Non-Biblical Citations and Allusions." *Studia Philonica Annual* 25 (2013): 139–67.

Litwa, M. David. "The Deification of Moses in Philo of Alexandria." *Studia Philonica Annual* 26 (2014): 1–27.

Livneh, Atar. "Jewish Traditions and Familial Roman Values in Philo's *De Abrahamo* 245–254." *Harvard Theological Review* 109 (2016): 536–49.

Long, Anthony A. *Hellenistic Philosophy: Stoics, Epicureans, Sceptics*. New York: Charles Scribner's Sons, 1974.

Long, Anthony A. "Language and Thought in Stoicism." In *Problems in Stoicism*. Edited by Anthony A. Long, 75–113. London: Athlone, 1971.

Long, Anthony A. "Socrates in Later Greek Philosophy." In *The Cambridge Companion to Socrates*. Edited by Donald R. Morrison, 355–79. Cambridge: Cambridge University Press, 2010.

Lutz, Cora E. "Musonius Rufus, 'The Roman Socrates.'" *Yale Classical Studies* 10 (1947): 32–147.

Macaskill, Grant. *Revealed Wisdom and Inaugurated Eschatology in Ancient Judaism and Early Christianity*. Leiden: Brill, 2007.

Mack, Burton L. *Wisdom and the Hebrew Epic: Ben Sira's Hymn in Praise of the Fathers*. Chicago: The University of Chicago Press, 1985.

Mackie, Scott D. "Seeing God in Philo of Alexandria: Means, Methods, and Mysticism." *Journal for the Study of Judaism* 43 (2012): 147–79.

Magness, Jodi. *The Archaeology of Qumran and the Dead Sea Scrolls*. Grand Rapids, MI: Eerdmans, 2002.

Mansfeld, Jaap. "Philosophy in the Service of Scripture: Philo's Exegetical Strategies." In *The Question of "Eclecticism": Studies in Later Greek Philosophy*. Edited by John M. Dillon and Anthony A. Long, 70–102. Berkeley, CA: University of California Press, 1988.

Mason, Steve. "Essenes and Lurking Spartans in Josephus' Judean War: From Story to History." In *Making History: Josephus and Historical Method*. Edited by Zuleika Rodgers et al., 219–61. Leiden: Brill, 2007.

Mason, Steve. *Flavius Josephus: Translation and Commentary*. Vol. 1b, Judean War 2. Leiden: Brill, 2008.

Mason, Steve. *Flavius Josephus: Translation and Commentary*. Vol. 9, Life of Josephus. Leiden: Brill, 2001.

Mason, Steve. "Jews, Judaeans, Judaizing, Judaism: Problems of Categorization in Ancient History." *Journal for the Study of Judaism* 38 (2007): 457–512.

Mason, Steve. *Orientation to the History of Roman Judaea*. Eugene, OR: Wipf and Stock, 2016.

Mason, Steve. "*Philosophiai*: Graeco-Roman, Judean and Christian." In *Voluntary Associations in the Graeco-Roman World*. Edited by John S. Kloppenborg and Stephen G. Wilson, 31–58. London: Routledge, 1996.

Mason, Steve. "Was Josephus a Pharisee? A Reconsideration of Life 10–12." *Journal of Jewish Studies* 40 (1989): 31–45.

Mason, Steve. "What Josephus Says about Essenes in His Judean War." In *Text and Artifact in the Religions of Mediterranean Antiquity*. Edited by Stephen G. Wisdom and Michael Desjardins, 423–55. Waterloo, Ontario: Wilfrid Laurier University Press, 2000.

Mattila, Sharon Lea. "Ben Sira and the Stoics: A Reexamination of the Evidence." *Journal of Biblical Literature* 119 (2000): 473–501.

Mattila, Sharon Lea. "Wisdom, Sense Perception, and Philo's Gender Gradient." *Harvard Theological Review* 89 (1996): 103–29.

McCarter, P. Kyle. *1 Samuel: A New Translation with Introduction, Notes and Commentary*. Garden City, NY: Doubleday, 1980.

McGuire, Meredith B. *Lived Religion: Faith and Practice in Everyday Life*. Oxford: Oxford University Press, 2008.

McPherran, Mark L. "Platonic Religion." In *A Companion to Plato*. Edited by Hugh H. Benson, 244–59. Chichester: Wiley-Blackwell, 2007.

Meeks, Wayne A. "Moses as God and King." In *Religions in Antiquity*. Edited by Jacob Neusner, 354–71. Leiden: Brill, 1968.

Mendels, Doron. "Hellenistic Utopia and the Essenes." *Harvard Theological Review* 72 (1979): 207–22.

Mendelson, Alan. *Secular Education in Philo of Alexandria*. Cincinnati, OH: Hebrew Union College Press, 1982.

Metso, Sarianna. *The Serekh Texts*. London: T&T Clark, 2007.

Metso, Sarianna. *The Textual Development of the Qumran Community Rule*. Leiden: Brill, 1997.

Middendorp, Theophil. *Die Stellung Jesu Ben Siras zwischen Judentum und Hellenismus*. Leiden: Brill, 1973.

Mieroop, Marc van de. *Philosophy before the Greeks: The Pursuit of Truth in Ancient Babylonia*. Princeton, NJ: Princeton University Press, 2015.

Mirguet, Françoise. *An Early History of Compassion: Emotion and Imagination in Hellenistic Judaism*. Cambridge: Cambridge University Press, 2017.

Modrzejewski, Mélèze. *The Jews of Egypt from Rameses II to Emperor Hadrian Joseph*. Translated by Robert Cornman. Princeton, NJ: Princeton University Press, 1997.

Momigliano, Arnaldo. *The Development of Greek Biography*. 2nd ed. Cambridge, MA: Harvard University Press, 1993.

Momigliano, Arnaldo. "J. G. Droysen between Greeks and Jews." *History and Theory* 9 (1970): 139–53.

Montiglio, Silvia. *Wandering in Ancient Greek Culture*. Chicago: The University of Chicago Press, 2005.

Morgan, Teresa. *Popular Morality in the Early Roman Empire*. Cambridge: Cambridge University Press, 2007.

Moyer, Ian S. *Egypt and the Limits of Hellenism*. Cambridge: Cambridge University Press, 2011.

Mroczek, Eva. *The Literary Imagination in Jewish Antiquity*. New York: Oxford University Press, 2016.

Mroczek, Eva. "Moses, David and Scribal Revelation: Preservation and Renewal in Second Temple Jewish Textual Traditions." In *The Significance of Sinai: Traditions about Sinai and Divine Revelation in Judaism and Christianity*. Edited by George J. Brooke et al., 91–115. Leiden: Brill, 2008.

Nadaff, Ramona A. *Exiling the Poets: The Production of Censorship in Plato's Republic*. Chicago: The University of Chicago Press, 2002.

Najman, Hindy. "Ethical Reading: The Transformation of the Text and the Self." *Journal of Theological Studies* 68 (2017): 507–29.

Najman, Hindy. "How Should We Contextualize Pseudepigrapha? Imitation and Emulation in *4 Ezra*." In *Flores Florentino*. Edited by Anthony Hillhorst et al., 529–36. Leiden: Brill, 2007.

Najman, Hindy. "Jewish Wisdom in the Hellenistic Period: Towards the Study of a Semantic Constellation." In *Is There a Text in This Cave? Studies in the Textuality of the Dead Sea Scrolls*. Edited by Ariel Feldman et al., 459–72. Leiden: Brill, 2017.

Najman, Hindy. *Losing the Temple and Recovering the Future: An Analysis of 4 Ezra*. Cambridge: Cambridge University Press, 2014.

Najman, Hindy. *Past Renewals: Interpretative Authority, Renewed Revelation and the Quest for Perfection in Jewish Antiquity*. Leiden: Brill, 2010.

Najman, Hindy. "Reconsidering *Jubilees*: Prophecy and Exemplarity." In *Enoch and the Mosaic Torah*. Edited by Gabriele Boccaccini and Giovanni Ibba, 229–43. Grand Rapids, MI: Eerdmans, 2009.

Najman, Hindy. *Seconding Sinai: The Development of Mosaic Discourse in Second Temple Judaism*. Leiden: Brill, 2003.

Najman, Hindy. "Text and Figure in Jewish *Paideia*." In *Authoritative Scriptures in Ancient Judaism*. Edited by Mladen Popović, 253–65. Leiden: Brill, 2010.

Najman, Hindy. "Towards a Study of the Uses of the Concept of Wilderness in Ancient Judaism." *Dead Sea Discoveries* 13 (2006): 99–113.

Najman, Hindy. "The Vitality of Scripture within and beyond the 'Canon.'" *Journal for the Study of Judaism* 43 (2012): 497–518.

Najman, Hindy. "A Written Copy of the Law of Nature: An Unthinkable Paradox?" *Studia Philonica Annual* 15 (2003): 54–63.

Najman, Hindy and Tobias Reinhardt. "Exemplarity and Its Discontents: Hellenistic Jewish Wisdom Texts and Greco-Roman Didactic Poetry." *Journal for the Study of Judaism* 50 (2019): 460–96.

Newman, Judith H. *Before the Bible: The Liturgical Body and the Formation of Scriptures in Early Judaism*. Oxford: Oxford University Press, 2018.

Newman, Judith H. "The Democratization of Kingship in Wisdom of Solomon." In *The Idea of Biblical Interpretation*. Edited by Hindy Najman and Judith H. Newman, 309–28. Leiden: Brill, 2004.

Newman, Judith H. "Embodied Techniques: The Communal Formation of the *Maskil*'s Self." *Dead Sea Discoveries* 22 (2015): 249–66.

Newman, Judith H. "Liturgical Imagination in the Composition of Ben Sira." In *Prayer and Poetry in the Dead Sea Scrolls and Related Literature*. Edited by Jeremy Penner et al., 311–26. Leiden: Brill, 2011.

Newman, Judith H. "Priestly Prophets at Qumran: Summoning Sinai through the *Songs of the Sabbath Sacrifice*." In *The Significance of Sinai: Traditions about Sinai and Divine Revelation in Judaism and Christianity*. Edited by George J. Brooke et al., 29–72. Leiden: Brill, 2008.

Newman, Judith H. "Speech and Spirit: Paul and the Maskil as Inspired Interpreters of Scripture." In *The Holy Spirit, Inspiration and the Cultures of Antiquity: Multidisciplinary Perspectives*. Edited by Jörg Frey and Jon R. Levison, 243–64. Berlin: de Gruyter, 2014.

Newsom, Carol A. "Models of the Moral Self: Hebrew Bible and Second Temple Judaism." *Journal of Biblical Literature* 131 (2012): 5–25.

Newsom, Carol A. "Positive Psychology and Ancient Israelite Wisdom." In *The Bible and the Pursuit of Happiness: What the Old and New Testaments Teach Us about the Good Life?* Edited by Brent A. Strawn, 117–36. Oxford: Oxford University Press, 2012.

Newsom, Carol A. "The Sage in the Literature of Qumran: The Functions of the Maśkîl." In *The Sage in Israel and the Ancient Near East*. Edited by John G. Gammie and Leo G. Perdue, 373–82. Winona Lake, IN: Eisenbrauns, 1990.

Newsom, Carol A. *The Self as Symbolic Space: Constructing Identity and Community at Qumran*. Leiden: Brill, 2004.

Nickelsburg, George W. E. and James C. VanderKam. *1 Enoch: A New Translation Based on the Hermeneia Commentary*. Minneapolis, MN: Fortress, 2004.

Niditch, Susan. *The Responsive Self: Personal Religion in Biblical Literature of the Neo-Babylonian and Persian Periods*. New Haven, CT: Yale University Press, 2015.

Niehoff, Maren R. *Jewish Exegesis and Homeric Scholarship in Alexandria*. Cambridge: Cambridge University Press, 2012.

Niehoff, Maren R. "Mother and Maiden, Sister and Spouse: Sarah in Philonic Midrash." *Harvard Theological Review* 97 (2004): 413–44.

Niehoff, Maren R. "Parodies of Educational Journeys in Josephus, Justin Martyr, and Lucian." In *Journeys in the Roman East: Imagined and Real*. Edited by Maren R. Niehoff, 203–24. Tübingen: Mohr Siebeck, 2017.

Niehoff, Maren R. "Philo and Plutarch as Biographers: Parallel Responses to Roman Stoicism." *Greek, Roman, and Byzantine Studies* 52 (2012): 361–92.

Niehoff, Maren R. "The Symposium of Philo's Therapeutae: Displaying Jewish Identity in an Increasingly Roman World." *Greek, Roman, and Byzantine Studies* 50 (2010): 95–117.

Nightingale, Andrea Wilson. "Sages, Sophists, and Philosophers: Greek Wisdom Literature." In *Literature in the Greek and Roman Worlds: A New Perspective*. Edited by Oliver Taplin, 156–91. Oxford: Oxford University Press, 2009.

Nissinen, Martti. "Wisdom as Mediatrix in Sirach 24: Ben Sira, Love Lyrics, and Prophecy." In *Of God(s), Trees, Kings, and Scholars*. Edited by Mikko Luukko et al., 377–90. Helsinki: The Finnish Oriental Society, 2009.

Nongbri, Brent. *Before Religion: A History of a Modern Concept*. New Haven, CT: Yale University Press, 2013.

Norden, Bryan W. van. *Taking Back Philosophy: A Multicultural Manifesto*. New York: Columbia University Press, 2017.

Nussbaum, Martha C. *The Therapy of Desires: Theory and Practice in Hellenistic Ethics*. Princeton, NJ: Princeton University Press, 1994.

Orsi, Robert A. *Between Heaven and Earth: The Religious Worlds People Make and the Scholars Who Study Them*. Princeton, NJ: Princeton University Press, 2005.

Orsi, Robert A. *The Madonna of 115th Street: Faith and Community in Italian Harlem, 1880–1950*. 3rd ed. New Haven, CT: Yale University Press, 2010.

Pavie, Xavier. *Exercices spirituels: leçons de la philosophie antique*. Paris: Les Belles Lettres, 2012.

Pellah, Robert N. *Religion in Human Evolution: From the Paleolithic to the Axial Age*. Cambridge, MA: Belknap Press of Harvard University Press, 2011.

Pellah, Robert N. "What Is Axial about the Axial Age?" *European Journal of Sociology* 46 (2005): 69–89.

Penner, Jeremy. *Patters of Daily Prayer in Second Temple Period Judaism*. Leiden: Brill, 2012.

Perdue, Leo G., ed. *Scribes, Sages, and Seers: The Sage in the Eastern Mediterranean World*. Göttingen: Vandenhoeck & Ruprecht, 2008.

Perdue, Leo G., ed. *The Sword and the Stylus: An Introduction to Wisdom in the Age of Empires*. Grand Rapids, MI: Eerdmans, 2008.

Petersen, Anders Klostergaard. "Dissolving the Philosophy–Religion Dichotomy in the Context of Jewish Paideia: Wisdom of Solomon, 4 Maccabees, and Philo." In *Second Temple Jewish "Paideia" in Context*. Edited by Jason M. Zurawski and Gabrielle Boccaccini, 185–204. Berlin: de Gruyter, 2017.

Poliakoff, Clare and Michael Poliakoff. "Jacob, Job, and Other Wrestlers: Reception of Greek Athletics by Jews and Christians in Antiquity." *Journal of Sport History* 11 (1984): 48–65.

Pomeroy, Arthur J., trans. and ed. *Arius Didymus: Epitome of Stoic Ethics*. Atlanta, GA: Society of Biblical Literature, 1999.

Popović, Mladen. *Reading the Human Body: Physiognomics and Astrology in the Dead Sea Scrolls and Hellenistic-Early Roman Period Judaism*. Leiden: Brill, 2007.

Pouchelle, Patrick. *Dieu éducateur: une novelle approche d'un concept de la théologie biblique entre Bible Hébraïque, Septante e littérature grecque classique*. Tübingen: Mohr Siebeck, 2015.

Raja, Rubina and Jörg Rüpke. "Appropriating Religion: Methodological Issues in Testing the 'Lived Ancient Religion' Approach." *Religion in Roman Empire* 1 (2015): 11–19.

Rajak, Tessa. "The Maccabean Mother between Pagans, Jews, and Christians." In *Being Christian in Late Antiquity*. Edited by Carol Harrison et al., 39–56. Oxford: Oxford University Press, 2014.

Rajak, Tessa. *Translation and Survival: The Greek Bible of the Ancient Jewish Diaspora*. Oxford: Oxford University Press, 2009.

Rappaport, Roy A. *Ritual and Religion in the Making of Humanity*. Cambridge: Cambridge University Press, 1999.

Riaud, Jean. "Les Thérapeutes d'Alexandrie dans la tradition et dans la recherche critique jusqu'aux découvertes de Qumran." *Aufstieg und Niedergang der römischen Welt* 2/20/2 (1987): 1189–295.

Rogers, Justin M. "The Philonic and the Pauline: Hagar and Sarah in the Exegesis of Didymus the Blind." *Studia Philonica Annual* 26 (2014): 57–77.

Rogerson, John. *A Theology of the Old Testament: Cultural Memory, Communication, and Being Human*. 1st Fortress Press ed. Minneapolis, MN: Fortress, 2010.

Rosen-Zvi, Ishay. "The Wisdom Tradition in Rabbinic Literature and Mishnah *Avot*." In *Tracing Sapiential Traditions in Ancient Judaism*. Edited by Hindy Najman et al., 172–90. Leiden: Brill 2016.

Rowe, Christopher Kavin. *One True Life: The Stoics and Early Christians as Rival Traditions*. New Haven, CT: Yale University Press, 2016.

Royse, James R. "The Works of Philo." In *The Cambridge Companion to Philo*. Edited by Adam Kamesar, 32–64. Cambridge: Cambridge University Press, 2009.

Runia, David T. "Eudaimonism in Hellenistic-Jewish Literature." In *Shem in the Tents of Japhet: Essays on the Encounter of Judaism and Hellenism*. Edited by James L. Kugel, 131–57. Leiden: Brill, 2002.

Runia, David T. "The Idea and the Reality of the City in the Thought of Philo of Alexandria." *Journal of the History of Ideas* 61 (2000): 361–79.

Runia, David T. "Philo of Alexandria and the Greek *Hairesis*-Model." *Vigiliae Christianae* 53 (1999): 117–47.

Runia, David T. "The Reward for Goodness: Philo, *De Vita Contemplativa* 90." *Studia Philonica Annual* 9 (1997): 3–18.

Russell, Daniel C. "Introduction: Virtue Ethics in Modern Moral Philosophy." In *The Cambridge Companion to Virtue Ethics*. Edited by Daniel C. Russell, 1–6. Cambridge: Cambridge University Press, 2013.

Sahlins, Marshall. "Two or Three Things That I Know about Culture." *The Journal of the Royal Anthropological Institute* 5 (1999): 399–421.

Salminen, Joona. "Asceticism and Early Christian Lifestyle." PhD dissertation. University of Helsinki, 2017.

Sanders, Jack T. *Ben Sira and Demotic Wisdom*. Chico, CA: Scholars Press, 1983.

Sanders, Seth L. *From Adapa to Enoch: Scribal Culture and Religious Vision in Judea and Babylon*. Tübingen: Mohr Siebeck, 2017.

Satlow, Michael. "'And on the Earth You Shall Sleep': 'Talmud Torah' and Rabbinic Asceticism." *The Journal of Religion* 83 (2003): 204–25.

Satlow, Michael. *How the Bible Became Holy*. New Haven, CT: Yale University Press, 2014.

Satran, David. "Daniel: Seer, Philosopher, Holy Man." In *Ideal Figures in Ancient Judaism: Profiles and Paradigms*. Edited by George W. E. Nickelsburg and John J. Collins, 33–48. Chico, CA: Scholars Press, 1980.

Schams, Christine. *Jewish Scribes in the Second-Temple Period*. Sheffield: Sheffield Academic Press, 1998.

Schiffman, Lawrence H. "Halakhic Elements in the Sapiential Texts from Qumran." In *Sapiential Perspectives: Wisdom Literature in Light of the Dead Sea Scrolls*. Edited by John J. Collins et al., 89–100. Leiden: Brill, 2004.

Schipper, Bernd U. and D. Andrew Teeter, eds. *Wisdom and Torah: The Reception of "Torah" in the Wisdom Literature of the Second Temple Period*. Leiden: Brill, 2013.

Schnabel, Eckhard J. *Law and Wisdom from Ben Sira to Paul*. Tübingen: Mohr, 1985.

Schniedewind, William M. *A Social History of Hebrew: Its Origins through the Rabbinic Period*. New Haven, CT: Yale University Press, 2013.

Schofield, Alison. *From Qumran to the Yaḥad: A New Paradigm of Textual Development for the Community Rule*. Leiden: Brill, 2009.

Schwienhorst-Schönberg, Ludger. *"Nicht im Menschen gründet das Glück" (Koh 2,24): Kohelet im Spannungsfeld jüdischer Weisheit und hellenistischer Philosophie*. Freiburg: Herder, 1994.

Scott, Bernard Brandon. "Jesus as Sage: An Innovative Voice in Common Wisdom." In *The Sage in Israel and the Ancient Near East*. Edited by John G. Gammie and Leo G. Perdue, 399–415. Winona Lake, IN: Eisenbrauns, 1990.

Scott, Susie. *Making Sense of Everyday Life*. Cambridge: Polity, 2009.

Sellars, John. *The Art of Living: The Stoics on the Nature and Function of Philosophy*. Aldershot: Ashgate, 2003.

Sellars, John. *Hellenistic Philosophy*. Oxford: Oxford University Press, 2018.

Sellars, John. "Review of John M. Cooper, *Pursuits of Wisdom*." *Mind* 123 (2014): 1177–80.

Sellars, John. "Review of Pierre Hadot, *What Is Ancient Philosophy?*" *Classical Review* 54 (2004): 69–70.

Sellars, John. "Stoic Cosmopolitanism and Zeno's Republic." *History of Political Thought* 28 (2007): 1–29.

Sharples, Robert W. "The Problem of Sources." In *A Companion to Ancient Philosophy*. Edited by Mary Louise Gill and Pierre Pellegrin, 430–47. Oxford: Blackwell, 2006.

Shaw, Teresa M. *The Burden of the Flesh: Fasting and Sexuality in Early Christianity*. Minneapolis, MN: Fortress, 1998.

Shweder, Richard A. et al. "The 'Big Three' of Morality (Autonomy, Community, Divinity) and the 'Big Three' Explanations of Suffering." In *Morality and Health*. Edited by Allan Brandt and Paul Rozin, 119–69. New York: Routledge, 1997.

Sloterdijk, Peter. *You Must Change Your Life: On Anthropotechnics*. Translated by Wieland Hoban. Cambridge: Polity, 2013.

Sneed, Mark R. "'Grasping after the Wind': The Elusive Attempt to Define and Delimit Wisdom." In *Was There a Wisdom Tradition? New Prospects in Israelite Wisdom Studies*. Edited by Mark R. Sneed, 39–63. Atlanta, GA: Society of Biblical Literature, 2015.

Sneed, Mark R. "Is the 'Wisdom Tradition' a Tradition?" *Catholic Biblical Quarterly* 73 (2011): 50–71.

Sneed, Mark R. "A Taste for Wisdom: Aesthetics, Moral Discernment, and Social Class in Proverbs." In *Imagined World and Constructed Differences in the Hebrew Bible*. Edited by Jeremiah W. Cataldo, 111–26. London: T&T Clark, 2016.

Snyder, H. Gregory. *Teachers and Texts in the Ancient World: Philosophers, Jews and Christians*. London: Routledge, 2000.

Sommer, Benjamin D. "Did Prophecy Cease? Evaluating a Reevaluation." *Journal of Biblical Literature* 115 (1996): 31–47.

Sorabji, Richard. *Emotion and Peace of Mind: From Stoic Agitation to Christian Temptation*. Oxford: Oxford University Press, 2002.

Stegemann, Hartmut and Eileen M. Schuller. *Qumran Cave 1.III: 1QHodayot^a, with Incorporation of 4QHodayot^{a-f} and 1QHodayot^b*. Discoveries in the Judaean Desert 40. Oxford: Clarendon, 2009.

Sterling, Gregory E. "'Athletes of Virtue': An Analysis of the Summaries in Acts (2: 41–47; 4:32–35; 5:12–16)." *Journal of Biblical Literature* 113 (1994): 679–96.

Sterling, Gregory E. "Philosophy as the Handmaid of Wisdom: Philosophy in the Exegetical Traditions of Alexandrian Jews." In *Religiöse Philosophie und philosophische Religion der frühen Kaiserzeit: Literaturgeschichtliche Perspektiven*. Edited by Rainer Hirsch-Luipold et al., 67–98. Tübingen: Mohr Siebeck, 2009.

Stern, Menahem. *Greek and Latin Authors on Jews and Judaism*. 2 vols. Jerusalem: The Israel Academy of Sciences and Humanities, 1974.

Stewart, Anne W. *Poetic Ethics in Proverbs: Wisdom Literature and the Shaping of the Moral Self*. Cambridge: Cambridge University Press, 2015.

Stone, Michael E. and Theodore A. Bergren, eds. *Biblical Figures outside the Bible*. Harrisburg, PA: Trinity Press International, 1998.

Stoneman, Richard. *The Ancient Oracles: Making the Gods Speak*. New Haven, CT: Yale University Press, 2011.

Strawn, Brent A. "Comparative Approaches: History, Theory, and the Image of God." In *Method Matters: Essays on the Interpretation of the Hebrew Bible*. Edited by Joel M. LeMon and Kent H. Richards, 117–42. Atlanta, GA: Society of Biblical Literature, 2009.

Stroumsa, Guy G. "From Master of Wisdom to Spiritual Master in Late Antiquity." In *Religion and the Self in Antiquity*. Edited by David Brakke et al., 183–96. Bloomington, IN: Indiana University Press, 2005.

Stuckenbruck, Loren T. "The Legacy of the Teacher of Righteousness in the Dead Sea Scrolls." In *New Perspectives on Old Texts*. Edited by Esther G. Chazon et al., 23–49. Leiden: Brill, 2010.

Svebakken, Hans. *Philo of Alexandria's Exposition of the Tenth Commandment*. Atlanta, GA: Society of Biblical Literature, 2012.

Swanton, Christine. *Virtue Ethics: A Pluralistic View*. New York: Oxford University Press, 2003.

Sweet, Ronald F. G. "The Sage in Akkadian Literature: A Philological Study." In *The Sage in Israel and the Ancient Near East*. Edited by John G. Gammie and Leo G. Perdue, 45–65. Winona Lake, IN: Eisenbrauns, 1990.

Sweet, Ronald F. G. "The Sage in Mesopotamian Palaces and Royal Courts." In *The Sage in Israel and the Ancient Near East*. Edited by John G. Gammie and Leo G. Perdue, 99–107. Winona Lake, IN: Eisenbrauns, 1990.

Szesnat, Holger. "'Mostly Aged Virgins': Philo and the Presence of the Therapeutrides at Lake Mareotis." *Neotestamentica* 32 (1998): 191–201.

Taekema, Sanne. "What Ideals Are: Ontological and Epistemological Issues." In *The Importance of Ideals: Debating Their Relevance in Law, Morality, and Politics*. Edited by Wibren van der Burg and Sanne Taekema, 39–57. Brussels: Peter Lang, 2004.

Taylor, Joan E. *The Essenes, the Scrolls, and the Dead Sea*. Oxford: Oxford University Press, 2012.

Taylor, Joan E. "Introduction." In *The Body in Biblical, Christian and Jewish Texts*. Edited by Joan E. Taylor, xv–xxi. London: Bloomsbury T&T Clark, 2014.

Taylor, Joan E. *Jewish Women Philosophers of First-Century Alexandria: Philo's "Therapeutae" Reconsidered*. Oxford: Oxford University Press, 2003.

Taylor, Joan E. "4Q341: A Writing Exercise Remembered." In *Is There a Text in This Cave? Studies in the Textuality of the Dead Sea Scrolls*. Edited by Ariel Feldman et al., 133–51. Leiden: Brill, 2017.

Taylor, Joan E. and David Hay. "Astrology in Philo of Alexandria's *De vita contemplativa*." *ARAM Periodical* 24 (2012): 293–309.

Taylor, Joan E. and Philip R. Davies. "The So-Called Therapeutae of '*De vita contemplativa*': Identity and Character." *Harvard Theological Review* 91 (1998): 3–24.

Temmerman, Koen de. "Ancient Biography and Formalities of Fiction." In *Writing Biography in Greece and Rome: Narrative Technique and Fictionalization*. Edited by Koen de Temmerman and Kristoffel Demoen, 3–25. Cambridge: Cambridge University Press, 2016.

Temmerman, Koen de and Kristoffel Demoen, eds. *Writing Biography in Greece and Rome: Narrative Technique and Fictionalization*. Cambridge: Cambridge University Press, 2016.

Termini, Cristina. "Philo's Thought within the Context of Middle Judaism." In *The Cambridge Companion to Philo*. Edited by Adam Kamesar, 95–123. Cambridge: Cambridge University Press, 2009.

Terrien, Samuel. "Job as a Sage." In *The Sage in Israel and the Ancient Near East*. Edited by John G. Gammie and Leo G. Perdue, 231–42. Winona Lake, IN: Eisenbrauns, 1990.

Tervanotko, Hanna and Elisa Uusimäki. "Sarah the Princess: Tracing the Hellenistic Afterlife of a Pentateuchal Female Figure." *Scandinavian Journal of the Old Testament* 32 (2018): 271–90.

Thomas, Samuel I. *The "Mysteries" of Qumran: Mystery, Secrecy, and Esotericism in the Dead Sea Scrolls*. Atlanta, GA: Society of Biblical Literature, 2009.

Thonemann, Peter. *The Hellenistic Age*. Oxford: Oxford University Press, 2016.

Tigay, Jeffrey H. *Deuteronomy: Devarim*. Philadelphia, PA: Jewish Publication Society, 1996.

Tolonen, Anna-Liisa and Elisa Uusimäki. "Managing the Ancestral Way of Life in the Roman Diaspora: The Mélange of Philosophical and Scriptural Practice in 4 Maccabees." *Journal for the Study of Judaism* 48 (2017): 113–41.

Too, Yun Lee. "Introduction: Writing the History of Ancient Education." In *Education in Greek and Roman Antiquity*. Edited by Yun Lee Too, 1–21. Leiden: Brill, 2001.

Trebilco, Paul R. *Jewish Communities in Asia Minor*. Cambridge: Cambridge University Press, 1991.

Tropper, Amram D. *Wisdom, Politics, and Historiography: Tractate Avot in the Context of the Graeco-Roman Near East*. Oxford: Oxford University Press, 2004.

Tso, Marcus K. M. *Ethics in the Qumran Community: An Interdisciplinary Investigation*. Tübingen: Mohr Siebeck, 2010.

Tzoref, Shani. "*Pesher* and Periodiziation." *Dead Sea Discoveries* 18 (2011): 129–54.

Ulrich, Eugene. "The Jewish Scriptures: Texts, Versions, Canons." In *Early Judaism: A Comprehensive Overview*. Edited by John J. Collins and Daniel C. Harlow, 121–50. Grand Rapids, MI: Eerdmans, 2012.

Uusimäki, Elisa. "'Happy Is the Person to Whom She Has Been Given': The Continuum of Wisdom and Torah in *4QSapiential Admonitions B* (4Q185) and *4QBeatitudes* (4Q525)." *Revue de Qumran* 26 (2014): 345–59.

Uusimäki, Elisa. "In Search of Virtue: Ancestral Inheritance in the Testament of Qahat." *Biblical Interpretation* 29 (2021): in press.

Uusimäki, Elisa "Itinerant Sages: The Evidence of Sirach in Its Ancient Mediterranean Context." *Journal for the Study of the Old Testament* 44 (2020): 315–36.

Uusimäki, Elisa "Mapping Ideal Ways of Living: Virtue and Vice Lists in 1QS and 4Q286." *Journal for the Study of the Pseudepigrapha* 30 (2020): 35–45.

Uusimäki, Elisa "A Mind in Training: Philo of Alexandria on Jacob's Spiritual Exercises." *Journal for the Study of the Pseudepigrapha* 27 (2018): 265–88.

Uusimäki, Elisa "Sages as Mediators of Divine Knowledge in Jewish Antiquity." In *The Textualization of Revelation*. Edited by Jonathan Stökl and Hanna Tervanotko. London: Bloomsbury T&T Clark, forthcoming.

Uusimäki, Elisa "Spiritual Formation in Hellenistic Jewish Wisdom Teaching." In *Tracing Sapiential Traditions in Ancient Judaism*. Edited by Hindy Najman et al., 57–70. Leiden: Brill 2016.

Uusimäki, Elisa *Turning Proverbs towards Torah: An Analysis of 4Q525*. Leiden: Brill, 2016.

Uusimäki, Elisa "Virtues and Practical Wisdom in the Book of Proverbs." *Journal for the Study of Diaconia* 2 (2017): 62–79 (in Finnish).

Uusimäki, Elisa "Wisdom Texts from the Dead Sea Scrolls." In *The Wiley Blackwell Companion to Wisdom Literature*. Edited by Samuel L. Adams and Matthew J. Goff, 122–38. Hoboken, NJ: Wiley-Blackwell, 2020.

VanderKam, James C. "Greek at Qumran." In *Hellenism in the Land of Israel*. Edited by John J. Collins and Gregory E. Sterling, 175–81. Notre Dame, IN: Notre Dame University Press, 2001.

VanderKam, James C. "Mantic Wisdom in the Dead Sea Scrolls." *Dead Sea Discoveries* 4 (1997): 336–53.

Veijola, Timo. *Leben nach der Weisung: Exegetisch-historische Studien zum Alten Testament*. Edited by Walter Dietrich and Marko Marttila. Göttingen: Vandenhoeck & Ruprecht, 2008.

Verheyden, Joseph, ed. *The Figure of Solomon in Jewish, Christian and Islamic Tradition: King, Sage and Architect*. Leiden: Brill, 2013.

Vermes, Geza and Martin D. Goodman. *The Essenes: According to the Classical Sources*. Sheffield: Sheffield Academic Press, 1989.

Vesely, Patricia. *Friendship and Virtue Ethics in the Book of Job*. Cambridge: Cambridge University Press, 2019.

Wassen, Cecilia. "On the Education of Children in the Dead Sea Scrolls." *Studies in Religion/Sciences Religieuses* 41 (2012): 350–63.

Wassen, Cecilia. *Women in the Damascus Document*. Atlanta, GA: Society of Biblical Literature, 2005.

Weaver, John B. "The Noble and Good Heart: καλοκαγαθία in Luke's Parable of the Sower." In *Scripture and Traditions*. Edited by Patrick Gray and Gail R. O'Day, 151–72. Leiden: Brill, 2008.

Weeks, Stuart. "'Fear God and Keep His Commandments': Could Qohelet Have Said This?" In *Wisdom and Torah: The Reception of "Torah" in the Wisdom Literature of the Second Temple Period*. Edited by Bernd U. Schipper and D. Andrew Teeter, 101–18. Leiden: Brill, 2013.

Weeks, Stuart. "Is 'Wisdom Literature' a Useful Category?" In *Tracing Sapiential Traditions in Ancient Judaism*. Edited by Hindy Najman et al., 3–23. Leiden: Brill, 2016.

Wegner, Judith Romney. "Philo's Portrayal of Women: Hebraic or Hellenic?" In *"Women like This": New Perspectives on Jewish Women in the Greco-Roman World*. Edited by Amy-Jill Levine, 41–66. Atlanta, GA: Scholars Press, 1991.

Weinfeld, Moshe. *Deuteronomy and the Deuteronomistic School*. Oxford: Clarendon, 1972.

Weitzman, Steven. "Was Moses Our Teacher a Good Teacher?" n.p. Cited 9 July 2020. Online: https://www.thetorah.com/article/was-moses-our-teacher-a-good-teacher.

Whitmarsh, Tim. *Beyond the Second Sophistic: Adventures in Greek Postclassicism*. Berkeley, CA: University of California Press, 2013.

Whybray, Roger Norman. *The Intellectual Tradition in the Old Testament*. Berlin: de Gruyter, 1974.

Whybray, Roger Norman. "The Sage in the Israelite Royal Court." In *The Sage in Israel and the Ancient Near East*. Edited by John G. Gammie and Leo G. Perdue, 133–9. Winona Lake, IN: Eisenbrauns, 1990.

Williams, Travis B. *History and Memory in the Dead Sea Scrolls: Remembering the Teacher of Righteousness*. Cambridge: Cambridge University Press, 2019.

Winston, David. "Sage and Super-Sage in Philo of Alexandria." In *The Ancestral Philosophy: Hellenistic Philosophy in Second Temple Judaism*. Edited by Gregory E. Sterling, 171–80. Providence, RI: Brown University Press, 2001.

Winston, David. "Theodicy in Ben Sira and Stoic Philosophy." In *Of Scholars, Savants, and Their Texts: Studies in Philosophy and Religious Thought*. Edited by Ruth Link-Salinger et al., 239–49. New York: Lang, 1989.

Witherington, Ben. *Jesus the Sage: The Pilgrimage of Wisdom*. Edinburgh: T&T Clark, 1994.

Wright, Benjamin G. "Ben Sira and Hellenistic Literature in Greek." In *Tracing Sapiential Traditions in Ancient Judaism*. Edited by Hindy Najman et al., 71–88. Leiden: Brill, 2016.

Wright, Benjamin G. "Ben Sira on the Sage as Exemplar." In *Praise Israel for Wisdom and Instruction: Essays on Ben Sira and Wisdom, the Letter of Aristeas and the Septuagint*. Edited by Benjamin G. Wright III, 165–82. Leiden: Brill, 2008.

Wright, Benjamin G. "Conflicted Boundaries: Ben Sira, Sage and Seer." In *Congress Volume Helsinki 2010*. Edited by Martti Nissinen, 229–53. Leiden: Brill, 2012.

Wright, Benjamin G. "From Generation to Generation: The Sage as Father in Early Jewish Literature." In *Biblical Traditions in Transmission*. Edited by Charlotte Hempel and Judith M. Lieu, 309–32. Leiden: Brill, 2006.

Wright, Benjamin G. "Joining the Club: A Suggestion about Genre in Early Jewish Texts." *Dead Sea Discoveries* 17 (2010): 289–314.

Wright, Benjamin G. *No Small Difference: Sirach's Relationship to Its Hebrew Parent Text*. Atlanta, GA: Scholars Press, 1989.

Wright, Benjamin G. "Solomon in Chronicles and Ben Sira: A Study in Contrasts." In *Rewriting Biblical History: Essays on Chronicles and Ben Sira*. Edited by Jeremy Corley and Harm van Grol, 139–57. Berlin: de Gruyter, 2011.

Wright, Benjamin G. "Wisdom, Instruction, and Social Location in Sirach and *1 Enoch*." In *Things Revealed: Studies in Early Jewish and Christian Literature*. Edited by Esther G. Chazon et al., 105–21. Leiden: Brill, 2004.

Wright, Benjamin G. and Lawrence M. Wills, eds. *Conflicted Boundaries in Wisdom and Apocalypticism*. Atlanta, GA: Society of Biblical Literature, 2005.

Wyss, Beatrice et al., eds. *Sophisten in Hellenismus und Kaiserzeit*. Tübingen: Mohr Siebeck, 2017.

Yli-Karjanmaa, Sami. "Philo of Alexandria." In *Brill's Companion to the Reception of Plato in Antiquity*. Edited by Harold Tarrant et al., 115–29. Leiden: Brill, 2018.

Yli-Karjanmaa, Sami. *Reincarnation in Philo of Alexandria*. Atlanta, GA: Society of Biblical Literature, 2015.

Zurawski, Jason M. and Gabrielle Boccaccini, eds. *Second Temple Jewish "Paideia" in Context*. Berlin: de Gruyter, 2017.

Index of Ancient Sources

HEBREW BIBLE

Genesis — 32
1:26–8 — 138n61
2–3 — 58
5:18–24 — 29
18:11 — 34
41:8 — 22
41:33 — 22
41:39–40 — 22

Exodus
7:11 — 22
7:22 — 22
8:3 — 22
8:14 — 22
12:2 — 52
15 — 91
28:3 — 21
31:3–5 — 21
34:29 — 68, 105
35:25–6 — 21, 23
35:31–5 — 21
36:1 — 21
36:4 — 21

Numbers
12:3 — 156n101
33:3 — 52

Deuteronomy — 22, 50–1, 56, 148n4, 148n9
1:15 — 22
4:5–6 — 51, 80
4:6 — 134n8
4:9 — 51
4:23 — 51
4:36 — 50
5:1–2 — 50
6:4–8 — 50
6:12 — 51
6:20–5 — 50
8:1–6 — 50
11:8–31 — 50
17:18–19 — 139n61
18:11 — 149n17
27:1–8 — 148n7
27:9–30:20 — 148n7
29:1–3 — 51
30:11–14 — 51
30:15–16 — 12
31:1–8 — 51
31:9–13 — 51
31:16–18 — 51
31:19–22 — 51
31:20–32:44 — 51
31:24–9 — 51
32:1–44 — 51
32:2 — 51
32:18 — 51
32:29 — 134n8
32:45–7 — 51
33:1–29 — 51
33:10 — 52
34:5–8 — 51
34:9 — 51
34:10 — 51

Joshua
1:7–8 — 148n4
1:8 — 108, 172n139

Judges — 51
5:29 — 23

1 Samuel
1:23 — 24
1:23–31 — 24
1:25 — 24
9:9 — 149n17
18:14 — 154n85
18:15 — 154n85
25:2–43 — 24
28:7 — 149n17

2 Samuel		29:14	21, 127n5
1:19–27	148n8	40:3	108
13:3	127n5	40:20	134n11
14:1–24	24	44:25	21
14:2	24	47:10	127n5, 135n17
14:14	24	48:17	50
14:17	21	54:13	50
14:20	21		
16:23	22	*Jeremiah*	22
17:23	22	8:2	149n17
20:16–22	24	8:8–9	21
20:18	24	9:16	23
		9:22–3	21
1 Kings	30, 46	10:9	134n11
3:1–15	138n60	18:18	22
3:5–15	21	21:2	149n17
3:6–9	153n67	32:33	50
3:12	21	37:7	149n17
3:16–28	21		
3:28	21	*Ezekiel*	
4:2–6	135n16	14:3	149n17
5:9–14	21, 48	14:7	149n17
7:14	21	20:3	149n17
10:1–9	22	20:31	149n17
11:1–13	30	27:8–9	134n11
19:21	46	28:1–10	134n11
21:27	135n20	28:11–19	134n11
22:5–8	149n17		
22:8	53	*Hosea*	
		10:12	104
2 Kings	30		
1:2	149n17	*Amos*	
3:11	149n17	5:13	154n85
8:8	149n17		
12:3	52	*Jonah*	
12:11	135n14	3:5	135n20
22:8–10	135n14		
22:13	149n17	*Micah*	
22:18	149n17	4:2	50
Isaiah	174n162	*Psalms*	66, 70
2:3	50	1:2	108
5:21	21	14:2	154n85
8:19	149n17	19	148n3
11:2	21	19:5–6	151n46
19:3	149n17	32:1	154n85
19:11	127n5	32:8	50, 66
19:11–15	135n17	41:2	154n85
28:23–9	134n11	42:1	154n85

44:1	154n85	10:5	154n85
45:1	154n85	10:19	154n85
47:8	154n85	14:35	154n85
51:8–9	153n67	15:24	154n85
52:1	154n85	16:20	154n85
53:1	154n85	17:2	154n85
53:3	154n85	19:14	154n85
54:1	154n85	21:12	154n85
55:1	154n85	22:17	24, 53
71:17	50	22:17–24:22	132n63
72	153n67	25:1	25
74:1	154n85	25:16–17	61
78:1	52, 154n85	26:12	21
88:1	154n85	30:1–4	25, 46
89:1	154n85	30:1–31:9	132n63
94:10	50	30:1–33	147n161
119	148n3	31:1–2	24, 54
119:105	151n46	31:1–9	24–5, 46
142:1	154n85	31:10–31	24
		31:26	24
Job	2, 12, 41, 132n63, 134n9, 147n161, 171n162	*Qoheleth*	2, 12, 18, 24–5, 40, 43, 45–8, 50, 54–7, 64, 73–7, 79–80, 119–20, 132n63, 150nn23–5, 150n31, 150n34, 150n36, 171n121
1:1	21		
1:8	21		
12:2	21		
12:12	21		
15:18	53	1:1	54
22:2	154n85	1:2	54
26:2–3	21	1:10	55
28	147n161	1:12–14	25
38:4	147n161	1:13	55, 77
		1:16	55
Proverbs	2, 12–13, 22, 24–5, 41, 46, 48, 53–4, 56, 66, 73–4, 81, 83, 119, 127n5, 136n24, 147n161, 171n121	2:1–11	55
		2:1–26	55
		2:3	25
		2:16	64
		2:18–23	150n36
LXX Proverbs	77, 159n132	3:1–8	55
1:1–7	53	3:10–14	75
1:2–4	24, 74	3:16–21	55
1:6	24	4:7–12	55
1:8	54	4:17	75
1:20–33	24, 53	5:6	75
5:12–14	54	5:9–14	55
6:20	54	7:18	75
8:1–36	24, 53	7:25	25
9:1–12	24, 53	8:1–17	45
10–29	136n24	8:12–13	75

8:17	75	8:2–5	52
11:5	75	8:7	52
12:1–7	55, 77	8:7–8	53
12:9	25, 54, 56, 73		
12:9–10	25, 55	*1 Chronicles*	30
12:9–14	55	10:13–14	149n17
12:10	75	13:3	149n17
12:12	25, 56	27:32	135n14
12:13	75		
12:13–14	158n162	*2 Chronicles*	30, 148n11
		1:7–12	138n60
Daniel	22–4, 154n88	2:6	21
1:4	23, 154n85	9:22–3	22
1:8	23	17:3–4	149n17
1:12	23	17:7–9	52
1:15–17	23	17:8	52
1:16	23	24:11	135n14
1:17	23	25:20	149n17
1:19–20	23	30:22	154n85
1:20	23	35:3	52
2:2–3	23		
2:10–12	23	JEWISH APOCRYPHA	
2:13–47	23		
9:3	23	*Tobit*	
9:22	66	1:8	54
10:2–3	23		
11:33	154n85	*1 Maccabees*	
11:33–5	154n88	2:49–64	152n53
11:35	154n85	15:22–3	138n53
12:3	154n85, 154n88		
12:10	154n85, 154n88	*2 Maccabees*	
		2:21	126n1
Esther		8:1	126n1
1:13	22	14:38	126n1
4:3	135n20		
		4 Maccabees	85–6
Ezra	22, 52–3, 56	1:1	86
7:1–11	52	1:30	86
7:6–10	52	1:30–3:18	152n53
7:7	149n14	5:22–4	86
7:8–9	52	5:34	148n3
7:10	52–3	7:6–7	86
7:11–12	52	9:8	168n88
7:14	52–3, 149n16	16:20–3	152n53
7:25	53, 149n16	17:12	168n88
8:31	52	17:16	168n88
		18:6–19	54
Nehemiah	22, 53, 56	18:10–19	149n22
8:1	52		
8:1–12	52		

Wisdom of		4:17–18	63, 153n72
Solomon	3, 30–1, 40, 44, 46–8,	4:31	64
	119, 138n61	6:5–17	152n52
1:4–5	153n67	6:18	60
2:4	64	6:29	26
6:12	151n46	6:31	26
6:12–21	31	6:37	60
6:22–5	30	7:3	136n29
7–8	30	7:9	62
7–9	30	7:10	62, 64
7:1–22	153n67	7:14	62
7:7	30	7:15	136n29
7:10	151n46	7:20–1	136n29
7:15–22	30	7:21	154n85
7:17–20	138n60	7:22	136n29
7:17–22	30	7:31	62
7:22	30	7:32	64
7:22–3	138n60	7:32–5	64
7:26	151n46	7:33	64
7:29	151n46	8:8	26, 61
8:7	30, 138n60	10:10	64
8:13	30	10:23	154n85
8:17	30	12:1–2	64
8:17–21	30	13:15–19	152n59
9	30	13:22	154n85
9:1–18	30, 47	14:11 LXX	62
9:6	30	14:20–1	61
9:7–8	30	15:1	60
10–19	152n53	16:24	61
18:4	151n46	17:11	60
		17:25	62
Sirach	3, 13, 18, 25–7, 40–1,	18:25	64
	45–50, 56–65, 72–80,	18:30	61
	120, 145n144, 149n22,	18:30–3	61, 152n63
	151n39, 151n49, 152n51,	18:31	152n63
	152n57, 153n74,	18:32–3	152n63
	158n123, 171n121	19:6	61
LXX Sirach	77, 153n76, 159n130	19:20	60
MSA	152n57, 153n76	21:11	60
MSB	151n49, 152nn60–1,	21:15	61
	154n78	21:25	61
Prologue	25–6, 59, 65, 121	22:23	64
1:9–10	65, 75	22:25–23:6	136n38
1:26	60	22:27–23:6	153n66
3:5	62	23:1–6	62
3:21–4	74, 152n62	23:6	61
4:1–10	64	24	26, 59
4:7	64	24:1–12	65
4:10	64	24:1–22	63, 153n72

24:23	47, 51, 60, 64	42:5	136n29
24:23–7	58	42:15	136n38
24:30–1	58	42:15–43:33	47, 61
24:30–4	25, 58, 136n38	42:17	61
24:32	159n130	42:23	61
24:32–4	58	43:27	61
24:33	63	43:32	136n38
24:34	26	44:1–15	60
25–6	136n38	44:1–49:24	60, 75
27:8	26	44:15	60
29:1–20	64	44:17	60
29:2	64	45:4	60
29:12	64	46:1	60
30:4–6	43	46:7	60
31:12–32:13	61	47:12	154n85
32:8	61	47:12–23	135n14
33:2–3	60	47:14	60
33:16–19	136n38	50:25–6	136n38
33:25–32	136n29	50:27–9	59
34:1	63	50:28	61
34:1–8	63	51	136n38
34:5	63	51:1–12	47, 62, 153n66
34:6	63	51:13–14	62
34:9–13	25, 65, 136n29, 136n38	51:13–25	26
35:1–4	62	51:18–19	64
35:4	64	51:23	25
35:10–12	62		
36:1–19	62	*Baruch*	
37:15	62	3:9–4:4	3
37:29	61		
38:1–3	63	JEWISH PSEUDEPIGRAPHA	
38:8	62		
38:9	62	*Ahiqar*	20, 77
38:11	62		
38:24–5	25	*Apocalypse of Zephaniah*	
38:24–34	46, 57	9:4	152n53
38:34	57, 61		
38:34b–39:8	25	*Aristobulus*	86
38:34b–39:11	26, 74	2–4	162n19
39:1	61, 63		
39:1–3	59	*Artapanus*	86
39:1–15	59	3	162n18
39:4	25, 65, 75, 136n29	4	162n20
39:5–8	47, 62		
39:6	63	*1 Enoch*	171n123, 171n126
39:7	63	12:4	29
39:9–11	25, 64	15:1	29
39:12–13	136n38	37–71	29
39:32–5	136n38	42:1	137n51

42:1–3	65	Community Rule (S)	67, 103–4, 106, 109–12, 137n41, 137n46, 155n97, 156n102, 171n123
71:16–17	29		
92:1	29		
2 Enoch	171n123, 171n126		
53:2	137n50	1QS	27, 65, 67–9, 106–8, 137n44, 155nn96–7, 156n101, 156nn104–5, 172n130, 172n136
Eupolemus	145n144		
4 Ezra			
7:106–10	152n53	1:1	67
		1:1–2	106
Jubilees	51, 137n49, 159n142, 171n126, 173n143	1:1–3	65
		1:5	106
4:21–4	137n50	1:11–12	107
24:18–20	151n46	1:18–2:19	103
25:1–3	54	2:24	106
		2:25–3:1	170n108
Letter of Aristeas	85, 138n55	3:3–4:26	72
31	85	3:5–6	170n108
32	138n55	3:13	67
39	138n55	3:13–14	68
46	138n55	3:13–15	67
121–2	138n55	3:13–4:26	67, 106, 146n152, 158n122, 171n123
200	85		
235	85	3:14	172n136
296	85	3:15	106
		4:2–11	106
Philo the Epic Poet	145n144	4:22–3	68
		5:1	65, 67
Pseudo-Philo (LAB)		5:1–20	67
33	54	5:3–4	106–7
		5:4–5	107
Testament of Abraham		5:7–8	65
B 11:3	29	5:23–6:3	103
		5:24	107
Theodotus	145n144	6:1–8	103
		6:6–8	108
DEAD SEA SCROLLS		6:8	173n140
		6:8–7:25	103
Aramaic Levi Document		6:12	173n148
(ALD)	171n123	6:13–14	107
		6:13–15	170n108
Beatitudes (4Q525)	27, 171n122	6:18	107
2 ii	51	6:20	173n148
2 ii 3–4	109	8:1	107
14 ii 14–16	27	8:2	106
4Q528	171n122	8:8–9	107
4Q534	171n128	8:9	107

8:10	107	11:3–5	47, 68, 74
8:10–11	172n134	11:5–7	73
8:11–12	105	11:6–9	156n101
8:12–16	108	11:9–11	156n101
8:15–16	65, 105	11:10–11	107
8:16–9:2	103	11:11–15	156n101
8:18	107	11:15–20	70, 107
8:20	107		
8:21	107	4QS	67, 155n97
9	27		
9:3	170n109	4QS^b (4Q256)	155n97
9:3–11	170n108	9:1	155n94
9:5	107		
9:9	107	4QS^d (4Q258)	155n97
9:12	69	1:1	155n94
9:12–14	27	2:10	108
9:12–21	69	8:5–9	28
9:12–21a	27, 67		
9:12–11:22	27, 74, 171n123	4QS^e (4Q259)	137n46
9:12–11:25	72	3:7–10	27
9:13	47, 69, 171n120	4:2–7	28
9:13–14	68		
9:13–21a	68	4QS^f (4Q260)	155n97
9:14–16	68, 157n111		
9:16–19	73	4QS^j (4Q264)	155n97
9:18	171n120		
9:18–19	68, 107	*Damascus Document*	
9:19–20	108	(D)	103–4, 109–12,
9:21–4	28		173n148, 174n152
9:21–6	28	CD (Genizah)	
9:21b–5	67–8	1:1	110
9:23–4	68	1:10–11	104
9:26–10:8	70, 156n107	2:2	110
9:26–11:22	67	2:15–16	109
10–11	27, 157n111	3:1–16	157n121
10:1	69	3:12–14	105
10:5–11:22	28	3:18–20	173n146
10:8–11	70	4:6–10	170n108
10:11–17	70	6	151n46
10:12	107	6:2–3	109
10:17–24	28	6:7	104
10:18–11:2	70	6:11–7:9	103
10:24–5	68, 74	7:4–8	103, 110
10:26–11:1	68	10:4–6	110
11	47	10:10–13	110
11:2–3	28	11:18–22	110
11:2–15	70	12:1–20	110
11:3	72, 151n46	12:19	103
11:3–4	69	12:21	173n148

12:22–13:2	103	1QH^a	70, 72, 156n111
13:2	110	1:1	156n111
13:6–8	110	4	157n111
13:9	173n146	5	70
13:16–17	111	5:12	47, 70
13:17–18	110, 173n151	5:13	70
13:22	69, 173n148	5:19–20	157n114
14:7–8	110	5:35–6	157n114
14:12–16	110	6:8–12	157n111
15:14–15	110	7	27, 70
19:3	103, 110	7:21	70
20:4	109	7:21–8:41	156n104
20:10	109	7:23–37	70
20:13	109	12:6–7	105
20:27–34	104, 170n108	20	27, 70
		20:7	47, 70
4QD^a (4Q266)		20:7–12	70
5 i 17	69	20:7–14	156n107
6 ii 1–13	111	20:12–14	70
9 iii 4–5	111	20:14	70
9 iii 6–7	110	20:14–17	156n104
9 iii 15	69	20:15–16	71
		25:34	70–1
4QD^b (4Q267)		25:36–7	71
9 vi 4–5	110–11	26:6–16	157n118
4QD^d (4Q269)		4QHod^a (4Q427)	
9:1–2	111	7 i–9	157n118
9:4–8	111	8 ii 10	70
		8 ii 17	70
4QD^e (4Q270)			
2 i 16–19	111	4QHod^b (4Q428)	
2 ii 15–17	111	12 ii 3	156n111
4:1–9	111		
7 i 12–13	110	Instruction	137n41, 155n90, 171n122
4QD^f (4Q271)			
3:15	111	1QInstr (1Q26)	171n122
4QD^g (4Q272)		4QInstr^a (4Q415)	171n122
1 ii 7–10	111	2 ii	173n151
4QpapD^h (4Q273)		4QInstr^b (4Q416)	171n122
5:4–5	111	2 ii 15	154n86
Genesis Apocryphon (1QapGen ar)		4QInstr^c (4Q417)	171n122
18:24–21:4	171n123	2 i 25	155n90
Hodayot (H)	137n41, 156n104, 156n111, 157n112, 171n123	4QInstr^d (4Q418) 81:17	171n122 155n90

4QInstr^e (4Q418a)	171n122	1–2 ii	109
4QInstr^f (4Q418c)	171n122	1–2 ii 4	157n121
4QInstr^g (4Q423)	171n122	*Songs of the Maskil*^{a–b} (4Q510–11)	71–2, 137n41, 171n123
Mysteries	4	4QShir^a (4Q510)	
1QMyst (1Q27)	171n122	1:4–5	71
1 i 5–6	151n46	1:4–9	71
		1:8–9	71
4QMyst^a (4Q299)	171n122	4QShir^b (4Q511)	
4QMyst^b (4Q300)	171n122	2 i 1	71
		8:4	71
4QMyst^c (4Q301)	171n122	8:6–10	71
		63–4 ii 3–4	72
Pesher Habakkuk (1QpHab)		*Songs of the Sabbath Sacrifice*	47, 71–2, 137n41, 171n120
2:5–10	104, 171n120		
2:7–9	104		
7:1–5	104		
7:3–5	104, 171n120	4QShirShabb^a (4Q400)	71
7:5–14	106	1 i 1	157n115
Psalms Scroll^a (11Q5)		3 ii 8	157n115
21:11–17	171n121		
22:1	171n121	4QShirShabb^b (4Q401)	71
27	157n121	1–2:1	157n115
Ritual of Marriage (4Q502)	174n152	4QShirShabb^c (4Q402)	71
1–3:6	174n152		
14:6	174n152	4QShirShabb^d (4Q403)	71
19:2–3	174n152	1 i 30	157n115
Rule of Blessings (1QSb)	70, 72, 137n41	1 ii 18	157n115
1:1	70	4QShirShabb^e (4Q404)	71
1:1–2	70		
3:22	70	4QShirShabb^f (4Q405)	71
5:20	70	20 ii 6	157n115
Rule of the Congregation (1QSa)	110	4QShirShabb^g (4Q406)	71
1:4–5	110, 174n153	1:4	157n115
1:6–8	170n108, 174n153		
1:7	110	4QShirShabb^h (4Q407)	71
1:27–8	109		
2:16	109		
Sapiential Admonitions B (4Q185)	171n122		

11QShirShabb
  (11Q17)   71
7:9   157n115

MasShirot   71

Testament of Qahat
  (4Q542)   112
1 i 7–10   157n121
1 i 10–13   157n121
1 i 12–13   112

War Scroll (1QM)   137n41, 155n96
1:1   155n96

*Ways of Righteousness*ᵃ⁻ᵇ
  (4Q420–1)   137n41, 171n122

4QWaysᵇ (4Q421)
1 ii 10   66
1 ii 12   66
1 ii 11–12   115n90

Wiles of the Wicked Woman
  (4Q184)   171n122, 174n152
1   174n152

Words of the Maskil
  to the Sons of Dawn
  (4Q298)   66, 72, 137n41,
                 171n122
1–2 i 1   66–7
1–2 i 1–3   67
3–4 ii 4–10   67
3–4 ii 9   171n120

Other Dead Sea Scrolls
2QJob (2Q15)   171n121
2QBen Sira (2Q18) 171n121
4QDeuteronomyᵠ
  (4Q44)   148n8
4QJobᵃ (4Q99)   171n121
4QJobᵇ (4Q100)   171n121
4QJobᶜ (4Q101)   171n121
4QProverbsᵃ
  (4Q102)   171n121
4QProverbsᵇ
  (4Q103)   171n121
4QProverbsᶜ
  (4Q103a)   171n121

4QQoheletʰᵃ
  (4Q109)   171n121
4QQoheletʰᵇ
  (4Q110)   171n121
4QtgJob
  (4Q157)   171n121
4QpPsalmsᵃ (4Q171)
  3:15–16   104
4QFlorilegium
  (4Q174) 1 i 6–7   170n109
4QHoroscope
  (4Q186)   171n128,
                 172n136
4QEnochᵃ
  (4Q203) 8:4   137n50
4QpapAdmonitory Parable
  (4Q302)   171n122
4QMeditation on Creation
  A (4Q303)   171n122
4QMeditation on Creation
  B (4Q304)   171n122
4QMeditation on Creation
  C (4Q305)   171n122
4QZodiac (4Q318) 171n128
4QAdmonFlood
  (4Q370)   171n123
4QSapiential Hymn
  (4Q411)   171n122
4QSapiential-Didactic Work
  A (4Q412)   171n122
4QComposition concerning
  Divine Providence
  (4Q413)   171n122
4QInstruction-like
  Composition A
  (4Q419)   171n122
4QInstruction-like Composition
  B (4Q424)   171n122
4QSapiential-Didactic Work
  B (4Q425)   171n122
4QSapiential-Hymnic Work
  A (4Q426)   171n122
4QHodayot-like Text
  (4Q433a) 2:2   156n111
4QSelf-Glorification Hymn
  (4Q471b)   157n118
4QThe Two Ways
  (4Q473)   171n122
4QSelf-Glorification Hymnᵇ
  (4Q491c)   157n118

4QDaily Prayers		2.122–3	100
(4Q503) 2 ii 14	137n50	2.127	100
4QVisions of Amram[c] (4Q545)		2.128	100
4:18–19	157n121	2.129–33	100
4QPhysiognomy ar		2.136	100
(4Q561)	171n128	2.137–42	100
6QpapProverbs		2.143–4	100
(6Q30)	171n121	2.143–6	100
11QtgJob (11Q10)	171n121	2.145	100
11QTemple Scroll[a]		2.147	100
(11Q19)	171n126	2.147–9	100
SirMasada	152n60,	2.150–3	100
	171n121	2.151	100
		2.152–3	100
ANCIENT JEWISH WRITERS		2.154–8	100
		2.159	100
Josephus	18, 83–6, 96, 99–102,	2.160–1	101
	114–15, 121–3,	2.567	169n97
	140n85, 161n6,	3.11	169n97
	162n16, 166n77,	5.145	169n97
	168nn93–5,		
	169nn96–7,	Contra Apionem	161n8
	169n101, 169n104	1.176–82	161n11
		2.171–5	169n101
Antiquitates judaicae	101	2.196	101
1.5	101	2.258	169n101
1.10–17	101		
1.14	169n101	Vita	101
1.19	169n101	8–12	101
1.25	169n101	10–12	85
1.154–7	169n101		
8.42–4	169n101	Philo of Alexandria	6, 11, 18, 30–4, 40,
8.208	135n14		44–5, 47–8, 51, 77, 79,
10.190	135n19		83–5, 87–99, 101–2,
13.171–2	169n102		114–15, 119, 121–3,
13.171–3	85		140nn78–9, 140n82,
15.371–9	101		145n150, 147–8n2,
18.11–25	85		162n13, 163n38,
18.18–22	101		164n46, 164n49,
18.23–5	162n16		165n54, 166n75,
20.262	101		167n80, 167nn82–3,
20.263	168n94		169n96
Bellum judaicum	99, 101, 168nn94–5,	De Abrahamo	
	169n97	1	32
1.78–80	169n97	3–4	33
2.113	169n97	23	32
2.119–66	85, 100	52–3	140n85
2.120	100	52–4	33, 140n83, 159n140
2.120–1	101	164	93

206	141n91	18–20	90
248–50	141n94	21	92
256–7	140n73	23–4	90
		25	91

De agricultura

		25–39	95
160	31	26	88–9
160–1	32	27	91
		28	88–9, 91, 93, 162n15

De cherubim

		28–9	91
10	141n91	29	93
40	34	30	88, 91
120–1	94	31	89
		31–2	91

De confusione linguarum

		32–3	91
69–70	140n85	34	88, 91
77–8	94	35	89
77–88	166n72	37	91
106	94	39	89–90
181	159n140	40	165n57
		40–89	95

De congressu eruditionis gratia

		57–62	92
22	34	58	92
23–4	34	58–64	165n57
35	159n140	63–4	88
35–6	140n85	63–5	92
44	167n82	66	91
67	163n39	67	88
69–70	32	68	89, 91, 165n57
74–6	34	69	88–9, 91
79	31	70–4	91
80	34	72	91
145	34	73–4	165n57
		75–7	91

De vita contemplativa

	11, 18, 87, 89, 90, 92, 95, 114, 121–3, 163n32, 166n75
1	85, 88–90, 93, 97
2	88, 92, 95
3–9	92
10	93
10–11	94
11	93, 95
12	95
13	90, 94
13–17	92
13–20	95
16	88
16–17	90
17	165n61

76	89
78	89, 93
80–9	88, 91
88	89
88–9	88
89	88
90	93–5

De decalogo

65	140n82

Quod deterius potiori insidiari soleat

10	159n140
19–21	168n91
59	141n91

72	163n39	2.91	31
147–8	168n92	2.99–102	140n73
		3.1	165n64
De ebrietate		3.18–19	33, 148n2, 159n141
49	32	3.86	167n86
		3.129	140n79
De fuga et inventione		3:129–32	140n73
30–40	168n91	3.135	159n140
51–2	34	3.144	32
128	141n91	3.207	31
172	139n72	3.217–18	141n91
183	31	3.222	34
		3.244	141n91
De gigantibus		3.244–5	141n96
26	159n140		
54	163n29	*Legatio ad Gaium*	
60–3	32	156	162n15
61	94–5	245	85
62	140n83	281–4	138n53
Quis rerum divinarum heres sit		*De migratione Abrahami*	
62	141n91	46	79
88	165n64	59	94
121	139n72	67	140n79
252–3	33, 148n2, 159n141	93	165n61
275	31	128–9	139n72
		153	32
Hypothetica	97–9, 168n90	167	168n88
11.1–8	97–8		
11.2	99	*De vita Mosis*	
11.3	99	1.1–3	32
11.6–9	99	1.29	32
11.11	99	1.155–6	140n79
11.13	99	1.157	94
11.14–17	99	1.158	140n79
11.18	99	1.158–9	33
		2.27	167n82
De Iosepho		2.216	162n15, 164n51
1	33, 159n140	2.288	32, 140n82
26	140n85		
28	32	*De mutatione nominum*	
		12	140n83, 140n85
Legum allegoriae		34–8	31
1.43–6	151n46	88	140n85
1.57–8	139n69	181–5	139n72
1.92	140n78		
2.1	140n82	*De opificio mundi*	
2.38	141n88	3	94, 165n65
2.82	141n91	8	32

128	164n51	*De sacrifiis Abelis et Caini*	
142	94	8	140n79
165	141n88	59	141n91
		92	140n82

De plantatione
36	93	*De sobrietate*	
98	140n73	56–7	32
151	163n39	65	140n85

De posteritate Caini
		De somniis	
62	141n91	1.106–7	31
86	163n39	1.120–6	140n85
88	32	1.131	168n88
		1.167–9	159n140
De praemiis et poenis		1.168	140n83
5	168n88	1.168–71	140n85
51	159n140	2.127	162n15
65	159n140	2.229–30	32
108–9	168n92	2.235	32

Quod omnis probus
		De specialibus legibus	
liber sit	97, 167n80	1.28	140n140
13	31	1.59	163n29
43	139n72	1.201	141n88
45–6	32	2.43–5	94–5
72–96	97	2.44	32
75	97	2.45	94
75–9	97	2.46	32, 167n86
75–91	97	2.62	164n51
80	97, 175n167	2.124	141n87
80–1	97	2.229	31
83	98	2.230	31
83–4	98	3.185	93
85–7	97	4.223	141n87
88	98		
88–91	99	*De virtutibus*	
97	32	51	33
115–17	167n80	64–5	85
121–31	163n39	190	94, 165n64
		195	140n73

De providentia
2.16	79

RABBINIC LITERATURE

Mishnah
m. Avot	124, 136n25

Quaestiones et solutiones in Exodum
1.7	141n87

Bavli
b. B. Bathra 12a	158n125
b. Sanh. 11a	63

Quaestiones et solutiones in Genesim
1.25	141n88
3.16	167n86
4.15	34
4.74	32

Midrash
Gen. Rab. 47:1	141n96

Index of Ancient Sources

ANCIENT NEAR EAST

Adapa	20, 42
Dûr-Sharrukîn Cylinder	148n11
Instruction of Amenemope	132n63
Šimâ Milka	78, 159n136

NEW TESTAMENT

Matthew	80
5:1–7:29	160n146
5:17–48	80
5:48	80
10:1–11:1	160n146
10:9–10	80
11:19	80
11:28	80
12:42	80
13:1–53	160n146
13:54	80
18:1–19:2	160n146
23:10	80
24:1–26:1	160n146
Luke	80, 160n147, 162n21
2:46–47	160n147
5:17	80
9:23–25	80
9:57–62	80
12:33	80
12:49–53	80
14:7–14	80
14:26	80
17:20	80
24:19	80
Acts	162n21
2:5–11	138n53
1 Corinthians	160n144
Galatians	
3:24	148n3
Hebrews	
11:2–39	152n53

EARLY CHRISTIAN WRITERS

Athanasius	176n14
1 Clement	
4:7–6:4	60, 152n53
9:2–12:8	152n53
Clement of Alexandria	176n14
Stromata 1	167n82
Eusebius	168n89
Historia ecclesiastica	
2.17.3	88, 163n28, 163n36
2.18.7	163n28, 163n36
Praeparatio evangelica	
8.6–7	168n89
8.10.3–4	162n19
9.27.4	162n18
13.12–13	162n19
13.13.8	162n20
Evagrius	176n14
Hegesippus	96
Hippolytus of Rome	96
Refutatio omnium haeresium	
9.18–28	166n77
Justin Martyr	
Dialogue 1–9	169n107

CLASSICAL SOURCES

Alciphron	
Letters 3.64	144n141
Aristophanes	
Clouds	
132–83	139n66
361	142n108
Testimonia	
1	39
Aristotle	15, 36–7, 41, 84–5, 93, 146n158, 162n13, 167n86
Magicus	167n82

Index of Ancient Sources

Nicomachean Ethics
1138b35–1139a1	127n5
1113a25–33	37
1141a9–1141b23	37
1145b8	164n49
1166a1–15	37
1176a16–22	37
1176b	93
1177a27–35	37
1177a–b	162n13

Rhetoric — 39
2.20	146n158
11.1	39
11.4–7	39

Arius Didymus
II.7	37
II.7.5b10–11	38
II.7.5b12	143n124
II.7.5b11m	143n124
II.7.5b11s	143n124
II.7.11d	143n130
II.7.11g	37–8
II.7.11k	38
II.7.11m	143n130

Aurea carmina
40–4	16

Cicero — 95
Brutus
307–10	169n107
315–16	169n107

De finibus
III.75–6	143n125

De legibus
1.23	95

De re publica
3.33–7	95

Tusculanae disputationes
5.108	166n69
5.114	165n56

Clearchus of Soli — 84–5, 161n8, 161n11

Diodorus of Sicily
Bibliotheca historica — 161n8
1.92.5	162n24
2.58.1	168n92
9.1	168n88

Diogenes Laertius (D.L.) — 37
1.1–11	167n82
1.13	36
1.22	36
1.41–2	36
2.3.6	165n56
2.66	144n132
6.63	166n69
6.70	16
6.72	166n69
6.103	175n167
7.10–11	39
7.33	166n70
7.92	164n49
7.102	143n127, 167n86
7.117–18	143n126
7.119	38, 47
7.121	143n130
7.131	168n92
7.166–7	16
8.1	168n92

Dio of Prusa — 96

Epictetus — 37
Discourses
1.9.1–2	166n71
2.10.3	166n71
3.12	16

Enchiridion
51.3	39

Fragmenta
2	143n125

Georgias of Leontini — 141n90

Hecateus of Abdera
Aegyptica — 161n8

Homer — 31, 34, 78, 144n136, 165m61
Iliad
13:5	165n61
13:6	165n61

Odyssey
12	34

Horace
Epistulae I.12.12   165n56

Iamblichus
Vita Pythagorae   167n83

Joannes Stobaeus
Extracts, Sayings,
    and Advice   37

Lucian of Samosata
Vitarum auctio 20   143n124
Adversum
    indoctum 17   144n142

Marcus Aurelius
Meditations   16
    2.16   166n71
    3.11   166n71
    4.4   166n71
    4.32   166n71
    10.15   166n71

Martial
Epigram 11.56   163n37

Megasthenes   84–5, 161n 8
Indica   167n82

Musonius Rufus   133n80
On Clothing and
    Shelter   164n47
On Exercise   16, 168n92
On Food   164n50
On Furnishings   164n47
On Training   163n37

Plato   15, 35–6, 38, 40–1, 45,
    77, 86, 144n136,
    144n138, 147n163,
    162n13
Apology
    19E   142n109
Gorgias
    507b   162n24
Hippias Major
    283a   165n56
Laws
    631c   138n60

Phaedo
    69c   138n60
    81c   163n37
Phaedrus
    245b–249d   165n67
    264c   165n61
Protagoras
    342e–343b   35
    349b   132n67
Republic
    387d12   144n132
    387d–e   36
    416d   167n83
    443E   139n69
    457d   168n92
    462c   167n83
    600a   36, 39
    605c–606b   36
Symposium   39, 144n138, 165n57
    199c–201c   142n106
    203e–204b   142n106
    204c   163n30
Theaetetus
    176b   36, 47
Timaeus
    90a–d   163n37

Pliny the Elder   96, 166n77
Naturalis historia
    5.17.4   166n77

Plutarch   37, 39–40
De fortuna Alexandri
    329a–d   166nn70–1
De fraterno amore
    487B   39
De liberis educandis
    2A–C   140n84
    7D   141n90
De profectibus in virtute
    82F   143n122
    84D–85B   40
De Stoicorum repugnantiis
    1033c–d   143n130
    1043b–e   143n130
De tranquillitate animi
    472A   143n124
Pericles
    16   165n56

Septem sapientium
  convivium   36

Porphyry
De abstinentia 4   167n82

Seneca   95, 165n67
Ad Helviam
  9.1–2   165n67
  9.7   95
De beneficiis
  7.2.1   16
De ira
  3.36.1–3   16
De otio
  4.1   95
Epistulae
  15.1   93
  20.2   38
  28.4   95
  41.4   143n125
  92.30–3   165n67
  94.50–1   143n122
  116.5   143n130
Naturales quaestiones
  1.7–8   165n67

Sotion
Succession of the
  Philosophers 167n82

Strabo
Geographica
  15.1.59–60   167n82
  16.2.29   79

Theognis   152n52

Theophrastus   84, 161n8

Thucydides
History 2.43.1–4   60

Xenophon
Memorabilia 4.8.11 162n24
Symposium   165n57

Zeno
Republic   166nn70–1

OTHER ANCIENT LITERATURE

Aranyaka   163n37

Index of Modern Authors

Adams, Samuel L. 128n18
Aitken, James K. 153n64
Albrecht, Janico 129n36, 130n37
Alesse, Francesca 139n64
Alexander, Loveday 162n21
Alexander, Philip S. 128n24, 156n102, 157nn117–18, 172n136
Amir, Yehoshua 141n87
Angel, Joseph L. 71, 156n102, 157nn119–20
Annas, Julia 38–9, 133n1, 142n106, 142n110, 142n112, 142n115, 143nn129–31, 144n133
Annus, Amar 145n151
Avram, Wes 167n84

Babbitt, Frank Cole 144n142
Bakker, Arjen 173n149, 174n161
Barbour, Jennie 150n25
Barclay, John M. G. 129n30, 164n54, 168n89
Barney, Rachel 142n108
Barthélemy, Dominique 155n93
Barton, Carlin A. 126n1
Barton, John 13, 131nn53–6, 131n60, 172n135, 174n161
Baumgarten, Albert I. 162n16
Beavis, Mary Ann 164n44
Becker, Adam H. 160n145
Beentjes, Pancratius C. 151n49
Belfiore, Elizabeth S. 144n136
Ben-Dov, Jonathan 158n122
Benedikt, Eckhardt 161n4
Benner, A. R. 144n141
Ben Zvi, Ehud 146n157
Bergren, Theodore A. 146n157
Berthelot, Katell 145n150
Bickerman, Elias J. 26, 77–8, 136nn33–4, 159nn133–5
Bledsoe, Seth A. 134n4
Blenkinsopp, Joseph A. 133n1, 134n8, 134n12, 136n25, 136n27, 148n10, 149nn14–15
Boccaccini, Gabriele 131n59

Borchardt, Francis 152n51
Borgen, Peder 139n62, 140n84, 141n92
Boyarin, Daniel 126n1
Brouwer, René 134n1, 142n116, 143n119
Brooke, George J. 105, 147n160, 154n88, 158n123, 170n111, 170n116, 171n120, 171n124, 172n135, 172n140, 173n144
Brown, Eric 166n69
Brown, Peter 147n164
Brown, William B. 12, 130nn48–9, 131nn50–2, 150n27, 150n34–5
Busine, Aude 142n103
Buxton, Richard 142n98

Camp, Claudia V. 130n42, 135n22, 149n22, 160n148
Carmignac, Jean 155n93
Carr, David M. 130n41, 145n148, 148n4, 149n22
Cavell, Stanley 146n155
Charlesworth, James H. 137n44
Chazon, Esther G. 173n141
Christensen, Line Søgaard 149n12, 176n16
Clark, Stephen R. L. 134n2
Cohen, Yoram 159n136
Collins, Adela Yarbro 162n19–20
Collins, John J. 127n7, 127n12, 129n30, 131n61, 137n51, 146n152, 146n157, 162n18, 167n79, 168n93, 169n106, 170nn111–13, 171n126, 172n134
Colson, F. H. 139n67, 139n70, 140n74, 140n76, 140nn80–1, 140n83, 163n32, 165n66–7
Cooper, John M. 132n70, 133n74, 142n105, 162n13
Cosby, Michael R. 146n157
Crenshaw, James L. 131n61, 150n37
Cribiore, Raffaella 76, 159n129
Csordas, Thomas J. 126n2

Davies, John K. 161n9
Davies, Philip R. 163n31

Dawson, David 165n60
Demoen, Kristoffel 163n36
deSilva, David A. 152n54, 152n56
Di Lella, Alexander A. 151n43, 151n47
Dillon, John M. 139n64
Dimant, Devorah 138n58, 170nn117–18
Doniger, Wendy 146n151
Douglas, Mary 174n161
Downing, Francis Gerald 160n144
Droysen, Johann Gustav 129n28
Duhaime, Jean 172n133
Dunderberg, Ismo 160n150, 176n12

Edelman, Diana V. 146n157
Elgvin, Torleif 156n109, 170n111
Emlyn-Jones, Christopher 144n132, 144n136
Engberg-Pedersen, Troels 136n30, 150n32, 164n43

Falk, Daniel K. 157n111
Feldman, Louis H. 141n85
Finkelberg, Margalit 159n135
Fiore, Benjamin 143n119
Fishbane, Michael 53, 149n18
Fobes, F. H. 144n141
Fontaine, Carole R. 149n22
Fowler, Harold North 142n113
Fox, Michael V. 43, 53, 126n4, 127n5, 131n61, 132n62, 136n24, 145n149, 149nn19–20, 150nn28–31, 150n36
Fraade, Steven D. 107, 133n82, 168n91, 170n110, 170n115, 172nn137–9, 174n153, 175n170, 176n9, 176n11
Fraser, Peter M. 138n54
Freeman, Kathleen 141n90
Freese, J. H. 144n137, 146n158
Frymer-Kensky, Tikva 141n91

Gammie, John G. 133n1
García Martinez, Florentino 128n22, 170n119
Gasparini, Valentino 129n36
Gillihan, Yonder M. 145n145
George, Andrew R. 159n136
Goff, Matthew J. 3, 58, 127n8, 127n11, 128n18, 151n42, 173n151
Goldberg, Shari 164n48
Goodman, Martin D. 166nn76–7

Grabbe, Lester L. 133n1, 134n12, 135n16, 150n26
Graver, Margaret R. 140n73, 143n126
Gribetz, Sarit Kattan 165n67
Grossman, Maxine L. 110–11, 174n152, 174n154, 174n157
Gruen, Erich S. 7, 87, 128n25, 129n27, 129n30, 138n53, 146n157, 162n26–7

Hadas-Lebel, Mireille 167n82
Hadot, Pierre 15, 38, 115, 132n71, 133n72, 133n76, 133n79, 133n1, 139n65, 142n106, 144n132, 144nn134–5, 144n141, 147n1, 159nn137–8, 159n141, 175n171, 176n18
Hägg, Tomas 163n36, 163n41, 164n45
Hall, David D. 129n31
Hamori, Esther J. 149n17, 172n131
Harding, James E. 152n52
Harmon, A. M. 144n142
Harrington, Daniel J. 127n8, 151n39, 155n91
Harrington, Hannah K. 174n155
Harris, Rivkah 134n7
Hartog, Pieter B. 129n30, 159–60n142, 170n119, 175n164, 175n4
Hatch, Edward 159n130
Hawley, Robert 66, 154n84
Hay, David M. 89, 163n30, 163nn33–5, 164n42, 164n53, 165n58, 166n73
Hempel, Charlotte 113, 154n86–8, 173n148, 175n165–6
Hengel, Martin 129n25, 160n143, 174n162
Henze, Matthias 154n88
Hicks, R. D. 144n140
Hogan, Karina Martin 77, 131n59, 159nn131–2, 169–70n108
Horst, Pieter van der 145n144

Inowlocki, Sabrina 168n89

Jaeger, Werner 131n58, 158n128
Japhet, Sara 148n11
Jassen, Alex P. 173n145
Jokiranta, Jutta 129n30
Jong, Albert de 158n122

Kampen, John I. 127n8, 155n91, 174n159
Kamtekar, Rachana 142n115

Ulrich, Eugene 147n160
Uusimäki, Elisa 127n8, 131n60, 132n62, 135nn14–15, 136n29, 139n61, 141n86, 141n96, 146n159, 148n8, 153n75, 154n82, 158n121, 158n123, 159n141, 161n1, 162n17, 171n125, 172n132, 173n147, 174n160, 175n3

VanderKam, James C. 138n52, 171n128, 175n164
Veijola, Timo 148n9
Verheyden, Joseph 135n14
Vermes, Geza 156n102, 166nn76–7
Vesely, Patricia 131n60

Wassen, Cecilia 173n148, 173n150, 174n153, 174n156
Weaver, John B. 169n103
Weeks, Stuart 128n14, 158n126
Wegner, Judith Romney 141n93
Weinfeld, Moshe 148n9
Weitzman, Steven 148n6
Whitaker, G. H. 139n70, 140n76, 140n81, 165n66

Whitmarsh, Tim 132n66, 175n6
Whybray, Roger Norman 134n13, 136n23
Williams, Travis B. 170n114
Wills, Lawrence M. 127n9
Winston, David 139n71, 140n73, 140n79, 154n79
Witherington, Ben 160n144
Wright, Benjamin G. 13, 26, 42, 46, 57, 127n9, 128n15, 130n42, 131n57, 136nn31–2, 136nn36–8, 137n39, 138n59, 144n144, 145n148, 147n162, 149n21, 150n37, 151nn40–1, 151n44, 151nn49–50, 152n52, 152nn57–8, 152n60, 153nn65–6, 153nn70–3, 153n76, 154n78, 154n81, 160n143, 160n148
Wyss, Beatrice 142n107

Yli-Karjanmaa, Sami 139n66, 166n68

Zurawski, Jason M. 131n59

www.ingramcontent.com/pod-product-compliance
Lightning Source LLC
Chambersburg PA
CBHW062219300426
44115CB00012BA/2131

Keady, Jessica M. 9, 130n39, 174n158
Kerferd, George B. 133n1, 142n99,
  142n101, 142n104, 142n111, 142n116–18, 143n119, 143n122, 143n128
Kidd, Ian G. 143n122
Kieweler, Hans Volker 152n52
Knibb, Michael A. 138n57
Kolarcik, Michael, S.J. 138n60
Kooten, George H. van 162n21
Koskenniemi, Erkki 139n63, 140n77, 145n150
Kosmala, Hans 137n41
Kovacs, Judith L. 160n150, 176n12
Kraemer, Ross Shepard 164n44
Kraft, Robert A. 6, 128n20, 166n77
Kramer, Samuel Noah 134n5
Krüger, Thomas 136n26, 150n24
Kugel, James L. 137n49, 150n33
Kynes, Will 127n10, 128n16

LaCoste, Nathalie 138n58
Lange, Armin 127n8, 137nn40–1, 171n123, 171n127
Larsen, Matthew D. 164n52
Legaspi, Michael C. 130n40, 132n64, 132n67, 150n23, 161n8
Lemaire, André 130n43, 136n30
Levinas, Emmanuel 97
Levine, Lee I. 7, 113, 128n25, 129n26, 129n29, 174n163
Lewis, Thomas A. 130n44
Lichtheim, Miriam 132n63
Lim, Timothy H. 128n23
Lincicum, David 145n150
Litwa, M. David 140n82
Livneh, Atar 141n95
Long, Anthony A. 143n123, 143n126, 144n138
Lutz, Cora E. 133n80

Macaskill, Grant 172n129
Mack, Burton L. 123, 152n54–5, 175n5
Mackie, Scott D. 165n62
Magness, Jodi 161n5
Mansfeld, Jaap 139n64
Mason, Steve 86, 126n1, 133n73, 160n144, 160n147, 161nn6–7, 162n21, 162nn22–4, 167n85, 168n93, 168n95, 169nn98–9, 169n101, 169nn104–5, 175n169

Mattila, Sharon Lea 141n88, 154n70
McCarter, P. Kyle 135n21
McGuire, Meredith B. 9, 129n31, 129nn34–5
McPherran, Mark L. 132n67
Meeks, Wayne A. 140n77
Mendels, Doron 167n78
Mendelson, Alan 139n68, 140n75
Metso, Sarianna 155n93, 155n97, 156n107
Middendorp, Theophil 145n150, 152n52
Mieroop, Marc van de 141n97
Milik, József T. 155n93
Mirguet, Françoise 64, 153n77
Modrzejewski, Mélèze 129n30
Momigliano, Arnaldo 129n28, 163n36
Montiglio, Silvia 135n15
Morgan, Teresa 146n157
Moyer, Ian S. 129n28
Mroczek, Eva 57, 135n14, 151n38

Nadaff, Ramona A. 144n136
Najman, Hindy 28–9, 117, 128n17, 128n19, 128n21, 137n47–9, 140n78, 145n147, 147n1, 148n5, 153n69, 154n80, 165n65, 173n142, 175n1
Newman, Judith H. 26, 30–1, 69, 128n23, 136n35, 138n61, 151n48, 153n66, 153n74, 156n104, 157n113, 157n118, 171n120, 173n145
Newsom, Carol A. 27–8, 127n9, 131n56, 137nn42–3, 137nn45–6, 154n83, 155n89, 155n92, 155nn95–7, 156n103, 156n105, 156n108, 156n110, 157nn111–12, 157n116, 160n1, 172n130, 175n168
Nickelsburg, George W. E. 138n52, 146n157
Niditch, Susan 9, 130n38
Niehoff, Maren R. 140n74, 141n87, 141n94, 159n135, 163n38, 165n57, 169n107
Nightingale, Andrea Wilson 133n1, 142nn100–2, 142nn108–9, 144n138
Nissinen, Martti 153n72
Nongbri, Brent 126n1
Norden, Bryan W. van 132n66
Nussbaum, Martha C. 132n69

Oldfather, W. A. 144n139
Orsi, Robert A. 8, 129nn31–3, 130nn46–7

Pavie, Xavier 133n74
Pellah, Robert N. 176n15
Penner, Jeremy 156n107
Perdue, Leo G. 133n1, 136n28, 138n56
Petersen, Anders Klostergaard 132n68, 176n16
Poliakoff, Clare 168n88
Poliakoff, Michael 168n88
Pomeroy, Arthur J. 143n121
Popović, Mladen 158n122, 172n136
Pouchelle, Patrick 131n59
Preddy, William 144n132, 144n136

Rackham, H. 142n114
Raja, Rubina 129n36
Rajak, Tessa 138n53, 149n22
Rappaport, Roy A. 126n3
Reed, Annette Yoshiko 160n145
Reinhardt, Tobias 154n80
Riaud, Jean 164n43
Rogers, Justin M. 141n92
Rogerson, John 147n165
Rosen-Zvi, Ishay 176n8
Rowe, Christopher Kavin 162n21
Royse, James R. 166n75
Runia, David T. 83, 93, 161n3, 162n14, 164n46, 165n59, 165n63, 167n83
Rüpke, Jörg 129n36
Russell, Daniel C. 161n2

Sahlins, Marshall 44, 146n153
Salminen, Joona 176n14
Sanders, Jack T. 152n52
Sanders, Seth L. 134n4, 145n146, 158n122
Satlow, Michael L. 124, 128n23, 176n10
Satran, David 135nn18–20
Schams, Christine 137n50, 138n55, 149n13
Schiffman, Lawrence H. 158n123
Schipper, Bernd U. 127n9, 173n147
Schnabel, Eckhard J. 173n147
Schniedewind, William M. 148n11
Schofield, Alison 170n111
Schuller, Eileen M. 157nn111–12
Schwienhorst-Schönberg, Ludger 145n150
Scott, Bernard Brandon 160n144
Scott, Susie 147n1
Sellars, John 89, 132n69, 133nn74–5, 133nn77–8, 133n81, 138n61, 142n106,
159n137, 159n139, 161n12, 163n40, 166n69, 166nn71–2, 166n74
Sharples, Robert W. 143n120
Shaw, Teresa M. 176n13
Shweder, Richard A. 167n87
Sloterdijk, Peter 176n17
Sneed, Mark R. 81, 127n6, 127n13, 160n149
Snyder, H. Gregory 81, 127n6, 127n13, 160n149
Sommer, Benjamin D. 153n68
Sorabji, Richard 133n74, 159n138
Stegemann, Hartmut 157nn111–12
Sterling, Gregory E. 129n30, 139n69, 167n78
Stern, Menahem 161n8, 161nn10–12
Stewart, Anne W. 13, 131n56
Stone, Michael E. 146n157
Stoneman, Richard 142n98
Strawn, Brent A. 146n156
Stroumsa, Guy G. 158n125
Stuckenbruck, Loren T. 170n114
Svebakken, Hans 164n49
Swanton, Christine 127n5
Sweet, Ronald F. G. 134n3, 134n6
Szesnat, Holger 164n42, 164n48

Taekema, Sanne 130n45, 175n2
Taylor, Joan E. 99, 126n2, 130n43, 141n89, 161n5, 161n7, 162n25, 163n28, 163n31, 163n37, 164n42, 164n48, 165n55, 165n58, 165n61, 167nn82–3, 168nn90–2, 169n96, 169n100, 169nn105–6
Teeter, D. Andrew 127n9, 173n147
Temmerman, Koen de 163n36, 164n45
Termini, Cristina 139n64
Terrien, Samuel 134n9
Tervanotko, Hanna 141n96
Thomas, Samuel I. 68, 156n100
Thonemann, Peter 129n25
Tigay, Jeffrey H. 148n8
Tolonen, Anna-Liisa 146n159, 162n17, 175n3
Too, Yun Lee 151n45, 158nn127–8
Trebilco, Paul R. 129n30
Tropper, Amram D. 175n7
Tso, Marcus K. M. 131n60, 172n131, 174n159
Tzoref, Shani 171n120